A History of Medieval Heresy and Inquisition

A History of Medieval Heresy and Inquisition

Second Edition

Jennifer Kolpacoff Deane

ROWMAN & LITTLEFIELD
Lanham • Boulder • New York • London

Associate Acquisitions Editor: Katelyn Turner
Assistant Acquisitions Editor: Haley White
Published by Rowman & Littlefield
An imprint of The Rowman & Littlefield Publishing Group, Inc.
4501 Forbes Boulevard, Suite 200, Lanham, Maryland 20706
www.rowman.com

86-90 Paul Street, London EC2A 4NE

British Library Cataloguing in Publication Information Available

Library of Congress Cataloging-in-Publication Data

Names: Deane, Jennifer Kolpacoff, 1970-author.
Title: A history of medieval heresy and inquisition / Jennifer Kolpacoff Deane.
Description: Second edition. | Lanham, Maryland: Rowman & Littlefield, | Series: Critical issues in world and international history | Includes bibliographical references and index.
Identifiers: LCCN 2022015018 (print) | LCCN 2022015019 (ebook) | ISBN 9781538152935 (cloth) | ISBN 9781538152942 (paperback) | ISBN 9781538152959 (epub)
Subjects: LCSH: Church history—Middle Ages, 600–1500. | Heresy. | Inquisition.
Classification: LCC BR163 .D43 2022 (print) | LCC BR163 (ebook) | DDC 272/.2—dc23/eng/20220608
LC record available at https://lccn.loc.gov/2022015018
LC ebook record available at https://lccn.loc.gov/2022015019

Contents

Acknowledgments vii

Introduction ix

Chapter One: Good Christians, "Cathars," and Historical Evidence 1

Chapter Two: Poverty, Preaching, and the Poor of Lyon 35

Chapter Three: Lawyer Popes, Mendicant Preachers, and New Inquisitorial Procedures 65

Chapter Four: Spiritual Franciscans, the Poverty Controversy, and the Apocalypse 103

Chapter Five: Mysticism, Lay Religious Women, and the Problem of Spiritual Authority 135

Chapter Six: Medieval Magic, Demonology, and Witchcraft 169

Chapter Seven: Wyclif, the Word of God, and Inquisition in England 203

Chapter Eight: Reform, Revolution, and the Lay Chalice in Bohemia 235

Epilogue 277

Index 281

About the Author 297

Acknowledgments

Since this volume first appeared in 2011, the field of medieval history has experienced dynamic growth and change—particularly around the themes of religious belief, spiritual practice, and the pursuit of ideals both inside and beyond ecclesiastical institutions. In other words, it has been an exciting time to be a medievalist interested in heresy and inquisition, and I'm grateful for the many opportunities to continue learning from colleagues both near and far. Special thanks to the participants in the sessions that Anne E. Lester and I organized at the 2015 International Medieval Congress at Leeds, whose research has informed many of the needed updates to the volume. To all those who have written to me about the book over the years, whether to share what has been useful or to offer corrections and suggestions for improvement, a sincere thank you; it has been deeply gratifying to hear that students continue to find it valuable and accessible, and I hope the new edition will be similarly useful.

Of the many generous colleagues and programs to whom I owe thanks over the last decade, I can list only a few here. For her editorial support and consistent encouragement over a decade, many lively conversations about matters large and small, and the initial suggestion to write a revised version, I thank Susan McEachern of Rowman & Littlefield. My sincerest thanks to Sandy Kill, interlibrary loan manager extraordinaire, whose lightning speed and efficiency (even when dealing with multiple languages and all those diacritical marks) make her a truly invaluable colleague. Alisande Allaben and John Hamerlinck in the grants management office shepherded many of my applications through programs such as the UMN Morris Faculty Research Enhancement Funds and the University of Minnesota Imagine Fund and Grant-in-Aid of Research.

On a personal level, I'd like to express my deep gratitude to Laura Burks and Sharon Severance of the Division of Social Science at UMN Morris, for their support, efficiency, good humor, and friendship over the years; I appreciated you in 2011 and I couldn't do without you now. To the J's (JE, JG, JL, and JR), my mother and my sister, thank you for the light and laughter during an exceptionally difficult couple of years. To my daughters, Lucy and Tess, for all you are. And to my mentors, past and present, *gratias tibi.*

Introduction

THE CONTOURS OF AUTHORITY IN MEDIEVAL CHRISTENDOM

Reflecting on events that occurred in southern France around the year 1022, a monk named Adémar of Chabannes penned a brief account of "Manichaean" heretics "who appeared throughout Aquitaine leading the people astray. They denied baptism and the Cross and every sound doctrine. They abstained from food and seemed like monks; they pretended chastity, but among themselves they practiced every debauchery. They were ambassadors of Antichrist and caused many to turn away from the faith."[1] A century and a half later, in the 1160s, the famous Rhineland abbess and prophet Hildegard of Bingen preached thunderously against *Cathar heretics* who hypocritically appeared pale, chaste, and austere, but were "scorpions in their morals and snakes in their works."[2] More than fifty years after Hildegard's death, the Italian Franciscan friar James Capelli wearily remarked, "We know that they [heretics] suppose their behavior to be virtuous and they do many things that are in the nature of good works; in frequent prayer, in vigils, in sparsity of food and clothing, and—let me acknowledge the truth—in austerity of abstinence they surpass all other religious." Yet he warned his reader that "under this cloak of good works" their sweet words steal away the hearts of the foolish.[3]

These three short accounts should provoke some questions, and probably different questions for different readers. One might ask, for example, "Who were these people, these Manichaeans, Cathars, and heretics? Where did they come from, and what did they believe and practice? And why were they so upsetting to contemporaries as to draw comparison to scorpions, snakes, and even the Antichrist?" Some might wonder why these authors were so invested in and angry about the beliefs of ostensibly pious people. Others might pose slightly different questions that focus less on the story of what happened and more on the credibility and usefulness of the accounts themselves (in other words, on the method, or *how* we piece the story together): "How relevant are similarities between reports from the eleventh, twelfth, and thirteenth centuries? Is it good reporting to lump together accounts from such different regions as the lands of modern-day France, Germany, and Italy? Are the writers here actually talking about the same group? How accurate is their information, and how slanted are their particular points of view?" Such questions have kept many a medieval historian awake at night, as has the kaleidoscopic, even conflicting, array of responses generated over the past century of scholarship.

Before moving on to sketch a bird's-eye view of the landscape of medieval Europe and the contours of religious, political, and social authority during these centuries, we should begin with the heart of the matter and confront three key challenges. For despite the apparently straightforward title *A History of Medieval Heresy and Inquisition*, this volume actually argues that heresy and inquisition were anything but simple or uncontested categories (among both medieval contemporaries and modern scholars).

CHALLENGE NUMBER ONE: DEFINING HERESY

First, the peculiar challenge of studying heresy is that, as John Arnold put it, "heresy only exists where there is an orthodoxy to name it. The two are an inseparable binary, and 'heresy' is forever both a boundary and a fluctuating category."[4] To put it another way, "heresy" is an artificial category designed by authorities who regarded themselves by definition as "orthodox" or "not heretic." It is a category that developed over the course of the medieval centuries as the Church itself became a more sophisticated administrative institution and a framework by which an endless variety of beliefs could be uniformly condemned, contained, and thus controlled. From one point of view, however, heresy was even necessary: after all, St. Paul had warned, "there must also be heresies among you" so that the righteous can be known by contrast.[5] Indeed, the early Christian world was fraught with struggles for authority and disputes about the proper way to follow the model of Christ and his apostles. Doctrinal arguments abounded over issues such as the nature of Christ, the meaning of God's words, and the best means for implementing them in the material world, and each group labeled the others as heretical.

Thus the process of establishing Christian authority and the scriptural canon laws was lengthy, controversial, and finalized only in the great early councils such as Nicaea in 325 CE. Over time, "orthodoxy" was established in contrast to such heresies as Arianism, Donatism, or Pelagianism—but only once there was sufficient organization and hierarchy for councils to rule on the acceptability of hitherto circulating doctrines. From these earliest Christian centuries were birthed a set of lurid and remarkably enduring stereotypes of heretics not only as hypocritical and secretive foes but even as orgiastic, bestial, murderous baby eaters—ludicrous and baseless accusations that would nonetheless echo painfully across the medieval centuries.

Figure I.1. St. Matthew the Evangelist, Gospel of Ebbo, Archbishop of Reims, from the Monastery of Hautevilliers, before 823. *Source*: **Bibliothèque Municipale, Epernay, France. Erich Lessing/ Art Resource, NY.**

Between approximately the fifth and tenth centuries, as small and scattered communities struggled daily for survival, local priests and Benedictine monks sought to embed Christian practice in their pagan or only lightly Christianized flocks. Heresy was not much of a concern during these years: vibrant lay religiosity was not a potent historical force in the West, canon law was in its infancy, and Church hierarchies and structures were still largely occupied with the challenge of conversion and implementation of basic Christian observance. Only in the eleventh and twelfth centuries (for reasons discussed below) did the medieval clergy begin to encounter uncomfortably novel forms of preaching and lay piety; for guidance, they turned to ancient Church fathers such as saints Augustine and Jerome and absorbed their descriptions of early Christian heresy. Thus clergy encountering what they began to deem religious dissent in the eleventh and early twelfth centuries presumed that these were simply new outbreaks of old heresies. However, authorities became increasingly aware of new spiritual expressions and practices once the floodgates of lay piety opened in the twelfth and thirteenth centuries.

This is not, however, to suggest that anyone at any time was liable to end up accused of heresy. Clergy of all ranks recognized that laypeople often held uninformed or mistaken beliefs about Christian doctrine and its apparently paradoxical theology of incarnate divinity, virgin birth, and resurrection from the dead. Religious training for the rank and file in medieval Christendom was generally limited to a few prayers or points of doctrine, and up until the late twelfth century, scripture was the sole domain of Latinate clergy. Moreover, the clerical task was always to save souls, to restore lost sheep to the pastoral flock. As a consequence, the theologically ignorant or confused were not at risk of condemnation for heresy, so long as they accepted the corrected teaching provided by their spiritual supervisor.

What, then, constituted heresy in the eyes of medieval contemporaries? Derived etymologically from the Greek *haeresis* ("choice"), the core of heresy as defined by the Church was disobedience rooted in pride and the willful rejection of orthodoxy *after* correction: the deliberate choosing of error over truth. In the mid-thirteenth century, for example, the bishop of Lincoln, Robert Grosseteste, defined heresy as "an opinion chosen by human perception contrary to holy Scripture, publicly avowed and obstinately defended."[6] Although not all victims of inquisitorial condemnation matched this description, choice represented the kernel of the matter for the clergy: a heretic obstinately refused correction, pridefully choosing instead his or her own interpretation of religion and thus boldly usurping the spiritual authority of the holy Church, of scripture—challenging even God himself. Discerning right from wrong was never a simple matter and usually devolved ultimately into a negotiation over authority, particularly over the institutional Church and its claimed responsibility to interpret scripture, dispense sacraments, and channel God's will on earth. The dialogue over what constituted heresy, therefore, was never simple; multiple voices emerged in an archipelago of diverse contexts and environments that varied enormously over time and place. Because the categories of "heresy" and "orthodoxy" lay very much in the eye of the beholder, they present a vexing but invigorating challenge for historians whose task is to reconstruct the past. But whose past? And according to which sources?

CHALLENGE NUMBER TWO: QUESTIONING SOURCES

Historians rely upon a variety of primary sources (i.e., materials close at hand to the events in question) in order to understand what individuals in the past thought, did, and believed; what their world was like; and what it meant to them. For the topic of medieval constructions of heresy, a range of sources exists for studying the topography of belief deemed heretical by the medieval Church. Orthodox literature includes conciliar decrees and records, treatises, canon law, annals, chronicles, histories, and even letters. In addition, specifically inquisitorial sources generated by the burgeoning record-keeping apparatus of such tribunals in the thirteenth and fourteenth centuries make up an extensive trove of documents. However, these are of course largely hostile accounts driven by an orthodox agenda. So what are the possibilities and pitfalls of such material for historians? On the one hand, inquisitorial sources frequently incorporated the assertions, claims, and defenses of the accused into the work itself, providing tantalizing scraps of evidence as to their own points of view. On the other hand, the layers of intimidation, threat of violence, and textual intervention by scribes combine with the inquisitors' ideological and institutional biases to render such materials unusually problematic. Historians must resist assuming that any individual voice can be easily or accurately understood through such intrusively filtered reported speech. Thus, as Edward Muir and Guido Ruggiero put it, "even as he snitches on the dead, the historian's fundamental obligation is to respect them in their own terms rather than in those of the judicial record that brings their experiences to view."[7] Historians have paid particular attention to this central problem in recent years, and we will consider it throughout the volume.

But how, then, can we hope to learn about spiritual ideas and practices from the perspective of people who rarely wrote texts, those termed "heretics" by others but who believed themselves truly religious and righteous? Due largely to the scrupulous editing and translation work of nineteenth-century scholars, historians now have access to a wide variety of spiritual and theological sources that, although still penned by elites, represent a sympathetic rather than hostile perspective: collections of biblical sources; vernacular translations; creeds, rituals, and professions of faith; treatises and doctrinal discussions; and sermons. Town records, chronicles, letters, and other indirectly related materials also provide insight into the world of those accused of heresy. Where possible, these may all be triangulated with inquisitorial records and other sources of information to reconceptualize the spiritual landscape of the high and later Middle Ages.

Emphasizing the complexity and diversity of the medieval past, therefore, I draw in this volume upon a variety of types of sources while acknowledging that none of them is exclusive, inclusive, or necessarily any more "true" than others. Peter Novick has characterized the challenge of determining objectivity and truth in history as "nailing jelly to the wall," and it is an apt image.[8] Readers are thus urged to ask themselves continually, "How do we know?" and "Where does this information or interpretation come from?" Historians must be able to defend their arguments based on primary source evidence, and it is my hope that readers will critically analyze and question this material along the way.

CHALLENGE NUMBER THREE: LANGUAGE AND LABELS

What's in a name? For those concerned with membership in "the ferment of heretical wickedness" (as Innocent expressed it in 1215), a great deal. Labels are sticky—they linger and cling, particularly the names and categories that institutions assign to assess, control, and supervise human beings. Perhaps obviously, no one ever called herself a "heretic," for the term implies obstinate deviation from the truth and, as of the thirteenth century, actual treason from righteousness. For a modern equivalent, one might consider the term *terrorist* and the ideological, political, legal, and authoritative gaps between those who wield it and those to whom it is attributed. Even the most radical dissenters of the Middle Ages typically considered themselves reformers, adherents of a more austere, pure, and true tradition from which the Church itself had deviated. For that reason, I avoid using the term *heretic* except as employed by clerics and inquisitors, as well as their broad (and broadly derogatory) names for groups such as the Cathars, Waldensians, and Free Spirits. Such terms not only convey a false sense of uniformity but also bear the uncanny power to manufacture out of whole cloth communities that never existed as such—in some cases because they imply conscious association and affiliation between what may only be superficially similar practices and people; in others, because (as in the case of Free Spirits) the movement was largely imaginary in the first place. Thus, when presenting issues from the point of view of adherents, believers, and leaders, I adopt the nomenclature they chose for themselves: often the simple terms Good Christians, Poor Men, or the Known. Any confusion that may result is, I believe, a reasonable price to pay for avoiding the forced categorization of medieval people into historically distorted and reductive labels.

It should also come as no surprise that the label *Inquisition* is equally problematic, suggesting an institutional coherence and official unity that never existed in the Middle Ages. Avoiding the looming capitals of "The Inquisition," we will instead refer to inquisitors, the inquisitorial process, or inquisitorial tribunals (one example of a specifically deputized but nonetheless decentralized approach to combating heresy). As we trace the birth and transformation of the category of medieval heresy, therefore, we will simultaneously pursue the reemergence and consequences of *inquisitio* as a legal process in the West.

SCHOLARLY PERSPECTIVES ON HERESY AND INQUISITION

So one person's wicked heretic was another's pious Christian, and between the ever-shifting sides of the debate emerged a complex array of theories, texts, and techniques for claiming righteousness. What does that mean for historians of medieval religion? It means that we have a lot to argue about, particularly in the recent burst of scholarship influenced by interdisciplinary studies and methods including anthropology, sociology, gender studies, and literary theory. Some of the most influential studies and arguments, however, are classics rooted in the traditional historical exercise of scrupulous research and analytical insight. In 1972, for example, Robert E. Lerner published *The Heresy of the Free Spirit in the Later Middle Ages*, which demonstrated that the so-called Free Spirit heresy (long considered by medieval and modern scholars alike as an organized and dissenting league of deviants) was instead a nebulous array of individuals whose spiritual ideas were closely related to popular contemporary interest in apostolic poverty and the mystical joining of God and humanity. Lerner also drew attention to the recurring medieval stereotype of heretics as depraved lechers and ritual murderers, observing that "just as fearful children imagine the most lurid shapes in the dark, so can grown men believe in patent fables concerning movements that they fear and do not understand."[9]

Having inspired decades of subsequent scholarship, Lerner's study in particular has provoked medieval historians across multiple disciplines to ask whether, how, or to what extent various heresies actually existed. It is a matter of serious debate in the field today, the stuff of vibrant conference sessions and pointed book reviews. At one extreme are those who perceive heresy as an imaginary construct manufactured by medieval clerical elites and perpetuated by modern historians; at the other, those who study heretics and emphasize the experience of self-consciously dissenting communities. These two poles are separated by a wide terrain of plausible arguments and interpretations, fertile historical territory enriched by bold new scholarship on inquisitorial perspectives, theories of Christian violence, and microstudies of local persecuting contexts. It is in this scholarly middle ground that I have rooted my own research. And although some scholars will no doubt take issue with the approach set forth in this volume, this is as it should be: an argument that provokes no response is unlikely to be a very interesting or useful one. Readers will therefore find a variety of scholarly perspectives reflected in the short bibliographies following each chapter and are encouraged to continue to grapple with these questions as they see fit.

It is the purpose of this volume to trace the main themes and issues at the heart of current debates over heresy and inquisition, to chart the process by which new central medieval ideals and institutions transformed the legal and social order, and to convey the extent to which, for all parties involved, proper order and salvation itself was on the line. We do the past a disservice if we simply dismiss the medieval Church and its inquisitorial history as a grotesque relic of a barbaric era. Far from popular conceptions of a dark age, central medieval Europe (c. 1050–1300) witnessed a cultural efflorescence of universities, cathedrals, literature, urbanization, and long-distance trade. So how do we square that with the fact that Christians scrutinized the hearts and minds of other human beings, consigning many to die in agony at the stake? We might start by committing ourselves to approaching the past on its own terms, setting aside preconceptions we may have about the morality or justice of religious persecution and scrutinizing instead the "how" and "why" behind the encounters themselves. But before we can unpack the logic behind medieval heresy and inquisition, it will be useful to take a closer look at these centuries and orient ourselves in the historical terrain of western Europe between 500 and 1500 CE.

LANDS AND LEADERS IN MEDIEVAL EUROPE

The contours of medieval Europe were decisively shaped by both geographical conditions and the blended historical legacies inherited from its Roman and Germanic predecessors. After the dissolution of the Roman imperial structure by the end of the fifth century, the lands we call Europe were inhabited by a wide range of peoples, including Visigoths, Ostrogoths, Lombards, Franks, and Anglo-Saxons, all increasingly accustomed to encountering Romans through trade or war. Although the Romans had established city outposts such as Londinium (London), Colonia (Cologne), and Corduba

(Córdoba) and linked them to the Mediterranean center with both roads and administrative representatives, urban life and long-distance contact slowed, faltered, and eventually disappeared for most of the early Middle Ages. Local rulers such as the Frankish Clovis (c. 500 CE), Pepin (c. 750 CE), and Charlemagne (c. 800 CE) sought to extend their rule and influence through alliances with the pope in Rome. By the ninth century, the pope had accrued the authority to make kings and crown emperors (much to the disgust of the

Map I.1. Europe c. 1250. Reprinted from Barbara Rosenwein, ***A Short History of the Middle Ages*****, Third Edition.** ***Source*****: Copyright © 2009 by University of Toronto Press Incorporated. Reprinted with permission of the publisher.**

Greek emperors in cosmopolitan Constantinople, who regarded Western rulers as uncouth backwater upstarts).

Meanwhile, Benedictine monks and missionaries sworn to poverty, obedience, and chastity had set themselves the task of founding spiritual communities in distant, often dangerous communities. By the tenth century, European lands from Italy to England were dotted with agriculturally productive monastic foundations that served as vital community service centers. Often the only literate people west of Rome, Benedictine monks meticulously copied books in their writing rooms or *scriptoria*, not only preserving the practice of literacy in the West but also rescuing in the process much ancient Latin literature for posterity. Some missionaries, such as St. Boniface (c. 750 CE), headed into uncharted territory in what is now Germany, preaching and persuading, often by superimposing Christian concepts on local beliefs. Conversion is hard to quantify or verify, however, and scholars disagree about the extent to which the various peoples of early medieval Europe actually embraced or practiced Christianity as such.

By the ninth century, this fusion of secular lordship, papal authority, and Benedictine dynamism had forged a distinctively Christian political matrix across the central western lands. Thus the inherited legacies of Roman, Germanic, and Christian influences were crystallized in a potent alliance of lords and popes, which laid the foundations of later medieval Europe. That said, the historical terrain was as diverse as its geography. For example, the northern islands of modern-day Ireland and England developed distinct linguistic, cultural, and political patterns and were shaped by their proximity to the increasingly aggressive Scandinavians; in contrast, fiercely independent and wealthy trading city-states emerged in the Italian peninsula, deeply influenced by the ancient trade routes linking China, the Middle East, and India to the Mediterranean. In the eighth century, invading Muslim Arabs joined the older communities of Romans, Germanic peoples, and Sephardic Jews to foster uniquely diverse cultural contexts in the Iberian Peninsula and Sicily. The fertile lands bordering the northern Mediterranean (modern-day southern France) embraced both walled cities and defensive mountain fortresses, decentralized and proud communities in which aristocratic influence was firmly embedded in local culture and custom.

Finally, the geographically diverse lands of what is now northern France, Germany, Austria, the Czech Republic, and Slovakia found themselves under increasingly powerful royal or noble control; secular leaders tried to maximize their economic position by milking taxes from the peasantry from the villages of coast, mountain, and plain and, as we will see, vigorously sought to wrest political authority away from their erstwhile partner, the Church. Regions such as the Rhineland provinces of Mainz, Strasbourg, and Trier found themselves in still different circumstances as both urban and rural centers occupied ecclesiastical lands under the political sway of a prince-archbishop. Given this extraordinary regional diversity, it should come as no surprise that we will pay particular attention to specific local geographies and how the unique political, religious, and cultural environment of each region nurtured distinct flavors and shades of spiritual controversy.

MEDIEVAL COMMUNITIES

If one can generalize about the vast majority of people inhabiting the western lands of early medieval Europe (perhaps a hazardous venture in itself), it might be to suggest that their lives were shaped by several overlapping spheres of influence. The first would be their immediate household, consisting not only of blood kin (i.e., children, spouse, siblings, or grandparents), but also other kinds of members—adopted kin, servants, helpers of one sort or another—and even animals, all living together in various types of dwellings, particularly during cold winter months. Beyond the household was the village, ranging in scale from tiny to large and usually consisting of houses, fields, local vendors, and perhaps a market center and a church. Villages were often linked to one another by well-trod paths (sometimes following ancient Roman roads), which were in turn connected to cities and shrines, ports and pilgrimage destinations.

A third sphere of influence that intersected with both household and village, particularly in the lands of England, northern France, and Germany, was the manor—noble lands on which free peasants or unfree serfs (who were bound to the land) lived and worked. Residents of manorial villages served the noble by producing crops and paying taxes and were subject to his legal authority. And finally, the parish or Christian administrative unit overlapped with all of these, staffed with a more or less capable local priest who led services, provided sacraments, heard confession, and generally instructed the laity as to the proper path to salvation. Invested with the authority to mediate between God and humanity, clergy were thought to hold the keys to salvation and divine will, a power explicitly and exclusively wielded by the men of the Church. In terms of daily responsibilities, however, such lofty ambitions often translated (for motivated priests) into grueling local service, just as in many circumstances it devolved into lax or nonexistent spiritual supervision by uninterested or poorly trained clergy.

To guide their pastoral work, early medieval clergy frequently used manuals compiled by colleagues that listed various sins and the appropriate penance suitable for cleansing the sinner's soul and reconciling him or her back into the pious fold. These early penitentials suggest that clergy were more worried about sins such as murder, assault, drunkenness, sexual misbehavior, and magical practices than they were about doctrinal observance. In striking contrast to the blaring urgency of late medieval antiheretical manuals, the seventh-century *Penitential of Theodore*, compiled by an English priest and archbishop, treats heresy more as an administrative problem among clergy than a lurking, secret evil: "If one, without knowing it, permits a heretic to celebrate the Mass in a Catholic church, he shall do penance for forty days. If [he does this] out of veneration for [the heretic], he shall do penance for an entire year." And if the clergyman allowed a heretic to celebrate Mass "in condemnation of the Catholic Church and the customs of the Romans, he shall be cast out of the Church as a heretic, unless he is penitent; if he is, he shall do penance for ten years."[10] Theological disputes among clergy in these early centuries tended to focus on issues such as the nature of the Trinity and calendrical timing rather than matters of scriptural interpretation and pious observance.

No sketch of medieval European spiritual topography is complete, however, without considering one more vital point of intersection and influence: namely, the belief in sacral joinings of heaven and earth that underpinned Christian theology. Peter Brown wrote that "the genius of late antique men lay in their ability to map out, to localize, and to render magnificently palpable . . . those few, clearly delineated points *at which the visible and invisible worlds met on earth*" [emphasis added].[11] Across the subsequent medieval centuries, these joinings of the visible and invisible—precise coordinates fusing the mundane and sublime, the corrupt and perfect, the temporal and eternal—became increasingly contested sites, ranging from relics and saints' shrines to Christ's blood, the sacraments, and scripture. This certainty in the spiritual efficacy of particular places, practices, and people represents a vital undercurrent in medieval culture and a crucial factor in later disputes over religious authority and heresy. We will return to these joinings throughout the volume, particularly in the form of bread and wine, sacraments, and the scriptural Word of God.

INTENSIFICATIONS IN THE CENTRAL MIDDLE AGES (1050–1300)

The mid-eleventh century opened a dramatic new phase in European history, one that can be summarized in terms of a broad and deep intensification along numerous historical axes, all of which are directly relevant to the issue of heresy and inquisition. After centuries of monastic and peasant agricultural labor, for example, extensive new lands had been claimed and cleared by the eleventh century. New farming techniques and practices produced an agricultural boom that in turn sparked a population explosion. Within a few centuries, the population of western countries had multiplied by factors ranging from two to seven or eight. By 1300, the overall population of medieval Europe had doubled, an astonishing increase in less than two hundred years.

Spurred by this growth and the consequent revival of trade networks (both local and long-distance), urban centers were revitalized for the first time since the Roman centuries. Although there were no rivals to the rich and cosmopolitan eastern cities of Constantinople, Baghdad, Samarkand, or Hangzhou, medieval cities such as Oxford, Marseilles, and Bologna began to incorporate expanding populations and commercial prospects. Forever complicating the traditional Christian order of "those who fight, those who pray, and those who work," merchants entered the socioeconomic scene, linking rural and urban communities to the vast trade networks in and beyond Europe.

One particularly visible and enduring consequence of this new commercial vitality was the outpouring of funds into two particularly Christian institutions: cathedrals and universities. This was the age of Gothic architecture, the stunning (and stunningly expensive) investments in soaring, light-filled urban cathedrals, seats of local episcopal authority and scripture in stone to be read by an awed, largely illiterate laity. Requiring vast economic resources and decades to construct, urban cathedrals represented a joining—not only of heaven and earth in a sacred architectural space, but also of the local community and Christendom, linked through the commanding ecclesiastical

Figure I.2. Plowing in the Middle Ages, 1028 CE From "De Universo" by Rabanus Maurus. Cod. 132. ***Source*****: Photo by Alfredo Dagli Orti. Library of the Abbey, Abbey, Montecassino, Italy. Bildarchiv Preussischer Kulturbesitz/Art Resource, NY.**

authority of bishops, canons, clergy, and monks. Small schools emerged under the wings of the cathedrals, many of which blossomed in the twelfth and thirteenth centuries into full-fledged universities dedicated to the study of medicine, canon law, theology, and the liberal arts. The University of Bologna took an early lead in law, producing an unsurpassed generation of scholars whose work set the stage for later European legal, constitutional, and even inquisitorial frameworks. Graduates of the University of Bologna also ended up on the papal see, applying their legal training to the ecclesiastical problems and challenges of the day. The University of Paris would become the preeminent institution (followed by the Rhineland University of Cologne) in theological studies, its faculty and graduates profoundly shaping late medieval intellectual and political discourse.

After the twelfth century, popes, kings, bishops, nobles, civic councils, and inquisitors began to draw routinely upon the concentrated brainpower and cultural influence of university faculty; not surprisingly, connections between university academics and inquisitors would also become stronger

Figure I.3. The Foire du Lendit (Fair on the Plain of St. Denis); Miniature from the Grandes Chroniques de France, fol. 122 verso. France, late 14th c. ***Source*****: Musée Goya, Castres, France. Erich Lessing/Art Resource, NY.**

and more complex over time. Thinkers pondered new ideas with colleagues and students, though their paths could lead them in very different directions. By the fifteenth century, not only did some of the Church's greatest inquisitorial experts come from faculty ranks, but so too did several of their most bitter foes. As we will see, the universities in Oxford and Prague would become particular sites of controversy over heresy, orthodoxy, and spiritual authority.

Beyond the universities, however, the central Middle Ages also experienced a flourishing of intellectual life and an explosion of new vernacular literary forms, ranging from heroic epics and short romances to courtly love poetry, mystical treatises, rules, manuals, parental guides to life, and even bawdy student accounts of drinking and debauchery. Shortly after the thirteenth-century courtly allegorical poem *The Romance of the Rose* was set down in French, Dante Alighieri penned his *Divine Comedy* in fourteenth-century Italy, and the Flemish mystic Hadewijch recorded her visionary experiences in Middle Dutch. Little wonder that this was also the age of vernacular translations of scripture, texts outlawed by the Church but of enormous spiritual significance to eager lay readers and listeners. Vernacular communication also extended to preaching, as invigorating speakers from all walks of life set aside impenetrable Latin for the homey familiarity and humility of the native tongue. Interest in the art of preaching not only spawned a huge literature of guides and *exempla* but also prompted vernacular communication between clergy and laity that would prove vital to certain disputes over heresy, particularly in regions such as Bohemia, where fierce linguistic and ethnic rivalries between Czechs and Germans added bitter fuel to the fire.

During the high medieval centuries, secular leaders intensified their grasp on local communities: in centralizing kingdoms such as France and England, among the fragmented principalities in the German lands whose nobility fended off weak imperial authority, and within the feuding oligarchies of Venice, Florence, and the other northern Italian city-states. Political intensification in the secular realm was mirrored—and eventually provoked directly—by an expansion of papal power at the end of the eleventh century. Heir to St. Peter, the rock upon whom Jesus built his church, the pope had over the preceding centuries wielded increasingly more spiritual *and* political authority; early medieval popes crowned kings and emperors, commanded armed forces, and even possessed a wide strip of central Italian lands known as the Papal States. Although evidence suggests that the papacy had fallen into disarray by the ninth and tenth centuries, frequently occupied by disaffected sons of wealthy Roman families, a series of vigorous and capable pontiffs ascended the see beginning in the mid-eleventh century. Among the many consequences were religious intensifications ranging from a consolidation of papal power, the successful and wide-ranging implementation of Church reform, and the igniting of lay religious enthusiasm across Christendom.

Figure I.4. The Classroom of Henricus de Allemania at the University of Bologna. Last folio from the Liber ethicorum by Fra Henricus de Allemania. Illuminated manuscript page by Laurentius de Voltolina. Parchment, 18 cm × 22 cm. Inv. Min. 1233. ***Source*****: Photo by Joerg P. Anders. Kupferstichkabinett, Staatliche Museen, Berlin, Germany. Bildarchiv Preussischer Kulturbesitz/Art Resource, NY.**

The reformer pope whose influence irrevocably set the stage for later notions of heresy and inquisition was Gregory VII (r. 1073–1085), who embarked upon a passionate campaign to correct what he saw as unacceptable failings within the clergy and to restore the spiritual credibility of the Church. Particularly troubling to him was secular influence over religious matters: the buying and selling of church positions, for instance, or the granting of ecclesiastical offices by lords on whose lands the churches lay. Equally galling was the endemic sexual activity of clergy, either with wives or mistresses. Thus Gregory VII and his curia initiated a wide reform, not only issuing new spiritual policies prohibiting both practices but alternately commanding and inviting lay Christians to hold local priests to higher expectations. Although the reforms were met in many places with entrenched resistance, papal insistence and pressure from newly involved local laity gradually turned the tide. Priestly behavior became an object of scrutiny, and laypeople (influenced by the many other intensifications of their day) began to take greater notice of spiritual matters. Although the Church still held the keys to the kingdom, its priestly gatekeepers were being held to a new standard.

Pope Gregory VII's reformist agenda to purify Christendom and enhance papal authority was continued under the pontificates of his successors, notably Urban II (r. 1088–1099) and Innocent III (r. 1198–1216). Both men employed the concept of armed pilgrimage (later termed "crusade") to battle infidels and heretics, sought to heal relations between the increasingly alienated Greek and Latin Churches, and to seize the holy city of Jerusalem, that supreme geographical umbilicus joining heaven and earth. Both also shared Gregory VII's commitment to building the papal monarchy, dominating secular authority, and ensuring proper social and spiritual order within Christendom. Yet they faced significantly different conditions: Urban actively encouraged, even agitated, the stream of new lay piety prompted by the Gregorian reforms (directing it toward crusade and penitential pilgrimage); in contrast, Innocent found himself a century later trying to build a dam against the rushing floodwaters of Christian enthusiasm and innovation, for by the end of the twelfth century, Christian women and men across Europe found themselves inspired by the freshly repopularized words of the scripture to express and enact its apostolic model.

LIVING CHRISTIAN IN THE WORLD

How is one to live well in the tempting, troubling, turbulent material world? This has never been an easy question to answer, but it loomed particularly large in the hearts and minds of medieval Christians after the twelfth century. The answers provided by the early medieval Church no longer satisfied, particularly as the urban and commercial intensifications of the age fostered growing literacy, textual production, and circulation of ideas. Illegal vernacular translations of scripture began to appear by the end of the twelfth century, and small, like-minded groups formed "textual communities" to hear the Word in their own tongue.[12] Sometimes these clusters formed unique ideas, as reflected in accounts of the first significant group accused of heresy in the medieval West—the community at Orléans in 1022 (recounted above by Adémar of Chabannes).

According to sources, a group of perhaps twenty men and women (including clergy, nuns, and members of the nobility) developed a belief in a secret and spiritual *gnosis,* or *knowing*, transmitted by the laying on of hands. Immediately purged of all sin, members were said to believe that they received the Holy Spirit and its gift of utter scriptural understanding and rejected sacraments and the theological paradoxes of incarnation, virgin birth, and resurrection. Orléans was an important educational and political center, and neither its local nor royal potentates could tolerate such a scandal; after resisting interrogation and considerable pressure to recant, all but two of the members were locked in a cottage outside the city walls and burned alive. It was the first capital condemnation for heresy in more than seven centuries, and it would become the opening salvo in a quickly escalating European dialogue over proper faith, order, and authority.

Some new eleventh-century religious expressions took itinerant form, as charismatic preachers wandered the western roads to preach penitence and personal salvation, often provoking a defensive stance among local clergy. In the early twelfth century, for example, an ascetic renegade Benedictine known as Henry the Monk appeared in Le Mans, where he preached Gospel-based penitence (and, according to clerical records, may also have challenged the Church's institutional and sacramental authority). Henry married off repentant prostitutes to local young men, seemingly inspiring a type of individual *and* communal conversion rooted in the scriptural call to moral rehabilitation and spiritual rebirth. As his teachings spread through southern France, Church authorities pursued and eventually imprisoned him—though not before the renowned abbot and mystic Bernard of Clairvaux (1090–1153) challenged him to a public disputation.

As some solitary individuals and scattered communities began to emphasize the rule of the Gospel in various ways, others sought to develop forms of life or even religious orders that, although appearing novel to the Church, were deeply rooted in the apostolic model of both the active and the contemplative life. We will encounter many of these in the following chapters, ranging from preachers, masters, and followers to adherents, men and women who would ultimately be sorted and classified into the categories of "heretical" and "orthodox." Urban centers in particular exhibited a centripetal religious force, drawing them not only to mendicant friars eager to serve underrepresented populations, but to a dazzling variety of organizations, institutions, and inspired individuals. Christian devotionalism would soon crescendo among some, manifesting in intense Eucharistic piety (involving extremely frequent communion and adoration of the elevated host), prayers by rosary or proxy, pilgrimage, penance, emotional contemplation of Christ's suffering, ecstatic mystical longing for union with the divine, and so on. Each of these practices evolved out of earlier traditions, yet their efflorescence in the fourteenth and fifteenth centuries represents yet another consequence of the central medieval transformations.

New pious expressions and opportunities were not limited to men: by the fourteenth century, women had long been joining formal nunneries under official rules and entering informal lay religious communities for a (perhaps temporary) stint of prayer and service, also seeking visionary or mystical connections with God, studying scripture, teaching or training children, serving the poor, and writing or even preaching about their experiences. Complex and often contradictory notions of gender were of course deeply enmeshed with ideas about piety; none remained static over the millennium prior to 1500. Due to the powerful legacy of Greco-Roman and Christian misogyny in Europe, gender has proven a particularly illuminating axis of analysis in the study of medieval religious history, and much work remains to be done. For example, whereas medieval scholarship of the past century first drew attention to the outpouring of religious enthusiasm among women and posited a particular affinity between women and heresy, recent research has challenged that assumption and offered nuanced new approaches to the workings of sex and gender in medieval religion.

As we will see, the central and later medieval centuries were marked by a deep intensification of hostility toward women. By the thirteenth century, elite thinkers had not only codified long-standing Western notions of feminine inferiority but also theologically articulated the unique danger of women's weakness. Strategically deploying a new understanding of female minds and bodies as potential channels of demonic power, scholars simultaneously undermined existing possibilities for feminine authority and cast them as literal joinings of hell and earth. Throughout the following chapters, we will consider how medieval gender assumptions were wielded and challenged over time, noting in particular key fourteenth- and fifteenth-century anxieties about women and mystical authority.

Intensification of other hostilities and anxieties also pervades the centuries between 1050 and 1500. As political leaders articulated new theories about the sovereignty of states in the face of earthly opponents, theologians began to consider, in increasingly precise ways, the sovereignty of Christendom in the face of spiritual opponents—namely, the devil. Anxieties about demonic and satanic influence had sharply escalated by the later medieval centuries, as did apocalyptic expectation and fear of the looming End of Days foretold most famously in the book of Revelation.

One particularly brutal consequence was that Jews were targeted with increasing frequency and brutality from the late eleventh century on, vulnerable scapegoats for local Christian fear and fury. Despite centuries of largely uncontroversial coexistence in early medieval European communities, cultural intensifications after the eleventh century birthed the bitter legacy of anti-Semitism. Crusading armies robbed and murdered local Jews on the way to battle "the infidel," and neither secular nor sacral authorities were able to put a stop to the violence. Rumors circulated for generations about Jewish murders of Christian children or theft and desecration of the Eucharist host, entirely fictive stories paralleled by the ancient stereotypes of cannibalistic and baby-eating heretics.

When the Great Mortality—the bubonic plague—arrived in Europe in 1348, sweeping away up to a third of the population, conspiracy theories about Jews poisoning water supplies spread like wildfire. Although some contemporaries pointed out that Jews were also dying of the plague and therefore were probably innocent of the crime, entire Jewish communities were slaughtered by enraged mobs. Although the Church did not initiate or encourage local violence against Jews, at the Fourth Lateran Council (1215) Innocent made clear the inferior, degraded status of Jews within the Western sociospiritual order, mandating that they wear special identifying markers on their clothing and forbidding them to interact with or hold any authority over Christians. By the later Middle Ages, living Christian had for many become conflated with aggression against increasingly classified and categorized out-groups.

THE FORMATION OF A PERSECUTING SOCIETY?

In a classic study published in the late 1980s, R. I. Moore argued for what he termed "the formation of a persecuting society" during these centuries, interpreting the central Middle Ages as a particular historical crucible of

Figure I.5. The Jews of Cologne Burned Alive, a Consequence of the Lie Spread by Bishop Hinderbach about the Alleged Ritual Killing of a Boy Named Simon in Trent [South Tyrol] in 1475. Michael Wolgemut, colored woodcut, from the *World Chronicle* by Hartmann Schedel, 1493. *Source*: Bildarchiv Preussischer Kulturbesitz/Art Resource, NY.

hostility against marginalized populations (including heretics, Jews, lepers, and homosexuals) that set the stage for later European discrimination and mass atrocities. At the heart of his argument is the claim that a new class of men emerged at this time, clerks (or clergy in official capacities), whose consolidation and cultural influence represent a revolutionary transformation in the West: the development "of an administrative class whose members identified their interests with those of their patrons and not their families, [who] laid the foundation for the reshaping of European society and culture."[13] Thus, the medieval social order had already become complicated by the end of the twelfth century: between those who rule and those who pray there emerged the clerical administrator, a learned, celibate, and likely ambitious man endowed with the cultural power to think, categorize, and write (always on behalf of greater authorities). We might think of these men as those who classify. Although the power to order and record may not at first glance appear as dramatic as physical violence, the pen ultimately controlled the sword in later medieval Europe. Nowhere was this truer than in the burgeoning ranks of thinkers and writers who administered the intensifying agendas of popes, archbishops, kings, and lords.

Thus when reading the following chapters, readers might keep in mind the link between this new cultural workforce and the birth of inquisitorial categories, procedures, techniques, and texts and consider whether the medieval relationship between cultural intensification and persecution might offer lessons for other times and places. Meanwhile, nonnoble merchants and their noble-like wealth continued to vex the Church; laywomen and men of all conditions continued to both adopt and adapt features of the world around them; Jews inhabited an increasingly dangerous no-man's-land of economic, religious, and physical vulnerability; and the poor, dispossessed, afflicted, or otherwise marginalized eked out an existence aided only by the promise of salvation and perhaps a few coins or scraps of Christian charity.

Finally, "[a]t the centre of the whole religious system of the later Middle Ages lay a ritual which turned bread into flesh—a fragile, small, wheaten disc into God. This was the eucharist: host, ritual, God among mortals."[14] The transformation of grain and grape into body and blood, the mystery of the incarnate Word, and the other astonishing joinings of heaven and earth in Christendom represent a pulsing spiritual vein linking the men and women of fortified towns of southern France, urban Rhineland, Alpine villages, Bohemian towns, the English countryside, and beyond. Such connections were not limited to sacred places, objects, or rituals but could also cohere within individual people modeled on Christ's own divine materiality. Thus living saints, or ascetic human preachers, were increasingly perceived through the high and later Middle Ages as incarnate textuality, representing a vibrant, vital conduit between the human and the divine.[15] And it was

Figure I.6. *Christ on the Cross*, **Jan van Eyck. 43 cm × 26 cm. Inv. 525 F.** *Source*: **Property of the Kaiser Friedrich-Museums-Verein. Photo by Joerg P. Anders. Gemaeldegalerie, Staatliche Museen, Berlin, Germany. Bildarchiv Preussischer Kulturbesitz/Art Resource, NY.**

within communities, through relationships with others, that their messages resonated.

By recognizing the deep certainty in such saving channels linking heaven and earth, we can better understand the growing passion with which people on all points of the institutional and theological spectrum struggled to claim them. Access to and interpretation of these joinings increasingly preoccupied Christians who, more or less consciously, reflected on them as they worked, played, worshiped, listened, birthed, loved, feuded, traveled, suffered, begged, prayed, and marveled. Their multitude of voices has echoed only faintly across time to our day, muted by the increasingly strident tones and techniques of institutional authority; Adémar of Chabannes, Hildegard of Bingen, James Capelli, and other trumpets of orthodoxy would soon be joined by many others, elite figures privileged in their power to record and shape history. Yet evidence does survive of the others if we pay careful attention. So we now begin our exploration of medieval heresy and inquisition in the first of a series of specific contexts in which dramatic controversies over Christian belief, piety, and authority erupted in the eleventh and twelfth centuries—controversies whose consequences would reverberate excruciatingly through centuries of European history to come.

SUGGESTIONS FOR FURTHER READING

Chazan, Robert. *The Jews of Medieval Western Christendom, 1000–1500*. Cambridge: Cambridge University Press, 2006.

Frugoni, Chiara, William McCuaig, and Arsenio Frugoni. *A Day in a Medieval City*. Chicago: University of Chicago Press, 2006.

Grundmann, Herbert. *Religious Movements in the Middle Ages: The Historical Links between Heresy, the Mendicant Orders, and the Women's Religious Movement in the Twelfth and Thirteenth Century, with the Historical Foundations of German Mysticism*. Translated by Steven Rowan. Notre Dame, IN: University of Notre Dame Press, 1995.

Janin, Hunt. *The University in Medieval Life, 1179–1499*. Jefferson, NC: McFarland Press, 2008.

Little, Lester. *Religious Poverty and the Profit Economy in Medieval Europe*. Ithaca, NY: Cornell University Press, 1983.

Lynch, Joseph. *The Medieval Church: A Brief History*. New York: Longman, 1992.

Moore, R. I. *The First European Revolution: 970–1215 (The Making of Europe)*. Malden, MA: Blackwell, 2000.

———. *The Formation of a Persecuting Society: Authority and Deviance in Western Europe, 950–1250*. Second edition. Malden, MA: Blackwell, 2007.

Rivard, Derek A. *Blessing the World: Ritual and Lay Piety in Medieval Religion*. Washington, DC: Catholic University of America Press, 2009.

Swanson, R. N. *Religion and Devotion in Europe, c. 1215–1515*. Cambridge: Cambridge University Press, 1995.

Ward, Jennifer. *Women in Medieval Europe, 1200–1500*. New York: Longman, 2003.

NOTES

1. Walter L. Wakefield and Austin P. Evans, *Heresies of the High Middle Ages* (New York: Columbia University Press, 1991), 74.

2. Beverly Kienzle, "Defending the Lord's Vineyard: Hildegard of Bingen's Preaching against the Cathars," 163–82, in *Medieval Monastic Preaching*, ed. Carolyn A. Muessig (Leiden: Brill, 1998), 172.

3. Wakefield and Evans, *Heresies*, 304.

4. John Arnold, review of *The Corruption of Angels: The Great Inquisition of 1245–1246*, by Mark Gregory Pegg, *H-France Review* 1, no. 31 (November 2001).

5. 1 Corinthians 11:19.

6. Quoted in Matthew Paris, *Chronica majora*, ed. Henry Richards Luard, 5 vols. (Rolls ser., London, 1880), v, 400; see also Gratian, *Decretum*, C. 24, q. 3, cc. 27–31, *Corpus iuris canonici*, ed. Emil Friedberg, 2 vols (Leipzig, 1879–1881), I, cols. 997–98.

7. Edward Muir and Guido Ruggiero, eds., *History from Crime*, trans. Corrada Biazzo Curry, Margaret A. Gallucci, and Mary M. Gallucci (Baltimore, MD: Johns Hopkins University Press, 1994), viii.

8. Peter Novick, *That Noble Dream: The "Objectivity" Question and the American Historical Profession* (Cambridge: Cambridge University Press, 1998), 7.

9. Robert E. Lerner, *The Heresy of the Free Spirit in the Later Middle Ages* (Notre Dame, IN: University of Notre Dame Press, 1991), 34.

10. Patrick Geary, ed., *Readings in Medieval History*, 3rd ed. (Peterborough, ON: Broadview Press, 2003), 265–66.

11. Peter Brown, *Society and the Holy in Late Antiquity* (Berkeley: University of California Press, 1989), 6.

12. On the concept of "textual communities," see Brian Stock, *Listening for the Text: On the Uses of the Past* (Philadelphia: University of Pennsylvania Press, 1997).

13. R. I. Moore, *The First European Revolution, c. 970–1250* (Malden, MA: Blackwell, 2000), 195.

14. Miri Rubin, *Corpus Christi: The Eucharist in Late Medieval Culture* (Cambridge: Cambridge University Press, 1992), 1.

15. R. N. Swanson, "Literacy, Heresy, History and Orthodoxy: Perspectives and Permutations for the Later Middle Ages," 279–93, in *Heresy and Literacy, 1000–1530*, ed. Peter Biller and Anne Hudson (Cambridge: Cambridge University Press, 1996), 286.

Chapter One

Good Christians, "Cathars," and Historical Evidence

Alarmed reports of heresy first sounded in 1143, in a letter from the German-speaking Rhineland region of northern Europe. Written by Eberwin, head of a monastery near Cologne, the letter anxiously sought guidance from the famous abbot and spiritual luminary of the age, Bernard of Clairvaux. In explaining the situation to Bernard, Prior Eberwin described a group of local people whose unusual religious opinions had brought them to the attention of the greater community. With equal parts dismay and disgust, Eberwin described their practices. "This is the heresy of those people," he began:

> They say that theirs alone is the Church, inasmuch as only they follow in the footsteps of Christ. They continue to be the true imitators of the apostolic life, seeking not those things which are of the world, possessing no house, or lands, or anything of their own, even as Christ had no property nor allowed his disciples the right of possession.[1]

Not only do they falsely claim apostolic purity and righteousness, Eberwin continued, but they diverge from proper Christian observance in matters of personal and sacramental behavior as well: The heretics forbid milk and anything born of sexual intercourse; they reject marriage as fornication; they believe that baptism should be performed by the laying on of hands; and they assert that anyone among them who is baptized in this way has the power to baptize others in turn. Denying the spiritual efficacy of ordained priests, the prior lamented, the heretics follow figures called the "Elect"—men and women who have been baptized by hand, intently observed by their communities, and who serve as a model to their "listeners" and "believers." Refusing to believe that saints can intercede for their souls, the heretics reject the value of prayers for the dead and even deny "that there is purgatorial fire after death," teaching instead that souls go immediately to heaven or hell upon death. Thus, complained Eberwin, do these wild beasts and monsters "render void the priesthood of the Church and condemn its sacraments."[2]

What was the fate of these people, according to the letter? The prior informs Bernard that some of the heretics returned to the Church after performing penance, whereas others (including their "bishop" and his assistant) "held their ground against us in an assembly of clergy and laymen, in the presence of the lord archbishop himself and some great nobles . . . defending their heresy with the words of Christ and the Apostle [Paul]."[3] That the debate reportedly continued for three days without resolution suggests that local clergy and secular authorities were focused more on persuasion than coercion; the intent of both sides was evidently to convince the other through argument and appeals to scripture.

However, as would often be the case in early responses to religious innovation, violence in Cologne erupted at the hands of local laity, "whereupon, against our will, they were seized by the people, who were moved by rather too great zeal, and thrown into the fire and burned." According to Eberwin, the accused heretics' deaths were a consequence of local Christians' escalating anger and exhausted patience. Yet the prior also injected an unexpected note of admiration into the letter, marveling that the accused "met and bore the agony of the fire not only with patience but even with joy." Where did these people, these "limbs of the devil," get courage and faith "such as is scarcely to be found even in men most devoted to the faith of Christ"?[4]

Even for Eberwin, therefore, the so-called heretics shared much in common with pious Christians: assurance in the authority of scripture, adherence to the apostolic model, acceptance of preaching and debate as a means of persuasion, appreciation for ascetic endurance, and spiritual joyfulness even in the face of persecution. It is an important point, for those termed unorthodox by their enemies (whether in twelfth-century Cologne, fourteenth-century Montpellier, or fifteenth-century Prague) viewed themselves not as enemies of the true Church, but as defenders of its pure and original form—one that many medieval reformers believed had become bloated and corrupt. Although the black-and-white categories of "heresy" and "orthodoxy" would become increasingly rigid and bureaucratically determined over the course of the later Middle Ages, in reality there was no such clear opposition or demarcation.

READING EBERWIN, ECKBERT, AND HILDEGARD

As one reads texts from this period, or arguably from any historical context, it is important to avoid taking an "either/or" position on the material. For example, instead of simply accepting Eberwin's perspective of this group as wicked people intent upon destroying the Church, one should pay attention to his language and then ask some questions: How does he describe the heretics? Why might the ideas described by Eberwin appeal to someone in this time? Why could such claims and actions be threatening to contemporaries? What was his purpose in writing to Bernard, an ecclesiastical leader who would be canonized only a few decades later? And what kind of evidence does the text provide about the past? All documents are arguably influenced by the agenda or bias of their author, whether explicitly or implicitly, and Eberwin's sole purpose in writing the letter was to inform a learned authority about what he regarded as a group of terrible deviants. Can we thus believe what he says at face value, or is it possible that he distorts, exaggerates, or unintentionally reports false information having himself been misinformed? There is certainly room for doubt, which brings us to questions of method.

Two basic rules for historians will be useful here. First, never read sources in isolation: one must always check one document against other sources of information, triangulating evidence before drawing firm conclusions. Second, one must always read both hostile and sympathetic accounts as critically as possible—that is, reading "against the grain" to figure out not only what the author intended to communicate to the reader but what is inadvertently conveyed through assumptions, omissions, and other, less obvious aspects of the text. We cannot simply accept the content of Eberwin's letter at face value, as proof that there were wicked heretics in the German Rhineland in 1143, but we *can* conclude that something was happening that so unsettled the prior that he invested time, energy, and ink in the appeal to the famous Bernard of Clairvaux.

To evaluate the credibility and significance of Eberwin's report, we can look for other independent accounts of the "something" that was going on in the mid-twelfth-century German Rhineland. A second piece of evidence is that Abbot Bernard of Clairvaux was simultaneously harnessing his own considerable resources and talents against what he perceived as the growing forces of evil in France. Clearly sympathetic to Eberwin's message that the "heretics have a very large number of adherents scattered widely throughout the world," he preached a sermon in 1144 intended to paint an unforgettable picture of the horrors inflicted by heresy. Drawing on a vivid passage from the Song of Songs (2:15) that reads, "Catch for us the foxes, the little foxes that ruin the vineyards, our vineyards that are in bloom," Bernard equated Christendom with the vineyard of the Lord. Heretics, in contrast, were "malicious foxes . . . who slink about in the shadows" and plunder God's vine. The association of heresy with secret sin was an ancient one, but Bernard's combination of Old Testament verse, beastly imagery, and contemporary spiritual concerns forged a new and enduring archetype in Christendom, one that would serve as a staple of antiheretical polemic for centuries to come. His writings thus reveal a great deal regarding *perceptions* of heresy in his day, which is not the same as heresy itself.

A third piece of evidence appears again from the hand of an abbot in the German Rhineland, but twenty years after Eberwin's letter to Bernard. In 1163, Abbot Eckbert of the monastery at Schönau, referred to a community "examined and convicted by learned men . . . , condemned by secular authority," and burned at the stake.[5] Although it is plausible that Eckbert was referring to yet another group (perhaps a remnant of the first, or refugees fleeing persecution elsewhere), he might also have had the original investigation from 1143 in mind; in either case, his account helps to substantiate Eberwin's claims of the presence of some kind of dissenting community in the region punished by laity, whether via formal authority or mob violence.

A fourth source (also written by Eckbert) is even more revealing: In what would be the era's first thorough polemical response to the heretics, he penned for the archbishop of Cologne a treatise called *Sermons against the Cathars*, a document consisting of thirteen sermons that refuted the heresy point by point and concluded with an excerpt from St. Augustine's *On the Manichaeans* to lend ancient and authoritative weight to the text. Eckbert claims to have come into personal contact with some of the heretic missionaries during the 1150s and retained a clear sense of their doctrines years later. He also suggests that this new type of dissent was not limited to Cologne, for it had appeared by now in the Rhineland city of Mainz, where a community of approximately forty known adherents had reportedly been able to practice their beliefs for some time.

What other evidence might one find for "something" of religious novelty going on in the Rhineland? A historian might read through the letters, sermons, and other surviving documentation left by educated religious figures of the twelfth century to see what themes or memes kept arising. And it turns out that individuals at the highest level in the late twelfth-century Western Church picked up on and amplified these concerns about heresy, adding more detail to our picture. Perhaps the most vivid example is Eckbert's contemporary, Hildegard of Bingen (d. 1179); a famous mystic and abbess of a Benedictine convent, she was also the only approved female preacher in the medieval Church. And Hildegard blamed the apparent upswell of heresy on lazy, corrupt clergy. In a public sermon preached in Cologne, she thundered against complacent priests whose laxity she claimed had allowed wicked heretics to multiply:

> You ought to be the corners of the Church's strength, holding her up like the corners that sustain the boundaries of the earth. But you are laid low and do not hold up the Church, retreating instead to the cave of your own desire. And

> because of the tedium brought on by your riches, avarice, and other vain pursuits, you do not properly teach your subordinates. . . . Wake up![6]

The heretics, she warned, are hypocritical servants of the devil who will walk about "with wan faces," clothed in sanctity and ready to seduce devout Christians. Tellingly, she emphasized that the heretics will not *appear* sinful, will not look or act "like rabid and unclean animals," but will seem "saintly and filled with the Holy Spirit."[7] To Eberwin's question "How do these wicked people have such faith and courage?" Hildegard has a clear response: they do not have faith and courage, but only the superficial *appearance* of it. Why is the sham piety of these servants of the devil able to lead people astray? Again, her response is clear: because to unsuspecting Christians, they *seem* better than priests of the day who are not living up to the expected moral and spiritual code. By the later twelfth century, therefore, it was already difficult for Church leaders to distinguish between piety and pretense, holiness and hypocrisy.

Hildegard's writings also add another layer of complication to the historical record, since they discuss *perceptions of* heresy. So how do we figure out what was really happening with "heresy" in the twelfth-century German Rhineland and beyond? Modern historians have found themselves at odds on a number of different issues, particularly having to do with the relationship between names and labels on the one hand, and their relationship to actual human beliefs, behaviors, and communities on the other.[8] It is a problem that we will encounter regularly in the pages and chapters ahead.

NAMING AND NAME CALLING

Language presents one of the most significant challenges facing modern readers of medieval heresy, and not simply because materials are usually written in Latin or sometimes in medieval vernaculars such as German, French, Czech, or Italian (quite different languages from their modern counterparts). Rather, the very words employed by people to describe themselves or others complicate the way in which we read historical sources. It is from Eckbert's letter and Hildegard's sermon that we first run across a specific, pejorative name for heretics that would echo for centuries through inquisitorial and historical records: Cathar. The origins of the term are unclear, perhaps deriving from the Greek word *katharos* (meaning "pure") or, less plausibly, the German *Katze* ("cat"; long associated in Europe with sin, sexual perversion, and witchery). Whatever its origin, the term became a staple in the language of orthodox opponents and was repeated by myriad clerical observers throughout the Middle Ages.

Medieval historians who study social and religious cultures have spent a lot of time and energy debating the term and associated problems over the last twenty years or so. One problem is that the term *Cathar* was never employed by those accused of heresy, who might refer to themselves and their leaders variously as believers, adherents, Friends of God, the Known, Good Men, Good Women, and Good Christians, to give only a few of the labels expressed in a variety of vernacular and dialectic forms. A second problem is that the term suggests a kind of consistency or uniformity of belief, one that is rarely present in the historical record. A third is that the label comes to us through the writings of Church officials and other authorities, and particularly often from inquisitors' pens—hardly a neutral perspective, if such a thing even exists in the written record.

One might reasonably say that this is a semantic concern and that one name is as good as another; in other words, who cares? But labels are powerful and capable of transmitting powerful and misleading assumptions under the guise of self-evident truth. Moreover, they are difficult to shake off once applied. The assumption behind the term *Cathar*, whether wielded by inquisitor or historian, not only is derogatory but implies that anyone labeled as such was somehow equivalent to another—that all were self-conscious members of an organized movement who accepted the same ideas and doctrines as other so-called Cathars in other places and times. As awareness of the new ideas spread, the names to designate heresy multiplied: Eckbert, for example, reported that those called Cathars in Germany were called "Piphles" in Flanders and "Texerant" in France.[9] The underlying assumption is that they were—regardless of local variations—part of the same general category of heretic. But were they? Would they have had any sense of being affiliated with like-minded people or fellow "believers" whom they had never met? It's an important question, and one that is easy to overlook when confronted with a broad umbrella label such as "Cathar."

Part of the problem is that nineteenth- and twentieth-century historians began to employ "Cathar" as a convenient term to represent what they regarded as a particular type of person and belief community from the twelfth through fourteenth centuries. Uncritical use of the term suggested uniformity where there was none; thus did loosely overlapping or even unrelated rings of belief across diverse time periods and regional contexts seem in retrospect a coherent movement, a consciously organized and internally consistent "anti-Church." That assumption is unwarranted: the self-identified Good Christians accused of such beliefs were deeply embedded in local communities and family structures but only rarely linked in any formal, institutional, or self-conscious manner to like-minded individuals elsewhere in Europe.

Although Catharism as an organized pan-European church movement never existed, however, there can be no doubt that there was something happening that caught contemporaries' attention at this time. One might think instead of deep, lingering sociospiritual and political currents that showed up in different forms across regional pockets such as southern France and northern Italy. A particularly common current was anticlericalism in various forms, skepticism about the sacramental authority of the priesthood, and a hunger for models of apostolic purity.

Another, according to some contemporary reports (and some modern historians), was a shared underpinning of such ideas in *dualism*. To map some key changes over time and place, the following sketches the nature of dualist belief and practice as reported in the twelfth- and thirteenth-century historical record and the role of social and political networks for the growth of heresy (or perceptions thereof). Additionally, we will return frequently to consider issues of evidence and interpretation about which historians still vigorously debate.

ORIGINS OF WESTERN DUALISM

Religious dualism, as the name suggests, is rooted in opposition and the division of all things into one of two camps: light or dark, good or evil, spiritual or material. In its absolute form, dualism posits two different, independent, and equally matched deities (usually God and the devil) in eternal opposition. Mitigated or moderate dualism assigns greater power to God, assigning the force of darkness to the devil, usually a fallen angel like Lucifer, who "owns" the wicked and material world. Far from being unique to the medieval centuries, dualist ideas appeared in most of the religions of salvation that took root in the classical world: in the teachings of the Persian Zoroaster (sixth century BCE), in Greek religion and philosophy (including that of Pythagoras and Plato), and in the syncretic blend of Manichaeism (third century CE). Moreover, certain Gnostic communities of early Christian thinkers, influenced by a variety of Persian, Jewish, Greek, and Egyptian sources, articulated a form of dualism in which souls were imprisoned in human bodies until released by *gnosis* (meaning "secret knowledge").

Thus as Christian doctrine developed and spread via missionaries and monasticism to the lands of western Europe in the late antique and early medieval period, so grew a tendency to emphasize the contrast between spirit and matter, the link between flesh and sin, and the omnipresent threat of the forces of evil. Several groups or movements that embraced a dualist doctrine, such as the Messalians and Paulicians, were eventually condemned by the Roman Church in the early medieval era. Yet mainstream Christianity contained elements that resonated with dualist thought: Jesus's teachings speak of separate kingdoms of God and of men, for example, as in John 18:36 ("My kingdom is not of this world . . . my kingdom is from another place"); of the contest between the love of God and the desire for things of this earth; and of freedom of the spirit and bondage to Satan. The dualism underpinning the faith of Good Christians and their followers was no novelty, which provoked many antiheretical authors to associate them with the Manichaeans of St. Augustine's day (fourth/fifth century) and to thus presume incorrectly that their medieval communities were a direct remnant of an ancient threat to the Church.

The origins of the communities described by Eberwin, Eckbert, and Hildegard are still controversial, first because the sources are not entirely reliable, and second because historians are reluctant to mistake coincidence for causality. For example, while some historians believe that members of the Bogomil Church that emerged in parts of Macedonia and Bulgaria in the early tenth century directly influenced the growth of Western dualism, others disagree vehemently, arguing that no such contacts were ever in place—nor are they necessary in order to understand the variety of Western communities in the twelfth century. In other words, one should be cautious about presuming direct connection simply because ideas in two places appear similar.

Yet direct contacts between high medieval East and West clearly existed, as demonstrated in the traveling mission of a Bogomil bishop, Papa Nicetas, from Constantinople, who visited dualist communities in Lombardy and Languedoc during the late 1160s or early 1170s, bringing with him a man named Mark and several other Italians. After meeting with adherents in Albi and France, Nicetas apparently had contact with three further communities in Toulouse, Carcassonne, and Agen. All bore some level of local organization. When a Dominican friar and former Good Christian named Rainier Sacconi surveyed the realm in the mid-thirteenth century, he reported sixteen "bishoprics," including two in the East (Bulgaria and Drugunthia): "All [the others] sprang from the last two named," he claimed.[10] Nicetas and his companions from the East did not create Good Christian communities in the West but seem to have visited existing communities in an attempt to reinforce administrative structures and to convince adherents to adopt their own theological slant on the nature of evil.

Rather than attempting to draw direct linear connections between Eastern and Western dualism in the eleventh and twelfth centuries, however, we do better to imagine pockets in western Europe in which local pieties and doctrinal skepticism had already begun to take root independently by the late eleventh century. Preachers, missionaries, and other travelers contributed to the spread of ideas, finding certain areas more or less receptive than others. Ironically, it seems that Pope Gregory VII's call for clerical reform and an active lay Christian apostolate in the late eleventh century inadvertently encouraged anticlericalism and dug new, unapproved channels of religious reform in the twelfth. The central idea of apostolic purity and clarified rituals evidently appealed widely across Christendom and became entrenched in particular regions of western Europe. Thus locales such as the northern Rhineland, southern France, and northern Italy, characterized by decentralized political authority and cultural tendencies toward localism and relative tolerance, represented fertile ground for new ideas.

DUALISM AMONG THE GOOD CHRISTIANS

Followers of the Good Christians were likely more influenced by the living example of their perfected leaders and the pressures of local circumstances than by dualist doctrine or theology; nonetheless, it is worth exploring the fundamental worldview in which many of the beliefs attributed to them were rooted. The primary manifestation of Western dualism was an interpretation of the world with parallels to the Christian story of humanity's fall from grace and expulsion from Eden. Offering a persuasive answer to the age-old question, "Why does God allow evil in his world?" Good Christians simply turned the question around: the material world could *not* be God's, as anyone paying attention to the horror of earthly life must acknowledge, and it therefore must be the realm of Satan.

According to sources from both sympathetic and hostile witnesses, Good Christians and their adherents were said to believe that goodness existed only in the spiritual realm, where a benevolent God resides in heaven. In contrast, they associated the visible, tangible world with darkness and evil and believed it to be either the creation of—or in the hands of—an evil deity. In moderate dualism, Satan was understood to be a fallen angel; in the more radical forms of dualism, he was understood to be an evil god coeternal and equal to the Lord God. Good Christians and their adherents believed that suffering in the world was a natural outcome of the world's inherent and unredeemable wickedness: thus collapses the paradox of a loving God inexplicably causing human pain, because the deity responsible for human circumstances (whether an independent god of evil or a fallen angel) is explicitly evil.

Medieval dualism was expressed and reaffirmed through stories that helped to buttress believers' view of the world about them. According to one such dualist myth, Satan seduced angels out of the good God's heaven and shut them up in bodies of flesh and clay. The world itself and all the human bodies in it were prisons in which the previously undifferentiated, sexless angels were trapped, corrupted, and mesmerized to forget their heavenly origins. Thus Good Christians are said to have believed that upon death, the angelic human soul left the body and transmigrated into the womb of the next available pregnant female, whether animal or human. To redeem these souls and rescue them from the endless cycle of rebirth, the good God sent an angel—identified by many medieval dualists with Jesus Christ—to remind those trapped in the corruption of the physical world of their true identity and angelic nature. The world would end only when the final angelic soul had been released, finally disentangling the spiritual and material worlds. Thus humanity and human choices to embrace either the world of flesh or the world of the spirit represent a battleground in which the irreconcilable forces of good and evil eternally clash. On a textual basis, believers generally rejected the Old Testament as Satan's book and adhered only to the precepts of the New Testament, the book of the angelic Jesus and the good God.

From an orthodox point of view, the theological implications of dualism were appalling: if the world and everything in it were eternally evil, then God could not have been responsible for its creation; if Christ did not assume human form or physically suffer on a cross of wood, there could be no crucifixion or resurrection; baptism by water, a natural element of the material world, could offer no salvation; and the Eucharist is no miracle of presence but only corrupted grain and grape. Where the Good Christians understood themselves as rooted in a pious tradition, their opponents perceived instead an utter negation of fundamental Christian principles.

Like many medieval critics of the ecclesiastical system, the Good Men and Good Women challenged the central paradoxes of Catholicism through skepticism. For example, a believer in France is said to have stated that "the body of Christ, even though it had been as great as the Alps, would have been long ago consumed by those who had eaten of it."[11] More crudely, others reportedly pointed to the natural outcome of consuming the wafer, observing that it must pass through the body and come to a disgusting end and asserting that such could not happen if God were in it. These objections remind us that theology and doctrine are only abstractions and therefore only part (perhaps a very small part) of the stories of medieval belief. Individual human beings absorb, create, modify, transform, and breathe new life into the atmosphere around them; belief is not static, and people of the past were more than the accumulation of ideas attributed to them. So how did individual people develop and embrace new ideas to enact in their daily lives? Or, to put it another way, how did men and women in such communities answer the enduring question, "How is a good Christian to live in the world?"

Perhaps most significant was the issue of sacraments. In contrast to the many sacred intersections in traditional medieval Christianity (for example, relics, pilgrimages, prayers, saints, sacraments, and, above all, the Eucharist), the Good Christians limited the fusion of profane and divine to a single moment: the *consolamentum*—baptism by the Holy Spirit via the laying on of demonstrably holy hands instead of through the corruption of material water. Indeed, there was widespread belief that the ritual was bequeathed by the angelic Jesus.

Communities influenced by dualism fell into two distinct tiers of unequal size. The Elect (or *perfecti* [perfects], as inquisitors called them) were a highly ascetic minority. Because the *consolamentum* was the only means of salvation and was to be administered only once, those who accepted it in their youth faced an austere and difficult path. The Good Men and Women sometimes traveled from one community to another or, particularly among the Good Women in Languedoc, established houses that functioned as social centers for local sympathizers. Once ordained, however, a member of the Elect had to remain in that exalted condition of purity, untarnished in the midst of the carnality and corruption of the material. In contrast to the traditional Church's position that sexual intercourse between married people was licit for procreation, the Good Christians insisted that pregnancy was an evil that served only to trap more angelic souls in flesh prisons.

Because there was no gradated system of penance to atone for misdeeds as in Catholicism, the Good Men and Women had to avoid all sins in order to remain unsullied—from lying to larceny, from eating a morsel of meat to murder. As Rainier Sacconi put it, "If their prelate, especially their bishop, may secretly have committed some mortal sin . . . all those upon whom he has imposed his hand have been misled and perish if they die in that state."[12] The stakes were thus enormously high, for followers believed that leaders who sinned had no spiritual authority with which to perform the all-important *consolamentum*. To meet the challenge, the Elect were said to hold themselves to uncompromising standards. Despite periodic accusations of orgies and obscene behavior (smears deployed against religious dissenters and political enemies far beyond the medieval centuries), even hostile observers noted that the Good Men and Women adhered rigorously to the spiritual and behavioral standards of their faith and provided a potent spiritual model for their adoring followers.

An additional ritual called the *apparellamentum* provided an outlet for the extremely minor transgressions that even the most scrupulous of souls commits. The *apparellamentum* was a collective confession of faults by the Elect at which supporters and believers might also gather. According to a surviving Occitanian version of the service, the Elect would ritually confess their offenses (such as distraction, malice, and laziness), followed by the prayer "O Lord, judge and condemn the imperfections of the flesh. Have no pity on the flesh, born of corruption, but show mercy to the spirit, which is imprisoned."[13] Only significant sins required reconsoling, an event that apparently occurred with less frequency than one might imagine given the manifold pitfalls and temptations of human life.

The great appeal of these ideas lay in the pure lives of the spiritually disciplined Elect, who essentially stood in for the behavior of the community at large: whereas in the Catholic tradition, monks and nuns withdrew from the world to dedicate their lives to prayer and service, the Good Christians pursued a similar vocation *in the world*. As discussed further below, most families in sympathetic villages or towns had a Good Man or Woman who either lived with relatives or in one of dozens of local houses; in no case, however, were these spiritual leaders isolated or walled off from the greater community. Close bonds of kinship, friendship, worship, and neighborly association linked the Good Men and Women to their followers and their followers to one another. Indeed, some scholars argue that this open and public model of sanctity influenced the emergence in the early thirteenth century of Catholic mendicant orders (Franciscan and Dominican), whose apostolic example of preaching in the world explicitly contrasted with the isolated life of monks.

Such a rigorous and ascetic path was not possible for (or desired by) all people, most of whom wished simply to live well with family and faith in their local communities, to marry and raise children, to enjoy the simple pleasures of life, and to enter heaven upon their deaths. Reinforcing this distinction between the Elect and believers was a ritual various sources describe as the *melioramentum* ("adoration"), in which the believer knelt before a Good Man or Woman, exchanged a greeting, and pleaded for his or her prayers and intercession with God. Because only the elite, perfected leader was free from sin, only his or her prayers were believed to be heard by God. Whether such actions were self-conscious and religiously inflected rituals or were instead traditional courtesies into which inquisitors read suspicious meaning probably varied over time and place; scholars will no doubt continue to debate the matter. At any rate, we know that lay believers looked to their elite for inspiration, intercession, instruction, and, most important, the imposition of the *consolamentum* at the end of their own lives.

These basic elements of belief and behavior among Good Christians and their followers developed in a wide variety of economic, social, political, regional, and religious circumstances in the twelfth and thirteenth centuries. To better understand the intimate meanings of the faith and its relationship to other local institutions and practices, let us consider two regions where support for the Good Men and Women was particularly vigorous: Languedoc (in modern-day southern France) and the cities of the central and northern Italian peninsula.

SOCIETY AND RULERSHIP IN LANGUEDOC

In the twelfth and thirteenth centuries, the lands of what is now southern France were divided among territorial lords such as the counts of Toulouse and Foix and the viscounts of Trencavel. In contrast to the centralizing political tendencies of neighboring lands under strong royal control, these counties were characterized by fierce independence and dense networks of local allegiances and alliances. Cultural and political differences with the northern realms were paramount—even the name "Languedoc" ("language of *oc*," or Occitan) emphasized the region's distinctiveness. Curving along the Mediterranean coast and pushing inland to the Dordogne River, Languedoc extended west to the Pyrenees and east past Avignon, with a diverse geography ranging from the lush plains of lower Languedoc to the mountainous terrain of Provence between the Pyrenees and Alps.

In Languedoc, social and political factors were so deeply interconnected with religious influences as to be virtually inextricable; as bishops, popes, and inquisitors would later discover, rural nobility provided protection for the Good Christians and their followers, support nourished by local solidarity. By contrast, northern regions under strong royal rule (such as France and England) tended to foster bonds between nobility and churchmen, shaping an environment of cooperative unity against the common threat of heresy. Historians have long debated the various reasons for the flourishing of different pieties in Languedoc, pointing in turn to fragmented political authority, socioeconomic conditions, laxity among bishops and priests, anticlericalism, the distractions of chronic warfare, the tightly knit family structures, and a certain local laissez-faire attitude on the part of the nobility and citizens alike regarding matters of faith. What is evident, however, is that no single event or cause was responsible for fostering new religious perspectives in so many towns and villages. Rather, one must imagine a constellation of factors that served to feed and perpetuate appreciation for the Good Christians in cities such as Toulouse, Carcassonne, and Béziers; villages such as Fanjeaux and Lavaur; and mountainous rural outposts such as Montaillou and Montségur.[14]

Of particular significance to the history of the Elect and their adherents in this region, however, is the family of Toulouse, whose counts had ruled the city and surrounding countryside since the late ninth century. Among its most famous members was Count Raymond IV, a leader of the First Crusade who founded the Latin county of Tripoli (in modern-day Lebanon) in the early twelfth century. According to some historians, one of the most important preconditions for the growth of heresy in Languedoc was the slow deterioration of the counts' authority since that time and the political anarchy created by competing rival claims (including those of the kings of France, England,

and Aragon). When the response to heresy escalated toward violence in the early thirteenth century, the pope would hold Count Raymond VI of Toulouse particularly accountable for the crime of sheltering the heterodox. Moreover, the Trencavel viscounts, who held an important cluster of lands in the center of Languedoc, tried to strengthen their position by developing strategic alliances alternately with the mutually hostile counts of Toulouse and Barcelona. Regional power had been consolidated throughout the region by dynastic alliances and marriage, but such webs of kinship could not fully temper the political disorder. Moreover, the local practice of partible inheritance—dividing land among children rather than transferring unified territories to a single heir—served to fragment authority further. Such conflicts lent Languedocian politics a distinct flavor, one that would foster defensive and protectionist tendencies.

Thus, day-to-day life in the lands of Toulouse and many other parts of Languedoc were routinely disrupted in the high Middle Ages by warfare, the predations of mercenaries, and a tendency toward lawlessness among secular lords. According to one thirteenth-century archbishop, a significant reason for the appeal of early Good Christians was that they successfully persuaded the rough and financially predatory nobility of the mountain villages to stop preying on merchants and other travelers and even to establish more peaceful relations with neighboring communities.[15] In other words, new religious ideas may have been accompanied by improved local conditions—a compelling motive for relative openness and tolerance.

Perhaps surprisingly, religious toleration was indeed a characteristic feature of the region: Jews were treated well, particularly in comparison with other regions of western Europe, and so too were those who voiced any one of a variety of different religious points of view. The label "heretic" seems to have had little meaning in twelfth-century Languedoc, and the local clergy apparently did not possess the ability, desire, or resources to combat the charismatic piety of the Good Christians. Once ecclesiastical attention was focused upon heresy in these lands, however, much was made of the failure of Languedocian bishops and priests. A Catholic council at Avignon in 1209 sharply rebuked clergy who were "indistinguishable from laymen in conduct";[16] a few years later, Pope Innocent III would also blame the rise of heresy on clerical laxity, calling the bishops of Languedoc "blind creatures, dumb dogs who no longer bark"[17] and removing several elite clergy from their positions. Although there were perhaps failures in leadership, however, not all the criticism was fair: most of the clergy in local areas were operating in hampered conditions, often impoverished to the point of incapacity, poorly educated, and likely demoralized by the abuse heaped upon them by nobility. No evidence points to a lower standard of morality among these clergy than among those in orthodox areas. Indeed, few Catholic clergy anywhere in western Europe looked particularly holy in comparison to the ascetic, inspiring Good Men and Women.

GOOD CHRISTIANS IN LANGUEDOC

Support and defense from local nobility lent "heretical" communities and their leaders strength and durability in the twelfth and early thirteenth centuries. Leaders were allowed to travel untroubled between communities under the control of a particular family (or group of families) and thus to preach and conduct rituals in safety. Supported financially by gifts, hospitality, and legacies from believers, the Good Men in particular could move in relative freedom between their homes and far-flung communities. Not only were rural populations dependent upon the goodwill of their lords unlikely to risk retaliation by protesting religious irregularities, they were just as likely to be part of the local spiritual matrix themselves. Although the enduring nature of such beliefs in Languedoc is largely attributable to the protective influence of nobility, the social makeup of communities devoted to their Elect was complex. Northern manifestations of such beliefs in France and the Rhineland tended to be associated with the lower classes (particularly with weavers and other cloth workers), but in the south the faith appealed to a wide cross-section of society: nobles, merchants, artisans, professional men of various backgrounds, and peasants all participated.

Map 1.1. Languedoc and Provence. Reprinted from Louisa A. Burnham, *So Great a Light, So Great a Smoke: The Beguin Heretics of Languedoc*. *Source*: **Copyright © 2008 by Cornell University. Used by permission of the publisher, Cornell University Press.**

The environments most conducive for sustaining the faith in Languedoc were the castles and fortified villages of powerful local nobility, homes of men and women whose webs of kinship provided influence over large territories and thus protection to the Good Men and Women. Although we have seen that some isolated regions may have been organized along a hierarchical ecclesiastical model, it would be a mistake on multiple levels to speak of a heretical Church. Far more significant to the shape and rhythm of life among Good Christians was the social milieu of families and villages in which new ideas took root and developed over the generations and in which one may discern "an intimate, intensely local, and deliberately unadorned way of living with the holy."[18] The knight Bernart Mir Arezat recalled, for example, that his village of Saint-Martin-de-la-Lande in the Lauragais contained as many as ten houses of Elect during his childhood, men and women who could move about, teach, and perform their rituals in complete freedom.[19] Believers interrogated by inquisitors in the thirteenth century routinely claimed that "earlier" (i.e., in the twelfth century) the faith had been virtually a family legacy: "One was born a Cathar just as one's neighbor might be born a Catholic—the family's religious options were thus conditioned, even if this did not rule out the possibility of later divergence."[20] That Occitanian families proved remarkably receptive to the religious spirit of the Good Christians poses a challenge to the traditional interpretation of Catharism as antisocial, dour, and essentially negative.

As evident in the tens of thousands of trial records, women played an influential role in the faith, not only as welcome followers who reared their children to venerate their ascetic leaders, but very often as admired Good Women themselves. Historians believe that nearly half the houses of Languedocian supporters were occupied by women who actively participated either as Good Women or their adherents. A young woman named Arnaude de Lamothe stated that as a child, "one day two heretical women whose names I do not know arrived at Montauban at the house of my mother, Astorgue. Those heretical women preached there, in my presence, and in the presence of my sister, Peirone, of my mother . . . and Lombarde, widow of my uncle Isarn d'Auzac."[21] Later sent to a female house in Villemur, both sisters apparently pursued religious careers as Good Women.

Yet the relationship between faith, sex, and gender was vexed, and the Good Christians did not appeal to all women any more than their message resonated for all men. For example, a woman named Aimersent from the village of Cambiac reported to inquisitors in 1246 that when she was an adolescent, her "paternal aunt, Gérauda of Cabuet, took her to Auriac, to the house of Lady Esquiva, the wife of the knight Guilhern Aldric. And she saw two heretics [female] in the said house . . . and all of them . . . adored the said heretics, genuflecting three times while saying, 'Bless, Good Ladies, pray for these sinners.'" The pregnant Aimersent said further that she listened to the preaching of the women for a long time, but that she was later embarrassed when they told her that the baby in her belly was the devil "and everyone began to laugh at this."[22] The passage has a ring of authenticity to it, especially in the young woman's discomfort at the others' laughter.

Female Elect played a variety of roles within Languedocian communities, and it can be difficult (perhaps impossible) to distinguish between personal or family engagements and religious purposes. Good Women traveled for the birth of children, family gatherings, and social visits, but also to preach and provide or receive training. Dulcie Faure of Villeneuve-la-Comtal, for example, left her husband to stay with the Good Woman of her own village and later moved to Castelnaudary to a house directed by Blanche of Laurac;[23] after another year, she entered formal training at yet another community founded by Blanche in the village of Laurac. Whether *bonas femnas* or simply *credenzas* (or believers), women of Languedoc diffused the faith in personal contacts and conversation, family ties, teaching relationships, and regional networks. Particularly strong were ties between mothers and daughters and aunts and nieces, whose commitment to their spiritual principles shaped not only generations of family religiosity but also served to bind different households as girl children matured and moved into either a husband's household or one of the community's homes or sisterhoods.

Brotherhoods of Good Men, or *bon omes*, as they were called in the local tongue, also existed throughout Languedoc, although males were more likely to travel between communities than to be settled in a single household. Such male brotherhoods often retained strong communal or familial ties to women within the faith as well. In the village of Les Cassès, for example, the brothers Pierre and Bernart Bofilh lived together as Good Men, raising Bernart's two young sons. Both sons grew up and remained within those circles—one as a believer and one as a deacon. Their sister, Pagane, evidently spent her childhood with her mother in an all-female community and grew up to become a Good Woman in a sisterhood at Saint-Paul-Cap-de-Joux. At Fanjeaux, the brothers Guilhabert and Isarn de Castres held positions of high esteem in their faith community, and their three sisters lived together in a sisterhood of Good Women.[24]

The number of pious houses in twelfth-century Languedocian towns and villages is extraordinarily high (reports of fifty to seventy in a single town, for example), though it would have been difficult to distinguish between specifically religious and private communities. As in Matthew 18:20, "For where two or three are gathered in my name, there am I in the midst of them": the formally regulated status and privileges of monasteries in the Catholic tradition had no clear equivalent among the Good Christians and their followers. In Languedoc, therefore, a large number of adherents' families claimed one or several members of the leaders, those ascetic and devout individuals who not only remained in the community but whose active example no doubt strengthened the bonds of both immediate and extended family.

Thus according to one historical view, the Good Christians' faith reflected a complex constellation of needs and desires: it provided an explanation for evil in the world and validated ascetic and apostolically inspired leaders whose single sacrament could release believers into the spiritual world upon their deathbed. It mirrored contemporary Catholic concerns about the temptations of the flesh and the corruption of the material world, but to the question of how a Christian is to live in the world, it offered a novel answer: to trust in the leadership of a demonstrably holy circle of individuals, in the saving power of the deathbed *consolamentum*, and in the attainability of one's ultimate release from the world of flesh.

From another scholarly perspective, however, the Good Men and Women's power is better understood as a highly localized web of affection and social belonging knit by routines and personal charisma. In other words, the "something" going on regarding apparently dissenting religious views was arguably more about social connections, localized rituals and communal belonging than it was about esoteric belief or doctrine. And Languedoc was not the only region in which such currents were reported by the end of the twelfth century, so let us turn east from the Midi to explore the political background, social development, and familial embedding of similar ideas in a very different setting: the cities and villages of the northern Italian peninsula.

GOOD CHRISTIANS IN NORTHERN ITALY

Although the urban centers of northern Italy might at first glance appear to be a far cry from the fortified rural villages and walled cities of Languedoc, both regions were politically decentralized, shaped by fertile plains and mountain ranges, fiercely resistant to outside authorities, and characterized by strong local and familial ties. And just as the power vacuum in Toulouse and the particular circumstances of rural nobility and local networks played a key role in the flourishing of Good Christians and their adherents in Languedoc, so too did a unique set of political and social factors shape the history of Catharism (as it was soon called by authorities) in twelfth- and thirteenth-century Italy. Once again, we are dependent largely upon inquisitorial documents triangulated with other source material, whose careful mining by scholars has recently yielded new insights.

Three elements merit consideration here. First is the conflict between imperial and papal forces, a fierce struggle birthed in the eleventh-century era of Gregorian reform and one that would serve to distract authorities in the

Map 1.2. Cathars in Italy. Reprinted from Malcolm Lambert, *The Cathars. Source*: **Copyright © 1998 by Malcolm Lambert. Reprinted with permission of the publisher, Blackwell Publishing.**

twelfth century from the threat of heresy. As Emperor Frederick Barbarossa (r. 1154–1190) and his foe, Pope Alexander III (r. 1159–1181), battled it out for influence in Italy, scant attention or resources were paid to issues of religious observance or local networks of spiritual resistance. Second is the earlier influence of Pope Gregory VII on Italian communities, where his reform movement opened issues of spiritual principle to circles previously excluded from such discussions and encouraged Christian laity to hold their clergy to a higher moral standard. Third, and of arguably equal significance for understanding the appeal of and concern about religious innovation in the northern peninsula, is the "Patarene" lay movement of the mid- to late eleventh century, a reformist uprising stirred by the preaching of a deacon named Ariald who called on humble citizens to unite against the reportedly simoniacal, unchaste, and degenerate clergy of the archdiocese of Milan. Although the reformers were explicitly pro-Church and not perceived as explicitly heretical (again, the boundary between heresy and orthodoxy had not yet been defined), the derogatory name "Patarene" would come be applied to a variety of heretical groups in the twelfth century, including communities of Cathars. In the 1150s, the Italian tradition of radical reform was continued by a charismatic canon named Arnold of Brescia, who seized control of Rome on a platform of evangelical poverty and a Patarene-like reform agenda and was executed in 1155. For decades after his death, Arnold's message of anticlericalism and moral reform continued to resonate in the peninsula.

What, then, is the relationship between these early religious movements and later twelfth-century heresy in the region? And according to the record, how did Cathar-like communities first come to or emerge in the Italian cities? In contrast to the relatively mysterious origins of the Good Christians in Languedoc, there is specific evidence of the faith's beginnings in Italy. According to the account of a thirteenth-century inquisitor from Lombardy named Anselm of Alessandria, Cathar ideas were transplanted directly from northern France in the mid-twelfth century via an encounter between a missionizing notary and a small but enthusiastic local community. Anselm reports that a "certain notary" from northern France met a gravedigger called Mark at Concorezzo, northeast of Milan, who was persuaded to join his ranks, along with a local weaver named John, a smith named Joseph, and an unnamed person whom they "led astray" in Milan. Directed by the notary, the little group visited a group of transplanted northern French believers at a village called Roccavione on the overland route from Languedoc to Italy. Mark the gravedigger received the *consolamentum* there from the bishop, was made a deacon, and returned to Concorezzo to preach. "As a result of his preaching in Lombardy, then in the March of Treviso and later in Tuscany, the number of heretics greatly increased."[25]

The geographical pattern is curious, because one might expect Italian dualism to have emerged via contact with Constantinople, Greece, or Bulgaria rather than northern France. Although there is certainly reason to question the veracity of the story, penned as it was more than a century later and without verifiable documentation, believers in such communities cared deeply about their history, enough so that one should not dismiss out of hand the unexpected legend of northern French origins.

As was the case in Languedoc, the evident receptiveness and openness of local communities to such ideas is as important as the exact nature of initial contacts and conversions. The chronology is also compelling: Mark and his friends were apparently actively missionizing and converting Lombardy and surrounding regions during the 1160s, coincident with Barbarossa's fierce wars with the pope, whose authority the emperor kept weakening by promoting rival claimants to the see. Local cities were sucked into the conflict, as was Milan, which opposed the emperor and was destroyed in 1162. It was a terrible time for citizens of the cities, and residents were furious at the callousness of the great lords and desperate for both social and spiritual stability. When Barbarossa withdrew from Italy in 1167, support for the pope and his hierarchy of all-too-frequently sinful clergy was miserably low. "It was," as Malcolm Lambert has put it, "the springtime of Italian Catharism."[26]

An account of the life of Galdinus, archbishop of Milan (r. 1166–1176), provides a glimpse into the preaching, teaching, and private missionizing that must have characterized the spread of new beliefs during these decades. The author records that the archbishop set himself to combat that "deadly plague and by many discourses and much preaching . . . recalled the people . . . and, by instructing them in the fundamentals of the Catholic faith in so far as he was able . . . advanced his cause by both word and example."[27] Galdinus's example was probably the more effective tool, because Italian Cathars observed in their ascetic Elect a striking contrast to the wealth, pleasures, and power of local clergy. Evidently he was restricted to verbal persuasion because there is no record of judicial action at this early date.

It was in Italy that Papa Nicetas of Constantinople evidently first encountered leaders from Languedoc. The message he bore was dire: the Elect status of "Mark the gravedigger"—and thus most of the Italian leadership—was uncertain because of a flaw in the chain of perfected authority through which he had received the *consolamentum.* Orthodox Catholicism had centuries earlier rejected the principle of Donatism, an ancient heresy that claimed any sacraments performed by a sinful priest were invalid. Twelfth-century Good Christians, with their emphasis upon fierce ascetic purity, were not convinced. Nicetas lodged such doubt and concern among the little northern Italian community that Mark and probably many of the other Italian elites accepted a renewed *consolamentum* from their persuasive visitor before accompanying him to the council in Toulouse.

Beyond the original foundations in Concorezzo and Milan established by Mark and his associates, communities were soon founded in Vicenza, Desenzano, Bagnolo, Cremona, Florence, and Spoleto, while dozens of groups also cropped up in the north and extended sporadically down through Orvieto and Viterbo to Rome and even Naples. Because inquisitors began their work much later and with somewhat less intensity than those operating in Languedoc, we have comparatively little information about the early history of communities in Italy. Scholars familiar with the surviving documents are convinced, however, that a key to twelfth- and thirteenth-century Italian heresy lay in the mismatch between escalating popular religious enthusiasm and the limited available channels for expression sanctioned by the institutional Church.

In Italy, the new currents were a deeply urban phenomenon that gained a foothold amid political battles between communes and Church, socioeconomic disorder, and the bonds and ties of family, kinship, and workshop. Ideas reached sympathetic ears not only by preaching and mission, but also via networks of artisans and family connections. In Florence, for example, members came from a cluster of upwardly mobile banking and mercantile families as well as laborers, servants, purse makers, doctors, and other professionals. And as in Languedoc, members' households served as community centers, schools, and hospices. The flux of Italian society fostered the spread of belief, not only because the traditional Church could not expand with (or effectively respond to) the needs of a burgeoning lay population, but also because the long-standing transience of merchants, nobles, patricians, and preachers throughout the peninsula maintained a social instability that fermented localized forms of religious observance. Only with the foundation of the mendicant orders in the early thirteenth century would the Church have a compelling response to those needs. During the intervening decades, however, this localized alternative would appeal to a cross-section of urban society ranging from nobles to artisans, merchants, moneylenders, matrons, patrons, and even priests. In contrast to Languedoc, however, few peasants seem to have participated in the Italian scene.

Indeed, the struggle over "Catharism" was at the very heart of a set of crucial changes in thirteenth-century Italian towns, including the creation of independent civic institutions, the restructuring of Catholic orthodoxy, and the narrowing of gender roles. Heretical involvement became a means of participating in and expressing a position vis-à-vis such changes because the dualist condemnation of the material body opened up possibilities for critiquing the broader hierarchy of authority in the material world. Thus when the believers of Viterbo came into conflict with the commune of Rome over a series of political issues, the pope backed his own city and was able to use heresy to justify a forceful response; in turn, the citizens of Viterbo launched scathing critiques of the Church that drew on their own faith. Likewise, when an argument between the city of Orvieto and the pope erupted over the right to control a nearby fortress, the pope responded with interdict while the Cathar Orvietans made plans to expel Catholics from the city. That the Cathars of Italy shared a significant theological profile with the Good Christians of Languedoc is suggested by many texts, including the statement of an Orvietan furrier named Stradigotto recorded by a Franciscan inquisitor in 1268–1269:

> That this world and all visible things were created by the devil; that human souls are spirits that fell from heaven and will only be saved through the hearts of the Cathars; that there will be no future resurrection of humankind; that the priests of the Roman Church do not have the power to absolve men who have confessed and are contrite from sin; that those living in matrimony are living in a state of damnation; that baptism in material water as it is performed in the ritual of the Roman Church does not aid in salvation.[28]

However, it is equally apparent from other reports that, just as in France, most Italian believers were drawn to the faith not because of its abstract dualist cosmology but out of admiration for a pure spiritual ideal perhaps lacking in the world of thirteenth-century Italy.

Men and women thus raised children within their communities, embraced spiritual bonds along with familial traditions, and adored the holy Good Men and Women who brought the ancient apostolic to life in the most local and intimate of circles. Most of those interrogated later by inquisitors did not embrace or even necessarily understand complex dualist theology (any more than most Catholics grasped the subtleties of orthodox doctrine), but they did frequently seek the simple sacrament of the *consolamentum* and criticize the Catholic clergy. Yet boundaries between their spiritual position and that of the Catholic Church were not necessarily firm or exclusive: for example, one believer named Armanno Punzilupo confessed to the Catholic clergy,

Figure 1.1. Medieval Orvieto. ***Source*:** **Photo by Nate Risdon.**

did penance, and was even venerated as a local saint for some time after his death; similarly, two Orvietans interrogated by inquisitors reported following both their own Elect and the Franciscan friars, clearly eager for the spiritual benefits offered by both circles.[29]

As to the presence of "Catharism" (or perhaps Cathar-ish ideas) beyond the realms of Languedoc and Italy, the evidence is scattershot. Diverse sources suggest a substantial presence of people associated with such ideas in the north, and communities were known to have taken root in Burgundy, Champagne, Flanders, Never, Vezelay, Auxerre, Troyes, Besançon, Metz, Rheims, Rouen, and Arras. Apparently, however, circles of belief did not spread enough in the northern lands to require the extensive organization established in Toulouse.

In contrast, these currents never successfully traveled to England; a boat of immigrant missionaries who arrived at the English shore in the winter of 1166 were promptly interrogated by Henry II and his clergy, rejected, and set adrift to die. Their antisacerdotal and antisacramental beliefs sound similar to that of "Good Christians," but the key point is that no new religious missions could make headway where clerical and secular power were united. As the English chronicler William of Newburgh put it, "Pious harshness purged the kingdom of that pestilence [and] preserved it from ever again intruding."[30] Even in regions less geographically insular than England, traveling preachers and missionaries made little headway in the north during the twelfth and thirteenth centuries.

CONVERSATIONS AND COUNCILS (1143–1209)

As we learned from Eberwin's letter to Bernard, Church officials in the German Rhineland were slow to persecute in the mid-twelfth century, and early Catholic responses to the Good Christians were also typically characterized by debate, dialogue, and directive: "The verbal jousts between the orthodox and the heretics, and among the heretics themselves, reflect the religious vitality of the region."[31] This is not to suggest tolerance, however, which could never be an option for Catholic leadership charged with protecting the spiritual health and vitality of Christendom. In 1145, Abbot Bernard of Clairvaux had already launched a preaching campaign in Albi in an attempt to convert the "Cathars" back to the orthodox fold, apparently believing that local nobility had allowed the heresy to thrive. Although he met with some success in Albi, he was disappointed after moving east of Toulouse. After he healed the son of a heretic and preaching to the gathered people of the church, his voice was drowned out by local knights clashing their armor in an unsubtle display of resentment. Bernard left in anger, noting later that the land was "in need of a great deal of preaching."[32] In 1148, Pope Eugenius III forbade anyone to protect or assist heretics in southern France, a warning sternly reissued by the pope more than a decade later. And in 1163, the pope and cardinals attending the Council of Tours issued legislation targeting heretics and their protectors.

During this time, Church spokesmen made serious, ongoing attempts to engage the Good Christians in public debates, an approach deemed in keeping with traditional ecclesiastical authority. In 1165, for example, a discussion was convened at Lombers (a castle near Albi) at which each side chose spokesmen to defend their position: evidence that the Catholics took the event seriously is the prestige and quality of those in attendance (the bishop of Albi, along with another bishop, three abbots, a layman, and a wide range of ranking observers, including Raymond Trencavel, Viscount of Béziers). Speaking on behalf of the Good Christians was Sicard le Cellerier, reportedly bishop of the Cathar church of Albi. According to contemporary sources, nearly the whole population of Lombers and Albi was present to witness the squaring off of Good Christian and Catholic. The debate disintegrated into a shouting match, however, as the Catholics hurled condemnations at the *bon omes* for refusing to accept the Old Testament or to give oaths, while the Good Men insulted their opponents as "ravening wolves, hypocrites, and seducers, lovers of salutations in the marketplace, of the chief seats and the higher places at table, desirous of being called rabbis and masters."[33] Although the outcome of this meeting was not one of mutual understanding, one must acknowledge the willingness of both sides to engage in verbal persuasion.

Further evidence that churchmen wanted to convince rather than coerce in these years lies in the mass of texts intended for instruction and debate, a documentary statement of faith in the process of conversion and the ultimate triumph of truth. Lambert describes the author of one such compilation as

> a dogged orthodox opponent grappling against his own reconstruction of Cathar theology with scriptural weapons, often soundly chosen, but failing to understand that Catharism generally attracted untrained minds, whose emotions were stirred by the contrast between the rigorous, ascetic *perfecti* and a relaxed local clergy of limited training, and who were drawn to their vivid metaphors and narratives.[34]

Within a few years, popes and archbishops had begun to recognize that such converts were not easily moved by logical, scripture-based argument.

By the final quarter of the twelfth century, elite ecclesiastical opinion had begun to shift in favor of more aggressive methods. In 1178, responding to decades of papal and archiepiscopal criticism, Count Raymond V of Toulouse requested help against the heretics in his realm in what was probably an attempt to curry favor with the Church in a tough political climate. The subsequent Catholic mission (led by a papal legate and the abbot of Clairvaux) resulted in the indictment of only a handful of people, but it was apparently sufficient to convince Abbot Henry of Marcy that more coercion would be needed. Support for such measures was soon forthcoming. At the Third Lateran Council in 1179, the threat of force was now made explicit, not only against Cathars but against a wide variety of other religious expressions deemed heretical (many of which will be addressed in subsequent chapters). The pope's message was clear:

> Since in Gascogne [Gascony], in the territory of Albi, in Toulouse and its neighborhood, and in other places, the perversity of the heretics, whom some call Cathari, others Patarini . . . has assumed such proportions that they practice their wickedness no longer in secret as some do, but preach their error publicly and thus mislead the simple and the weak, we decree that they and all who defend and receive them are anathematized.[35]

Note the fusion here of Cathari and Patarini and the implied homogeneity of the two labels. Five years later, Pope Lucius III issued the decretal *Ad abolendam* (*In Order to Abolish), which further criminalized a wide range of heretics and their defenders and called upon the vigilance of local bishops for enforcement.*

POPE INNOCENT III AND A NEW STANCE ON HERESY (1198–1209)

In the first week of January 1198, ninety-two-year-old Pope Celestine III died in Rome. The election of his successor would represent a turning point in the history of the medieval papacy as well as a watershed for the Church's position on heresy. Only thirty-seven years old at the time of his election, Pope Innocent III (r. 1198–1216) came from a wealthy and powerful Italian family and had been trained at the finest universities in theology and canon (Church) law. Brilliant, dynamic, and energetic, the young pope would spend his eighteen years in office not only aggrandizing the power of the papacy but also strengthening the ecclesiastical unity of Christendom. His pontificate would be characterized by bold campaigns into new doctrinal, legal, and even geographical regions, particularly through the use of the crusade as a means of extending Christian authority. The identification and conversion of heretics back to the orthodox fold represented for the first time a key element of the papal agenda, though Innocent's approach would shift and evolve markedly over time in response to changing circumstances in Languedoc, Lombardy, and beyond.

Innocent's approach to the problem of heresy in Christendom was novel, rooted in a keen recognition that much of what appeared as dissent was better understood as misplaced or misguided enthusiasm. Whereas Bernard of Clairvaux drew on the Song of Songs to depict heretics as "little foxes in the vineyard," Innocent drew famously on a parable from the Gospel of Matthew (13:24–30) to develop the more subtle metaphor of a farmer carefully distinguishing between wheat and tares (weeds) in his field. Convinced that the proper tending of Christendom's spiritual soil required scrupulous sifting through suspected heretics' beliefs and behaviors, he developed alternative paths for those willing to submit to the Church's authority. For example, in 1201 he rehabilitated and reorganized the Italian lay Humiliati, who had been shifted into hereticated territory by continuing to preach after the Third Lateran Council in 1179, and charted a similar path with other reformist communities (which will be discussed in chapter 2) a few years later.

In his early years on the see, therefore, the new pope explored a wide variety of canonical resources and possibilities in order to heal the growing rifts within the Church. The threat of force was never entirely distant, however: just as the parable of the tares concludes with the burning of the weeds that threaten God's wheat, so too did Innocent perceive heresy as a deep and utterly destructive enemy—and the "tares" were not only the believers themselves but also those who protected them. Interested in explaining and persuading where possible so that there could be no misunderstanding, the pope wrote letters such as one sent to the people of Treviso in 1207, in which he spelled out precisely what constituted Cathar beliefs, how they were wrong, and why they must be eliminated. It had little effect, perhaps as he anticipated.

In fact, Innocent had moved almost immediately upon his election against the "defenders, receivers, fautors and believers of heretics"; in 1199, he issued the bull *Vergentis in senium* (*Inclining toward Decay*) specifically aimed at secular and sacral authorities in the northern Italian city of Viterbo, in which he stripped from those found guilty all civic or clerical rights of office as well as the right to inherit or to leave an inheritance to children. Innocent's legal basis for such punitive action was his innovative but draconian equation of heresy with the imperial crime of conspiracy, for which he reached back eight hundred years to a precedent from the year 397: if treason against secular power and the civic realm is so dreadful as to deserve the death penalty (or worse, according to those old imperial laws), he argued, how much more appalling is conspiracy against ecclesiastical power and God's own community. *Vergentis in senium* provided the pontiff a weapon against the autonomy of the heretically inclined Italian cities, whose influence he perceived as increasingly malignant.

Fourteen years into his pontificate, Innocent also lambasted Emperor Frederick II for his failure to defend orthodoxy during campaigns in Italy: "Not only do you not capture the aforementioned little foxes" (note that we are back to vineyard imagery), "you favour and defend them to the extent that with you they are changed from little foxes to lions, from locusts to horses ready for war."[36] Sporadic efforts through his first decade in office to chastise lax clergy, create enduring alliances, and rally support for orthodoxy bore little fruit. The peculiarly chaotic political circumstances in the Italian peninsula and the disjuncture between secular and Church authorities made immediate reform an impossibility.

Innocent's response to heresy in Languedoc followed a different course, one shaped largely by the political circumstances that characterized the region. One of his earliest actions as pope had been to commission Cistercian monks to preach widely throughout the south of France, a campaign predicated on the value of persuasion and instruction as a means of converting straying souls back into the orthodox flock; Innocent referred to the effort as the "enterprise of peace and faith." In 1204, a public debate was held in Carcassonne, in which Catholics, Good Christians, and papal legates all participated, but the outcome was as unproductive as the debates thirty and forty years earlier; each side knew the arguments of the other but was not about to be persuaded. Some progress was made during these early years negotiating with larger populations, as at Toulouse when the town leaders and populace swore to repudiate heresy; such strides came at a price, however, because the oath at Toulouse had been secured in exchange for key political liberties that infuriated the local count, Raymond VI.

In 1206, the pope seized upon yet another approach to conversion by preaching. Petitioned by the Castilian bishop Diego of Osma and a canon named Dominic de Guzmán (the future St. Dominic) for the right to preach, the pope agreed to back their service as ascetic wandering preachers in Languedoc. The pope believed that their scrupulous way of life might impress local Cathars accustomed to venerating elite Good Christians. Adopting the apostolic model of the "sending of the seventy" (Luke 10:1–20), Innocent also divided territory up among the preachers so that they could cover as much land as possible as they traveled from village to village, preaching their message of conversion and orthodoxy. Dominic and his colleagues made inroads between 1206 and 1208, not only convincing some local adherents to embrace traditional Catholicism but also establishing new institutions such as the nunnery at Prouille to care for females displaced from their all-important familial ties and domestic structures. One wonders what the consequences of ongoing, apostolically inspired preaching campaigns might have been had they not been cut short in 1209 by the shift from verbal persuasion to violent crusade.

THE ALBIGENSIAN CRUSADE IN LANGUEDOC (1209–1229)

The circumstances leading up to Innocent's call for a crusade against the heretics of Languedoc in 1209 centered upon the political situation of Count Raymond VI of Toulouse. Unwilling to take the oath to repudiate heresy in Toulouse a few years earlier, Raymond fell squarely in the camp of those who "protected" heretics, though his concerns were by all accounts political and territorial, not spiritual. Encroachment by any external authorities rubbed him the wrong way (as it did most of the southern lords), and Raymond had been particularly unwelcoming to the abrasive Cistercian Pierre de Castelnau, whom Innocent had sent as his agent to Raymond's lands. For various reasons, including the ongoing use of mercenaries who stole Church wealth and his defense of Cathar heretics, Pierre excommunicated Raymond VI in 1207. Angry words followed, but the pope agreed with the decision and apparently began to consider sending an armed expedition to take control of a rebellious region teeming with disobedience (and thus heresy). For years Innocent had been actively planning and supervising crusading missions to the Iberian Peninsula in the west and the Levant in the east, expeditions that proved more successful in some cases than in others. It was perhaps only a matter of time before the instrument of crusade was wielded against "heretical" lands within the borders of Christendom.

Pierre de Castelnau was murdered in January 1208, probably by one of Raymond's officers; although it is unlikely the count would have been so politically clumsy as to order the execution himself, he failed to express sufficient innocence and sorrow, and Innocent was forced to respond. Raymond VI was no Cathar, but his oppositional stance (and now his appearance of guilt for murdering a papal legate) could no longer be tolerated. After unsuccessfully seeking help from the king of France, he ordered agents to begin preaching crusade throughout northern France against the southerners. Turning once again to militant Old Testament language as well as the Church fathers, he summoned loyal Christians to avenge the crime against God and drew on St. Augustine's articulation of the accepted criteria for a just war. According to Augustine (and thus Innocent), the faithful were obligated through the original covenant to take action against those who rebelled against God; Pierre de Castelnau had not only been murdered, he had been martyred. Innocent made clear his certainty that the legate's death was a sacrifice that should awaken true Christians everywhere: "We believe it is expedient that one man should die for it rather than it should all perish; for it is indeed so contaminated by the contagion of heresy that it may well be recalled from error more readily by the voice of the blood of its victim than by anything he could have done had he gone on living."[37]

In response to Innocent's call for a crusade, papal legates assembled an army that included powerful dukes, counts, archbishops, and other lords, all primarily from northern France. The army's aim was to destroy the holdings of the local lords and seize their lands, whether they were "Albigensians" (as the "heretical enemy" came to be called by the crusaders) or simply tolerant thereof. To elicit as much support as possible, crusaders who enlisted for forty days were given the same indulgences as those who signed on for an expedition to Palestine.

Although deeply entangled with the notion of heresy, the Albigensian Crusade was at heart a crusade of conquest, firmly linked to political ambitions and territorial concerns. It raged for twenty years in agonizing cycles of warfare and retreat until French royal intervention forced an end through a complex combination of sieges, treaties, and marriage alliances. Count Raymond VI lost nearly all his lands, tens of thousands of people (Good Christians, believers, Catholics, and combinations thereof) were slaughtered without recourse to trial, and local bishops and clergy were replaced with new men who were deeply committed to eradicating heresy and the social links that fostered it in Languedoc.

Signed in 1229 by exhausted and battle-sick representatives of both sides, the Treaty of Paris did not mark the end of the Good Christians in Europe, only the crumbling of the southern noble stronghold in the strategic lands of Languedoc. The primary—and unintentional—victor was the French throne, which absorbed extensive southern territories that had until then been independent lands. But it broke the momentum of localized power and familial bonds in Languedoc and set into motion a series of political and religious changes that made possible its ultimate repression at the hands of a new power.

As will be discussed in chapter 3, the first inquisitorial tribunals would emerge in the 1230s, in which special representatives traveled across the land to identify, interrogate, classify, and sentence heretics. These "inquisitors of heretical depravity" would prove a more effective strategy for uprooting outlawed ideas and individuals; by the 1320s, the communal fabric of Languedoc had been shredded, social and familial bonds torn apart, and the Good Men and Women hounded largely out of existence. Yet the history of the crusade has not been forgotten: visitors to southern France today will still encounter a vibrant tourist trade proudly rooted in "Catharism" as a local tradition, one closely tied to regional resistance to the overweening power of Paris and the north. And for many reasons, it is a tradition few people from this region are interested in surrendering.

So we return to the questions with which this chapter began: What is a heretic? According to whom? To what extent was heresy or any "-ism" a thing in itself? Where does it belong in our understanding of medieval Europe? How can we know what people believed and felt nine hundred years ago? And to what extent does it matter? These questions, and the competing perspectives vehemently argued by scholars in recent years, will echo across the chapters ahead as well. Perhaps even more important than these questions, however, is the spirit one brings to the material—ideally, a willingness to approach the past with respect, to allow for context and complexity, and to honor the stories of individual human beings whose vivid, singular lives were more than any historical label can adequately capture or contain.

Figure 1.2. Expulsion of the Albigensians from Carcassonne in 1209. ***Source*****: From Les Chroniques de France. British Library, London, Great Britain. HIP/Art Resource, NY.**

SUGGESTIONS FOR FURTHER READING

Barber, Malcolm. *The Cathars: Dualist Heretics in Languedoc in the High Middle Ages*. Essex, UK: Pearson Education, 2000.

Biller, Peter, and Anne Brenon. *Heresy and Literacy, 1000–1530*. Cambridge: Cambridge University Press, 1994.

Bruschi, Caterina. *The Wandering Heretics of Languedoc*. Cambridge: Cambridge University Press, 2009.

Lambert, Malcolm. *The Cathars*. 1998. Reprint, Malden, MA: Blackwell, 1999.

———. *Medieval Heresy: Popular Movements from the Gregorian Reform to the Reformation. Third edition. Malden, MA: Blackwell, 2001.*

Lansing, Carol. *Power and Purity: Cathar Heresy in Medieval Italy*. Oxford: Oxford University Press, 1998.

Moore, John C. *Pope Innocent III: To Root Up and Plant*. Notre Dame, IN: University of Notre Dame Press, 2009.

Pegg, Mark. *The Corruption of Angels: The Great Inquisition of 1245–1246*. Princeton, NJ: Princeton University Press, 2005.

Peters, Edward, ed. *Heresy and Authority in Medieval Europe*. Philadelphia: University of Pennsylvania Press, 1980.

Reyerson, Kathryn, and John Victor Drendel, eds. *Urban and Rural Communities in Medieval France: Provence and Languedoc, 1000–1500*. Leiden: Brill, 1998.

Sackville, L. J. *Heresy and Heretics in the Thirteenth Century: The Textual Representations*. York: York Medieval Press, 2011.

Sennis, Antonio, ed. *Cathars in Question*. York: York Medieval Press, 2016.

Sparks, Chris. *Heresy, Inquisition, and Life Cycle in Medieval Languedoc*. York: York Medieval Press, 2014.

Taylor, Claire. *Heresy, Crusade and Inquisition in Medieval Quercy*. York: York Medieval Press, 2011.

Thompson, Augustine. *Revival Preachers and Politics in Thirteenth-Century Italy: The Great Devotion of 1233*. Oxford: Oxford University Press, 1992.

Wakefield, Walter, and Austin P. Evans, eds. *Heresies of the High Middle Ages*. New York: Columbia University Press, 1991.

NOTES

1. Walter L. Wakefield and Austin P. Evans, *Heresies of the High Middle Ages* (New York: Columbia University Press, 1991), 129.

2. Wakefield and Evans, *Heresies*, 131.

3. Wakefield and Evans, *Heresies*, 128.

4. Wakefield and Evans, *Heresies*, 129.

5. Wakefield and Evans, *Heresies*, 244.

6. Hildegard of Bingen, *The Letters of Hildegard of Bingen*, trans. Joseph Baird and Radd Ehrmann (Oxford: Oxford University Press, 1998), 1:57–59.

7. Wakefield and Evans, *Heresies*, 336.

8. For more on current debates in the field, see the 2016 volume *Cathars in Question* (York Medieval Press, 2016), which contains essays by fourteen scholars each articulating a different perspective on the Cathar question. The contributors refer often to each other and a nonspecialist reader can quickly begin to see how the different interpretive camps are aligned; just as important, the essays in toto illustrate why these questions matter deeply to historians on a methodological and ethical level. John Arnold's essay, "The Cathar Middle Ages as a Historical and Methodological Problem" (pp. 53–78), offers a particularly thoughtful and balanced assessment.

9. Malcolm Lambert, *Medieval Heresy: Popular Movements from the Gregorian Reform to the Reformation*, 3rd ed. (Malden, MA: Blackwell, 2001), 65.

10. Wakefield and Evans, *Heresies*, 336.

11. Edward Peters, ed., *Heresy and Authority in Medieval Europe* (Philadelphia: University of Pennsylvania Press, 1980), 124. On the source itself, see Christopher Kurpiewski, "Writing beneath the Shadow of Heresy: The *Historia Albigensis* of Brother Pierre des Vaux-de-Cernay," *Journal of Medieval History* 31 (2005): 1–27.

12. Wakefield and Evans, *Heresies*, 336.

13. Wakefield and Evans, *Heresies*, 485.

14. Emmanuel LeRoy Ladurie's classic 1975 study *Montaillou: The Promised Land of Error* makes fascinating use of an inquisitorial register to reconstruct life in an early fourteenth-century life of a village.

15. Malcolm Lambert, *The Cathars* (Malden, MA: Wiley-Blackwell, 1998), 41.

16. Lambert, *Cathars*, 67.

17. Walter L. Wakefield, *Heresy, Crusade and Inquisition in Southern France, 1100–1250* (Berkeley: University of California Press, 1974), 66.

18. Mark Pegg, *The Corruption of Angels: The Great Inquisition of 1245–1246* (Princeton, NJ: Princeton University Press, 2005), 130.

19. Pegg, *Corruption of Angels*, 86.

20. Anne Brenon, "Catharism in the Family in Languedoc in the Thirteenth and Fourteenth Centuries: An Investigation Based on Inquisition Sources," 291–314, in *Urban and Rural Communities in Medieval France: Provence and Languedoc, 1000–1500*, ed. Kathryn Reyerson and John Victor Drendel (Leiden: Brill, 1998), 296.

21. Brenon, "Catharism in the Family," 296.

22. Pegg, *Corruption of Angels*, 74.

23. Brenon, "Catharism in the Family," 300.

24. Brenon, "Catharism in the Family," 302–3.

25. Wakefield and Evans, *Heresies*, 169.

26. Lambert, *Cathars*, 81.

27. Lambert, *Cathars*, 81.

28. Carole Lansing, *Power and Purity: Cathar Heresy in Medieval Italy* (Oxford: Oxford University Press, 2001), 4.

29. Lansing, *Power and Purity*, 16, 96.

30. Wakefield and Evans, *Heresies*, 151.

31. Malcolm Barber, *The Cathars: Dualist Heretics in Languedoc in the High Middle Ages* (Essex, UK: Pearson Education, 2000), 63.

32. R. I. Moore, *Origins of European Dissent* (Toronto: University of Toronto Press, 1994), 113.

33. Wakefield and Evans, *Heresies*, 191–92.

34. Lambert, *Cathars*, 81.

35. Edward Peters, ed., *Heresy and Authority in Medieval Europe* (Philadelphia: University of Pennsylvania Press, 1980), 169.

36. Lambert, *Cathars*, 95.

37. Barber, *Cathars*, 108.

Chapter Two

Poverty, Preaching, and the Poor of Lyon

"If you wish to be perfect, go, sell your possessions, and give the money to the poor, and you will have treasure in heaven; then come, follow me!" These words from the Gospel of Matthew (19:21) lay at the heart of the apostolic model of life that broadly captured the hearts and imaginations of Christians in the twelfth century. More specifically, they also prompted the decision of one man in the French city of Lyon to embrace a new way of life—an event shaped by local circumstances that nonetheless bore surprisingly long-term historical consequences for the religious history of western Europe. For although Church authorities held the apostolic model in high regard, particularly among those who continued to advocate ecclesiastical reform in the Gregorian spirit, anxieties mounted over issues of implementation of that model and authority for its supervision.

> In these years, increasingly heated dialogues were erupting about the *vita apostolica* and its relationship to the hierarchical Church, disputes largely rooted in the Gregorian reform and the eleventh century's call for an active, dynamic Christian laity. Who was fit to adopt the *vita apostolica* and its mandate of poverty and preaching? What might the spiritual consequences of amateur lay preaching be on Christendom? And who possessed the right to regulate and restrict such behaviors? On the one hand were passionate laymen and women recently converted to a new spiritual vigor and eager to answer Jesus's call; on the other hand were equally committed priests, bishops, and popes charged with saving souls through the sacraments and scripture, men wary of those who demanded access to a role long deemed exclusively clerical and to the texts in which their authority was rooted. Not only did the traditional three-part medieval social order of "those who labor, those who pray, and those who fight" offer no space for laypeople who looked and acted like clergy, but attempts to transcend or blur those old divisions were perceived as deeply troubling. To put it more simply, the "ordering of Christian society did not leave room for the sudden, inconvenient, inappropriate experience of late conversion."[1]

The apparent usurping of power and authority by unqualified people bothered the clergy, as did fears that unwitting souls would be seduced to their doom by wicked laymen masquerading as priests or by depraved women garbed in cloaks of false virginity and piety. All agreed that at stake was nothing less than salvation—but wherein lay the true authority? Was it found in the scriptural call to action or in the official Church that had so long mediated that scripture? As more lay Christians gained access to the Bible through vernacular translations in the twelfth and thirteenth centuries, the imperfect match between ecclesiastical hierarchies and the language of scripture lent a new and increasingly strident tone to reformist tendencies.

VALDÈS AND THE POOR OF LYON

According to an anonymous chronicler in the city of Lyon (in what is now east-central France), an unusual event took place in the year 1173. A local man named Valdès, said to have "amassed a great fortune through the wicked practice of lending interest," one day heard a minstrel singing about the life of St. Alexius. An early Christian saint who exchanged a wealthy life for one of begging and spiritual bliss, Alexius and his story so transfixed Valdès that he invited the minstrel to his home in order to learn more. In the chronicler's view, the conversation must have been riveting, for the next day Valdès sought a different kind of expert and consulted a local theologian about the state of his soul. When Valdès asked him what the most certain way of reaching God was—in other words, how best to live as a Christian—the theologian quoted him Christ's words to the wealthy man as reported by Matthew, as cited above. According to the account, Valdès was at this moment fully converted, and he followed Jesus's instructions to the letter. He gave up his material possessions, provided for his wife and daughter (who were apparently not urged to follow his new lifestyle), and adopted the life of an itinerant preacher.

Valdès was neither the first nor the last of such preachers, as the apostolic ideal of poverty, preaching, and piety had long inspired men and women and would continue to do so through and beyond the Middle Ages. Since the early twelfth century, reports circulated of fiery, impassioned preachers inspired by the Gregorian reform: men such as Tanchelm, Henry of Le Mans, and Peter of Bruys, for example, called for spiritual and social reform and sometimes met violent ends at the hands of unappreciative mobs. By Valdès's day, however, circumstances had changed remarkably. Not only had urbanization and long-distance trade complicated the traditional social order by inserting a new class of merchants, but heated religious passion among the laity was beginning to disrupt the order of Christendom as well. On the one hand, the papacy's invitation to laity to critique clergy who fell short of expected moral standards set a previously unknown precedent of lay involvement in ecclesiastical matters. But on the other, the moral fervor of good Christians who criticized their local clergy in order to reform and improve the Church could begin to look very much like the anticlericalism of "Good Christians." As noted in the previous chapter, new ideas and growing controversy over Catharism spread across the West during Valdès's lifetime, sparking councils, debates, and public preaching both for and against the lifestyle of the Good Christians and their believers. It is within the context of concern about proper piety and secret heresy, about how to live as a Christian in the world, that Valdès's message took root in and beyond Lyon.

Yet to embrace the apostolic life in the twelfth century meant the loss of not only wealth but also one's place in the social order, of the security and protection that communal belonging offered. In the chronicler's account, Valdès's family, friends, and associates were disturbed by his new role—not least by his distribution of his wealth to the poor—and concluded that he must be crazy. Valdès is said to have protested, "My friends and fellow townsmen! Indeed, I am not, as you think, insane, but I have taken vengeance on my enemies who held me in bondage to them, so that I was always more anxious about money than about God and served the creature more than the Creator."[2] Continuing on in this chosen path, he reportedly soon attracted both female and male followers to his model of voluntary poverty and vivid piety: "[L]ittle by little, both publicly and privately, they began to declaim against their own sins and those of others."[3]

Accounts of his conversion and influence must be read critically, however, and with an eye toward the context in which they emerged. First, historians today look skeptically upon the oft-repeated claim that Valdès was a usurer or wealthy merchant, given the lack of corroborating evidence, though the story's appeal certainly points to medieval concern about the new commercial class and Christian wealth. Second, the lay preacher's popular success and early freedom from harassment hinged upon certain local factors unique to Lyon. The chronicler does not, for example, reveal what recent research has uncovered: that the city had been riven for decades by political conflict between the archbishop of Lyon and a powerful count, hostilities that not only erupted in physical battle but also played into the fierce simultaneous struggle for sovereignty between emperor and pope. The question of archiepiscopal succession split the Lyon cathedral chapter into competing loyalties, and it was not until the papally engineered election of a new archbishop in 1165 (the Cistercian Guichard de Pontigny) that an uneasy political balance was restored. In exchange for peace with the count, Archbishop Guichard committed himself to reforming the church of Lyon, a program staunchly resisted by many local clergy. Allies were necessary, and they were to be found among the laity: specifically in men such as Valdès, whose fervent commitment to apostolic principles Guichard believed could be productively channeled for reformist ends. Once contextualized within the framework of these political and ecclesiastical circumstances, the medieval account of Valdès's rise to prominence, encounter with papal authority, and later hereticization illuminates the multiple agendas and tensions at play in twelfth-century Christendom.

Let us return, then, to the medieval sources, whose reports (if not always precisely or factually accurate) do reveal contemporary concerns and priorities. According to our Lyon chronicler, one of Valdès's first actions upon his conversion was to hire two priests to copy and translate into the French vernacular many books of the Bible and extracts from key patristic writings. After studying the sacred texts and learning many of them by heart, Valdès committed himself to the goal of evangelical perfection in the footsteps of the apostles. The translation of scripture into the French vernacular was a vital step toward making portions of the Bible accessible to laypeople, a process that would continue for centuries. Bolstered by scripture, Valdès insisted to those who criticized him that he was seeking his own salvation in accordance with Christ's injunctions and trying to teach others that all hope must rest in God rather than in riches. One may also perceive here the reforming archbishop's influence, or at least hearty agreement.

The message was compelling and clearly spoke deeply to the hearts of men and women in Lyon, for many followers adopted his way of life and preached the Gospels that he shared with them. Those who followed Valdès referred to themselves in the simple terms that would appeal to many such circles: the Poor, Friends, the Known, or sometimes (confusingly for historians) even Good Christians. In its early years, the small cluster of new friends had no residence but wandered in pairs, barefoot or shod only in sandals, following the model of preaching and poverty set forth in Mark 6:7: "He called the twelve and began to send them out two by two, and gave them authority over the unclean spirits."

Men found it an easier path to follow than did women, not only because the original apostles were male but because of powerful medieval cultural anxieties around female bodies and taboos regarding women's movement in public. For many contemporaries, the absence (or rejection) of protective walls and male supervision automatically put women in the same category as prostitutes. Put simply, the assumption was that women "on the loose" were "loose women," actual or potential. Such prejudices and pressures did not, however, prevent large numbers of women from seeking to follow the apostolic model in a variety of forms.

In its early years, the movement evidently counted women among its preachers, and female teachers were documented well into the groups' later years. Horrified clergy responded not only with general accusations of sexual disorder but also with scriptural prohibitions such as 1 Timothy 2:11–14: "Let a woman learn in silence with full submission. I permit no woman to teach or to have authority over a man; she is to keep silent. For Adam was formed first, then Eve; and Adam was not deceived, but the woman was deceived and became a transgressor." Historians disagree as to how best to interpret the dearth of evidence regarding women among Valdès's early followers, but there was evidently a comparative inclusiveness and openness in the movement's early years, a flexibility that soon hardened under ecclesiastical pressure into a more traditional gender model that precluded female preaching.

THE POOR OF LOMBARDY

Within a short time, opponents of the apostolic group became more vocal, launching critical attacks against the people they had begun to call Vaudois or Valdesi (anglicized to Waldensians). Nonetheless, the circle grew as the group traveled, preached, and passed on their scriptural translations to communities in southern France and northern Italy. One of the first significant regions in which the Poor found welcome was Lombardy, a region dotted with cities in which, as we have seen, the competing pieties of different communities had long—and often violently—intersected with volatile local politics. Historians are certain that Valdès and his followers had direct contact with communities

Figure 2.1. *Liber generationis*/**Gospel of Matthew.** *Source*: **Hill Monastic Manuscript Library HAStK 7002 30 f.124r. Historisches ArchivArchiv der Stadt Köln and the Hill Museum & Manuscript Library.**

that soon came to be known as the "Poor of Lombardy"; it is unclear, however, whether emissaries from France founded the latter or whether they simply forged bonds with an existing group of spiritually dynamic laity seeking to follow the Gospels.

Before the onset of ecclesiastical repression in the latter part of the twelfth century, early groups of the Poor in Lombardy were able to establish themselves firmly in local city structures, with public meeting places and schools and a formal administrative structure similar to that of the Church. In contrast to the itinerant, impoverished groups in Lyon and Languedoc, the northern Italians seem to have developed a far more sedentary, even quasi-monastic style of life; within a few decades, sources would report at least eight "schools" or centers in Milan alone. A commitment to manual labor on the part of the Italian Poor represented yet another distinction between the Lombards and Languedocians. Valdès himself was said to have insisted that the Italian brethren "could have no peace with him unless they separated themselves from the 'congregations of labourers' who were then in Italy."[4] The combination of manual work with religious devotion was not new and certainly had its own place within the reformist and Gospel-based tradition of medieval piety. But the issue seems to have functioned symbolically to represent the growing division between the western wing, who closely followed Valdès's initial model, and the more adaptable Lombards, whose distance from the founder afforded them greater flexibility in applying spirituality to daily life.

One of the major targets of the Poor in both France and Italy was the Good Christians or Cathars (as they were indeed called locally), similarly embedded in family, social, and political networks in both Languedoc and Lombardy. As largely sincere Catholics inspired by reformist impulses and scripture, Valdès and his followers shared the clergy's dismay at the specter of heresy, and they launched preaching campaigns against the dualists. Before long, the Poor included not only laymen and laywomen but also clergy compelled by their simple vision of Christian life and service. The movement's best-known and most eloquent voice belonged to the theologian Durand of Huesca, a committed member of the early Poor who wrote the only major theological work in the movement's history: the *Liber Antiheresis* (*Book against the [Cathar] Heresy*), which is discussed in detail below. Like his spiritual brothers and sisters, Durand's faith was orthodox in content; what ultimately set them all apart from ordinary lay Christians was the emphasis upon apostolic poverty and preaching.

EARLY ECCLESIASTICAL RESPONSE

By the late 1170s, Valdès of Lyon had witnessed the creation of apostolic communities in Languedoc and Lombardy committed to the Gospel, voluntary poverty, preaching, and antiheretical exhortation. Given the complex religiopolitical context of reform, heresy, and concerns about lay spirituality discussed above, it will come as no surprise that the groups were not entirely welcomed by the clergy. Although the Poor thought of themselves as models of orthodoxy, setting a fine apostolic example and no doubt encouraged for a period of time by the reforming archbishop, many Church officials looked upon them with mounting distrust. First, any profession of poverty tended to make the clergy look bad; even if the lay brothers and sisters were not explicitly denouncing the wealthy Church, an implicit criticism lay in the striking contrast between a voluntarily impoverished and nearly barefoot Christian and a richly garbed cleric. Observant laypeople certainly began to think that the former were more Christlike than the latter. Nor did one necessarily have to read between the lines to get the message: in his *Liber Antiheresis*, Durand of Huesca not only excoriated Cathars but also scathingly criticized the "greed, simony, pride, avarice, feasting . . . lechery, and other disgraceful acts" of the Catholic clergy.[5] Very much men and women of their day, the Poor effectively channeled through both word and deed an early critique of wealth that would subsequently reach a climax in the later Middle Ages. As we will see in later chapters, accusations of heresy would frequently erupt where poverty and piety intersected—where one group's claims to a uniquely righteous path clashed with that of the hierarchical Church.

A second potent objection to the Poor, however, was that they preached. Laypeople were not allowed to preach without the consent of their local clergy (a privilege rarely forthcoming) due to the deep-rooted assumption that untrained and theologically ignorant preachers would spread error and confusion and sow the seeds of spiritual destruction. In a certain sense, scripture was regarded as too important to be shared directly with masses incapable of comprehending its meaning; such texts could not be directly open to every Christian because the Word of God demands prudent and scrupulous study beyond the capacity of even many educated men. False teaching and incorrect understanding could provide a foothold for the devil, after all (we will return in a later chapter to this growing late-medieval preoccupation with battling the devil and his encroachment into Christian sovereignty). Thus although laymen and women were allowed, or even required as Christians, to *exhort* others to right action, Church authorities maintained a firm, if not always clear, distinction between urging right action and explaining doctrine.

From a modern perspective, the suppression of speech may seem like a crime in itself, and it can be tempting to dismiss the actions of the medieval clergy as merely self-interested and defensive. The issue is, however, not so simple. One might consider, for example, modern stipulations as to who may legally practice law or prescribe medicine: society would be poorly served—and certain vulnerable populations quite seriously damaged—if left in the hands of amateurs, no matter how passionate or well intentioned. Moreover, in the Middle Ages the safety of souls was paramount to all other concerns. Thus although some clergy were doubtless jealously protecting their own spiritual authority out of self-interest, many were truly worried about the souls of their flock and the risk posed by unregulated preachers.

In contrast, the Poor and other apostolic movements insisted that lay preaching was not only in accordance with the Gospel but was in fact a requirement of Christian life: after all, had not Jesus enjoined them to "go into all the world and preach the good news to all creation" (Mark 16:15)? Certain clergy agreed, at least in a modified form. In fact, the absence of any controversy in Lyon during the 1170s reinforces the sense that the lay exhortation of Valdès and his small apostolic community was actually approved by Archbishop Guichard. Moreover, the fact that Valdès and a group of followers not only sought an audience with the pope in 1179 but actually managed to secure a face-to-face meeting at the Third Lateran Council points again to ecclesiastical influence shaping Valdès's spiritual career.

THIRD LATERAN COUNCIL (1179)

The encounter between the Poor of Lyon and ecclesiastical authorities at the council was a crucial turning point for both sides. Gathered in Rome under Pope Alexander III, the council addressed a variety of administrative issues, ranging from procedures for papal election and clerical ordination to taxation, education, and stipulating penalties for usury and heresy. A major goal of the council was to fight heresy (Cathars in particular), and because the Poor of Lyon wanted nothing more than to be commissioned as lay preachers for the cause, their interests overlapped. Moreover, Alexander thought well of Archbishop Guichard.

In Rome, however, the welcome they received was less than warm. Ecclesiastical officials in attendance were wary of the lay volunteers and of the threat their unlettered learning and unsupervised preaching posed to the spiritual health of Christendom. Some were also certainly resentful of the ragged band's dramatic poverty. Perhaps at Guichard's prompting, Valdès and his followers anticipated the problem and brought with them biblical and theological translations for inspection to demonstrate both orthodoxy and willingness to submit to papal supervision. Subjected by various officials to rigorous, even hostile questioning on complex theological matters, the Poor were effectively cross-examined with no preparation or adequate defense. For example, they were asked whether they believed in God the Father, the Son, the Holy Spirit, and the mother of Christ. It was a trick question, and there was no right answer for these laypeople: If they had said they did not believe in the mother of Christ, they would have been challenged on the statement. But upon affirming their belief in Mary, they were shamed for their "ignorance" in equating her with the three persons of the Trinity.

An English cleric and famous wit named Walter Map, who was present at the council, called the visitors "dabblers" who misperceived themselves as experienced persons: "Shall the Word be given to the ignorant, whom we know to be incapable of receiving it, much less of giving in their turn what they have received?" Mockingly, he continued, "Let waters be drawn from the fountains, not from puddles in the streets." Yet even the condescending Map could not maintain an entirely jeering stance, and his account ends with a surprisingly somber warning: "They have no fixed habitations. They go about two by two, barefoot, clad in woolen garments, owning nothing, holding all things common like the apostles, naked, following a naked Christ. They are making their first moves now in the humblest manner because they cannot launch an attack. If we admit them, we shall be driven out."[6] The implication is clear: the Church must drive them out first.

Unfazed by Map's hostility, however, Alexander seems to have recognized their potential use to the Church. Sources suggest that he approved Valdès's commitment to poverty and explicitly encouraged him to continue in that path. At no point was the group labeled heretical in this meeting, and there is no mention of them in canon 27 of the council, which condemned groups such as the Cathars, Publicani, and Patarenes. Yet the line had to be drawn at unlettered men preaching, and the pope followed canon law by ruling that the Poor of Lyon could preach only if local priests gave them permission to do so. Such authorization was not likely to be forthcoming in most parishes, although Alexander may well have understood that the archbishop was willing to offer the Poor some leeway.

Other contemporary lay groups of men and women inspired by the Gospels, however, were petitioning—unsuccessfully—for such spiritual privileges. For example, in the account of an anonymous clerical chronicler, we learn of a similar group of apostolically inspired laypeople called the Humiliati:

> At that time there were certain inhabitants of Lombard towns who lived at home with their families, chose a peculiar form of religious life, refrained from lies, oaths, and law suits, were satisfied with plain clothing, and presented themselves as upholding the Catholic faith. They approached the pope and besought

> him to confirm their way of life. This the pope granted them, provided that they did all things humbly and decently, but he expressly forbade them to hold private meetings or to presume to preach in public. But spurning the apostolic command, they became disobedient, for which they suffered excommunication.[7]

Like Valdès and his followers, the Humiliati sought approval for a simple and humble way of life rooted in the apostolic model, but their desire to preach and teach ran counter to the clerical monopoly on letters and learning. For members of both groups, there could be no compromise on the issue of preaching because God had commanded the apostles to "preach the Gospels to every creature." Moreover, the expanding threat of heresy in Languedoc and Lombardy reminded many of the need to spread orthodoxy and bring straying sheep back into the fold of mother Church. Preaching was an obvious tool—but in whose mouths?

At a diocesan synod in 1180 attended by leading clerical figures, Valdès presented a statement evidently aimed at proving that he was not a Cathar (still the Church's major concern). Typically, the formal document tells us more about the preoccupations of contemporary churchmen than the exact nature of an individual's beliefs. Valdès affirmed belief in the Trinity, incarnation, resurrection, sacraments, and asserted that "we humbly praise and faithfully venerate the ecclesiastical orders, that is, the episcopate and priesthood and the others of higher and lower degree, and all that is in good order appointed to be read and sung as holy in the Church."[8] At this point, there were zero doctrinal issues or points of dissent; Valdès and his community were in full theological accordance with the Church. Thus the document concludes with a proposal for the group's way of life, in which they affirmed renunciation of the world, voluntary poverty, and a literal interpretation of the Gospel's mandate to apostolic life. Preaching in terms of clerical *predicatio* was not permitted, but neither was the right of *exhortatio* explicitly forbidden; in sum, the text underscores early ecclesiastical willingness to accommodate the Poor within local structures of piety, reform, and priestly authority.

EXPULSION FROM LYON AND THE COUNCIL OF VERONA (1182–1184)

Such accommodation was short lived. In 1181 or 1182, Archbishop Guichard died and was replaced by Jean de Bellesmains, a man of very different background and outlook. A secular and hierarchically minded priest rather than Cistercian reformer, and a man with strong support from the local cathedral chapter, Archbishop Jean was in no mood to tolerate a motley band of ragged lay preachers. As Alexander had perhaps anticipated, the local clergy and the archbishop now refused to extend permission to preach, and the Poor were faced with the choice of disobeying the Church or compromising their principles. When the new archbishop of Lyon ordered Valdès to stop begging publicly and to go back to his wife and home, he is said to have refused, emboldened by scripture: "I will rise now and go about the city, in the streets and in the squares; I will seek him whom my soul loves" (Song of Songs 3:2); "We must obey God rather than any human authority" (Acts 5:29); and "Anyone, then, who knows the right thing to do and fails to do it, commits sin" (James 4:17). Valdès and his followers continued to preach and thus were expelled from Lyon in 1182.

Even at this point, however, the issue with the Poor of Lyon was not heresy but pastoral irregularity—and as such, an issue for the archbishop to settle as he saw fit. But obedience to ecclesiastical authority was increasingly becoming the cornerstone of orthodoxy in the late twelfth and early thirteenth centuries. Thus by resisting attempts by clerical authority to limit their preaching, the Poor would soon find themselves increasingly marginalized alongside the Cathars they so despised. A second step toward a break with the Church and the "creation" of heresy where none had previously existed occurred only two years later, when the death of Alexander in 1181 opened the way for a new pope with a different agenda. Tired of festering political disputes with the German emperor, Pope Lucius III (r. 1181–1185) also decided to take a stand on the brewing issue of heresy. At the Council of Verona (1184), the Poor of Lyon were not only listed as anathema in the decree *Ad abolendam* (*In Order to Abolish*) along with Cathars, Patarenes, and Humiliati, but were excommunicated for preaching without authorization. From this point on, the Poor were categorized as schismatics and firmly located within a legal status defined first and foremost by stubborn disobedience.

In *Ad abolendam*, Lucius also set forth a series of requirements to improve spiritual supervision and prevent future outbreaks of heresy: local bishops were now to visit twice a year any parish where heresy had been reported, to take an oath from three or more people of good reputation about local religiosity, and to initiate legal action against those denounced. Lay authorities were also encouraged to cooperate with such episcopal inquiries so that responsibility for the spiritual health and orthodoxy of a diocese was effectively devolved onto local authorities. Although this was not yet a formal system of antiheretical inquiry, it represented a watershed in terms of clerical perceptions of heresy and strategies to fight it. Yet the condemnation from the Council of Verona did little to quell the Poor. Valdès's community left Lyon in small groups of itinerant men and women and traveled through southern France and northern Italy, staunchly committed to defending Catholic doctrine and preaching against the Cathar heresy.

DISPUTATIONS, DEFECTIONS, AND DISAGREEMENTS (1191–1207)

Despite the condemnation at Verona, however, the major clerical strategies for dealing with the Poor rested for another thirty years in either pragmatic tolerance or attempts at persuasion. After being expelled from Lyon, for example, some of the Poor traveled south and were soon preaching near Narbonne. In an encounter remarkably similar to that at Lombers in 1165 (discussed in the previous chapter), spokesmen for the Church and for the Poor of Lyon met for discussion and debate in 1191. Our record of the encounter, in which the preachers were ultimately condemned, comes from a treatise by Abbot Bernard of Fontcaude near Narbonne. The prologue includes a reference to the sticky issue of nomenclature, for Bernard comes up with his own etymology for the Waldensians:

> At the time when Lord Lucius of glorious memory presided over the Holy Roman Church, new heretics suddenly raised their head who, choosing by chance a name with a forecast of the future, were called Waldenses, a name surely derived from "dense vale" (*valle densa*) inasmuch as they were enveloped in the deep, dense darkness of error.[9]

Although the treatise itself is not particularly striking, Bernard's prologue provides another interesting observation about what he perceived as the fundamental problem behind heresy. Explaining his authorial intentions in the same passage, he stated that he wrote the tract

> particularly to instruct or encourage some of the clergy, who, either because they are burdened by inexperience or for want of books, become an offense and a scandal to the faithful under their charge by their failure to stand against the enemies of the truth; for they neither confirm [their parishioners] in the Catholic faith nor refresh them with the nourishment of the Holy Scriptures, wherefore they languish like starvelings on the journey through this world. . . . [T]his, indeed, is the real cause of the greater evil we have described: that the ravening wolves, to wit, the demon-heretics and tyrants, are not being driven out of the folds of Christ's sheep either by the word of preaching or by the rod of discipline or strictness.[10]

Like Walter Map, Bernard was concerned about the persuasive power of the group's behavior and perhaps dubious about the ability of parish priests to launch an effective defense. For more than a decade, the Poor continued to roam, stirring the souls of listeners who likely had no idea that their humble preachers had been excommunicated and declared schismatics.

Already at this early date, however, new doubts and doctrinal extensions were emerging among certain communities, ideas that separated them from the original Poor. In a treatise attributed to Ermengaud of Béziers (a former Poor preacher and companion of Durand of Huesca), the Waldensians are said to deny purgatory and the value of any religious offerings for the dead, and to claim baptismal and Eucharistic sacramental authority for themselves.[11] Several early sources also claimed that the Poor regarded the taking of oaths as explicitly forbidden based on Matthew 5:34–37: "But I say to you, Do not swear at all, either by heaven, for it is the throne of God, or by the earth, for it is his footstool, or by Jerusalem, for it is the city of the great King. And do not swear by your head, for you cannot make one hair white or black. Let your word be 'Yes, Yes' or 'No, No'; anything more than this comes from the evil one." Since a suspect could be pressed simply to swear an oath, this belief would prove a useful litmus test for later authorities seeking to establish a person's beliefs or associations with believing networks.

Indeed, the early thirteenth-century forces of orthodox persuasion were about to secure a major victory against the recalcitrant Poor. In the autumn of 1207, a short time after Valdès's death, his followers suffered the first of what would turn out to be a series of crippling defections from their ranks. Arriving in the city of Pamiers in Languedoc, the formidable preacher Bishop Diego of Osma (a colleague of the future St. Dominic) discovered that a disputation was being held there between Catholics and the Poor. The bishop apparently joined the debate and succeeded in convincing the "Waldensian heretics" to admit their wrong, abjure their heresy, and agree to live as Catholics thereafter. The leader of the Poor on this day was none other than their greatest spokesman, Durand of Huesca.

Although we do not have an account of his conversion or the conversation between Durand and Diego, there are some interesting possibilities. Diego was one of the finest and most compelling preachers of his day, and Durand may simply have been impressed and convinced by the eloquent man, whose ambitions and goals were so similar to his own; yet it is likely there were other forces at work as well. One may have been that Durand was alarmed by an apparent drift of certain wings toward a more radical, anti-Catholic stance in the wake of the Verona decree (particularly the Donatist belief that only a sinless priest—or even a layperson—could properly effect the sacraments). Finally, the state of affairs in Languedoc on the eve of the Albigensian Crusade may have convinced Durand that the anti-Cathar forces must come together and no longer remain divided and opposed. Whatever the reasons, Durand of Huesca's conversion and concession to Church authorities were a major blow to Valdès's movement at a crucial moment, removing one of its most theologically sophisticated and moderate voices and promoting further division within its communities.

RECONCILIATIONS WITH ROME (1208–1212)

Within a few decades, papally deputized officials would begin tracking down networks of Cathars and Waldensians through the patient, exhaustive process of personal inquiry—but in the early thirteenth century, the papacy had not yet come to that point. Indeed, Pope Innocent III was in 1207 still busily trying to reconcile lay preaching groups back into the Church and to further extend his platform of Christian uniformity and vitality. A tireless organizer and administrator committed to the preservation and extension of European Christianity, he was quick to perceive opportunities to bring well-intentioned, piously motivated groups back into the fold of the Church.

Poor Catholics

The first of these was the group of Poor brethren led by Durand of Huesca, who had relinquished his affiliation with the group (if not his commitment to its principles) and returned to the Church in 1207. By December of the following year, Innocent informed local clergy in Narbonne that the small community had been received by the see as good Catholics. To prove their obedience, they had accepted a confession of faith much like the one embraced by Valdès in Lyon more than twenty-five years earlier, although with a few significant shifts of emphasis. Not only did the 1208 confession stress the expected tenets regarding the lawfulness of oaths and the requirement of authorization before preaching, but it also affirmed that a priest's personal sinfulness did not impede the spiritual efficacy of the sacraments he performed. It seems that during the intervening years, clergy began to suspect the Poor of a creeping, reconceptualized Donatism (an ancient heresy whose insistence on clerical sinlessness had unacceptable implications for the highly administrative, sacramental medieval church).

Not satisfied with simply eliciting confessions, Innocent took an innovative step to further ensure the group's reconciliation with orthodoxy. He created a new place for them within the Church as a semimonastic community of "Poor Catholics"; allowed to continue their renunciation of the world, now framed in terms of orthodox piety, they were to pray regularly, say the canonical hours, and, because most were sufficiently learned to hold effective disputations, commit themselves to reading, teaching, and preaching among the heretics. Garbed in plain and simple habits, they were to observe the traditional monastic requirements of chastity and obedience and to receive sacraments from the local Catholic clergy.

In his treatment of the Poor Catholics, the pope displayed a masterful diplomacy by not insisting the newly reconciled brothers immediately abandon all their former beliefs and behaviors; he granted limited permission for the "brethren remaining in the world" to avoid taking oaths and defended the Poor Catholics against hostile local clergy. No indication of their numbers survives, but evidently they did not represent all of the Poor preachers in Languedoc, for many would surface there in later encounters with inquisitors. Durand must have been disappointed in the decision of these brethren and sisters to refuse the opportunity to maintain both the group's original mission and unity with the Church.

Tensions between Catholic clergy and the recently rehabilitated group increased over the next few years. In the summer of 1209, the archbishop of Narbonne accused the Poor Catholics of not only maintaining their former heresy but using their new position to seduce ordinary people out of orthodox services. Innocent responded mildly, urging accommodation and scrupulosity on both sides, and in the years that followed he continued to secure acceptance for the Poor Catholics. Despite the pope's best efforts and the ongoing anti-Cathar preaching campaign of the new group, however, the Poor Catholics were not to survive; ongoing suspicion of their formerly suspect status and the new option of irreproachable mendicant orders in the second decade of the century (discussed in chapter 3) drained the group of its vitality. By the mid-thirteenth century, its members had disappeared, either due to death or movement into other religious orders. Pope Innocent's first attempt to avoid the mistakes of the Third Lateran Council had not proved particularly successful, but they were not his only effort.

The Reconciled Poor

At the same time, Innocent was eyeing another group of potential converts back to the Catholic Church—the communities in Lombardy. Durand himself had brought them to the pope's attention when, in 1209, he referred to about a hundred members of the Poor of Lombardy in Milan who sought reconciliation with the Church. After the local archbishop had demolished their school and seized the land on which it had been built, the group petitioned the pope for its return upon their conversion back to Catholicism. Innocent refused to barter land for proper spiritual observance, and the Poor eventually reconciled themselves to the Church prior to the summer of 1210. Adherents had to agree to a formal confession based, once again, on the exemplar of Valdès in 1180–1181 and the Poor Catholics in 1208. In this case, however, there were significant additional heretical tenets of which the group was either specifically accused or admitted having held. Among the apparent issues were that the Poor had embraced the Donatist tenet that only sinless priests could consecrate as well as corollary beliefs that righteous laypeople could preach, consecrate the Eucharist, and absolve penitents. In addition, the Poor agreed to stop performing lay sacraments and disrespecting local clergy, stipulations that suggest the Lombard communities had developed a more radical brand of piety than their associates in southern France. Thus the text sheds intriguing light on the beliefs of the northern Italian communities and their apparent divergence from the Occitan and French contexts.

Like the Poor Catholics of 1208, the Lombard Reconciled Poor (as they came to be called) received from Pope Innocent a document setting forth their new, approved way of life. And like Durand's group, they agreed to live chastely in impoverished communities devoted to study and to preach against heretics. However, there were some intriguing alterations that contrasted sharply with the Languedocian model. The Reconciled Poor were, for example, to work with their hands, to maintain possession of their more than eight houses, and in those houses, to hold regular readings and meals in silence. Scholars have observed that the new conditions actually resonated with the earlier preferences of the Poor Lombards before their conversion back to the Church: a commitment to manual labor and a more settled, quasi-monastic organization than those found in central or southern France. Yet the reconciled group faced the same fate as the Poor Catholics, its numbers gradually dwindling within a few decades by death or defection to other, less controversial orders.

Innocent's final attempt at reconciling with the Poor had failed. As explored in the next chapter, the pope would issue broad legislation against heretics "by whatever name" at the Fourth Lateran Council in 1215, marking a watershed in the institutional and antiheretical history of the Church. However, the pope's sudden death in 1216 meant that the problems of lay preaching, poverty, and the issue of obedience were not to be solved on his watch. Meanwhile, tensions within Poor communities threatened to further disrupt the now-hereticized groups.

INTERNAL DISSENT AND THE COUNCIL OF BERGAMO (1218)

Although a small portion of the Poor of Lombardy had reconciled with Rome in 1212, the majority remained deeply committed to the faith as practiced within local networks of family and friends. Differences between the beliefs and practice of the Poor in Languedoc and Lombardy reached a breaking point within a few years. In May 1218, six representatives from Languedoc and six from Lombardy met in the northern Italian city of Bergamo for a summit. According to an informative letter written by one of the Lombards, the conference was intended to explore common ground between the two groups and sought to mend a deep rift. Yet the letter concludes by acknowledging that several key issues met with no resolution, listing the various arguments and texts with which the Lombard group tried to persuade their "brothers, sisters and friends beyond the Alps" (*ultramontanes* [people beyond the mountains]) that the Italian position was the correct one.[12]

What were these pressing issues? First, the Lombards seem to have resisted the *ultramontanes'* insistence that only the traditions established by Valdès were appropriate. For example, Valdès had chosen not to appoint a leader but rather to rotate responsibilities among members for a given period of time; he did not create a separate hierarchy of ministers; and he evidently disapproved of manual work and labor as part of the Poor lifestyle, preferring the apostolic model of utter poverty and reliance upon the charity of others. According to the letter, the *ultramontanes* were willing to capitulate to the Italians' right to a more formal and work-oriented practice as well as to their insistence that baptism in water was vital for salvation and other points. The visiting delegation agreed that they should not force the Lombards into any practice that did not have scriptural authority, a concession in keeping with Valdès's own literal devotion to scripture.

On two points, however, the Lombards and *ultramontanes* simply could not agree. First, the Lombards rejected the French claim that Valdès and a companion named Vivetus were both absolutely in heaven; they refused to accord Valdès any special sanctity and insisted that he, like any other Christian, had to atone for his sins before going to heaven. The second issue was more theologically subtle and centered on the Eucharist—specifically, on the issue of who possessed the spiritual authority to perform the sacrament. According to the text, the crucial issue was the Italians' Donatist tendency to believe that the prayers and sacraments of sinful priests could not reach God and, therefore, that their wicked behavior or failure to atone for sin negated their ordination. In other words, the Italians demanded scrupulous living and piety from their priests as a necessary precondition of sacramental power (Donatism), a belief that flew in the face of centuries of Catholic theology.

Intriguingly, the Lombards defended themselves with the words of Pope Innocent, who was also deeply interested in affirming the central significance of the Eucharist. Quoting from one of the pope's letters, they cited: "Why do they not attend the words of Solomon? 'He that turneth away his ears from hearing the Law, his prayer shall be an abomination.' And the Lord, proclaiming through Malachi that the benediction of evil priests is to be reckoned a malediction, says: 'I will curse your blessings.'"[13] Innocent was no Donatist, of course, and would have been most displeased to discover that a heretical group was citing his own works in their defense. After all, orthodox theology insisted that even the most depraved priest could still perform the Eucharist and bring about transubstantiation.

In contrast to the Italian stance, the *ultramontane* Poor affirmed that prayers, consecrations, and other sacraments performed by a lawfully ordained priest (whether wicked, penitent, or sinless) would still be spiritually effective. No middle ground could be reached on the issue. Either the priest could or could not perform the sacrament, and the letter indicates that the two sides parted courteously but still divided. According to various writers in subsequent decades and centuries, the schism endured, perpetuated not only by geography but also by issues of behavior and belief. A text written by a hostile Italian nobleman in about 1235 excoriates the Italians:

> O Poor Lombards! You were once members of the Roman Church. Because that Church did not satisfy you, you joined the Poor Leonists and with them you were under the governance of Waldes, staying for some time under his rule. Afterward, you chose another leader and gave offense to Waldes and the Poor Leonists . . . and for several years you taught just what the Poor Leonists were teaching, asserting that you had no quarrel with them, but now there is the greatest discord between you two.[14]

Despite vehement disagreement on some key issues, the Lombards and *ultramontanes* did not separate into new splinter groups but chose instead still to conceive of themselves as connected to each other as part of a broader community. As circles of variously self-identified Poor or Friends spread far beyond the group's original lands in the thirteenth century, the question of their identity and ideas becomes considerably more complicated.

REGIONAL SPREAD IN THE THIRTEENTH CENTURY

By 1230, the first generation of Valdès's leadership was long gone, and Pope Gregory IX was preparing to launch new inquisitorial campaigns that would unravel the very family and social structures in which the group's beliefs were embedded. Over the previous half century, Valdès's conviction in the importance of an active role for Christian laity had jarred the institutional Church and challenged the clergy's privileged access to the Word of God. As Gabriel Audisio summarizes it,

> When one bears in mind, firstly, the importance of the spoken word in such an oral world; secondly, the role that a literature class could play; and lastly, the esteem the clerics enjoyed . . . within this society shaped by and dependent on the religious orders, only then can one assess the importance of Valdès and his followers and the challenge they, perhaps unconsciously, represented.[15]

Although the dates when members of the Poor brought their apostolic message to various regions of Europe cannot be known with any precision, it is evident that by the end of the thirteenth century, communities were deeply established far beyond Lyon, Languedoc, and Lombardy: in Quercy, Auvergne, Maine, and Burgundy to the north; Gascony in the west; and Provence and the Dauphiné to the east. Through subsequent waves of preaching and migrations, Valdès's message took root farther east as well—not only in isolated western Alpine and Piedmontese villages, but also deep into the Apulian and Calabrian regions of the Italian peninsula.

In the northeast, Poor were known to have settled in Metz, at the confluence of the Moselle and Seille rivers, and to have penetrated the Rhine region by the early thirteenth century. Inquisitors would later discover settled communities in the Rhineland cities of Trier, Mainz, and Strasbourg, in central and southern cities such as Fribourg and Augsburg, and in large swaths of rural villages and small towns across the northern and southern realms of the Holy Roman Empire. For complex reasons probably hinging on local spiritual conditions, social structures, and mounting anticlericalism, their ideas became deeply rooted in the easternmost lands of medieval Europe—from Austria in the southeast, where inquisitors reported that the heresy was embedded in forty different parishes, north to Saxony, Bohemia, and Moravia, and Poland, Silesia, and even rural Brandenburg and Pomerania in the northeast.

Originally an urban phenomenon rooted in the vibrant Lyonnais commercial scene, the later Poor would experience a significant extension of geography and shift in socioeconomic composition in the later thirteenth century. Although groups of Poor were still common in thirteenth-century cosmopolitan centers and large communities would thrive secretly in major cities (particularly along rivers such as the Rhine) until the late fourteenth century, there was nonetheless an increasing tendency for adherents to live in rural rather than urban settings. Once the Poor brethren's preaching mission was shut down by hostile authorities, however, preachers everywhere hushed their voices and went underground, effaced from public view.

The shift in geographical concentration also brought changes in socioeconomic composition. Although in its early years the Poor often included urban elites such as merchants and clerks, its later adherents represented a somewhat different variety of membership. In France and Germany, for example, thirteenth- and fourteenth-century documents report that although members of the Poor were occasionally skilled laborers (e.g., blacksmiths, carpenters, tailors, or weavers), most were likely to be peasants. Audisio observes that as a consequence,

> their way of life, and in particular the relations between the Poor . . . and the wealthy and lettered classes of society, were considerably altered. The latter

> ceased to be attracted by their ideas; they even became oblivious to them. The Waldensians' preaching, which had become discredited, no longer moved them, nor indeed did it reach them.[16]

On the other hand, large communities farther east in Bohemia frequently included not only craftsmen and innkeepers but schoolmasters, magistrates, and even judges: one really cannot draw simple connections between status and religious expression. Thus, when pursuing the question of who counted themselves as a member of the Poor, one must pay close attention to the variations in local circumstances.

Nevertheless, the new rural emphasis was undeniable, and a number of factors were responsible for this transformation. As discussed in the next chapter, mounting scrutiny in cities with highly trained clergy and friars doubtless forced many to relocate for safety, although presumably the itinerant masters could travel and visit rural villages in greater safety. Just as important, however, was the role of family ties in transmitting the faith: many women and men interrogated in the thirteenth and fourteenth centuries reported not only that they had been brought into the faith as children, but that their parents had also been raised within it. Once families established themselves in rural areas, therefore, so too did the primary structures for maintaining and passing on the belief—namely, parents, siblings, uncles, aunts, cousins, neighbors, and friends.

SOCIAL STRUCTURES AND DAILY LIVES

After the formal criminalization of heresy at the Fourth Lateran Council in 1215, the Poor sisters and brothers were forced to abandon their public mission. A message that had once been spread by preaching in city marketplaces, town squares, and local schools was suddenly restricted and its bearers harassed. Sources suggest that no member of the Poor was known to have preached publicly after 1230, a stunning reversal for a Christian group founded on the Gospel call to proselytize. Yet ecclesiastical proscriptions seem not to have dampened members' enthusiasm or their leaders' temerity behind closed doors. As ecclesiastical pressure mounted across the thirteenth century, the spiritual and social lives of the Poor conflated even further as members increasingly used their own homes as safe houses and secret meeting locations for the community and itinerant brethren.

Usually brought into the faith at a young age, the celibate masters (*Meister* in Germany; *barbes* in the south) underwent a rigorous apprenticeship of scriptural study and training in the art of preaching and teaching. Following Jesus's injunction to the Apostles to go forth two by two, a young trainee

Map 2.1. Spread of the Poor. Reprinted from Malcolm Lambert, *Medieval Heresy: Popular Movements from the Gregorian Reform to the Reformation*, **Third Edition.** *Source*: **Copyright © 2002 by Malcolm Lambert. Reprinted with permission of the publisher, Blackwell Publishing.**

would accompany a more experienced brother on his travels to observe his actions and learn the networks and locations of believers. In so doing, the young man would gather a rich array of experience and information, becoming not only familiar with but also familiar to his future flock. Masters were responsible for tending to an increasingly large and scattered number of members, which required extensive and grueling travel. Since the excommunication of 1215, voluntary poverty in the form of public begging was no longer an option, so the masters generally had to adopt a trade or craft, as much for disguise as income.

Upon arriving at the home of a "friend," the master, family, and other members of the community would come together for a shared meal, doubtless full of shared news and gossip from other towns and villages. Supper would be followed by preaching, confession, and absolution, a sacrament much on Christian minds since Pope Innocent III's decree in 1215 that it be performed at least annually. In return for these services, gifts were sometimes pressed upon the master, but just as often he brought presents and charity to his hosts. In isolated areas, the arrival of a master was cause for celebration, like a holiday—especially in rural regions of the Alps, Bohemia, or Silesia, where entire villages were steeped in the faith. In some regions, particularly Germany and Austria, some groups maintained schools or special meeting houses through the fourteenth century. Such schools provided a gathering spot for preaching, reading scripture, and various types of teaching. In Mainz, for example, a community that numbered at least in the dozens had a house called Spiegelberg where they held their gatherings for decades. Exactly how the relationship between these houses and "heretical" groups escaped the notice of local Catholics is uncertain, though it suggests either a tacit tolerance of the well-behaved Waldensians or the extent to which the group of "friends" managed to protect their secret. Both were probably the case to varying degrees across Europe.

Although practice varied, most later thirteenth- and fourteenth-century adherents in fact simply blended in with the local Catholic community: they took communion from the priest, confessed as required, prayed in church, and otherwise behaved like their neighbors. Some doubtless did so with some certainty in the rituals' spiritual value and perceived the masters' visits and additional preaching or confession as a special additional element of their piety, whereas others reinterpreted their own actions to distinguish themselves internally from their Catholic peers. Sources reveal, not surprisingly, that some members were uneasy about the distinction between the two camps: one believer told inquisitors, for example, that she had "two faiths," believing on the one hand that blessed water helped to wash away sin, and on the other hand that it did not, because of what the brethren told her.[17] Once again, we are reminded that the line between orthodoxy and heresy was always imaginary (an idea rather than a reality), and many ordinary people easily melded and merged a variety of beliefs or were able to adhere to contradictory ideas simultaneously. For others, probably a smaller percentage, it was a simple decision to look like their neighbors but to maintain the "true" faith in their heart: they went through the motions, explicitly rejecting the spiritual value of the practice, dissembling for safety until the master's next visit.

LATER PATTERNS OF BELIEF

In the early fourteenth century, the inquisitor Bernard Gui bluntly stated that the "principal heresy of the Waldensians was and still remains the contempt for ecclesiastical power."[18] Gui was only one of many inquisitors empowered by papal, episcopal, and other forms of ecclesiastical authority who would pursue the Poor and other heretical groups with mounting vigilance and bureaucratic technologies in the decades and centuries to come. Between approximately 1230 and 1400, new inquisitorial pressures would reshape the diverse phenomenon of the Poor into the construct of "Waldensian heresy"; in a wave of antiheretical activity across Europe, they would shatter the social systems of the Poor and virtually eliminate the faith from all but a few small lingering Alpine and other rural communities. Particularly in German-speaking lands, inquisitors such as Peter Zwicker would use the latest intellectual tools and theological techniques for discerning wrong belief, and in the process redefine the very categories of heresy, heretics, and good Christians. That process will be traced in chapter 3, but it is worth pausing here to reflect on the subsequent transformation of beliefs either claimed by or attributed to believers: in other words, the shift from early reformers (stubborn but orthodox) to later, often explicit critics of the Church.

We have already seen how early ecclesiastical pressure provoked the orthodox Valdès and his followers into heresy via disobedience on the preaching issue; the process would escalate dramatically once a formal inquisitorial apparatus and set of procedures began to officially define and delimit the nature of the heresy around 1230. Once the bloody Albigensian Crusade against heresy in the southern territories came to an end in 1229, ecclesiastical attention became trained upon the excommunicated Poor who still persisted. In 1231, Gregory IX established the first inquisitorial tribunal, staffed with trained men charged with seeking out and converting heretics—namely, the men and women of southern France and northern Italy whose beliefs were so deeply embedded in local social and familial structures. The process of inquiry would become increasingly complex, sophisticated, and self-referential, leaving behind a great wake of protocols, records, and transcripts.

Because our knowledge of the beliefs of the Poor is derived primarily from inquisitorial or other hostile sources, one must remember that we possess *at best* a faint and distorted echo of their voices. Nonetheless, historians must make do with the available evidence. So let us look past the regional variations and identities and set forth the main tenets of what came to be known by inquisitors and historians as Waldensianism between 1218 and approximately 1400. These tenets can be categorized in three main headings, each of which pertains in its own way to key intersections of divine and mundane: first, an attack on the authority of priests and the Church; second, a denial of the doctrine of purgatory and all its associated beliefs and practices; and third, an evangelical mission and morality rooted in the Gospels.

After the mid-thirteenth century, the Poor are increasingly represented as insisting that the ordination of a priest conferred no right to preach or administer the sacraments and that merit alone was the source of that authority. From this stance, which was far more radical than anything proposed by Valdès and the first generation of believers, it was a short step to the conclusion that the entire hierarchical Church had been poisoned by wealth and sin. History is a malleable and potent tool, and the early Poor developed a novel understanding and justification of their origins. Drawing on a legend circulating at the time, they claimed that the Church that Christ founded on Peter had remained pure until the early fourth century CE, when Emperor Constantine (motivated by a newfound and historically implausible piety) supposedly granted rule over Italy and the West to Pope Sylvester. On that day, it was said that an angelic voice lamented the sullying of the papal see with such vast new material and territorial possessions, crying out, "This day poison has been spread in the Church!" According to this legend, a pious associate of Pope Sylvester urged him to reject the imperial gift, known as the Donation of Constantine; excommunicated for his defiance, he went underground with a few followers to keep the fire of the true Church burning. And from that point on, according to legend, there was a continuous line of truly Christian priests and believers who remained hidden until the twelfth century, when Valdès brought the underground movement once more into the open.

Or so the story went, for the Donation of Constantine was a forgery. As proved by the fifteenth-century Italian Renaissance scholar Lorenzo Valla, the document originated with an eighth-century cleric working, presumably, under papal direction. In the twelfth century, however, the forgery had not yet been revealed, and the story resonated powerfully within increasingly anticlerical circles. And the Poor thus drew their own powerful conclusions from them: once poison was spread by the flow of riches, the Roman Church was no longer the Church of Christ and became instead the "whore of the Apocalypse" and the "synagogue of Satan." By the late fourteenth century, Valdès had been rechristened "Peter" by his followers because he had restored the Church that had been founded on the first Peter and because of his Petrine insistence on obeying God rather than men. This legend made all of Valdès's followers heirs of two great Peters, and thus the only true followers of Christ. All later references to "Pierre Valdès" or the anglicized "Peter Waldo" are part of this mythical tradition.

As they came under pressure, the doctrine of the Waldensians (as represented in inquisitorial sources) came increasingly to follow the earlier radical claims challenging major assumptions of medieval Catholic practice: for example, that saints cannot intervene for the living, the cult of saints has no value, and the Church cannot canonize saints. In keeping with their strict biblical literalism, the Poor also seem increasingly to have refused to take oaths. Others believed that all legal procedures were sinful because Christ had said, "Do not judge, so that you may not be judged" (Matthew 7:1). And yet others among them insisted that all warfare and capital punishment (including the execution of heretics) were strictly forbidden because of Exodus 20:13 ("You shall not murder") and Christ's injunction to "put your sword back into its place; for all who take the sword will perish by the sword" (Matthew 26:52). Moreover, because most of the believers read or listened to vernacular versions of scripture, they could usually offer the appropriate biblical chapter and verse to support their moral teachings. Indeed, many inquisitors would note the extraordinary ability of common "friends" to recite long passages of scripture.

As adherents began to embrace more fully the notion that the institutional Church was sinful and corrupt, it fell to meritorious laity to preach, hear confessions, and celebrate the Eucharist. However, the group's organization was shaped by a compromise between belief and reality. Although all people desiring salvation were admonished to follow Christ's model of apostolic poverty, in practice not everyone could live off alms and minister to the flock. Some were needed to provide support and to be the tender sheep. Thus the movement's organization curiously paralleled that of the Good Christians, distinguishing between the "friends" of both sexes and the elite masters. As this pressure was forging a new radicalism among many Poor communities, an emerging denial of purgatory helped strengthen their confidence in their own new stance and provided a strong platform from which to criticize the old one. Why did they refuse to accept the doctrine of purgatory? Because they found no explicit statement of it in scripture. And so for adherents, there were only two roads after death—to heaven or to hell.

But the denial of purgatory did not stop there, for it effectively dismantled an enormous structure of traditional Christian beliefs and practices and, to some extent, even the basic foundation of the Roman Church. If all souls went to heaven or hell, there was no point in praying for the dead—and no purpose in granting indulgences. (Indulgences were the remission of temporal punishment in purgatory in return for certain good works and had emerged out of the context of early crusading and associated fundraising efforts.) However, the income of most monasteries and churches was based on prayers for the dead; moreover, the theory of indulgences was a major force behind the Crusades, armed expeditions originally to claim the Holy Land, which began during the time of the reformer popes of the late eleventh century. Because the initial embrace of poverty by the Poor of Lyon had irritated the clergy, it is not difficult to understand why their newly strident criticism of ecclesiastical theory and practice was threatening.

GENDER ROLES AMONG THE POOR

The woman interrogated about her dual points of view was not unique as a female member of the Poor, and the role of women among such communities has been an issue of some controversy among historians. Some have identified an early period of opportunity and relative freedom followed by the imposition of traditional gender roles when ecclesiastical pressure heightened at the end of the thirteenth century. Others have argued that the (primarily clerical) sources for early female preaching among the Poor exaggerated the phenomenon, prompted by long-standing Western fears of female bodies and voices—in other words, that hostile clergy exaggerated the Poor's toleration of women's activity as another indication of the group's essential depravity. It is evident, however, that the Poor did not interpret the notion of the soul's spiritual equality as having any ramifications for life on earth, and thus largely traditional gender roles prevailed.[19]

However, two particularly interesting points about gender as it influenced women and men among the Poor merit consideration here. The first is that the Poor, in both early and late settings, placed little emphasis upon gender or sexual difference in their writings and beliefs. In contrast to the established Church, whose texts and theologies were deeply rooted in a binary model that set feminine depravity and weakness in contrast to masculine purity and strength, the Poor seem not to have considered the distinction between men and women particularly salient. Rather, it was the division between human and divine that preoccupied the Poor, and the power of the apostolic model available to all people to breach the agonizing gap between humanity and God, between sin and righteousness.

Thus it would seem that Valdès included women among his early community not because he was attempting to make a special point about the spiritual value of females, so long despised and marginalized in the Christian West. Rather, he seems to have perceived them first and foremost as Christians, virtuous laity who responded to his Gospel message and whose enthusiasm earned them a place within the early circle of ardent followers. Even after pressure from the Church raised the group's visibility, and thus the need to prove its own virtue and scrupulosity, there exists no evidence of particular backlash against women, no attempt to segregate and isolate women or to deploy the feminine as a metaphor for sin. In the case of the Poor, it is plausible that the common ground of a shared and suddenly outlawed apostolic mission was more significant than the divisions of gender or, for that matter, social status.

The second point concerns the roles played by women. Although clergy would make much of the distinction between theological preaching and common teaching, for example, the difference was blurred in practice. As the inquisitor and historian Bernard Gui described the group's early years:

> Although they were ignorant and unlettered, these people, both men and women, went from village to village, going into people's homes and preaching in public squares and even churches, the men in particular leaving behind them a host of misunderstandings and mistakes.[20]

The passage suggests not that women were necessarily better preachers than men, but that the latter were likely more inclined to sermonize on theological points and expound on scripture, whereas the former probably kept their messages to simple exhortation and encouragement to the Gospel model. Once groups were forced to withdraw from the public stage, women could still participate in the traditionally feminine sphere of home and hearth. Exhortative preaching did not require a large crowd, a podium, or a rehearsed sermon, and women in both early and later years could carry the message through conversation with family members and friends, over private meals, while tending to children, and even in school settings.

Teachers in schools or gatherings of the Poor included not only men but women as well, because education was a licit occupation for medieval women, particularly the role of teaching girls. And because most members were brought into the faith by parents and tended to marry within the community, women played a crucial role in maintaining existing relationships and bringing the occasional new convert into the fold. Once the primarily masculine worlds of public streets, markets, and roads were eliminated as a stage for the brethren's activity, the feminine realm of households and domestic settings became its setting.

Women among the Poor also periodically sought a lifestyle beyond the traditional home and joined sisterhoods or other forms of pious communities that somehow distinguished them from other female "friends." Living in pairs, trios, or even larger numbers, such women were sometimes called "sisters" and provided both domestic care and spiritual devotion to their fellows in the faith. A female believer named Guilhelma Michela of Auriac, for example, told an inquisitor in the 1240s that she "lived with Bernarda of Pomas and Rixen of Limoux and Crestina, the Waldensian [women] for four years or thereabouts." Not only did she hear their teachings and message, "she dressed, ate, drank, prayed and did other things as they did."[21] Teaching and preaching thus blended with domesticity and traditional female labor.

Such penitential Poor sisters would have doubtless recoiled in horror at the comparison, but it is worth noting that their deep yearning for a devoted lay Christianity in community makes them in practice virtually indistinguishable not only from many sisters in southern France associated with Catharism but also from the kaleidoscopic variety of lay religious women whose sisterhoods cropped up across Europe in the thirteenth and fourteenth centuries. Frequently viewed with skepticism or suspicion by male clergy, such pious households (as we will see in chapter 5) could range widely in size, scope, and service. As unofficial communities with no institutional scribes or chroniclers, their historical imprint is faint; yet as centers of lay piety and community that appeared simply as homes for good women, these penitential sisterhoods helped maintain the vital message and practice of the Poor throughout the thirteenth and fourteenth centuries.

CONCLUSION

In response to the question, "How is a Christian to live in the world?" the Poor brothers and sisters offered their own homely and Gospel-based answer: Follow us, even through likely persecution at the hands of the false Church, and you will go to heaven. It was an answer rooted in the certainty of apostolic simplicity and scriptural truth, one that would be echoed in various manifestations across late medieval Christendom. And as we will see in the next chapter, inquisitorial pressure (even in its most thoroughly developed practices) would never succeed in fully eliminating the Poor. Remnants lingered in pockets across Europe to meld with later movements such as Bohemian Hussites in the fifteenth century and Protestant reformers in the sixteenth, the faith virtually inextricable from proud local cultural traditions. Today, distantly related Waldensian descendant churches can still be found in Europe, in South America, in the United States, and even in Rome itself.

SUGGESTIONS FOR FURTHER READING

Audisio, Gabriel. *The Waldensian Dissent: Persecution and Survival c. 1170–1570*. Translated by Claire Davidson. Cambridge: Cambridge University Press, 1999.

Biller, Peter. *The Waldenses, 1170–1530: Between a Religious Order and a Church.* Aldershot, UK: Ashgate Variorum, 2001.
Biller, Peter. "Goodbye to Waldensianism?" *Past and Present* 192 (2006): 3–33.
Biller, Peter, and Anne Brenon, eds. *Heresy and Literacy, 1000–1530*. Cambridge: Cambridge University Press, 1994.
Cameron, Euan. *Waldenses: Rejections of Holy Church in Medieval Europe*. Malden, MA: Blackwell, 2000.
Lambert, Malcolm. *Medieval Heresy: Popular Movements from the Gregorian Reform to the Reformation*. Third edition. Malden, MA: Blackwell, 2001.
Lerner, Robert E. "A Case of Religious Counter-Culture: The German Waldensians." *American Scholar* 55 (1986): 234–47.
Shahar, Shulamith. *Women in a Medieval Heretical Sect: Agnes and Huguette the Waldensians*. Rochester, NY: Boydell Press, 2001.
Smelyansky, Eugene. *Heresy and Citizenship: Persecution of Heresy in Late Medieval German Cities.* New York: Routledge, 2020.
Välimäki, Reima. *Heresy in Late Medieval Germany: The Inquisitor Petrus Zwicker and the Waldensians*. York, UK: York Medieval Press, 2019.
Wakefield, Walter L., and Austin P. Evans, eds. *Heresies of the High Middle Ages.* New York: Columbia University Press, 1991.

NOTES

1. Euan Cameron, *Waldenses: Rejections of Holy Church in Medieval Europe* (Malden, MA: Blackwell, 2000), 14.
2. Walter L. Wakefield and Austin P. Evans, *Heresies of the High Middle Ages* (New York: Columbia University Press, 1991), 201.
3. Wakefield and Evans, *Heresies*, 200.
4. Cameron, *Waldenses*, 42.
5. Cameron, *Waldenses*, 27.
6. Wakefield and Evans, *Heresies*, 204.
7. Wakefield and Evans, *Heresies*, 159.
8. Wakefield and Evans, *Heresies*, 207.
9. Wakefield and Evans, *Heresies*, 211.
10. Wakefield and Evans, *Heresies*, 211–12.
11. Cameron, *Waldenses*, 33.
12. Wakefield and Evans, *Heresies*, 278–79.
13. Wakefield and Evans, *Heresies*, 287–88.
14. Wakefield and Evans, *Heresies*, 272–73.
15. Gabriel Audisio, *The Waldensian Dissent: Persecution and Survival, c. 1170–1570* (Cambridge: Cambridge University Press, 1999), 23.
16. Audisio, *Waldensian Dissent*, 37.
17. Peter Biller, "Goodbye to Waldensianism?" *Past and Present* 192 (2006): 29.
18. Bernard Gui, *The Inquisitor's Guide: A Medieval Manual on Heretics*, ed. Janet Shirley (Welwyn Garden City, UK: Ravenhall Books, 2006), 51.

19. Shulamith Shahar, *Women in a Medieval Heretical Sect: Agnes and Huguette the Waldensians* (Rochester, NY: Boydell Press, 2001), especially 26–45.

20. Audisio, *Waldensian Dissent*, 18.

21. Peter Biller, "The Preaching of the Waldensian Sisters," *Haeresis* 30 (1999): 135.

Chapter Three

Lawyer Popes, Mendicant Preachers, and New Inquisitorial Procedures

In the middle of the twelfth century, as new spiritual currents began to flow across western European family and social structures, St. Bernard of Clairvaux depicted heretics as sly animals stripping bare the vineyard of Christendom: "What shall we do to catch those most malicious foxes, they who would rather injure than conquer and who do not even wish to disclose themselves, but prefer to slink about in the shadows?"[1] Bernard was a spiritual giant of his age—abbot of the monastery of Clairvaux, theologian, adviser to kings, and mentor to saints—and as patron of the newly established Knights Templar and the driving force behind the Second Crusade, he was no pacifist. Yet his answer to the question, "What shall we do to catch the malicious foxes?" was that they should be taken not by force of arms but by force of argument.

Bernard was very much a man of his age. Verbal persuasion rather than physical coercion was the Church's early response to the new beliefs and behaviors dotting Christendom, and responsibility for such persuasion was left primarily in the hands of local bishops and priests. Although laypeople in the twelfth century periodically took matters into their own hands and lynched or burned accused heretics of their own accord, the Church had no official antiheretical process or structure in place even by the end of the century, when the Poor of Lyon and other groups were pleading their case before the pope. Ancient Christianity had grappled with new movements and splinter groups that became characterized informally as heresies, but the juridical category of "heretic" as a spiritual criminal characterized by a specific set of beliefs, behaviors, and penalties was a high medieval development. Within a century after the Gregorian reform, the legal and procedural climate of western Europe would change dramatically in both secular and sacral realms.

Twelfth- and thirteenth-century kings and emperors developed increasingly sophisticated bureaucratic and legal systems to manage their rapidly expanding realms (and to ensure that their authority was efficiently imposed), a process paralleled in the sacral sphere. After the failure of both localized preaching campaigns and twenty years of crusading to uproot heresy, innovative popes charted an astonishingly effective new approach to heresy.

In contrast to images presented in popular culture, however, no such thing as the "Medieval Inquisition" existed, either in terms of the name itself or the organized and efficient persecutory institution those capital letters suggest. Only "in polemic and fiction" did "The Inquisition" exist, "a single all-powerful, horrific tribunal whose agents worked everywhere to thwart religious truth, intellectual freedom, and political liberty."[2] This is the myth of "The Inquisition" that emerged over the past four hundred years, as a result of both deep hostilities between Catholic and Protestant writers of the intervening centuries and grisly cinematic renderings of dark-robed, pitiless inquisitors sending innocents to a fiery death.

In fact, the process of *inquisitio* did not theoretically allow for a sheer abuse of power; rather, checks and procedural layers were in place to ensure that justice was met. That said, significant gaps existed between theory and practice (as they do in all legal systems); and although deputized inquisitors were, for multiple reasons, never free to consign suspects to death willy-nilly, many thousands did face an excruciating and legally sanctioned death at the stake for the crime of heresy. So we are not concerned here with the myth of "The Inquisition," but the history of inquisition as a process that changed over time: the procedures and personnel, the techniques and technologies, the functions and frustrations of those appointed to preserve the vineyard of the Lord.

The turning point came in the 1230s, with the development of medieval inquisitorial activity from its origins in Roman law, an activity staffed by the mendicant and other monastic orders and fueled by growing administration, bureaucracy, and institutionalization in the West. The strategy, training, techniques, and technologies medieval inquisitors used were striking; not only representing an intriguing chapter in legal history, they also arguably played a key role in emerging Western notions of truth and power—as well as in the relationship between individuals and institutions. For inquisitors, the most important joining was that between Christians and Church, and their charge was to zero in on disobedience and bring prideful souls back into the flock. At risk was the very health of Christendom, and each "heretic" was a potential breach of hell, filth, and depravity into the world. Strong words—but then, as Christine Caldwell Ames reminds us, salvation was on the line.

Far from being a coherent machine, inquisitorial activity began in fits and starts, just after Bernard of Clairvaux's call to action. As noted previously, at the Third Lateran Council in 1179, the pope admonished Valdès of Lyon to stop preaching but encouraged his life of poverty. In 1184, Pope Lucius III presented in his decree *Ad abolendam* a thorough plan of action. Bishops were required to visit parishes suspected of heresy twice a year, to take oaths from respected residents about local religiosity, and to pursue legal action against anyone with apparently deviant beliefs. Lay authorities were encouraged to cooperate with bishops. Papal pronouncements did not, however, necessarily carry weight with the thousands of bishops throughout Western Christendom, each of whom could decide whether to adopt an active or passive approach to heresy.

THE BUILDING OF ANTIHERETICAL MOMENTUM (1198–1229)

There are moments in history when the influence of certain personalities is undeniable, when the agenda and drive of particular individuals are so potent that they become a powerful historical force in their own right. The early thirteenth century witnessed a kind of perfect storm of personalities that we must acknowledge if we are to understand the origins and development of medieval inquisition. For this reason, we will start with Pope Innocent III and his accommodation of new religious orders led by the extraordinary figures of Francis of Assisi and Dominic de Guzmán. We will then briefly consider the failure of violence as a means of uprooting heresy, the foundation of the first papal inquisition in the 1230s, its staffing by the mendicant orders, and the inquisitorial techniques and technologies employed to prosecute heresy.

As discussed in chapter 2, one of Innocent's first antiheretical measures during his pontificate (1198–1216) was the decree *Vergentis in senium*, which built on and extended the momentum of Lucius's *Ad abolendam* (1184). The significance of the decree is that it associated heresy with treason as defined in secular law, formally linking spiritual sin and legal crime for the first time. After 1199, those convicted of heresy were to have their goods confiscated and their children subjected to perpetual deprivation; the consequences of heresy were now juridically regulated and historically enduring.

The lawyer pope further clarified the penalty eight years later, just as the confrontations between Good Christians of all stripes, Cistercian preachers, and the Poor were heating up in Languedoc. In 1207, he issued the decretal *Cum ex officii nostri* (*We Decree*), which stated,

> In order altogether to remove from the patrimony of St. Peter the defilement of heretics, we decree, as a perpetual law, that whatsoever heretic . . . shall immediately be taken and delivered to the secular court to be punished according to

> law. . . . All his goods also shall be sold, so that he who took him shall receive one part, another shall go to the court which convicted him, and the third shall be applied to the building of prisons in the country wherein he was taken.[3]

Cum ex officii nostri would have a particular significance for the lands of Languedoc. Within a year of its issuing, it had become clear that Innocent's two-pronged approach of persuasion and coercion in southern France had failed. Although the Cistercian and Dominican preachers had indeed managed to gain some conversions (particularly the Dominicans, who appeared as holy and ascetic as the Good Men), the roots of local territorial and spiritual independence reached deep into the Languedocian soil. Efforts to pressure lords into enforcing spiritual obedience had met with resistance and were often perceived as the encroachment of unwelcome external powers on local lands. Innocent needed a new approach.

Fourth Lateran Council (1215)

In 1215, as the Albigensian Crusade raged in Languedoc, Innocent convened the Fourth Lateran Council, at which the multiple strands of his papal agenda were brought together in official form. The pope had long wanted to summon an ecumenical council because it was the ideal venue through which to recoup the bitter losses of the Fourth Crusade (1204) and reinvigorate the papal crusading program. Innocent's overarching goal had always been the reformation and rejuvenation of Christendom, which was manifested in several distinct projects: demanding higher moral standards for the clergy, implementing more regular sacramental participation by the laity, and the defense of Christianity against its many foes, including Jews, Muslims, and above all, heretics. Attended by hundreds of archbishops, bishops, abbots, priors, and other clergy, the council (supervised by Innocent) ultimately issued seventy canons on a wide range of issues, including an articulation of Trinitarian theology, procedures and penalties for pursuing heresy, the declaration of papal primacy over the patriarchs of the Church, the prohibition of new religious orders, regulations for the behavior and trials of clergy, arrangements for a new crusade to the east, and supervision of Jews and Jewish-Christian relations.

Of these, canon 3 was most important for the topic at hand because it officially anathematized heresy. Acknowledging the exasperating difficulty of labels and names, it thundered the following pronouncement against heterodoxy: "We excommunicate and anathematize every heresy setting itself up against this holy, orthodox and catholic faith which we have expounded above, and condemn all heretics by whatever names they go under; they have various faces indeed, but tails tied onto another, for they have vanity in common. Those condemned as heretics shall be handed over to the secular authorities present or to their bailiffs for punishment by the penalty deserved, clerks first being degraded from their orders. The goods of these condemned are, if they are laymen, to be confiscated."[4] The implication here is that whatever the name or flavor of belief, heretics are all the same in their willful and prideful disobedience to the Church and that they have as such forfeited their place (and possessions) in Christendom. Such clear-cut categorization of orthodox and heterodox admitted no shades of gray nor acknowledged any distinctions among groups deemed heretical, an important step in the bureaucratization of antiheretical activity.

Canon 3 also criticized preaching by laymen, though the old problem was reframed here in terms of unlicensed preaching by hypocrites and usurpers. Again, Innocent sought to exclude disobedient sons from the community of Christendom until they repented:

> Since some, under "the appearance of godliness, but denying the power thereof," as the Apostle says (II Tim. 3:5), arrogate to themselves the authority to preach, as the same Apostle says: "How shall they preach unless they be sent?" (Rom. 10:15), all those prohibited or not sent, who, without the authority of the Apostolic See or of the Catholic bishop of the locality, shall presume to usurp the office of preaching either publicly or privately, shall be excommunicated and unless they amend, and the sooner the better, they shall be visited with a further suitable penalty.[5]

Another decree of the Fourth Lateran Council with vital implications for heresy and inquisition was the mandate in canon 21 for all Christians to confess and take communion at least once a year, at Easter. Annual confession was crucial for the later development of inquisition, for the two were closely related: both involved inquiry into the moral and spiritual state of an individual, and both focused on the discovery and repentance of error for the sake of one's soul and the wider health of Christendom, the success of which was predicated on Christian obedience to clerical authority. Employing the metaphor of disease for sin, Innocent characterized the work of clergy as akin to that of a physician:

> Let the priest be discreet and cautious that he may pour wine and oil into the wounds of the one injured after the manner of a skillful physician, carefully inquiring into the circumstances of the sinner and the sin, from the nature of which he may understand what kind of advice to give and what remedy to apply, making use of different experiments to heal the sick one.[6]

The association of sin with sickness would take on particular resonance in the early thirteenth century, as would (in some circles) a symbolic parallel between inquisitors and physicians; as we will see, Dominican friars in particular understood their charge to be "Doctors of Souls," learned experts responsible for restoring depraved spirits rather than diseased bodies.[7]

Accommodating the Apostolic Model: The New Mendicant Orders

Even as Innocent was launching the crusade against "Albigensians" in southern France, however, he retained his original impulse to accommodate passionate apostolic Christians whenever possible. In 1209, as the first northern crusaders were heading toward Toulouse, an Italian merchant's son named Francis presented himself at the papal court to receive approval for his way of life. Much like Valdès of Lyon thirty years earlier, the young man had been suddenly inspired to a new spiritual vitality by the Gospel of Matthew 10:9:

> And as ye go, preach, saying, The kingdom of heaven is at hand. Heal the sick, cleanse the lepers, raise the dead, cast out devils: freely ye have received, freely give. Provide neither gold, nor silver, nor brass in your purses, Nor scrip for your journey, neither two coats, neither shoes, nor yet staves.

Compelled to give away his possessions and live an ascetic life of apostolic poverty, the charismatic Francis had stripped himself naked in the square of his hometown in a dramatic act of renunciation and since then had drawn numerous supporters and followers to him. In Rome, he placed himself at the pope's disposal and promised total obedience to the pontiff.

According to legend, Innocent was not initially amenable to the ragged penitent and refused to meet Francis; that night, however, he had a dream of a man holding up the crumbling Church. When Francis finally appeared before him, as the story went, Innocent recognized him as the man from the dream. Whatever the reason, Innocent had evidently learned from past mistakes through which the lack of papal discernment drove orthodox and passionate groups such as the Poor of Lyon needlessly into heresy. At this meeting, therefore, Innocent seized the opportunity to encourage Francis and his followers in their imitation of the Gospel, approving their mission of preaching and poverty and establishing them as a new religious order: the *Friars Minor*, or "little brothers," as Francis humbly wished them to be called. With Innocent's patronage, the Franciscan friars spread quickly throughout the towns of western Europe and became a rigorous example of Christian piety.

Such ideas were in the air in the early thirteenth century, and a parallel development emerged simultaneously yet independently in southern France, where the Spanish monk and preacher Dominic de Guzmán was debating Good Christians in Pamiers. Like Francis in Italy, Dominic had committed himself to a life of strict discipline and orthodox preaching according to the same apostolic model that had been inspiring men and women since the Gregorian reform. Dominic was particularly distressed by heresy and established a community of preachers in Toulouse to tend to Christian souls; given the contemporary circumstances, the persuasion of heretics away from error took on particular significance within their broad pastoral mission.

Immediately following Innocent's death in 1216, Dominic presented himself and his eager brethren (like Valdès and Francis before him) to the new pope to ask for recognition. Because another decree of the Fourth Lateran Council had prohibited new religious orders, the Dominicans were approved as an offshoot of the existing Augustinian canons by Pope Honorius III in 1216. Particularly devoted to theology and preaching, pairs of black-robed and barefoot Dominican preachers would become an increasingly common sight throughout Europe. Chaste, pale from fasting, fiercely ascetic, and licensed to preach against heresy, they and the Franciscans embodied the first effective argument against heretical *perfecti* and Waldensian masters.

Although many of Innocent's ambitions failed or were left incomplete, his pontificate had been a watershed in keeping with his earlier Gregorian predecessors. Innocent extended papal authority into all corners of Christendom and its Church, railed against secular rulers who challenged him, and explicitly clarified the status of out-groups (Jews, infidels, and heretics), whose very marginality reinforced the in-group of obedient Western Christians. He was succeeded by Pope Honorius III (r. 1216–1227) and Pope Gregory IX (r. 1227–1241); both men were leading Italian ecclesiastics whose pontificates would, as we will see, contribute mightily to the new inquisitorial approach to heresy in the thirteenth century.

NEW ANTIHERETICAL ATTEMPTS (1227–1231)

During the early thirteenth century, ecclesiastical officials and lay rulers continued to clarify their stance on heresy and to render the new legal strictures into practicable forms. Emperor Frederick II, for example, added new canonical restrictions on heresy to imperial law and mandated death by burning as the penalty for recalcitrant heretics. Thus the pyre became the universal punishment for lapsed or unrepentant heretics throughout Christendom as heated debates and dialogues about heresy and law continued. By mid-century, English scholar and bishop of Lincoln Robert Grosseteste had contributed an enduring definition of heresy as "an opinion *chosen* by human perception, *created* by human reason, founded on the Scriptures, contrary to the teachings of the Church, *publicly* avowed, and *obstinately defended*" (emphases added). His point was that heresy consisted not of error or theological confusion but

Figure 3.1. *The Dream of Pope Innocent III*, **1298.** *Source*: **Giotto di Bondone, mural, 270 cm × 230 cm. Upper Church, S. Francesco, Assisi, Italy. Erich Lessing/Art Resource, NY.**

Figure 3.2. *Members of the Dominican Order*, **Tommaso da Modena. Seminary, Treviso, Italy.** *Source*: **Copyright © DeA Picture Library/Art Resource, NY.**

was defined by the stubbornness and public pridefulness of a willful Christian gone astray.[8] By the end of the thirteenth century, these fierce conversations had produced a sophisticated body of juridical assumptions and procedures for dealing with heresy.

The distinguished canon lawyer Pope Gregory IX, who ascended the see after Honorius's death in 1227, quickly ascertained that the Church's battle with heresy was not going well—particularly in the south. By this time, the Albigensian Crusade had been raging for nearly twenty years, and the preaching campaigns of Cistercians and Dominicans had still not uprooted Good Christian communities and traditions in Languedoc; Innocent's measures, although foundational in so many ways, had not proven fully effective, and the pope needed a new strategy.

The Council of Toulouse (1229)

In 1229, two developments took place that deeply affected the spiritual politics of Western Christendom. First was the end of the Albigensian Crusade. After years of only marginal attention to the devastation of the southern lands, the French monarchy finally intervened in the Albigensian affair and ended the crusade with the Treaty of Paris; the complicated negotiations left the defeated southern lands placed largely under royal authority. Yet although the crusade had smashed some of the leading families of Languedoc and devastated its population, it had not eliminated heresy.

In the same year, the pope and his staff turned their attention sharply to the problem of lay support for heresy in Languedoc, and in November, the second major event took place: the Council of Toulouse. Guided indirectly by Gregory IX, the council issued eighteen canons (nearly half of the total) dealing explicitly with heresy, setting forth new techniques for uncovering stubborn "Cathar" errors. In this new set of tactics, laymen of good repute were deputized along with a local priest to "seek out the heretics in those parishes, by searching all houses and subterranean chambers which lie under any suspicion."[9] It was a fearsome approach, in which homes and buildings associated with heretics were to be destroyed and repentant heretics forced to wear crosses sewn to their clothing as a badge of their sin and relocated to a town with no heresy. Above all, these were instruments of social penalty aimed at disrupting community bonds and forming them anew into an explicitly orthodox pattern.

But perhaps most striking among the canons of the Council of Toulouse was the prohibition against possession of biblical texts, a key indicator of the perceived relationship between lay access to scripture and heresy:

> We prohibit that the laity should be permitted to have the books of the Old or the New Testament; unless anyone from motives of devotion should wish to have the Psalter or the Breviary for divine offices or the hours of the blessed Virgin; but we most strictly forbid their having any translation of these books.[10]

In contemplating Church control of scripture, it is worth remembering that biblical books (Latin or vernacular translations) were frequently glossed with marginal comments, and notations by "unlicensed" Christians could be misleading or downright unorthodox, particularly within books circulating among suspect communities like the towns and villages of Languedoc. Thus the prohibition of lay access to the Word was, from the perspective of the clergy, an attempt to safeguard lay Christians from error and, in turn, to protect scripture from lay Christians.

The First Inquisitors

By the end of the 1220s, Gregory IX was well aware of past failures—lackadaisical preaching and local heresy trials had proven ineffective, as were the more extreme measures of crusade and regional violence. What was needed, he decided, were specialists dedicated to painstakingly and relentlessly unraveling local heretical networks. In an early experiment, in 1227 he commissioned a secular priest named Conrad of Marburg, who had spent years preaching for crusading efforts and independently investigating heresy in Germany. Shortly thereafter, the pope also appointed a Dominican friar named Robert le Bougre, who had formerly been a "Good Christian" and converted before joining the order to smoke out heretics in northern France. Yet this first attempt at staffing papal inquisition was not a success; both men acted overzealously with little information, forced false confessions, and sent hundreds to the stake with little attempt at pastoral care or conversion.

Conrad, for example, notoriously forced stereotyped confessions of abominable practices and demonic worship from his victims and forwarded the accounts to the pope, who appears to have taken them at face value. In 1233, apparently in response to such reports, Gregory IX issued the decree *Vox in Rama* (*A Voice Was Heard in Rama*), in which he described a gathering of heretics in stereotypical terms already familiar from ancient smears against early Christians and other out-groups. Because of the tenacity of such demonic accusations (to which we will return in chapter 6), the passage is worth quoting at length:

> The following rites of this pestilence are carried out: when any novice is to be received among them and enters the sect of the damned for the first time, the shape of a certain frog appears to him, which some are accustomed to call a toad. Some kiss this creature on the hindquarters and some on the mouth; they receive the tongue and saliva of the beast inside their mouths. Sometimes it appears unduly large, and sometimes equivalent to a goose or a duck, and sometimes it even assumes the size of an oven. At length, when the novice has come forward, he is met by a man of marvelous pallor, who has very black eyes and is so emaciated and thin that, since his flesh has been wasted, he seems to have remaining only skin drawn over the bone. The novice kisses him and feels cold, like ice, and after the kiss the memory of the catholic faith totally disappears from his heart. Afterwards they sit down to a meal and when they have arisen from it, from a certain statue, which is usually in a sect of this kind, a black cat about the size of an average dog, descends backwards, with its tail erect. First the novice, next the master, then each one of the order who are worthy and perfect, kiss the cat on its hindquarters; the imperfect, who do not estimate themselves worthy, receive grace from the master. . . . When this has been done, they put out the candles, and turn to the practice of the most disgusting lechery,

> making no distinction between those who are strangers, and those who are kin. Moreover, if by chance those of the male sex exceed the number of women, surrendering to their ignominious passions, burning mutually in their desires, men engage in depravity with men. Similarly, women change their natural function, which is against nature, making this itself worthy of blame among themselves. . . . They even receive the body of the Lord every year at Easter from the hand of a priest, and carrying it in their mouths to their homes, they throw it into the latrine in contempt of the savior. . . . They acknowledge all acts which are not pleasing to the Lord, and instead do what he hates.[11]

Of course these crimes bore no relationship to reality, nor to any particular practices in Germany at the time; rather, they reflected ancient anxieties and fantasies in which the wickedness of one's declared enemies was presumed to manifest itself in the most heinous of all possible crimes: perverted, filthy sex. Nor have we seen the last of this stereotype, for we will encounter these accusations again later in the context of late medieval magic and witchcraft. The pope appears to have taken them to heart, however, lamenting the extent to which such horrors had become rooted in the German lands.

Equivalent to Conrad in terms of minimal procedural restraint was the career of Robert le Bougre, who worked in both French and Germanic lands through the 1230s. His methods led frequently to burnings, such as in the towns of Cambrai and Douai in 1236; in 1239, he was instrumental in the unprecedented simultaneous execution of over 180 people in Mont Aimé in Champagne. Yet he was no rogue inquisitor whose excesses slipped past the attention of authorities: the king of Navarre, the count of Champagne, and sixteen local bishops were all present at the spectacle. Evidently, therefore, Robert's methods appealed to some, probably resonating significantly with local fears, hatreds, and resentments.

In terms of the intended inquisitorial model of persuasion over coercion, conversion over condemnation, however, both Conrad and Robert were failures. Since the aim of antiheretical activity before and after the papal inquisition was to bring straying sheep back into the fold, execution of those still in error was a last measure; indeed, the goal was always to obtain confessions followed by sincere repentance and penance. Despite pockets of support, contemporary outrage rippled back to Rome, and Robert was ultimately suspended by the papacy, whereas Conrad was murdered by his enemies before the pope could step in. Another method had to be developed.

FROM *ACCUSATIO* TO *INQUISITIO*

Even before the disaster of Conrad of Marburg's commission, Gregory IX was looking to the mendicant orders for an effective new solution to the problem of "the little foxes." During the early 1230s, in one of his many attempts to find innovative solutions to fight heresy, he deputized some mendicant friars to staff antiheretical tribunals in Toulouse and Carcassonne; in doing so, he developed the single most effective approach for extirpating heresy in European history. Drawing on the ancient legal precedent of *inquisitio,* or inquiry, a process revived largely under the pontificate of Innocent III, Gregory IX reconceptualized antiheretical methods into a new model that would profoundly influence European law for centuries to come. Before we consider its organization and mission, however, let us consider what the legal shift entailed and what it meant for the goal of prosecuting heresy.

In the earlier Middle Ages, lay courts typically followed the process of *accusatio* (what has since been labeled "accusatorial procedure"), a system of law based largely on Germanic practices. As its name might suggest, the process began with a single accuser bringing a charge before the court. This person was then obliged to prove the charge, essentially acting in the role of prosecutor, while meeting the accused face to face. In such situations, early courts often turned to judicial ordeals for proof of guilt or innocence. For example, suspected criminals might be required to grasp hot irons, and in several days their wounds would be examined to determine whether they were healing properly (little to no healing was a sign of guilt), or suspects might be bound and dunked in water to see how quickly they rose to the surface (floating too quickly was a sign of guilt). Such methods were not entirely as irrational as they might initially seem. These rituals were performed publicly, and the ultimate determination of guilt or innocence often relied on the general acclamation of the gathered witnesses, who determined whether a burn was sufficiently scabbed over or a suspect had remained submerged for an adequate amount of time. Judgments in these cases might well have been informed by the deep knowledge people living in tightly knit communities usually had of their neighbors' general character as well as of the accused's own guilt or innocence.

The accusatorial process also contained a built-in protection for the one accused. When suspects were acquitted or found innocent of the charge, their accusers faced legal retribution for bringing false charges—the principle of *lex talionis* (the law of retaliation). Thus, in the absence of clear physical evidence or eyewitnesses, there was a strong barrier to making any accusation unless the accusers were absolutely sure that they stood in higher regard within their communities than did the accused. Certainly if an entire community regarded an individual with suspicion, punishment could occur, and it was often severe (and noninstitutional, with punishment meted out by the lay mob).

By the twelfth and early thirteenth centuries, a shift away from the accusatorial model was already underway. Rather than individuals facing the accused on the basis of firsthand knowledge, judges now took on the prosecutorial role based not on personal experience but on collected information pertaining to a suspect. Under inquisitorial procedures, guilt or innocence was proved by the active inquiry (*inquisitio*) of said judge into the details of a case. Although an investigation could still be initiated by an accuser, in most cases a deputized officer conducted an investigation on his own initiative, based largely on general reports of an individual's reputation—which could involve exactly the sort of vague disrepute that often hovered around those suspected of heresy.

In 1215, Innocent had decreed that the trial form of *inquisitio* was to replace *accusatio* broadly, and not only in cases of heresy: "The *inquisitio* was used at all levels, from the courts of archdeacons and rural archpriests or deans charging rustics with fornication or adultery to papally commissioned trials presided over by cardinals on charges brought against kings and queens."[12] Far from a minor legal detail, the shift from personal to official criminal inquiry went hand in hand with overarching trends toward bureaucratization in the high and later Middle Ages, and is thus a crucial strand to unravel in the history of premodern religious and institutional history.

THE BIRTH OF INQUISITORIAL TRIBUNALS IN THE 1230S

After the failure of Conrad of Marburg's commission (and even prior to Robert's excesses in France), Gregory IX shifted gears and recruited specially trained judge-inquisitors from the ranks of the Franciscans and Dominicans. The Dominicans demonstrated a particular affinity for the work, emphasizing as they did preaching, learning, and the unflagging care of souls. In 1231, Gregory IX took the first step by calling upon a Dominican prior in Regensburg, Germany, to pursue suspected heretics in the area. Shortly thereafter, he appointed papal inquisitors in Languedoc, and by 1233 he had directed the local Dominican priors to choose likely inquisitors from among their subordinates to staff tribunals established in cities throughout Europe.

In 1237, a tribunal was established at Carcassonne, and within a few years others were being set up in central Italy and Lombardy. By the early fourteenth century, Franciscans headed tribunals in Savoy, Provence, the Dauphiné, central and southern Italy, and Sicily; Dominicans took the rest of the territories, particularly Spain, Germany, and Bohemia. Operating independently from each other, however, these tribunals should not be thought of as interchangeable elements of a single office, or as even coordinated functions. Each scattered tribunal, staffed largely by mendicant papal delegates, worked locally, on its own authority, and without formal contact or communication with other tribunals.

Even though they were not part of a single, uniform institution, however, such tribunals did share features in common.[13] For example, the inquisitors were directly subject to the pope and therefore exempt from episcopal oversight, were licensed to proceed against suspects by virtue of the authority of their office, and were allowed to take depositions from people typically prohibited in canon law from testifying (including children, criminals, and accomplices); the accused who were summoned to testify were required to swear an oath making them liable to prosecution for perjury; and, in one of the most significant departures from *accusatio*, the accused were not told the names of those who testified against them. Thus, although the papally deputized *inquisitio* is perhaps best understood as a network of independently operating tribunals, inquisitors of heretical depravity did share a common understanding of the heretical threat, the seriousness of their task, and the techniques and procedures available to them. Although the tribunals operated independently, the training the friars received within their own orders also helped to establish some uniformity and consistency. And it was at these tribunals that precedents were set for inquisitorial activity over the next century.

Yet the fact remains that the process of *inquisitio* was never particularly suitable for ascertaining the inner beliefs and spiritual condition of Christians. *Inquisitio* simply meant that the judges launched cases themselves based upon reports of reputations in communities about which they initially had little knowledge, and that those summoned and accused had little recourse to defend themselves. Although the disconnect between deputized inquisitors and local villages was intended as an aid to their labor, ensuring that no ties of kin or kind would cloud their antiheretical mission, it also meant that inquisitors faced the daunting task of disentangling fact from fiction, certainty from suspicion, and dissemblance from mere confusion. Thus by the mid-thirteenth century, officials pursuing heresy under inquisitorial procedures needed new tools to secure confessions, contrition, repentance, and penance—in other words, to see into people's souls. By the end of the century, deputized inquisitors and their episcopal (or occasionally freelance) colleagues possessed a rapidly growing body of powers and texts to support their work. And despite the limitations of *inquisitio* as a legal process, it would prove far more effective in identifying, prosecuting, and punishing heresy than earlier methods of persuasion and crusade.

INQUISITORIAL PROFILES

Although the label "inquisitor of heretical depravity" suggests a certain uniformity of background and experience, the men who acted in an inquisitorial capacity came from a variety of backgrounds, worked in a number of different regions, and conducted their business in unique ways. In most regions, episcopal oversight remained strong, and, particularly in Germany, itinerant or freelance inquisitors outside of the papal bureaucracy took on the responsibility of pursuing heretics. Thus although the new thirteenth-century papal *inquisitio*, staffed largely with Dominicans and Franciscans, was a crucial development in our story, it never held a monopoly on medieval antiheretical efforts. And because each tribunal worked independently, we should consider the variety of local contexts to which the emerging new technologies of inquiry were adapted and aimed. We should also factor in the character and methods of individual inquisitors because, as the following profiles suggest, ecclesiastical agents were little closer to a fixed or homogenous group than were the "heretics" they pursued.

Étienne de Bourbon (c. 1195–1261)

One of the earliest appointed Dominican inquisitors of the thirteenth century, Étienne de Bourbon joined the friary in Lyon in about 1223 after his student years at the University of Paris. In keeping with the Dominicans' emphasis on preaching and teaching, he wrote many popular sermons as well as entertaining tales of his days as an undergraduate in Paris. A few years later (c. 1235), he was appointed inquisitor, working primarily in the valleys of the Saône and Rhone. He was present at Robert le Bougre's burning of 180 "Manichaeans" in 1239 and was convinced of the effectiveness of the death penalty as a tool for distinguishing between Christian and un-Christian.

Active in Lyon only a generation after Valdès's lifetime, the inquisitor gathered testimony from followers who had known the man personally and recorded one of the most reliable accounts of the movement's early years.[14] He also mockingly targeted superstition: "I also heard of a Spanish schoolman who believed in auguries. He was all ready for a journey to return to his homeland, when one of his companions stopped him from leaving by crowing outside the house door as if he was a crow. He thought it was an evil omen!"[15] Across his writings and *exempla*, he recounted many tales of inquisition and execution, gathered to disclose the wickedness of heresy and reinforce a "Christianity of fear"—a theological stance employing terror of sin as motivation for seeking salvation.[16] Étienne's collection would later serve as the basis of a similar collection of anecdotes, *De dono timoris* (*On the Gift of Fear*), written between 1263 and 1277 by the Dominican master general Humbert of Romans.

Rainier Sacconi (d. 1263)

In contrast to Étienne de Bourbon, whose path to the Dominican inquisitorial office was relatively straightforward, Rainier Sacconi's journey was more complicated. A native of Piacenza, one of the northern Italian cities torn by civic and spiritual turmoil, he described himself as a "former heresiarch" and was evidently deeply involved with local heretical circles. Around 1245, he was converted by the Dominican preacher Peter of Verona and made a surprise about-face by joining the order himself. Within ten years he had so demonstrated the sincerity of his conversion and extent of his abilities he was named inquisitor for Lombardy and the March of Ancona (1254–1259). In 1250, he composed the *Summa de Catharis et Pauperibus de Lugdano* (*Summa on the Cathars and the Poor of Lyon*), containing detailed information regarding heretical churches, communities, and catalogues of their tenets. The text became the most widely circulated tract on the Cathars and Waldensians in the thirteenth century and highly influential among both inquisitors and historians for decades and centuries to come.

Bernard Gui (c. 1262–1331)

Born at the time of his predecessors' deaths, Bernard Gui represents the second generation of Dominican inquisitors and was one of its most influential participants in both contemporary and historical terms. Having grown up in Limousin, he entered the friary of Limoges as a teenager and took official vows at the age of eighteen (c. 1280). His early years were spent studying grammar, logic, philosophy, and theology in both Limoges and Montpellier. After gaining a reputation for both his scholarship and administrative skills, by 1294 he had been made prior of the convent of Albi, followed by positions at Carcassonne (1297), Castres (1301), and Limoges (1305). Despite more than a half century of inquisitorial effort, orthodoxy had never been successfully enforced in the region, and Gui would become one of the most active and influential inquisitors of the era. Over his career, he pursued a wide variety of accused peoples with a rigorous and methodical system geared toward securing confessions and penitence. Records suggest that he pronounced 536 separate judgments, of which 45 were death sentences.

A theologian and career ecclesiastical diplomat as well as inquisitor, Gui was also a prolific writer whose works include volumes of sermons, a history of the Gauls, and a biography of Thomas Aquinas. Gui's extensive experience and secondary reading shaped his practical manual on inquisitions, *Practica officii Inquisitionis heretice pravitatis* (*Conduct of the Inquisition into Heretical Wickedness*).[17] Although the manual's date of composition is uncertain, scholars have made a persuasive case for the later years of his career, around 1323 or 1324. Just as a modern manual might include boilerplate templates for administrative purposes, so too did the *Practica* supply standard formulas for abjuration or recanting of heresy. In the following example, "N" simply stands for *Nomen* ("Name" in Latin):

> I, such a one, N., of such a place, such a diocese, on trial before you, N., inquisitor into the evil of heresy, with God's most holy gospels placed before me, utterly abjure all heresy which rebels against the Catholic faith of the Lord Jesus Christ and the holy Roman Church, together with every belief held by heretics of whatever sect condemned by the Roman Church, under whatever name, especially such and such a sect [this may be specified], including all support, help, shelter, defense or association with these persons, on pain of the punishment lawfully imposed on those who relapse into a heresy they have abjured in court.[18]

The manual opens with directions "of the manner, skill and method to be used in the examination and interrogation of heretics, believers, and their supporters," followed by specific categorizations of the errors of "today's Manichaeans," "the Sect of the Waldensians" (also known as "the Poor of Lyon" or "the Sandallers"), "the Sect of the False Apostles" (the Dolcinites), "the Béguin sect," and "the Jews." Although Jews were not initially associated with Christian heresy, the fourteenth century witnessed an escalation of the anti-Semitic hostility that had been formalized in the canons of the Fourth Lateran Council. Gui's manual refers repeatedly to the treachery of Jews, noting that "Christians who transfer or return to the Jewish rite . . . shall be proceeded against as heretics."[19] Because Gui also concerned himself with magic and demonology (discussed in chapter 6), he offered guidance for interrogating "sorcerers, fortune-tellers and those who summon demons." For his service, Gui was rewarded with promotion to procurator general of the Dominicans, in which capacity he served the new pope, John XXII, and with a bishopric in 1323. He died in office in 1331, still supervising the sixty-one parishes under his administration.

Jacques Fournier (d. 1342)

A contemporary of Bernard Gui, Jacques Fournier (who was to become Pope Benedict XII in 1334) was a Cistercian monk who studied at the University of Paris as a young man. In 1311 he became an abbot, and in 1317 he ascended the episcopal seat of Pamiers. Fournier's fierce persecution of Cathar communities in the mountainous regions under his spiritual authority is documented in the enormous *Register* preserved in papal archives. By all accounts, he was a vigilant, detailed, and tenacious inquisitor who picked up on discrepancies, posed penetrating questions, and (like his colleagues across Christendom) sought to save souls. From this mass of source material, Emmanuel Le Roy Ladurie famously reconstructed the local culture, spiritual climate, and consequences of inquisitorial activity in the small village of Montaillou:

> After dinner there would begin the long country-style evening around the fire. Those present included the hostess's two grown-up sons when they were not out keeping their sheep . . . there would also be a little group of passing *parfaits*, or some merry priests with their women . . . [t]he newcomers, to create a good impression, brought their own wine with them. Discussion would range over various topics. When only friends were present, the subject could be heresy. The veterans of Catharism would go over old memories: tricks played on the Inquisition by some woman heretic cleverer than its myrmidons; plots to murder a traitor or a bad daughter . . . ; or merely the problems of marrying off a son, questions of health or of removing a spell from some sheep which had been bewitched.[20]

The painful consequences of Fournier's antiheretical activity for Montaillou and other neighboring villages are considered at greater length below.

With the fall of the final Cathar stronghold in 1326, the inquisitor's career trajectory quickly escalated: in that year he was made bishop of Mirepoix, in 1327, cardinal, and in 1334, he was elected pope to succeed the deceased John XXII. The new Pope Benedict XII quickly adopted a reformist stance in Avignon, where he would play an important role in healing a growing rift between the papacy and Franciscans (see chapter 4).

Peter Zwicker (Mid-Fourteenth to Early Fifteenth Century)

Our final inquisitor was also no French Dominican, but a German-speaking Celestine monk named Peter Zwicker.[21] Of his origins we know little, for he first appears in the historical record as an independent inquisitor in the final decade of the fourteenth century. In 1391, he pursued Waldensians in the city of Erfurt, and for the next few years (1392–1394) he interrogated nearly two hundred suspects in Stettin, Pomerania, and Brandenburg. From there he moved on to Styria (1395) and Hungary (1400–1404). Rather than operating as a formally deputized "inquisitor of heretical depravity," Zwicker and colleagues (several of whom operated in fourteenth-century Germany) would request permission from local bishops to pursue heresy within the diocese.

One might think of this as an inquisitorial freelance or consulting position, which could produce results in dioceses in which bishops were otherwise occupied, needed assistance, or for whom heresy did not constitute a major concern. In the diocese of Cammin in the Uckermark (between Berlin and Stettin) in 1392, he recorded discovering communities of more than four hundred Waldensians. In the southwestern region and Switzerland, where the Poor flourished in urban rather than rural settings, he identified communities in Mainz in 1390, Augsburg in 1393, and Strasbourg, Bern, and Freiburg im Üchtland in 1399.

Like many of his peers, Zwicker compiled an extensive collection of recorded evidence as well as procedures focused on eliciting confessions and conversions. He also wrote an influential treatise on heresy, *Cum dormirent homines* (*While Men Slept* [the enemy came and sowed tares]). According to surviving source material, Zwicker seems to have been a talented preacher who used practical arguments and familiar, homespun images to communicate his message; at the same time, he was deeply concerned with the theology of heresy and brought all the intellectual and textual tools of his day to the task at hand. He was unusually successful in securing large numbers of conversions: by his own account "around a thousand Waldensian heretics were converted to the Catholic faith" within the space of two years; and a contemporary treatise noted that "Brother Peter within the space of one year called back to the faith around six hundred of these heretics."[22] Whether or not these numbers were accurate in a mathematical sense, they certainly communicate the contemporary sense that Zwicker was remarkably good at his job.

Other temporary or "freelance" inquisitorial officials also appear in the historical record. Bishops might allow itinerant inquisitors to conduct proceedings in their dioceses, particularly if such had proven successful in neighboring regions. Members of the cathedral clergy might also participate in local interrogations, armed with precise knowledge of the parish and its membership, and faculty from universities such as Heidelberg and Paris were frequently involved when theologians and canon lawyers were called to serve on various types of panels or hearings. Thus although the category of medieval inquisitor was developing more visible administrative contours, it was far from an exclusive designation.

READING INQUISITORIAL RECORDS

One of the most important elements of the development of medieval inquisitorial activity was its use of texts—its painstaking recording and copying of interrogations, their organization and cross-referencing for easy use, and the collection of supporting written materials on issues of law and theology. Each tribunal had archives of registers into which confessions and information were copied, and these provide some of our best sources for the history of inquisition. Notaries kept journals of day-to-day activities, summaries of penances, and full legal accounts of the most severe sentences. Staff also kept copies of relevant papal documents, acts of councils, and procedural documents in a kind of inquisitorial reference library, often aided by finding tools, indexes, and other means of retrieving needed information at a moment's notice.

Of particular value over the course of the later thirteenth and fourteenth centuries were procedure manuals for inquisitors, texts not so very different in structure and purpose from the confessors' manuals long used to aid priests in their pastoral aim of eliciting confessions and applying appropriate penance to their parishioners. One of the first was compiled at Carcassonne in the 1240s and provided a brief description of their pattern of investigation and sentencing, but they rapidly became more complex and elaborate after that. A decade later, another handbook (the *Ordo processus Narbonensis*) provides information on more than fifty-six hundred interrogations conducted by two inquisitors near Narbonne.[23]

Before we move on to consider at greater length the tools and techniques employed by inquisitors in their work and the consequences of those processes for those who found themselves under interrogation, it would be wise to pause and ask, How do we know any of this? Where does this information come from? And how reliable is it?

The answer is both simple and complicated, because much of our historical information about the Church's categories of heresy and antiheretical procedures comes from inquisitors' records. As we will discuss below, inquisitors developed scrupulous techniques of record keeping and copying in order to track the testimony of suspects and build documented cases against them over time. Thus inquisitors like those introduced above not only compiled lengthy registers of names, dates, geographical locations, kin relationships, and sentences, but also gathered them along with trial notes and records of testimony. Although many such collections were dispersed or disposed of over the centuries, a few remained in local archives or were fortuitously transferred to libraries for safekeeping. As a consequence, modern historians have access to several different collections of medieval inquisitorial sources, most of which have now been subjected to analysis by multiple scholars. Other examples of relevant surviving sources might include urban or monastic chronicles penned by local observers, episcopal or parish records, or scholarly treatises or histories referring to the events.

However, it should be evident that all of these represent elite or privileged perspectives, and none gives direct voice to the thousands of (largely illiterate) suspects interrogated over the centuries. Although the records may seem to report testimony directly, remember that the conditions under which they were written can hardly be described as conducive to free expression. The men and women being interrogated were usually not there out of choice, the inquisitors asked specific questions geared to elicit particular types of answers, and fear and intimidation certainly influenced the form of response given. Within a few decades of the establishment of papal inquisition, how-to guides or manuals began to circulate that further influenced the shape of interrogations and testimony by describing and reinforcing stereotyped profiles of certain heresies—Cathars believe this, Waldensians will say that, one can know a "master" by this statement, or one can trap a "perfect" by asking him this question. Having triggered the inquisitor's suspicion according to one of these profiles, a suspect was usually subjected to intense and predefined questioning *based upon that imagined category of heretic*. In other words, even if we had access to the exact words, inflections, gestures, and expressions of the conversation, the inquisitors' assumptions and power position always skewed the course and direction of interrogation.

The process of recording and translating testimony added further layers of obscurity onto this already problematic text: although interrogation took place in the vernacular, the notes or protocols were jotted down in Latin and later transformed into an official past-tense document written in the third person and in even more formal Latin. Thus, as a suspect carefully answered an inquisitor's questions (perhaps employing some of the evasive or manipulative strategies discussed below), a third party—the notary—was simultaneously translating the exchange into an entirely different linguistic structure. If you have ever tried to report a conversation exactly with all its nuances and gestures, you know how difficult it is: now imagine translating and abridging as you go. As a consequence, the utility of inquisitorial documents for historians is complicated. It is difficult to know whose voice we are hearing or to evaluate to what extent the words are shaped by the inquisitorial discourse itself, and we do the past a disservice if we pretend otherwise. Yet historians must make do with the available evidence, so with these qualifications in mind, let us proceed carefully to consider these records and the extent to which we may use them to enrich our understanding of the interplay between "heresy" and "orthodoxy" in the thirteenth through fifteenth centuries.

"INQUISITORS OF HERETICAL DEPRAVITY" AT WORK

So how did the "inquisitors of heretical depravity" conduct their work? Papally appointed inquisitors developed a relatively standard procedure for launching their investigations, which was adopted (and sometimes modified) by itinerant inquisitors and episcopal appointees. At first, one or two inquisitors, along with a small staff or entourage, would travel from one town or village to another in order to launch an investigation. However, such vulnerability quickly turned out to be unsafe in certain regions, and after years of suffering attacks, many inquisitors stopped traveling and began insisting that witnesses appear at tribunal headquarters instead. Some bolder souls, such as Zwicker, continued to travel. Enlisting the support of local clerics and secular officials, an inquisitor would generally preach a public sermon—a pointed one focused on the evils of heresy—and then call for people to come to him with confessions, accusations, or even mere suspicions. The message was repeated from the pulpits of parish priests who could be called into the service of the inquisitors, delivering summonses to individuals with whom they wanted to speak. No one over the age of twelve for women and fourteen for men was exempt, and failure to respond to a summons could result in excommunication. Because the purpose of the investigation was to identify the "little foxes" and turn them back into sheep, there would usually be a grace period of a week to a month during which time people could voluntarily confess in exchange for light sentences.

Interrogation

Once a list of suspects had been created, an inquisitor would proceed with his investigation, questioning the accused and calling people to testify or confess. Under this procedure, accusers were not responsible for the veracity of their accusations, and of course inquisitors would not suffer legal reprisals for proceeding with questionable investigations that ultimately resulted in acquittals. Interrogation was the same for suspects and those who responded to the general summons. It took place in the presence of at least two witnesses, and, interestingly, its purpose was not only to discover wrong beliefs and doctrines but—perhaps even more importantly—to reveal peoples' acquaintance with heretics and their sympathizers. It could be a daunting responsibility, as in the case of inquisitors Bernart de Caux and Jean de Saint-Pierre, who questioned more than fifty-four hundred men and women in Toulouse in 1245–1246.[24] Inquisitors were charged with the difficult task of uncovering *what a person knew, and about whom*—not only what they knew about Christian doctrine and orthodox praxis, but also what information they possessed about the beliefs and practices of their family members, friends, and neighbors. To put it another way, they sought potential joinings of hell and earth, and they hunted those joinings in people: in their errors, in their stubbornness and pride, and in their influence over others.

Inquisitors were deeply aware of the relationship between heresy and social or kin networks, and a major purpose of their interrogations was to unravel those bonds through well-informed probing. Canon 3 of the Fourth Lateran Council had already threatened anyone who received, defended, or supported heretics with excommunication; over time, these shades of guilt were codified into increasingly subtle categories. At the Council of Tarragon (1242), for example, eleven categories of transgression were set forth, ranging from heretics and believers to suspects, hiders, receivers, defenders, and relapsers (those who had already confessed, received penance, and fallen into their error again). The inquisitor's task was thus to assess and diagnose the spiritual status of those who filed through the makeshift interrogation rooms and to file away information about both their piety and personal connections.

Inquisitors' Questions

During the interrogation of suspected Waldensians in late-fourteenth-century Germany, for example, questions fell into three categories. First was the subject's origins and family, followed by his or her relationship to the heretical community, length of membership, and his or her frequency of interaction with known masters or believers. According to Gui, one should ask

> whether he has anywhere seen or met one or more heretics . . . whether he has received any such heretics into his house, and who they were; who brought them, how long they stayed; who came to see them; who took them away and where they went. Whether he heard them preach and what they said and taught.[25]

An elderly woman named Bernarta Verziana, when questioned by inquisitors in about 1245, recalled that when she was eight years old, she lived for a year with her aunt at a house for Good Women; a man named Arnaud Picoc testified that, years earlier, he heard two heretic cobblers say "that nothing about that which God had created will corrupt or pass away."[26] Such statements were carefully recorded and filed away for future use. Once the suspect was located within the network of familial and heretical ties, the inquisitors systematically inquired into the final category of belief and practice. In the case of the Poor, for example, follow-up questions might involve their understanding of purgatory, of the value of prayers for the dead, or of the efficacy of the clergy, or the inquisitor might ask them to give an oath, knowing the reluctance of many adherents to swear in any form.

Direct questioning was not the only strategy available to an inquisitor, because record keeping allowed for the tracking of others' confessions and testimony. After being summoned, people were often presented with evidence that others had supplied during interrogations. Such social pressure was very effective, particularly when the rewards for immediate confession were substantial compared with the steep penalties for recalcitrance and relapse. The stakes were dramatically heightened for tight-knit communities bound by local ties and the visits of a revered master, for every now and then someone high on the list of transgressors (such as a master) would convert and ask for reconciliation to the Church. In such scenarios, the price of absolution was to tell all she or he knew about other believers and supporters. These kinds of disclosures could create panic in a community. For example, the conversion of a former Good Man named Bernard dels Plas was said to have destroyed his hometown.[27]

Papal inquisitors particularly appreciated these kinds of leads, which could quickly unravel entire heretical networks. Some converts were actually so helpful that they were later employed on the inquisitorial staff themselves. The consequences for their former flocks were of course horrifying, because such close-knit solidarity meant immediate vulnerability when a member converted. In Germany one "frequently reads that thirty, forty, or fifty members . . . were brought before an inquisition, and there is unimpeachable evidence that hundreds of suspects were brought to trial on one occasion," a massive undertaking rooted in informers' testimony.[28] In Germany, inquisitors compiled a list of twenty Poor masters, of whom all but one had converted back to the Church by 1400; of these, five became priests and one even entered a monastery.

After the mid-thirteenth century, confessions could also be elicited through the application of torture. Because *inquisitio* was not a particularly effective means of determining inner thoughts and beliefs, in 1252 Pope Innocent IV permitted inquisitors to employ torture to elicit information or confessions. Like the inquisitorial process itself, torture was an ancient Roman legal practice revived in Europe in the thirteenth century, employed to determine guilt in cases of secret belief when no eyewitnesses were present. Practitioners were aware of its shortcomings, however, and protocols controlled its use: it was not to be unnecessarily brutal or to inflict permanent injury; a medical expert was required to be present, as was a notary to take down an official record; and the torture itself was to be traditional (such as stretching or searing the body) rather than any novel methods.

Confessions elicited under torture were not in themselves sufficient proof of guilt and had to be repeated by the suspect once removed from the place of torture. If a suspect recanted once the torture was lifted, however, it might be applied again later. That said, the role of torture in medieval inquisition should not be exaggerated. Despite its clear canonical legality, it is hardly mentioned in inquisitors' manuals and was not employed as a routine feature of interrogation. Readers might wonder whether inquisitors simply kept information about torture out of the records, but evidence suggests otherwise: torture was legal, much was at risk, and inquisitors so painstakingly recorded their approaches and techniques that conscious and collaborative silence regarding the application of physical force is most unlikely. Even when the balance shifted from persuasion to coercion, other methods (such as threats and imprisonment) seem to have proved more effective.

FORMS OF RESISTANCE

Although inquisitors held the upper hand in interrogations, deponents were not entirely helpless or without strategies for resisting such questioning. Over the centuries, the collected sources present evidence of the array of "weapons of the weak" employed by suspected heretics. Summoned Christians could, of course, choose to flee: several Poor interrogated in Mainz in 1390 fled to safety within sympathetic communities elsewhere on the Rhine. However, given the social solidarities of medieval communities and the difficulties of transience (particularly for women), flight was not always the option it might appear to be. Just as common was the decision to stay put and draw on the array of evasive measures employed consciously by canny suspects—and sometimes unconsciously by many deponents who simply did not understand the inquisitors' questions.

For example, the Aragonese inquisitor Nicholas Eymeric identified in his manual "ten ways in which heretics seek to hide their errors," including equivocation, adding conditions, redirecting the question, feigning astonishment, twisting the meaning of words, changing the subject, self-justification, feigning illness (including claims of "female trouble"), feigning stupidity or madness, and feigning holiness. Eymeric supplemented each of these with specific examples, apparently drawn from his own experience. Likewise, Gui offered a sample dialogue to illustrate how an accused Waldensian might dissemble, including not only linguistic tricks but also psychological manipulation of gesture and expression:

> When one of them has been seized and is brought up for examination, he comes as if without a qualm, as if conscious of no wrongdoing on his part, and as if he felt entirely safe. When asked if he knows why he has been arrested, he replies quite calmly and with a smile, "Sir, I should be glad to learn the reason from you." When he is questioned about the faith which he holds and believes, he replies, "I believe all that a good Christian should believe." Pressed as to what he means by "a good Christian," he answers, "One who believes as the Holy Church teaches us to believe and hold." When asked what he calls the Holy Church, he replies, "Sir, what you say and believe to be the Holy Church." If he is told, "I believe the Holy Church to be the Roman Church, over which presides our lord pope and other prelates subordinate to him," then he responds, "That I do believe," meaning that he believes that I believe this.[29]

One cannot help but sense Gui's exasperation.

In addition to the individual strategies of resistance outlined here (which also could include manipulation, lying, and playing inquisitors off one another), communities could act together in opposition to the inquisitorial process. As mentioned above, violence was sometimes directed at inquisitors and sometimes at defectors or informants. According to one of Zwicker's reports, heretics in one eastern town fixed a burned block of wood and a bloody knife to the town gates as a symbol of their intent to resist; in a nearby town a vicar and his family perished when accused heretics set fire to his home in retaliation for inquisitorial cooperation. Anti-inquisitorial riots sometimes broke out in Languedoc, particularly between 1295 and 1302, and in one case, a woman was silenced by cutting out her tongue. Yet violence was not an enduring or particularly frequent response either to inquisitors or their procedures—such eruptions tended to coalesce around particularly troubled times or contexts. Far more common was a passive but determined collective resistance rooted in the very local structures that inquisitors attempted to break: deep spiritual connections, durable kinship groups, and the defensive ties of village, town, and manor.

Penance

Once individual interrogations had been completed to the inquisitor's satisfaction and guilt was established, suspects were asked whether they wished to abjure their heresy. If so, they were given a penance, such as penitential crosses to wear, private devotions, or other forms of spiritual purgation. Inquisitors had a wide array of penitential options from which to choose, including badges of shame and other physical markers, pilgrimage, and various conditions of imprisonment.

The penance doled out by inquisitors served a double role: first, and most obviously, it was intended to purify penitent "heretics" and pave their way back into the orthodox community; second, and just as important for the inquisitors' purpose, penance served as a powerful method of social control. Such a flexible array of penitential punishments available to inquisitors allowed them to isolate, mark, humiliate, and segregate a social grouping—a powerful advantage in the tight-knit social worlds of medieval Europe, one that let them simultaneously purge transgressors of their sins, warn potential heretics of the dangers ahead, and demonstrate the spiritual authority of the institutional Church they represented.

Those found guilty but not imprisoned were frequently required to wear large yellow crosses on the front and back of their clothing as a sign of their lapsed spiritual status. Sometimes crosses were combined with another form of public shaming, in which the suspect's punishment became a form of public spectacle—for example, convicted heretics might be required to stand on scaffolds in front of the cathedral for a certain period of time or on special days or be subjected to public scourging by a priest. This kind of symbolic marking and isolation served to exclude the penitents from the local community, often exposing them to mockery and abuse, but it is important to note that the symbol of the cross also marked them specifically as members of—included in—the Church. The central error of heresy was to argue for a space outside or beyond the Church: the imposition of penance thus served simultaneously to bring penitents back *into* Christendom and to demonstrate the falsity of the heretics' position.

On a less visible level, confinement of various sorts was also a punishment frequently employed by inquisitors, who not only wielded it as penance but were allowed to use temporary imprisonment as a tool for pressuring suspects before and during interrogations. Once guilt was determined, lifelong imprisonment was a frequent penalty, though it could range from a kind of free-range condition within a prison's many rooms to a lockdown within a single cell. Of the sentences in Gui's register, nearly half were for various types of imprisonment (all of which nonetheless involved the forfeiture of property, and thus the disinheritance of one's children and successors). Houses associated with heresy were also frequently torn down as both a spectacle and a sign of the disgrace of heresy. Because prisoners were required to pay for their own upkeep, such a sentence was financially devastating to entire families.

Inquisitors took full advantage of the theatrical opportunities afforded them: for example, sentences were often not announced in private, but publicly at large gatherings attended by an impressive array of secular and ecclesiastical officials and local notables. Once the opening sermon was complete, the inquisitor would begin to hand out commutations or sentences to the accused among the gathered audience, building for dramatic effect from the least serious penance to the most draconian sentence. The inquisitors' public performance was not the only dramatic element of heretical penance, however, for the punishments themselves also served to enact the religious teaching and social marginalization crucial to the inquisitorial enterprise.

Penance did not always achieve its intended goal of conversion. The most extreme penalty available in antiheretical proceedings was death, reserved for relapsed or stubborn heretics. When someone found guilty of heresy refused to recant his or her errors or was found to have lapsed back into heresy, the person was deemed stubborn and recalcitrant and was "relaxed" to secular authorities for burning. The Church was not allowed to condemn anyone to death, and this pious fiction served to keep the inquisitors' hands theoretically free of blood. In reality, of course, they were perfectly aware of the fate to which they were handing men and women. Executions were carried out by officers of local secular rulers, and the only escape (one not always available) was a last-minute recantation. Evidence was also collected against people who had already died—if their heresy could be proved, their bones were exhumed from consecrated ground and burned so as to remove all trace of them.

Such executions were perhaps the greatest spectacle in the Church's arsenal, shocking and horrifying events even in a world accustomed to violence and public punishment. The building of the pyre, procession of the condemned, fixing of living human beings to the stake (often friends and family members together), taunting or weeping or praying by onlookers, and the scrutiny of the condemned's conduct for signs of weakness made for a powerful experience. Fire was the chosen means of execution because, as first legislated at the Council of Verona in 1184, it annihilated the body so that it could not be resurrected; canonical proscriptions against the clerical shedding of blood (reaffirmed at the Fourth Lateran Council in 1215) may also have been an influence.

In some cases only a single person or small group would be executed at once, whereas in other circumstances large numbers were burned together. The methods employed and the executioners' experience level also varied: sometimes people were affixed by the neck to a stake or bound by other parts of their body; often garbed in penitential clothing or other marks of humiliation, some had pitch applied to the body to make it burn faster while others did not. And while condemned heretics were generally given a final opportunity to recant before the fires were lit, other last-minute appeals were denied. Sometimes the smoke asphyxiated victims before the flames lapped at their clothing and limbs, but not always; contemporary accounts of the agonized screams of the victims who did not die until they were fully engulfed in flames make for difficult reading. The historian's job, however, is to understand *why* this spectacle was regularly and repeatedly staged across Europe in the later medieval centuries. As tempting as it may be to read the events as proof of medieval barbarism and irrationality, it is not that simple. The excruciating executions of condemned men and women were rooted in the period's confluence of precise Christian logic, deeply connected local bonds of society and spirit, and contests for authority: after all, Christ himself said that he came "not to bring peace, but a sword" (Matthew 10:34).

Executions were not as endemic as popular modern imagination might have it, however: of the 5,400 people interrogated in Toulouse between 1245 and 1246, only 206 were known to have been sentenced by inquisitors Bernart de Caux and Jean de Saint-Pierre. Of these, 184 received penitential yellow crosses, 23 were imprisoned for life, and none was sent to the stake.[30] Of the 633 imposed penalties for heresy described in Bernard Gui's inquisitorial register, the vast majority (about 90 percent) involved penitential yellow crosses, pilgrimages, imprisonments, or combinations thereof; only 41 (6.5 percent) of those Gui interrogated over the years were handed over to secular authorities for execution.[31] Authorities understood that burnings represented not victory but failure—the Church's inability to bring lost souls back to Christ. Moreover, the stoic and pious deaths of many a "wicked heretic" simply reinforced their status as martyrs to their own communities. Violence would thus never elicit the spiritual uniformity sought by medieval ecclesiastics.

SPIRITUAL AND SOCIAL CONSEQUENCES

Within a century and a half after the foundation of the papal inquisition (and parallel efforts of itinerant and episcopal authorities), the spiritual landscape of Christendom was forever altered. The Good Christians' mountain strongholds in southern France were eliminated by the mid-thirteenth century (Montségur fell in 1244, followed by the mass burning of more than two hundred people, and Quéribus fell to French knights a decade later), and focused inquisitorial efforts slowly but effectively disrupted the deep-rooted social bonds of kin and village. Between 1244 and 1300, local communities suffered tremendous blows (particularly in Languedoc at the end of the century) but were not wholly extirpated. Waves of prosecutions crested at the end of the century, culminating in the small village of Montaillou, presided over by the inquisitor (and future Pope Benedict XII) Jacques Fournier; the ideas of Good Christians had so intermingled with Catholic and local culture as to be virtually inextricable. The arrest of the entire village in 1308 demonstrates the extent to which Fournier was willing to go in order to eliminate heresy from his realm.

In Lombardy, regional political conditions shaped the eventual success or failure of papal inquisition. Franciscan inquisitors in Orvieto, for example, were local men who appear to have targeted people truly associated with heretical circles and imposed penalties sufficiently reasonable as to not provoke an outcry. In contrast, inquisitors in Bologna initiated mass trials and burnings and encountered significant hostility and resistance along the way. Sources suggest that the single most effective inquisitorial method in Lombardy for dismantling loyalty to "heretical" ideas was the imposition of financial penalties, thus stripping both wealth and security from families.

If the Good Christians of the south had been hounded out of existence in Europe by the mid-fourteenth century, the same could not be said of the Poor, for there were many communities in Europe that embraced one form or another of a now-familiar set of scripturally based reformist and anticlerical principles. Again, it would be a mistake to presume much uniformity across time and space at this point: by the fourteenth century, the sociospiritual lives of peasant villagers in Alpine communities differed significantly from those of artisans in the urban Rhineland or from merchants in Mediterranean ports. Nevertheless, many of these far-flung communities were in contact with one another through the travels and ministrations of their master, so it is not unreasonable to believe (as inquisitors did) that these were local manifestations of a broader sociospiritual tendency.

Communities of Poor or Waldensians were prosecuted widely in the thirteenth and fourteenth centuries, caught in the nets of papal inquisition in southern and northern France as well as farther north and east. Large populations in Germany, Austria, and Bohemia came under attack in the fourteenth century. Between about 1335 and 1355, the Dominican Gallus of Neuhaus tried what might have been thousands of people, including Poor members and lay religious women (discussed in chapter 5); of those trapped by interrogation techniques and careful record keeping, hundreds were certainly sent to secular authorities for burning. In the following excerpt from an interrogation of one Heinrich of Jareschau from 1349, we observe Gallus's methods for unraveling bonds of family and faith. Heinrich's brother, Gotzlin, had already been burned for heresy.

INQUISITOR: Have you now decided to tell the whole truth about the others who were in your sect?

HEINRICH: But I have already told you the whole truth.

INQUISITOR: Is your brother Henzlin the cutler a member of your sect?

HEINRICH: Henzlin is dead and I have not seen him for eight years.

INQUISITOR: Do you dare to swear to that?

HEINRICH: I do.

INQUISITOR: Then swear.

HEINRICH: I don't want to swear because you won't believe me anyway.

INQUISITOR: That's right, because you're a liar and a perjurer, and lie even under oath. In fact I know that your brother Henzlin was in the village of Jareschau three or four years ago and stayed with you for many days and that before then he stayed with you for half a year.

HEINRICH: My brother was not with me three years ago.

INQUISITOR: Then how long has it been since you've seen him?

HEINRICH: I haven't seen him for four years.

INQUISITOR: Was Henzlin a member of your sect?

HEINRICH: Yes.

INQUISITOR: And how did you know this?

HEINRICH: Whatever I say to you, you won't believe, so I won't say anything. [Then, after a pause] He was in our sect and entered it before me. . . .

The record is cut off, but we may presume that Heinrich went to the stake if he did not flee Bohemia immediately after the interrogation. For those interested in historical detective work, the story of Alexander Patchovsky's reconstruction of these texts from a couple of footnotes and manuscript scraps is an incredible account of scholarly sleuthing.[32]

Farther west, inquisitors Peter Zwicker and Henry Angermeier unraveled German communities through a wave of masters' conversions in the 1360s. Prosecutions continued periodically as the itinerant inquisitors wound their way across southern and western Germany, individual efforts rather than the outcome of any coordinated ecclesiastical program. In the early 1390s, a long-standing community in the thriving Rhineland city of Mainz found itself caught in a hinge between territorial politics, university authorities, and the ambitions of a local cleric eager to make a name for himself. In 1392–1393, a total of thirty-nine men (including clergy) and women were burned at the stake for Waldensian heresy in one of the largest single executions of its day.

POLITICS AND INQUISITION

Inquiring into heresy was not, however, limited to the purview of inquisitorial deputies or tribunals in the thirteenth and fourteenth centuries. As you will recall, there was nothing about the legal format of *inquisitio* in either its Roman or medieval form that limited it to religious cases or to use by ecclesiastical authorities. Secular leaders were quick to perceive its value, whether for spiritual purposes or politically self-seeking ends. For an example of the latter, we need look no further than the reign of French king Philip IV (r. 1285–1314). Philip and Pope Boniface VIII (r. 1294–1303) had been locked in a power struggle for years over the issue of clerical taxation, each attempting to secure his authority over the other. In 1303, Philip seized the upper hand by first persuading a council of French nobility and ecclesiastics to charge the pope with heresy and demonic magic and then sending soldiers to seize Boniface physically at his residence in northern Italy. The aged pontiff was so shaken by the experience that he died soon after, but the pseudo-inquisition continued; Philip pushed the new pope (Benedict XI) for a posthumous trial and continued to smear Boniface's name via an expanded list of trumped-up heresy charges. Ultimately no trial took place, however, because Philip and Benedict reached a mutually agreeable settlement on the issue of papal and royal authority, and the matter was dropped.

Philip manipulated the construct of "heresy" not only as a powerful political weapon but also for what historians have argued were explicitly financial purposes. Within a few years of the Boniface affair, Philip trained his sights on the military order of the Knights of the Temple of Solomon, better known as the Knights Templar. Founded as a crusading order in the Holy Land during the early twelfth century, the order had grown both in membership and wealth from many donations (particularly of land). Upon the fall in 1291 of Acre, the last Christian-controlled city in the Levant, foes of the popular order began to claim that its raison d'être had passed and that it should be disbanded. Philip saw an opportunity, once again, to use accusations of heresy to achieve his ends—in this case, the relocation of Templar wealth into the royal coffers. In 1307, he filed an array of charges against the Templars that included heresy, demonic magic, and sodomy and coordinated arrests across his lands; under brutal torture, many Templar knights confessed to the ludicrous charges.

Caught in a bind between royal pressure and "evidence" of heresy, Pope Clement V (r. 1304–1314) formally disbanded the order in 1312; the order's extensive possessions were then indeed placed under the control of the crown. Two years later, several Templar leaders (including its grand master, Jacques de Molay) were burned alive as relapsed heretics: not for new crimes, but for having recanted their earliest confessions. It was a purely political affair and serves as grim evidence of how powerful the late medieval construct of "heresy" had become. But the danger here lay not in the application of inquisitorial techniques, but rather in the absence of proper procedure. Indeed, the knights would have been safer in the hands of working inquisitors, men whose goal was almost always conversion rather than condemnation. In its disregard for due process, excessive use of torture, and politically charged context, the Knights Templar affair thus represents a precursor to the abuses for which later witch trials would become notorious. Nor would it be the last time accusations of heresy were wielded politically at the French court.

CONCLUSION

For centuries after the establishment of inquisitorial tribunals in the thirteenth century, inquisitors worked with a growing set of bureaucratic tools and texts to eradicate heresy from Christendom. Adopted widely as a legal technique in both secular and ecclesiastical courts, the process of *inquisitio* became increasingly more sophisticated and developed an ever more specific and detailed collection of methods, techniques, and materials. Moreover, the inquisitorial approach came to be associated particularly with suppressing dissent. As bureaucratic resources and textual tools grew in sophistication, so too did the rigidity of heretical stereotypes and constructs.

To its officials and proponents, papal and episcopal *inquisitio* was a necessary and vital function that employed appropriate procedures for identifying and correcting error, for saving souls, and, by extension, for saving Christendom. With the exceptions of Conrad of Marburg and Robert le Bougre, few of the inquisitors were fanatics. Most behaved properly according to the parameters of the role, in some cases even conservatively and carefully, and almost all functioned in accordance with the directives of both Church and secular leaders. Whether or not we may approve of those directives today is beside the point. In the intervening centuries, many, influenced by the Enlightenment and "progressive" rationality, have understandably decried the horrors of the inquisitorial process and lamented the thousands of people burned alive for their beliefs. Yet historians must approach the past on its own terms—our role is neither to excuse nor to excoriate, but rather to explain, to answer the question, "Why?" Gui answered that question:

> The end of the office of the inquisition is the destruction of heresy; this cannot be destroyed unless heretics are destroyed. . . . Heretics are destroyed in a double fashion: first, when they are converted from heresy to the true, Catholic faith . . . secondly, when they are surrendered to the secular jurisdiction to be corporeally burned.[33]

The development of inquisitorial administration and bureaucracy would pave the way not only for the expanded Spanish and Roman inquisitions of the fifteenth and sixteenth centuries, but also, as James Given has argued, for state structures in the early modern period as well. It is not an easy history to read about, and it is seductive to linger on the repugnance of their methods and the short-sightedness of their aims—not least perhaps because recent centuries have seen even greater brutality harnessed to European ideology and institutions. But inquisition is not a closed chapter: it is not irrelevant in the twenty-first century to understand how past societies have "made visible who walks in light and dark," nor to consider with what methods, costs, and consequences one has forced them to speak.

Bernard of Clairvaux might have been pleased if he could have seen the extent to which many of "the little foxes" or Good Christians had been destroyed by the late fourteenth century; Catharism had been destroyed, for example, its social networks damaged beyond repair. Yet Bernard would also have perceived ongoing problems in the Lord's vineyard as well. Lay and clerical Christians alike continued to heed the call to apostolic life, to respond to the appeal of vernacular scripture, to affirm and seek what they felt to be the vital intersections of heaven and earth. Pockets of Waldensians survived, and new spiritual threats mushroomed across Europe. By the end of the fifteenth century, innovative mystical writings challenged the institutional Church, theologians offered bold new interpretations of heaven and earth, laywomen formed spiritual communities, elite theorizing about supernatural forces provoked explosive new fears of diabolical agency in the world, and bold voices of reform (both English and Czech) erupted within the privileged ranks of priest and scholar, even igniting revolution.

Perhaps most striking is the extent to which these long-standing tensions over poverty, preaching, and access to and interpretation of scripture continued to rend the fabric of medieval Christendom in the fourteenth and fifteenth centuries—not only exacerbating rivalries between laity and clergy but even erupting within approved religious orders. As new threats emerged and the powers of both sacral and secular authorities intensified, so too did inquisitors stretch their strategies of detection and record-keeping techniques. In particular, antiheretical activity would soon unfold geographically beyond central Europe to the east and north, including the standing inquisitions of Bohemia, localized proceedings in Hungary and northeastern Germany, and the English adoption of much continental procedure under joint royal and ecclesiastical authority.[34] Such expansion was both accompanied and bolstered by an explosion of writing; antiheretical sources and related literature become quite overwhelming in the fourteenth and fifteenth centuries, defying simple generalizations of content and genre.

To maneuver our way through the vast web of sticky spiritual problems in the later Middle Ages, therefore, let us now descend from the bird's-eye view of inquisitorial activity and pick up with our exploration of a single vital thread in medieval piety, one central to so many debates over heresy and orthodoxy: apostolic poverty. Our next chapter explores how piety, reform, and arguments over scriptural authority ignited into heresy and inquisition not only among laymen and women but even among Franciscan friars themselves—the same order founded by St. Francis and approved by the vigilantly antiheretical Pope Innocent III.

SUGGESTIONS FOR FURTHER READING

Ames, Christine Caldwell. *Righteous Persecution: Inquisition, Dominicans, and Christianity in the Middle Ages*. Philadelphia: University of Pennsylvania Press, 2009.

Arnold, John. *Inquisition and Power: Catharism and the Confessing Subject in Medieval Languedoc*. Philadelphia: University of Pennsylvania Press, 2001.

———. "The Historian as Inquisitor: The Ethics of Interrogating Subaltern Voices." *Rethinking History* 2 (1998): 379–86.

Bailey, Michael D., and Sean L. Field, eds. *Late-Medieval Heresy: New Perspectives. Studies in Honor of Robert E. Lerner.* Woodbridge, UK: York Medieval Press, 2018.

Biller, Peter, and Caterina Bruschi. *Texts and the Repression of Medieval Heresy.* Woodbridge, UK: York Medieval Press, 2003.

Deane, Jennifer Kolpacoff, ed., and Steven Rowan, trans. *Herbert Grundmann (1902–1970): Essays on Heresy, Inquisition, and Literacy.* Woodbridge, UK: York Medieval Press, 2019.

Given, James. *Inquisition and Medieval Society: Power, Discipline, and Resistance in Languedoc*. Ithaca, NY: Cornell University Press, 1997.

Hill, Derek. *Inquisition in the Fourteenth Century: The Manuals of Bernard Gui and Nicholas Eymerich.* Woodbridge, UK: York Medieval Press, 2019.

Kelly, Henry Ansgar. *Inquisitions and Other Trial Procedures in the Medieval West.* Aldershot, UK: Ashgate Variorum, 2001.

Kieckhefer, Richard. *The Repression of Heresy in Medieval Germany*. Philadelphia: University of Pennsylvania Press, 1979.

Lawrence, C. H. *The Friars: The Impact of the Early Mendicant Movement on Western Society*. New York: Longman, 1994.

Le Roy Ladurie, Emmanuel. *Montaillou: The Promised Land of Error*. Translated and abridged by Barbara Bray. New York: Vintage, 1979.

Moore, Jill. *Inquisition and its Organisation in Italy, 1250–1350.* Woodbridge, UK: York Medieval Press, 2019.

Pegg, Mark Gregory. *The Corruption of Angels: The Great Inquisition of 1245–1246.* Princeton, NJ: Princeton University Press, 2001.

Peters, Edward. *Inquisition*. Berkeley: University of California Press, 1989.

Sackville, L. J. *Heresy and Heretics in the Thirteenth Century.* Woodbridge, UK: York Medieval Press, 2014.

Smelyansky, Eugen. *Heresy and Citizenship: Persecution of Heresy in Late Medieval German Cities.* New York: Routledge, 2020.

Sparks, Chris. *Heresy, Inquisition and Life Cycle in Medieval Languedoc.* Woodbridge, UK: York Medieval Press, 2014.

Summerlin, Danica. *The Canons of the Third Lateran Council of 1179*. Cambridge: Cambridge University Press, 2021.

NOTES

1. Walter L. Wakefield and Austin P. Evans, *Heresies of the High Middle Ages* (New York: Columbia University Press, 1991), 133.

2. Edward Peters, *Inquisition* (Berkeley: University of California Press, 1989), 3.

3. Edward Peters, ed., *Heresy and Authority in Medieval Europe* (Philadelphia: University of Pennsylvania Press, 1980), 178.

4. Patrick Geary, ed., *Readings in Medieval History*, 3rd ed. (Peterborough, ON: Broadview Press, 2003), 445.

5. Peters, *Heresy and Authority*, 177.

6. Peters, *Heresy and Authority*, 176.

7. Christine Caldwell Ames, *Righteous Persecution: Inquisition, Dominicans, and Christianity in the Middle Ages* (Philadelphia: University of Pennsylvania Press, 2009), see especially 5–10.

8. By referring to heresy as "founded on the Scriptures," Grosseteste explicitly excluded Muslims, Jews, and other non-Christians from the category of heretic.

9. Peters, *Heresy and Authority*, 194.

10. Peters, *Heresy and Authority*, 195.

11. Peters, *Heresy and Authority*, 115–16.

12. Henry Ansgar Kelly, "Inquisition and the Prosecution of Heresy: Misconceptions and Abuses," *Church History* 58, no. 4 (1989): 441.

13. James Given, *Inquisition and Medieval Society* (Ithaca, NY: Cornell University Press, 1997), 15.

14. Wakefield and Evans, *Heresies*, 208–10.

15. Étienne de Bourbon and A. Lecoy de La Marche, *Anecdotes historiques, légendes et apologues* (Paris: Librairie Renouard, H. Loones, 1877). Translation available at http://falcon.arts.cornell.edu/~prh3/262/texts/Guinefort.html.

16. Ames, *Righteous Persecution*, 213.

17. Derek Hill, *Inquisition in the Fourteenth Century: The Manuals of Bernard Gui and Nicholas Eymerich* (Woodbridge, UK: York Medieval Press, 2019).

18. Bernard Gui, *The Inquisitor's Guide: A Medieval Manual on Heretics*, ed. Janet Shirley (Welwyn Garden City, UK: Ravenhall Books, 2006), 158.

19. Gui, *Inquisitor's Guide*, 139.

20. Emmanuel Le Roy Ladurie, *Montaillou: The Promised Land of Error* (New York: Vintage Books, 1979), 247.

21. Reima Välimäki, *Heresy in Late Medieval Germany: The Inquisitor Petrus Zwicker and the Waldensians* (Woodbridge, UK: York Medieval Press, 2019).

22. Euan Cameron, *Waldenses: Rejections of Holy Church in Medieval Europe* (Malden, MA: Blackwell, 2000), 140.

23. Lucy Jane Sackville, "The *Ordo processus Narbonensis*: The Earliest Inquisitor's Handbook, Lost and Refound," *Aevum* 2 (2019).

24. Mark Gregory Pegg, *The Corruption of Angels: The Great Inquisition of 1245–1246* (Princeton, NJ: Princeton University Press, 2001).

25. Gui, *Inquisitor's Guide*, 43–44.

26. Pegg, *Corruption of Angels*, 88–89.

27. Given, *Inquisition*, 88.

28. Richard Kieckhefer, *Repression of Heresy in Medieval Germany* (Philadelphia: University of Pennsylvania Press, 1979), 57.

29. Wakefield and Evans, *Heresies*, 397–98.

30. Pegg, *Corruption of Angels*, 126.

31. Given, *Inquisition*, 66–71.

32. Robert E. Lerner, “A Case of Religious Counter-Culture: The German Waldensians,” *American Scholar* 55 (1986): 234–47.

33. Given, *Inquisition*, 71–72.

34. On the unfolding of inquisitorial activity to the Bohemian and Slavic east, a good starting point in English is still Henry Charles Lea, *History of the Inquisition of the Middle Ages*, vol. 2 (1888; reprint, New York: Cosimo Classics, 2005), though one must be alert to the marked anti-Catholic strain in his work.

Chapter Four

Spiritual Franciscans, the Poverty Controversy, and the Apocalypse

In the spring of 1317, the newly elected Pope John XXII sent a letter to the Franciscan brothers at the friaries of Narbonne and Béziers. It was a summons to appear at the papal court in Avignon within ten days in order to explain why they had violently taken over their houses and kicked out their superiors. When the sixty-one indignant friars appeared in Avignon, what they faced was more of an ultimatum than an actual hearing of their grievances. John insisted that they capitulate to papal authority, and with a little help from an inquisitor, most did. The four men who resisted were, after many hours of argument and exhortation, finally burned at the stake on May 7, 1318. Both the victims and the inquisitor were Franciscans—it was, as David Burr put it, "very much a family affair."[1]

How did an order founded by the saintly Francis and approved by Pope Innocent III end up in such a predicament? It is a complex story and an important one, not only as a thread in the fabric of medieval heresy and inquisition but also as a manifestation of the deepest religious challenges and currents of the day: the enduring attraction of the *vita apostolica*, the changing reach and effectiveness of papal authority, the possibilities and pitfalls of urban life and the new money economy, the ideal relationship between clergy and laity, and the proper role of scripture and the Gospel in Christendom. Although many decades would elapse before the tension between groups later known as the Spirituals and the Conventuals became overt, the seeds of division were arguably sown from the moment Francis of Assisi's ideals were institutionalized.

As discussed in chapter 3, the simple answer that Francis offered to the crucial question, "How is a Christian to live in the world?" was rooted in the apostolic tradition in scripture: a life of full humility and obedience, without excess, pride, or possessions. Ironically, however, the very appeal of the message and its embodiment in the ragged, austere, holy friars brought them into positions of authority and privilege within the institutional Church. The paradox of poverty was that the institutionalization and spread of Francis's ideals required that they be diluted, or even sacrificed, if the pope deemed it necessary for the greater vitality of Christendom. By the late thirteenth century, the struggle to square the material with the ideal would polarize the order into two general but loosely defined camps: proponents of radical poverty on the one side, and conservatives who defended a more moderate position on the other. Between the two poles lay friars and supporters along a complex spectrum of middling positions, which defies any attempt to split the order too simply into discrete and opposing camps.

INSTITUTIONALIZING IDEALS (1208–1226)

To understand how Franciscan friars committed to Christ's poverty ended up burned at the stake in 1318 for heresy, let us start at the beginning with Francis's apostolic vision and the early years of the movement he inspired. Paralleling the experience of Valdès in Lyon a generation earlier, this wealthy Italian cloth merchant's son was inspired at the turn of the thirteenth century by certain Gospel texts and an inner spiritual experience to convert himself from a life of easy sociability and luxury to one of severe yet joyful rigor, poverty, and service in the world. It was a magnetic model, and he drew many followers to him in a short period of time. Noting his total obedience to the Church, Innocent approved his life of apostolic poverty and itinerant preaching and welcomed his brothers, the Friars Minor, as an official new order of the Church. Fundamental to the new Franciscan identity was their founder's insistence on poverty, both individual *and* communal, a renunciation of the world in direct imitation of Christ and his apostles that set the friars apart from their individually impoverished but institutionally well-endowed Benedictine and Cistercian brothers.

During the first few years of the Franciscan Order's existence, leadership was relatively simple: Francis inspired his eager brothers (First Order) and sisters (Second Order) through the force of personal example, a spiritual model rooted in scripture. Indeed, the only other text shaping Franciscan practice in these early years was a compilation of key passages from the Gospels that, approved by Innocent in 1209, served as the basic rule for the order. Within a handful of years, however, the original band of thirteen impassioned new friars had reached into nearly every part of the Italian peninsula, and the brothers needed a more formal structure to organize their mission. At a chapter meeting at Assisi in 1217, the Italian peninsula was carved into six provinces, and preaching expeditions were planned to the future Franciscan provinces of Germany, France, Spain, and the Holy Land. To each province, the chapter assigned a head minister who was himself answerable to Francis, the unofficial but indisputable head of the order. It was an effective structure, and it fostered the order's explosive growth, reaching approximately thirty thousand men by the middle of the thirteenth century. In just over a decade,

Figure 4.1. *Innocent III Approving the Franciscan Rule*, **Giotto di Bondone.** *Source*: **Photo by George Tatge. Upper Church, S. Francesco, Assisi, Italy. Alinari/Art Resource, NY.**

therefore, the order's new numbers and diverse circumstances demanded a more complex administrative system and nuanced rule of life.

As anyone who has been part of a fledgling organization knows, periods of rapid expansion inevitably introduce logistical problems and difficult decisions. Within a few years, new responsibilities had already devolved onto men other than Francis: not only did the vast new scope and range of the order demand it, but also the simple fact that charismatic leaders are rarely skilled at (or interested in) the administrative and political skills necessary for successful institutionalization. But there are people with such a calling, and one of the most influential figures to shape early Franciscan history was Cardinal Hugolino, nephew of Innocent (and the future Pope Gregory IX, who would found the first inquisitorial tribunals in the 1230s). A warm supporter of Francis for some years already, Hugolino became the order's protector in 1219 and would play a significant role in the shaping of early Franciscan history.

THE CHALLENGE OF COMMUNAL POVERTY

A brief story will illustrate Hugolino's influence and provide a glimpse of the tensions to come within the order itself. In 1219, while Francis was away on a preaching mission with crusaders to convert the sultan of Egypt, an admiring supporter offered the Franciscan brothers in the city of Bologna the gift of a house. The friars gladly accepted, because the university city was a key location for the order's urban mission; when Francis returned to Italy, however, he was deeply disturbed by the gift and went to Bologna himself to personally drive the friars out of the house. From his point of view, to accept and own a house undermined everything the Friars Minor stood for and could not be tolerated. At this crucial moment, Hugolino stepped in to calm Francis and serenely announced that the house belonged to him rather than the order and that the friars had not compromised their ideals by owning property. However, he did welcome them to make *use* of the house. This legal distinction (some might call it a pious fiction) between ownership and use would become increasingly complex in its scope and implications. We will return to it shortly, for issues of ownership, authority, and use would lie at the heart of the order's most bitter quarrels for three hundred years.

Francis was always concerned about the potential for abuse and arrogance within hierarchy and clearly would have preferred a simple, egalitarian model in which brothers served others in a spirit of humility. Having stepped down from the responsibility of the day-to-day running of the order in the early 1220s, Francis nonetheless continued to impress his original convictions upon the community through the remaining five years of his life. In 1221, for example, he drafted a new Rule of the order in which he urged the brothers to observe their superiors' behavior carefully and to refuse obedience if orders contradicted Gospel, Rule, or their own spiritual conviction. Although friars who chose such a course were also directed to accept obediently whatever punishment or penalty ensued in order to maintain the order's unity, major consequences would unfold from Francis's insistence upon individual brothers' duty of refusal. The Rule of 1221 was never approved by the pope.

Two years later, however, Francis submitted a revised version that substantially reduced the earlier emphasis on righteous resistance to authority, although it too limited obedience to "those things which [the brothers] have promised the Lord to observe and which are not against their souls or our rule."[2] In addition, the Rule modified Francis's stance on apostolic poverty by allowing for the use of "spiritual friends" who could in certain cases pay for or donate materials to sick brothers. In 1223, Pope Honorius III approved this official Rule of the Friars Minor, known as the *Regula Bullata*. Of particular importance for the looming tensions over poverty was chapter 6, which addressed the crucial issue of friars and wealth. "The brothers should appropriate neither house, nor place, nor anything for themselves," it proclaimed,

> and they should go confidently after alms, serving God in poverty and humility, as pilgrims and strangers in this world. Nor should they feel ashamed, for God made himself poor in this world for us. This is that peak of the highest poverty which has made you, my dearest brothers, heirs and kings of the kingdom of heaven, poor in things but rich in virtues. Let this be your portion. It leads into the land of the living and, adhering totally to it, for the sake of our Lord Jesus Christ wish never to have anything else in this world, beloved brothers.[3]

Francis's position was clear: the brothers' voluntary poverty and their explicit rejection of the comfort and safety of provisions were to serve as a joyful demonstration of faith in God's promises. From this point of view, even mild encroachments such as communal ownership of books or the storage of grain and wine represented a direct assault on Christ's message in the Gospels and a rejection of the specific model of pure poverty therein.

For the women inspired by Francis's example, however, the matter was not so simple. The life of Chiara Offreduccio of Assisi (1194–1253), one of his earliest and most devoted followers, encapsulates both the opportunities and obstacles for female adherents. Having fled her well-to-do parents and the marriage they planned for her, Chiara (known in English as Clare) found refuge with her inspiration, Francis. After living for a short period of time in a house of penitents in Rome, she returned to the north and founded a rigorously ascetic women's community at the church of San Damiano in Assisi. Under her able leadership, Clare's Poor Ladies were soon formally recognized as nuns by the Church and institutionalized as the Order of San Damiano. After her death in 1253, they came to be known as the Order of St. Clare or the Poor Clares.

Throughout her lifetime, however, Clare struggled to win approval for the life she and her women desired: one of utter poverty, both personal *and* institutional. Even as Francis urged his brothers to embrace all the humility and dependence upon God implied by "poverty," he was loath to preach the same to his female followers. In order to ensure the virginity and physical seclusion of religious women, and in explicit contrast to the mendicant friars' active urban professionalism, nuns lived enclosed behind protective walls. Clare and her nuns accepted the rules of enclosure but fought bitterly for the right to own nothing as an order. In keeping with the Gospel message reinforced by Francis's own preaching, they argued and pleaded for corporate poverty so that their rugged determination might not be softened and cushioned by the institution's financial reserves.

Their requests were never granted. Voluntary poverty was a distinctly masculine privilege in this period, and the line between poor women and desperate or depraved women was deemed too fine to risk. Indeed, to many medieval contemporaries, all women were in effect potential prostitutes, and the stakes for supervision were thus extremely high. A rigorously ascetic lifestyle safely enclosed behind convent walls was an acceptable lifestyle for a thirteenth-century pious woman, but what if the order ran out of funds? Would the women have to beg to support themselves? Would they enter the public eye, exposing and shaming themselves and their brethren? What might they be forced to do—or be willing to do—if they were allowed to live always on the edge of hunger and destitution? Clare finally had to accept the order's restriction of feminine poverty. But one person's protective measure is another's prison, and Clare's capitulation was evidently reluctant.

The Third Order

Francis's message struck a chord not only with men and women committed to the lifelong choice of celibacy and ascetic rigor but also with laypeople who sought to link their daily lives to the inspiring model of the Franciscans. Such lay communities, "Third Orders" or "tertiaries" (in contrast to the First Order of friars and Second Order of nuns), had long been associated with monasticism, though primarily in terms of physical labor and domestic service to monasteries. Within early Franciscan circles, the motivation of tertiaries was more frequently penance and the expression of inner conversion to a newly revitalized spiritual life. Francis himself early on recognized and appreciated the devotion of his lay followers or "the brothers and sisters of penitence." As he addressed them in his *Letter to the Faithful*, Francis wrote, "We must never desire to be above others, but, instead, we must be servants and subject to every human creature for God's sake."[4] These urgings were formalized into an official Rule first in the 1220s; sixty years later, Italian penitents succeeded in eliciting a more definitive Rule to govern the Third Order. However, the history of these lay associations is anything but uniform or formal.

In 1289, the first Franciscan pope, Nicholas IV, issued the bull *Supra montem* (*Upon the Mountain*), a Rule combining existing and new tenets, including the requirements of humble dress, moderate fasting, observance of canonical hours, reception of the sacraments, and guidelines for prayer. Perhaps the most striking difference between the early and later Rule, however, is that the latter opens with a warning about heresy:

> Solicitous precautions must be taken, however, lest any heretic or one suspected of heresy, or even of ill-repute be in any way admitted to the observance of this life. And if it happen that such a one was found to have been admitted, he should be turned over to the inquisitors as quickly as possible, to be punished for heretical depravity.[5]

Indeed, inquisitors of the early fourteenth century would be greatly occupied by the task of discerning the overlap among Franciscans, Third Order members, and heresy. As those relationships were profoundly shaped by developments between 1226 and 1318, let us now return to Francis and the challenge of institutionalizing saintly ideals in the material world.

FRANCIS'S *TESTAMENT* AND ITS TEMPERING (1226–1230)

Shortly before his death in 1226, Francis took the final step of dictating a testament for his brothers and sisters in the faith. In this document, Francis not only recorded his memories of the earliest days of the order but also admonished the friars once more to live always as strangers and exiles in poverty and humility, to move on passively without protest if the clergy in some towns drove them out, and to avoid asking Rome for protection and privileges. Particularly important from an administrative point of view, however, was his request that the testament be always kept with and read with the Rule and insistence that no glosses or interpretations were to be made on either of them. These were serious limitations. Francis's *Testament* created a major problem for the order because a number of his instructions conflicted with what was already beginning to happen—not so much because of abuse or moral laxity in the order, but because of the very commitment its members had to implementing the Franciscan vision and mission. Many clergy did try to keep them out of cities and towns, so how could Franciscans carry out their preaching and teaching mission without papal protection? In a world of increasingly bewildering complexity, how could they extend the Rule to an army of new recruits unless expert theologians were allowed to interpret it and apply it to the new and various situations?

An anecdote regarding Francis's death neatly illustrates the difficulties here: he was adamant in his wish to die in the purest state of poverty, stripped of any property or possessions—yet modesty required that his body be covered. The solution came through the sensitive intervention of a colleague, who firmly insisted that he had only loaned Francis the patched and shabby garments on his dying body. Although free to *use* the ragged garment, in other words, Francis did not *own* it or have "dominion" that would allow him to pass it to another. Therein lay the heart of apostolic poverty, and Francis was said to have died joyfully once he was released from the burden of property. Whether or not the story is factually true, it encapsulates the reality of the Franciscan dilemma at the pivotal moment of its founder's death: How was one to translate the order's original and austere vision into a stable and enduring institution rooted in its precepts of poverty and humility?

Quo elongati (1230)

Four years after Francis's death, leaders of the order were already feeling the tug between the language of their founder's *Testament* and the daily exigencies of a rapidly expanding order. Deeply concerned and seeking guidance, they petitioned their old supporter Hugolino (now Pope Gregory IX [r. 1227–1241]) to determine whether the *Testament* was fully binding upon them and the order's organization. In the pivotal bull *Quo elongati* (*Further Away from the World*), the pope responded with a clear and unequivocal "no": the friars were not literally bound to the *Testament* and, despite Francis's insistence to the contrary, were indeed allowed to reinterpret the text. Equally important was Gregory IX's official new interpretation of Franciscan poverty: although the friars were themselves to live without property, they could *use* houses, books, and other material items owned by the papacy or a cardinal-protector. Such a statement might seem to resonate easily with Francis's own position vis-à-vis the borrowed habit, but a deep fault line ran through the concept of "use." The simple borrowed habit was ragged, patched, and unworldly, and Francis would certainly not have accepted a new, clean, or costly garment. But under *Quo elongati*, such distinctions were not made clear. What constituted appropriate "use" of goods and materials? How much austerity was sufficient to remain true to the apostolic model, and upon what guidelines could a friar rely? And who had the authority to decide such matters?

Gregory IX's issuing of *Quo elongati* was a crucial step because the order was evolving in ways that Francis could not have foreseen in 1208 (though the language of his *Testament* suggests that the potential for problems had become clear to him). How had the order changed, and in response to what circumstances? In the urban centers they entered across Europe, Franciscans found large populations swollen past the capacity of local clergy to serve them, Christians in need of not only preaching but pastoral care. Thus, as the friars' sterling reputation attracted increasingly educated (and perhaps increasingly ambitious) laymen and priests to join in the 1220s, they were drawn into elite positions far from the humble world of Francis and his original lay followers. Maintaining strict adherence to Francis's precepts as well as the order's Rule was not simple in these new conditions, even for the most spiritually committed of friars:

> A Franciscan confessor whose duties brought him to the homes of wealthy merchants might find himself dining well, since the rule instructed him to eat what was placed before him. A friar teaching at Paris might discover that his mission demanded a large, expensive library. Once Franciscans inserted themselves into the world, they found worldly comforts difficult to escape.[6]

Moreover, the papacy was happy to extend its protection and patronage to an order that could be utilized for the faith in so many ways: as preachers and teachers, bishops and cardinals, pastors and inquisitors. By the end of the thirteenth century, even the pope himself was a Franciscan.

But how did such transformations square with Francis's original insistence that friars were to be "pilgrims and exiles," serving the lord in humility and poverty? Friars agonized over whether it was "honorable to continue to claim the highest poverty and a peculiar fidelity to the life of Christ and the apostles, when in practice they used money, which Francis had forbidden, and enjoyed the fruits of property, which Francis had excluded?"[7] Far from establishing a permanent solution to the poverty issue, the moderate stance of *Quo elongati* added fuel to what would become an increasingly heated controversy.

By the middle of the thirteenth century, therefore, tension mounted between Francis's original vision of itinerant "high poverty" and the growing demand for a viable and self-sustaining institution to serve Christian spiritual needs. In the 1240s and 1250s, the official stance of the order and the papacy vacillated, shaped as much by the distinct personalities and preferences of individual leaders as by the principles set forth in the various authoritative texts (scripture, bulls, Rules, and other documents). Under Pope Innocent IV (r. 1243–1254), for example, the parameters of Franciscan poverty were simultaneously clarified and relaxed: the papacy was identified as the legal owner of all property given to the order, and procedures were established through which agents or intermediaries could handle transactions on behalf of the Franciscans.

FRANCISCAN LEADERSHIP (1244–1274)

Leadership within the order also fluctuated through mid-century, as illustrated by the careers of three of its ministers general, or supervisors: Crescentius of Iesi (1244–1247), John of Parma (1247–1257), and Bonaventure (1257–1274). Crescentius of Iesi, for example, displayed a relatively flexible adherence to primitive Franciscan rigor that infuriated a portion of the friars. A delegation of those angry brothers reported to the papacy that Crescentius and his supporters were engaged in soliciting fancy buildings, welcoming financial donations and privileges, and abandoning prayer in favor of what critics called the sterile knowledge of Aristotle. In other words, some friars insisted that Francis's austere and simple vision was being tainted by intellectualism and worldly concerns.

Already during the 1240s, dissent and opposition were brewing among the scattered Franciscan convents. According to later sources, Crescentius himself may have encountered a radical wing early in his career while he was still the provincial minister of the March of Ancona (in what is central Italy today). A Franciscan writing in the early fourteenth century reported that in the region "a sect of brothers who, . . . despising the institutions of the order and thinking themselves better than the others, wanted to live as they wished and attributed all to the spirit, wearing cloaks so short that they came up to their buttocks."[8] The vivid evocation of radical spiritualism symbolized in the short garments of local Franciscans indicates that the March of Ancona was home to one of the first pockets of vehement supporters of radical poverty. It would soon be joined by others, particularly in the Franciscan houses of Narbonne, Béziers, and Carcassonne, and in scattered communities to the north, to the east, and in the Italian peninsula.

Although we have no eyewitness accounts, multiple pieces of evidence suggest that by the 1250s the Franciscan Order was already polarizing into a conventional majority and a radical minority that, committed to Francis's vision and emboldened by his call to righteous disobedience, was unafraid to challenge hierarchical power. In response to Crescentius's laxity, the order effected an about-face in the election of 1247 by selecting a rigorous new minister general, John of Parma, who dedicated himself to restoring the friars to ascetic poverty and adherence to Francis's Rule. John set a vigorous example of the *vita apostolica*, traversing extensive territories on foot in a shabby garment, explicitly rejecting the ease and comfort afforded by his elite new position. Perhaps inevitably, given the increasingly riven condition of the Franciscan Order and his literal reliance upon Francis's *Testament* and Rule, John garnered as many enemies as supporters during his years in office. Ten years later, he delivered a stinging indictment of the order's laxity at the general chapter meeting in 1257. According to later sources, John charged the majority of brothers with neglecting their spiritual duties, seeking and hoarding wealth, donning multiple and expensive garments, and falsely depicting their ascetic colleagues as disobedient schismatics. Resigning his office in that year, John appears to have given up as hopeless the task of bringing the order back to scrupulous regularity.

For several years prior to his resignation, John had mentored a young Franciscan named Bonaventure, whom he placed at the University of Paris and nominated in 1257 as his replacement. Once Bonaventure became the master general of the order, however, relations between the two soured. Pressured by the brothers, the new Franciscan leader held a hearing to deliberate on John of Parma's case. Bonaventure sentenced his former mentor to imprisonment for life, though the punishment was later reduced and John withdrew to live out the rest of his life at a hermitage.

Among the major developments of Bonaventure's leadership were the Constitutions of Narbonne (1260), which tried to set standards for clothing, consumption, and comfort based on a reasonable interpretation of the Rule that also allowed Franciscans to complete the pastoral work set forth for them. Although considerably more moderate than John, Bonaventure also lambasted the order for handling money, its lavish lifestyle, and excessive interaction with the powerful and wealthy. For him, as for John, the problem was moral and behavioral slackness and a failure to conform to Francis's express intentions for the order. Particularly troubling for Bonaventure was the way in which Franciscans were now perceived: no longer admired but reviled and mocked for greed. His aim, therefore, was to rectify what he perceived as the failings of the order on the conservative rather than the radical end of the spectrum.

THE *USUS PAUPER* CONTROVERSY

By the early 1270s, St. Francis had been dead for nearly a half century, and despite the efforts of the various ministers general, the order entered a period in which tensions erupted into open conflict between those committed to strict adherence to the original poverty envisioned by Francis and those wanting to institutionalize his ideals in a firm, long-lasting material basis that required some minor accommodations. Although actual observance varied and brethren in some regions were evidently more vigilant than in others, the essential controversy was never about the value of poverty itself or even whether a Franciscan should be limited to a "poor" or "restricted" usage of loaned materials. All agreed that Franciscans must not own property (either individually or communally) and that friars should restrict themselves to a limited and thus "poor" use of loaned materials. The poverty controversy as generally expressed during the 1270s and 1280s focused not on whether poverty and "poor use" (*usus pauper*) were essential to Franciscan life, but rather on their place in the Franciscan *vow* of poverty, celibacy, and obedience. Here is the problem: because breaking this kind of vow constituted a mortal sin, it was important for the requirements of the vow to be clear. But how was one to define "restricted use"? How much is just enough? If there could be no hard-and-fast definition of "restricted use"—even of simple goods such as garments and food—how could the friars know when they had reached the limit of proper use and were thus endangering their souls? And was it not possible that the requirement of one friar's material situation might differ from another's? These were not easy questions to answer.

The side that came to be known as the Conventuals (the majority of the community) never suggested that a Franciscan was free to possess and own and use whatever he wanted. On the contrary, they fully agreed that poverty and simplicity were essential to Franciscan life; however, they did not want a potentially nebulous promise to be part of the vow. But others did, men who came to be known as Spirituals or Spiritual Franciscans. The fiercest protests came from Spiritual Franciscans in regions with which we are already familiar from the previous chapter—the religious hotbeds of northern Italy and southern France—men who were inspired not only by Francis's *Testament* but also by the writings of several contemporaries. They were criticized, hounded, and in some cases even imprisoned by their opponents, at whom they in turn slung barbed insults. In a kind of mirror to Gregory IX's attempt in 1230, Nicholas issued *Exiit qui seminat* (*A Sower Went Out*) in 1279 in an attempt to settle the debate. Simultaneously, of course, Nicholas was busy writing *Supra montem*, the new Rule for the Third Order, and cautioning the Franciscans to ensure that no heresy lay in the hearts of newly admitted tertiaries.

Thus the seeds of division had been sown long before four Franciscans died at the stake in Avignon in 1318. Far from being an obscure internal dispute, by 1300 the hostilities between Spiritual and Conventual Franciscans would have drawn in not only popes and cardinals but even emperors and lay supporters far beyond the Franciscan convents. Yet Spirituals, the laymen and laywomen they inspired, and inquisitors did not square off in the 1300s on poverty issues alone: instead, the simmering controversy would be ignited in the final decades of the thirteenth century by apocalypticism and the potent fusion of history, prophecy, and Franciscan ideals. Thus, although the particular fault line of the internal Franciscan argument was the issue of how to define and embody impoverishment in the world, the explosive epicenter of the Spiritual controversy was rooted—as it was for other emerging "heresies" elsewhere—in the impasse between competing notions of authority and obedience.

SPIRITUAL FRANCISCANS AND THE APOCALYPSE

Early Franciscan history was shaped by key texts, including the Gospel, the inspirational authority of Francis's letters and *Testament*, and the shifting voice of the papal see. At mid-century, the growing divisions within the order over issues of poverty and authority became entangled with yet another set of texts whose authority would become an explosive point of contention. By 1300, the spiritual deadlock between radical Franciscans and the clerical hierarchy was boldly reframed in epic dimensions by a single friar from Narbonne named Peter of John Olivi, whose apocalyptic and prophetic understanding of the Franciscan Order inspired passionate devotion among scattered communities of lay followers in southern France and Italy. Olivi in turn was deeply influenced by the bold historical and prophetic ideas of an abbot and mystic named Joachim of Fiore.

Because the fusion of Franciscan radicalism with apocalyptic thought was central to the later suppression of Spirituals and their supporters, let us briefly trace both men's influence and the reasons why their message was so appealing to certain Christians of the late thirteenth and early fourteenth centuries. Thus twelfth- and thirteenth-century Franciscan interpretations of the biblical past and anticipated future lit a new fuse on the powder keg of fourteenth-century spiritual controversy.

Joachim of Fiore's Stages of History (1135–1202)

In the middle of the twelfth century, a talented young man from Calabria, in southern Italy, began an administrative career at the royal publications office in Palermo. Unlike other members of the burgeoning bureaucratic community of his day, however, Joachim of Fiore underwent a profound conversion around 1167 that changed the course of his life and gave rise to a bold and innovative set of ideas about the divisions of Christian history and their meaning for the future.

After some years spent in contemplation as an ascetic hermit, Joachim entered the priesthood and joined a Benedictine monastery in southern Italy. By 1176, he had not only become the community's abbot but was already deeply steeped in biblical study and the search for patterns within scripture that would unlock the mystery of Christian past, present, and future. Like many mystics of the central and later Middle Ages (including some we will discuss in the next chapter), Joachim experienced flashes of insight and inspiration, often in the wake of mental uncertainty or spiritual anguish.

After one such revelation, for example, he reported suddenly comprehending in an instant the full meaning of the book of Revelation as well as seeing a hitherto unrecognized relationship between the Old and New Testaments. After obtaining permission from Pope Lucius III to write down what he had learned through revelation, Joachim set to work on a series of important books; these included explanations of the scriptural relationship between the testaments, the meaning of the Apocalypse, and (perhaps most influential) an ingenious map of Christian history that unfolded in richly meaningful patterns of twos and threes. The Calabrian mystic's framework for Christian history was, as we will see, profoundly relevant to the spiritual circumstances of the twelfth and thirteenth centuries. "Although it is given to few mortals to invent a single new important idea," notes Robert Lerner, "Joachim of Fiore invented three big ones."[9] A brief discussion of each will help to clarify why Joachite ideas became such a potent channel for Olivi, Spiritual Franciscans, and their followers over a century and a half later.

Joachim's first "big idea" was that the Old Testament was essentially a massive cryptogram of hidden meanings and patterns that could be deciphered only by the closest scrutiny; once discovered, however, those meanings served as signs and predictions of the entire course of Church history. That is, the Old Testament prefigured the New Testament in a series of perfect (if obscure) symmetries that could be interpreted to chart the chronology of salvation. Joachim mapped the history of the faith visually with the image of two parallel and temporally symmetrical trees: the tree on the left, associated with the Old Testament, represented linear time from Adam to Christ; on the right, the New Testament tree ascends from the period of a certain king of Judah to the second coming of Christ. The image is dazzlingly complex, every branch and leaf and detail a vivid metaphor of apostolic, ecclesiastical, or historical relationship, all of which are set in a precise chronological and generational framework of matching generations. Such calculations, rooted in his superb scriptural knowledge, prompted Joachim to predict that the Antichrist would arrive in 1260 and that (in keeping with traditional and entirely uncontroversial scriptural interpretation) his appearance would be followed by an uncertain period of time before the final End of Days.

At the heart of Joachim's second major idea was the mysterious book of Revelation and the force of the text's "full meaning" as vouchsafed to him in a vision. Let us consider the following cryptic yet important verses from Revelation 20:1–7:

1. And I saw an angel come down from heaven, having the key of the bottomless pit and a great chain in his hand.
2. And he laid hold on the dragon, that old serpent, which is the Devil, and Satan, and bound him a thousand years,
3. And cast him into the bottomless pit, and shut him up, and set a seal upon him, that he should deceive the nations no more, *till the thousand years should be fulfilled:* and after that he must be loosed a little season.
4. And I saw thrones, and they sat upon them, and judgment was given unto them: and I saw the souls of them that were beheaded for the witness of Jesus, and for the word of God, and which had not worshipped the beast, neither his image, neither had received his mark upon their foreheads, or in their hands; *and they lived and reigned with Christ a thousand years.*
5. *But the rest of the dead lived not again until the thousand years were finished.* This is the first resurrection.
6. Blessed and holy is he that hath part in the first resurrection: on such the second death hath no power, but they shall be priests of God and of Christ, and shall reign with him a thousand years.
7. *And when the thousand years are expired, Satan shall be loosed out of his prison.* [emphases added]

In contrast to centuries of previous biblical scholars who had assumed that Revelation recounted a series of separate visions chronologically disconnected, Joachim read the book as a single narrative unfolding in time. As a consequence, he contradicted the authoritative interpretation of St. Augustine that the saintly millennium referred to the reign of the current Church, insisting instead that (because it came at the end of the book and just prior to the Last Judgment) it was still in the Christian future. The thousand years of peace, therefore, was yet to come. Although it may not seem like a particularly earth-shattering claim, Joachim's interpretation represented a stunning paradigm shift in a world increasingly concerned with God's plans, Christendom's future, and the revelatory potential of scripture.

Joachim's third and perhaps most influential idea was also imparted to him in a vision, but it also grew out of contemporary interest in projecting Christian history into the future. Still seeking concordances and patterns, Joachim developed the claim that Christian history unfolded not only in the duality of Old and New Testament patterns but also in threes—the ages of the Father, the Son, and the Holy Spirit. Likewise locked into terrestrial time, these three "statuses" overlap at historical moments associated with key Christian figures such as John the Baptist or, later, St. Benedict. Joachim's historical model, therefore, began with the initial sphere of the time of the Father, followed by that of Christ, and would come to linear completion near

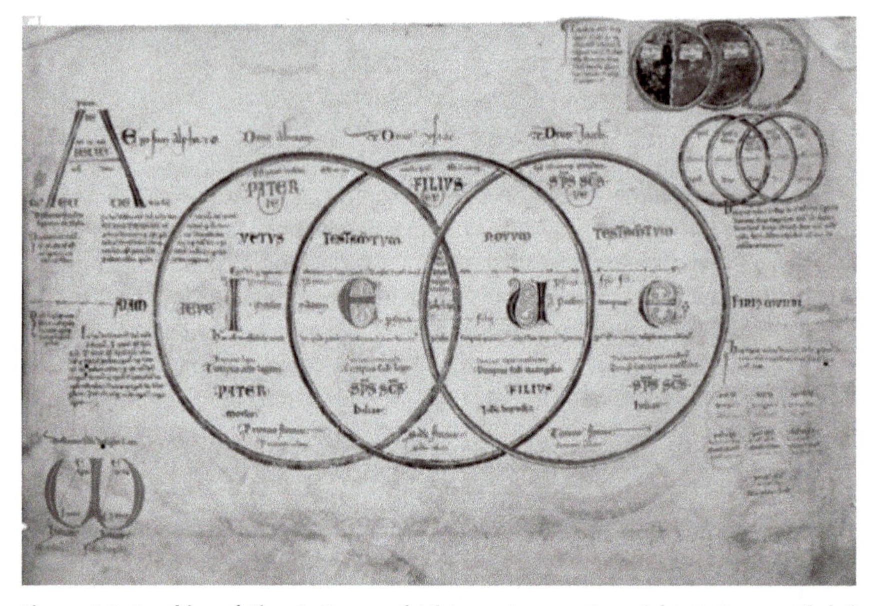

Figure 4.2. Joachim of Fiore's Stages of History. *Source*: **Copyright © Corpus Christi College Oxford.**

the end of the earthly time with the age of the Holy Spirit. Characterized by simultaneous simplicity and endless complexity, the Joachite pattern of unfolding stages represented one of the earliest global expressions of temporal and material progress. The future would bring battles, to be sure, with dragons, hellfire, and the Antichrist himself, yet the triumphant outcome at the End of Days was now a given and inscribed into human chronology.

But why were Joachim's theories so thrilling for certain circles of radical Franciscans and their followers in the late thirteenth and early fourteenth centuries? The answer lay in the precise conclusions drawn by the Calabrian mystic about his own historical time: the late twelfth century, he claimed, was "trembling on the brink of the third age," shifting from the age of Christ to that of the Holy Spirit; moreover, he predicted the emergence of a new monastic order that would represent the spiritual purity and progress of this third phase. Little wonder that many Franciscans (whose order was founded only a few years after Joachim's theories began to circulate) saw themselves and their mission reflected in his words, embracing the notion that their order was to be the midwife of a new Age of the Spirit. Joachite structures unfolded harmoniously into the realm of specifically Franciscan history, and Francis himself was associated by many with the angel of the sixth seal (Revelation 7:2). Bonaventure himself not only incorporated the claim into his own writings in 1263 but drew on a rich tradition of Joachite thought (a phenomenon studied by modern theologians, including Joseph Ratzinger, elected Pope Benedict XVI in 2005).

Yet there can be no doubt that Joachite ideas appealed most strongly to the radical wing of the Franciscan poverty movement and its various circles of lay followers throughout southern Europe. Particularly compelling was Joachim's claim that ecclesiastical hierarchies would be unnecessary in the final, perfected age of the Holy Spirit and that the current age shuddered on the brink of tremendous, wondrous change. Spiritual Franciscans and their supporters thus regarded Joachim as a prophet; most significant among these was the thirteenth-century Franciscan theologian, teacher, and thinker Peter Olivi—and whether he was a holy saint or heretical sinner depended entirely upon whom one asked.

Peter Olivi's Apocalypticism (1247–1298)

A native of Béziers who entered the Franciscan Order around 1259, Olivi studied at the University of Paris with some of the order's greatest scholars, including Bonaventure. After finishing his studies, he taught at a variety of friaries, including Narbonne, Florence, and Montpellier, attracting devoted students and writing on a wide variety of theological topics. As a leading Franciscan theologian, Olivi could not help but be directly involved in the explosive controversies of his day. Although his perspective was fairly moderate—he even criticized what he perceived as the excesses of the Spirituals—his stance on the *usus pauper* and his theological writings attracted criticism. In 1283 and again in 1285, he was accused by his more conservative colleagues of spreading heretical views, largely due to ideas inspired by the writings of Joachim of Fiore. Not surprisingly, it was Olivi's work on the *usus pauper* and apocalyptic scripture that brought him to the forefront of the poverty debate. Scholars still disagree over the doctrinal orthodoxy of writings such as his *Commentary on the Apocalypse* (1297), which garnered fierce criticism in its day for the application and extension of Joachite theories. A panel appointed to investigate his work three decades after his death concluded that many of his assertions were heretical, although scholars since have determined that Olivi, like so many other accused "heretics," was located more squarely in contemporary spiritual currents than his opponents had been willing to acknowledge.

Most troubling to his critics were claims about the historical significance of his own day: that, precariously perched at the tipping point of one age to another, the late thirteenth century would soon witness the total corruption and disorder of the institutional Church. Poverty and poor use were, for Olivi, at the heart of the issue, for the Church's greatest apocalyptic failing was its rejection of pure poverty as modeled by Christ and the apostles. The life of

Francis, unequivocally the angel of the sixth seal in Olivi's eyes, represented a key historical hinge on which the Christian future would turn. For supporters of the Spirituals, therefore, even the attacks and assaults on Franciscan poverty themselves took on an apocalyptic hue as painful but necessary precursors to the imminent new age.[10]

Yet Franciscan struggles in these tumultuous years were shaped as much by personalities as principles, and the appointment of a sympathetic minister general in 1287 ended the resistance to Olivi in his lifetime. Although the Franciscan Nicholas demanded in 1290 that brothers who created controversy in Provence be investigated, Olivi was left largely in peace to write and preach. In Florence he trained his most famous disciple, Ubertino of Casale, and after a few years returned to southern France, where he continued to read, teach, and write about poverty and the coming third age. The final years of his life were spent back in Narbonne, where he died in relative peace in 1298, unaware that for some his body would soon become a relic and his grave a pilgrimage shrine. He was acclaimed immediately by Spirituals and their lay supporters as a saint, and his tomb in Narbonne became a popular, though unofficial, pilgrimage destination.

To the Conventuals, however, he was a heretic. In 1299, the general chapter ordered all of his books gathered up and burned, and his supporters were rounded up as well. In the same year, the Council of Béziers made clear that it was becoming suspicious not only of Olivi but of his followers, called beguins (the accepted anglicized pronunciation is "buh-GEENS").[11] Meanwhile in Tuscany, his student Ubertino of Casale was preaching the Spiritualist message and calling attention to the increasing persecution of those who chose short cloaks and an austere lifestyle. Spiritualist appeals to the pope were blocked, and it was only through the intervention of sympathetic supporters that their call for help was heard. Arnold of Villanova, for example, a Catalan physician to kings and popes, pleaded with Pope Clement V to end the persecution of the Spirituals, "the sons of truth," and to mend the division in the order. Some years later, a young girl from Montpellier named Prous Boneta apparently visited Olivi's tomb and, while in prayer, received three spiritual gifts from God. In an inquisitorial deposition near the end of her life, she recalled experiencing a beautifully sweet aroma, a blessed flood of tears, and the sensation of a loving, warm mantle placed over her shoulders. Prous was not alone in her veneration of Olivi, "the angel whose face shone like the sun." Nor would she be alone at the stake, where she was burned for heresy in 1328 as a beguin. We will return shortly to these Olivi-inspired beguin communities as well as to the mounting inquisitorial attempts to unravel them.

The early fourteenth century was an epicenter of tension and controversy, not only within the Franciscan Order but more broadly across Christendom as the voices of spiritual reform, dissent, and innovation first heard in the eleventh and twelfth centuries swelled into a complex chorus of different religious tones, notes, and rhythms. And Joachite ideas and the expectation of a new spiritual age spread far beyond Franciscan walls. One particularly vivid example is the life and posthumous veneration of a saintly Milanese lay religious woman, or *pinzochera*, named Guglielma, rumored to have been the daughter of the king of Bohemia. After her death in 1281, her enthusiastic devotees claimed that she was the incarnation of the Holy Spirit, come to earth to found a new and saving church. In 1300, Dominican inquisitors interrogated dozens of citizens, after which several of her most ardent followers (including nuns) were sent to the stake.[12] It was a localized event, but one set in motion by the same spiritual undercurrents running deep across Western Christendom. Indeed, radical penitents and apostolically inspired critics cropped up across Europe, particularly in northern Italy, where a group founded by one Gerard Segerelli (a penitent and unsuccessful Franciscan applicant) became, under persecutorial pressure, a group of radicals hunted in Alpine hideouts. Bernard Gui described their belief that "this Gherardo was God's own plant springing from the root of faith and that through him God began to bring his Church back to the perfection, life, condition and poverty of the early Church, to the state in which it was when Christ entrusted it to the blessed apostle Peter."[13] The history of these particular "Apostolic Brethren" ended with the deaths of their leaders at the stake in 1307, but the broader impulse to combine religious revival, critique of the Church, and an expectant apocalypticism in the message of a single figure certainly did not perish with them.

THE FORGING AND FRACTURE OF THE CLEMENTINE SETTLEMENT (1309–1316)

These early years of the fourteenth century were a troubled time for the papacy. After the royally ordered assault on Pope Boniface VIII and his subsequent death, the papacy had been established in the southern French city of Avignon. Elected in 1305, Pope Clement V inherited a daunting array of problems, not least of which was the ongoing controversy within the Franciscan Order. In 1309, Clement was finally persuaded that the matter needed further investigation, and he invited spokesmen for both sides to a hearing over the next three years. Like a modern conference organizer, he issued a call for papers focusing upon four issues: (1) whether the Spirituals had been infected by heresy, (2) whether the Rule and papal bulls were being observed properly within the order, (3) Olivi's orthodoxy, and (4) the persecution in southern France. The explosion of polemical literature that resulted is

Figure 4.3. Palace of the Popes in Avignon. *Source*: **Photo by George Tatge. Alinari/SEAT/ Art Resource, NY.**

rich and complex, including the writings of Ubertino of Casale and his arguments about the issue of "restricted use."

Ubertino charged, for example, that the community held special luxurious dinners for leaders and scholars and that elite members were treated better than those of lower rank; that the order was using big, expensive buildings and placing itself too much in the decadent center of urban life; that individual brothers were not employing "restricted use" of books, but hoarding large boxes of them and refusing to let anyone else read them. He also attacked the practice of storing up surplus, of Franciscan barns filled with wheat and cellars filled with wine: "Do not think about tomorrow" (Matthew 6:34), he urged, but live instead in radical dependence and faith.

As for garments, he argued that regulation Franciscan habits were too fancy; that although shoes were prohibited except in case of dire necessity, many Franciscan elites wore them throughout the winter. In fact, he observed, it was only the Spirituals who routinely went barefoot, and they were persecuted for their effort, just as they were hounded for wearing the vile, short, patched tunic of Francis himself. Such injustice was a common complaint in the Spiritualist literature. Ubertino told the story of one Spiritualist who washed his tunic and hung it out to dry only to find it later in the latrine being used as toilet paper. Clothing was always a marker of social and spiritual status in the Middle Ages, but the Franciscans' garments had become particularly emblematic of both disputes within the order and also broader tensions within Christendom itself.

To settle the matter, Clement appointed a fourteen-member commission to advise him on the material he collected and then issued *Exivi de paradisi* (*When I Went Forth from Paradise*) on May 6, 1312. From one point of view, it was a victory for the Spirituals: Clement acknowledged the accuracy of most of Ubertino's points and commanded the order to clean up its act. But from another point of view, the bull was an attempt to end the controversy by simply closing the conversation: Clement's final word on poverty in the bull was a mandate to stop debating whether *usus pauper* was or was not part of the vow; his final word on clothing was to leave it in the hands of Franciscan superiors to decide how vile the garments should be; the brothers need only obey and their consciences would be clear. Yet Francis had specifically said that each friar has a responsibility to disobey superiors if they demand a violation of the Rule. Olivi did, too, and so the Spirituals did not find the pope's solution satisfying.

Clement's reconciliation of the order was off to a poor start, and it degenerated quickly in northern Italy and southern France. Spirituals in "short garments" resisted their superiors in Tuscany; in 1314, thirty-seven were excommunicated as "notorious apostates, schismatics and rebels; originators and proponents of a superstitious sect, and sowers of pestiferous doctrine."[14] Meanwhile, attempts to reconcile the divided order were viewed by the Conventual community as an unacceptable appeasement of wayward radicals. In Provence, matters escalated even more dramatically. Clement had fired the provincial minister and fifteen others who had persecuted the local Spirituals, prohibited their return to authority, and taken disciplinary action against them. He then assigned the Franciscan houses at Narbonne, Béziers, and Carcassonne to the Spirituals and ordered that they be assigned superiors acceptable to them.

The Conventuals were furious. And in one of those unforeseeable coincidences that periodically shape history, both the pope and the minister general died in 1314; their deaths created a two-year power vacuum during which chaos reigned and hostilities between the Spirituals and Conventuals mounted. According to the sources, the infamous sixteen of Provence who had been fired by Clement fought back to power and now deposed the Spirituals. Having neither pope nor minister general for support, the Spirituals actively undertook their own defense. With the support of laymen and women in Narbonne and Béziers, they physically drove the Conventuals out the convents, which became havens for escapees from other houses in Provence and neighboring areas. Within a month, 120 Spirituals had congregated there, defending their claim that their actions were just and that the Conventuals were disobeying a papal command. In turn, their opponents claimed that the Spirituals were disobedient, violent heretics—that they venerated and even worshiped the heretic Olivi, and that, like the Cathars and Waldensians before them, they were heretics for insisting that sinful clerics should not be obeyed. Calling for decisive action, the Conventuals deployed an image we have encountered before: "to keep the little foxes in sheep's clothing from sneaking in and destroying the vineyard."[15]

POPE JOHN XXII AND THE CONDEMNATION (1318)

Because the Franciscan poverty controversy was at heart a struggle over authority and the proper relationship among the friars, the Gospel, and the papacy, the deadlock could not be broken until the election of a new pope and minister general of the order. In 1316, the Franciscans chose as their leader Michael of Cesena from the University of Paris, a man with a moderate perspective on the controversy. But the turning point was the cardinals' selection of the new pope, a former chancellor of the kingdom of Naples who took the name John XXII (r. 1316–1334) and immediately trained his formidable gaze on the Franciscan problem. In 1317, as recounted at the beginning of the chapter, he summoned the Spirituals of Narbonne and Béziers to the papal court in Avignon.

We witness the events through the eyes of a Spiritual Franciscan whose account dramatically describes the pope in an imposing chair, surrounded by advisers; a crowd of Conventuals stirs angrily to one side, some dressed simply, others sumptuously; across from them are sixty-four friars in torn, patched, short habits. One could probably have cut the tension in the air with a knife as the two sides faced off. As the designated Spiritual spokesmen made their claims in turn, each was shouted down by opponents and then taken away to prison. After the third time this happened, a respected friar intervened. Elderly and frail, he was a friend and companion of Ubertino and had spent the winter at court defending the Spirituals. When he began to speak, the pope mockingly observed that it was a surprise to see him there, defending the right to observe the Rule strictly, when everyone knew that he himself wore five tunics. The friar responded politely that he was not wearing five tunics. "Are you calling me a liar?" asked the pope. And when the friar responded that no, perhaps the Holy Father was just mistaken, the pope sent him off to prison as well "to see how many tunics he was wearing." At that point the proceedings reportedly broke down entirely. The Spirituals clamored for justice, but all were thrown into prison for the following year.[16]

John worked quickly to bring the matter to a conclusion. In the bull *Quorundam exigit* (1317) he reaffirmed the stance of his predecessors, ruling that there could be no differences in dress within the order or claims to greater austerity by one faction or another; officials of the order would set the standard and all brothers were to obey it. Friars, he ordered, could store up supplies of bread and wine in granaries and cellars for their security and convenience; amounts would, once again, be determined by officials of the order. But the real significance of *Quorundam exigit* is that it became an exceedingly useful litmus test against which the orthodoxy (read: obedience) of the friars could be tested. As the pope put it, "Poverty is great, but chastity is greater, and the greatest of all is obedience if it is preserved intact."[17] Would the friars obey, accept the storing up of surplus possessions, and submit to orders that contradicted Francis's vision? The answer varied.

According to one source, the minister general himself interrogated the imprisoned Spirituals: in front of witnesses and a notary, he asked each one whether he would obey the precepts in *Quorundam exigit* and whether he believed that the pope possessed the authority to legislate on the matter. Many recanted, but twenty-six did not. And because a panel of thirteen theologians had all agreed that refusal to acquiesce constituted heresy, the recalcitrant brothers were handed over to the Franciscan inquisitor of Provence. By May, the inquisitor had persuaded all but five to recant; on May 7, 1318, two weeks after Easter, he issued his sentence. One of the five backed down at the eleventh hour and was sentenced to perpetual imprisonment. But that same day, the four friars who refused to recant were burned to death in front of the bishop, the heads of regional monasteries and convents, the twenty-one friars who had escaped the stake, and a motley crowd of Marseilleise onlookers. As will be discussed below, the four friars would soon be joined at the stake by laymen and laywomen who supported the Spirituals; both were persecuted throughout southern France by inquisitors for another decade.

John was not yet finished with the Franciscans, however. Influenced by Dominican theologians who argued that even the conservative friars' understanding of poverty fostered error, the pope began pressuring Michael of Cesena and other leading Franciscans to change the order's position. In 1322, apparently having made little headway through persuasion, he shattered the old distinction between ownership and use by transferring all possession of things given to the friars *and used by them* to the order. Franciscans were forced to accept ownership, to touch money, and they could no longer claim to possess nothing. The finishing touch from Avignon was the pope's declaration that, in contrast to what had previously been taught, it was heretical to teach that Jesus and the apostles did not have possessions. By 1322, in other words, the pope had heard enough from the mendicants about apostolic poverty.

In little more than a century after the Franciscan Order's birth, much had changed: the Spirituals had been driven from the order; the distinction between use and ownership was quashed; the Franciscans were a propertied order; and the previously orthodox doctrine of the absolute poverty of Jesus and the apostles was deemed heretical. And even the Conventuals were fighting the pope, as figures such as Michael of Cesena fled to the court of John's enemy, Emperor Louis of Bavaria, who was delighted to welcome him. Meanwhile, Spiritual Franciscan attitudes toward poverty and the Apocalypse had taken root among circles of the beguins, particularly in the now-familiar region of southern France. Frequently associated with the Franciscan Third Order, these men and women came under intense inquisitorial scrutiny after 1318. For more than a decade, inquisitors employed precise and effective strategies to unravel these close-knit communities, prompting ever-new tactics of resistance among the beguins. Over a hundred would die at the stake—wicked heretics to the Church but heroic martyrs to their friends and followers.

BEGUINS AND INQUISITORS (1318–c. 1330)

The term *beguin* held a variety of competing and sometimes contradictory definitions in Languedoc, as it did elsewhere. Bonaventure had referred to the sisters of the Order of Penitence as *beguines*. Lay religious women of all stripes were often termed beguines (as discussed in chapter 5), and in northern Italian lands, members of the Third Order were known as *Pizocari*, *pinzochere*, or *bizzoche*. These are general terms, not precise canonical descriptions of status, employed to cover a variety of essentially lay penitential forms of life. But in southern lands by the late thirteenth century, many of these were explicitly associated with the lay orders of the Franciscans.

In 1299, a provincial council held in Béziers that criticized the heretical Cathars also referred to people "commonly called Beguins"; not yet designated as heretics, the beguins were recognizable for penitential practice, for distinctive garb (a coarse dark cloak or habit), and for their certainty that the time of the Antichrist was nigh. Within a decade, sources demonstrate that *begui* had become a pejorative term linking heresy to local tertiaries. And by 1317, the term as employed in Mediterranean lands often bore the specific meaning of a Franciscan tertiary devoted to Peter Olivi and steeped in his potent theological blend of apostolic poverty and the Apocalypse.

According to contemporary observers, the beguins' appearance and behavior distinguished them within local communities: "[T]hey agreed that a Beguin went barefoot, wearing humble and long clothes, and walked around all day with a mortified face."[18] One source reported that "when they pray in a church or elsewhere they sit crouching down, hoods over their heads, facing an opposite wall or something similar or looking down to the ground. They are not often seen on bended knees and with folded hands, like other people."[19] Evidently, however, beguins were not marginalized within their own towns or villages but were rather fully embedded in local relationships, family structures, and institutions. Some lived in their own family homes, whereas others (often those committed to lives of celibacy) inhabited "houses of poverty" akin to those we encountered among other southern French communities in earlier chapters. In other words, the beguins were inspired by the Franciscans and sought to blend the apostolic model with various forms of lay life. In this respect, beguin circles appear to represent yet another hue in the spectrum of localized spiritual fervor influenced by the economic, political, and social shifts of the high Middle Ages.

Perhaps unsurprisingly, it is difficult to ascertain exactly what the status of a "tertiary" or "penitent" was, if such distinctions even held in the first place beyond specific times and contexts.[20] In some cases, it implied that the required oath had been taken and that the community was under the supervision of the local mendicants; in others, however, the terms were adopted or attributed informally. Not all beguins were formal members of the Franciscan Third Order, nor were all Franciscan tertiaries followers of the Spirituals and Peter Olivi. Indeed, Gui was careful to place among the number of the heretics "other faithful not of the Third Order, be they clerics, members of religious orders, or laity, as long as they believe and maintain as the beguins do on the aforesaid issues."[21]

Yet there were distinguishing characteristics of the beguins as well, shared beliefs that not only bound local clusters of believers into regional networks but soon became indelibly linked with heresy in the minds of clerics and inquisitors: the equivalence of St. Francis's Rule and the Gospel, the Christ-given importance of apostolic poverty, the imminence of the Antichrist's arrival, and the status of Olivi as an uncanonized saint. Indeed, Olivi and his apocalyptic condemnation of the institutional Church lay at the heart of beguin piety and ecclesiastical hostility. Embracing his Joachite understanding of the looming End of Days prophesied in Revelation, beguins interpreted the persecution of Spiritual Franciscans as proof that the Church had indeed become the Whore of Babylon, that the Antichrist was loosed, and that as members of the true Church, they now had a crucial role to play in the historical unfolding of salvation. When rebuked for inappropriate preaching, however, these beguins defended themselves by claiming that they were only "talking about God."

What appeared a fine distinction in the eyes of authorities seemed a clear divide to those seeking to legitimize their right to consider and converse about Christian mysteries. The right to talk about God was, of course, employed by many other contemporary communities and individuals we have thus far encountered; how much more urgent such conversations must have seemed in the early fourteenth century, when Joachim's timetable suggested that the Spiritual Franciscans and all their followers were about to take center stage in the Apocalypse.

Pursuing Beguins

Both the conservative Franciscan wing and the papacy sought to eradicate what they perceived as dangerous new ideas sprouting in the south and moving north. Michael of Cesena, for example, sought to have the "order of Fraticelli" annulled and to dismantle the link between beguins and tertiaries so as not to lend mendicant authority to any errors they might be preaching. Likewise unimpressed with claims of membership in the Third Order, in December 1317 John issued the bull *Sancta Romana* (*The Holy Roman Church*), which called for the persecution of those known as "*fraticelli*, or brothers of poor life, or *bizzochi* or *beguins*" scattered throughout southern France and Italy. The public deaths of the four Franciscan friars several months later must have dramatically underscored the seriousness of papal intent to eradicate heresy.

By early 1319, many men and women from places such as Marseilles, Montpellier, and Toulouse had been arrested and interrogated by inquisitors, usually in cooperation with local episcopal and secular authorities. Gui devoted more time in his inquisitorial manual to beguins than any other topic, specifically noting that they drew their "pestiferous errors and opinions" from the apocalyptic writings of Peter Olivi, and that they taught one another error in their vernacular language in "houses of poverty."[22] To ensnare a beguin, the experienced inquisitor urged colleagues to select questions subtly and in whatever combination or sequence would elicit the truth. Questions included: Do you believe that the Rule of St. Francis is one and the same with the Gospel of Christ? Have you ever held that Christ and the apostles had nothing either individually or in common? Can the pope insist that the Franciscan Friars Minor store wheat and wine for their common future needs? Did you know that the four friars burned in 1318 were heretics? Are you aware that male and female beguins (who call themselves Poor of the Third Order of St. Francis) were recently condemned? Do you believe that they were heretical? What have you heard regarding Peter Olivi, or the sixth period begun in the time of St. Francis, or about the coming of the Antichrist?[23]

These, of course, represent only a tiny fraction of the interrogation formulas provided by Gui's manual, which was intended to educate inquisitors about the heresy and how best to guide a suspect to confession, penance, and reconciliation. Not all would come, he acknowledged. Some would recant, but others would remain obstinate and choose the stake instead. Indeed, six beguins had already been sent to the stake by October 1318. After each burning, the horrifying news spread quickly throughout southern communities, setting various modes of resistance and response into action. As Louisa Burnham has vividly illuminated, networks of resistance grew under the pressure of inquisition and not only bound like-minded souls in different communities but even served to reinforce the sense of a common and historically imminent fight against the Antichrist.

Strategies of Resistance

Such networks and bonds were, of course, not unique to beguins: we have already seen them emerge from the familial and communal structures associated with Good Christians and the Poor. As discussed previously, the strategies employed by those interrogated differed significantly according to the contextual circumstances and individual temperaments. Some vehemently denied affiliation with beguins, whereas others admitted prior belief in Olivian ideas about poverty and apocalypticism and accepted penance. Yet others, such as the impassioned priest Bernard Maury of Narbonne, escaped (in his case only temporarily) by fleeing to other locations. Beguin communities are, for example, documented in western cities such as Barcelona and as far north as Metz—the latter certainly a consequence of flight from persecution and evidently one of many places where beguins mingled with sympathetic Poor and other like-minded souls.[24]

Such escape was made possible by safe houses along a kind of underground railroad, such as the home of Raimon and Bernarda d'Antusan.[25] Some who came under interrogation confessed or informed on others, yet the evidence suggests that just as many dissembled, evaded, lied to, and misled inquisitors. It was a dangerous strategy, of course, because inquisitors had become adept at recording and cross-referencing testimony in order to weed out stubborn or relapsed heretics. Many of the hundred or so beguins who died at the stake during these years were condemned as a consequence of a second, third, or subsequent interrogation. Those found guilty of lesser degrees of heresy received light penalties or prison sentences after abjuring.

Although the increasingly frequent sight of comrades' corpses on execution pyres certainly persuaded some back to the orthodox fold, it emboldened the resistance of others. For many beguins in the 1320s, the burning of beloved local figures, such as the holy woman Esclarmonda Durban, a fifteen-year-old girl named Amegiardis, the Franciscan friar Raimon Maistre, or the priest Bernard Maury, grimly reinforced their certainty that the Apocalypse was imminent. The public spectacle of execution thus invigorated rather than chilled beguin spiritual convictions, particularly when the condemned "died well," enduring the flames with patience, faith, and serenity. Likewise, the martyred bodies of the condemned served not as the intended warnings but were instead gathered secretly and transformed into holy relics treasured by persecuted survivors. Inquisitors would discover various body parts or objects belonging to executed beguins among the possessions of their "heretical" brothers and sisters.

Inquisitors and beguins thus brought different worldviews to their encounters, perspectives rooted in different Christian authorities, texts, and historical understanding. To inquisitors, beguins were impious heretics whose prideful disobedience threatened to unleash hell on earth. For beguins, Christian joinings of heaven and earth extended beyond sacraments, scripture, and traditional saints' relics to incorporate more recent holies, such as the writings of Francis, the grave of Olivi, the charred bones of their martyred companions, and the looming promise of a new historical age.

Yet by the early 1330s, inquisitorial techniques had effectively sundered and suppressed beguin networks; the intensity and focus of inquisitorial attention during these years underscores the seriousness with which the beguin threat was regarded and the extent to which the Church's inquisitors of heretical depravity had honed their profession over the preceding century. It is worth remembering, however, that the Church did not experience the burning of more than a hundred people at the stake as a triumph, representing as it did the annihilation rather than reconciliation of wayward souls.

CONCLUSION

Despite all his efforts, Pope John XXII had not fully uprooted the tendency toward apostolic rigor; it returned periodically in small scattered bands of Spirituals or Fraticelli hunted by inquisitors through the middle of the century, and in the spread of Spiritualist writings. The book of Revelation was on the minds of many, and increasingly the pope himself was identified by critics as the apocalyptic Whore of Babylon. One cannot avoid the sense that history had painfully come full circle from 1208 and Innocent III's willing embrace of Francis and his band of ragged "apostles." Over the century between the saint's death and the consigning of Spiritual Franciscans and beguins to the stake, multiple fault lines had converged: particularly divisive had been the challenge of institutionalizing pious ideals, reconciling competing interpretations of scripture, and settling the question of ultimate spiritual authority. A booming cash economy had exacerbated the tension between wealth and poverty, as had new understandings of history and the End of Days.

Various attempts to establish austere wings of the order were initiated and quelled until, in the early years of the fifteenth century, a rigorous movement of "Observants" emerged whose special regard for the Franciscan Rule set them apart from their brothers. At the Council of Constance in 1415, a division was actually approved between Observants and Conventuals, and in 1428 the pope restored the distinction between ownership and use, making the order propertyless once again. In 1517 (the same year in which Martin Luther's theses ignited the early Reformation), the pope finally split the Franciscans into two separate orders, formalizing a tendency that had been three centuries in the making. Since 1982, moreover, the Rule followed by religious members of the Franciscan Third Order is not *Supra montem,* with its initial antiheretical injunction, but rather Francis's *Letter to the Faithful,* which welcomes "all who love the Lord with their whole heart, with their whole soul and mind, and with all their strength [Mark 12:30] and love their neighbors as themselves [Matthew 22:39] and who despise the tendency in their humanity to sin." The order had changed over time both in purpose and in function, as institutions do; Francis himself could not have prevented it.

SUGGESTIONS FOR FURTHER READING

Ames, Christine Caldwell. *Righteous Persecution: Inquisition, Dominicans, and Christianity in the Middle Ages*. Philadelphia: University of Pennsylvania Press, 2008.

Armstrong, Regis J., and Ignatius Brady, eds. *Francis and Clare: The Complete Works*. New York: Paulist Press, 1982.

Burnham, Louisa. *So Great a Light, So Great a Smoke: The Beguin Heretics of Languedoc.* Ithaca, NY: Cornell University Press, 2008.

Burr, David. *Olivi and Franciscan Poverty: The Origins of the Usus Pauper Controversy*. Philadelphia: University of Pennsylvania Press, 1989.

———. *The Spiritual Franciscans: From Protest to Persecution in the Century after Saint Francis*. University Park: Pennsylvania State University Press, 2001.

Elliott, Dyan. *Proving Woman: Female Spirituality and Inquisitional Culture in the Later Middle Ages*. Princeton, NJ: Princeton University Press, 2004.

Given, James. *Inquisition and Medieval Society: Power, Discipline, and Resistance in Languedoc*. Ithaca, NY: Cornell University Press, 1997.

Lerner, Robert E. *The Feast of Saint Abraham: Medieval Millenarians and the Jews*. Philadelphia: University of Pennsylvania Press, 2001.

McGinn, Bernard. *Visions of the End: Apocalyptic Traditions in the Middle Ages*. New York: Columbia University Press, 1979.

Mueller, Joan. *The Privilege of Poverty: Clare of Assisi, Agnes of Prague, and the Struggle for a Franciscan Rule for Women.* University Park: Pennsylvania State University Press, 2006.

Nold, Patrick. *Pope John XXII and His Franciscan Cardinal: Bertrand de la Tour and the Apostolic Poverty Controversy*. Oxford: Oxford University Press, 2003.

Thompson, Augustine. *Francis of Assisi: The Life.* Ithaca, NY: Cornell University Press, 2013.

NOTES

1. David Burr, *The Spiritual Franciscans: From Protest to Persecution in the Century after Saint Francis* (University Park: Pennsylvania State University Press, 2001), 1.

2. Burr, *Spiritual Franciscans*, 3.

3. Translation by David Burr available at http://www.history.vt.edu/Burr/Francis/Frn_rule.html.

4. Regis J. Armstrong and Ignatius Brady, eds., *Francis and Clare: The Complete Works* (New York: Paulist Press, 1982), 70.

5. Robert M. Stewart, *"De Illis Qui Faciunt Penitentiam": The Rule of the Secular Franciscan Order: Origins, Development, Interpretation* (Rome: Istituto Storico Dei Capuccini, 1991), 209.

6. Burr, *Spiritual Franciscans*, 7.

7. Malcolm Lambert, *Medieval Heresy: Popular Movements from the Gregorian Reform to the Reformation* (Oxford: Blackwell, 2002), 209.

8. Burr, *Spiritual Franciscans*, 22.

9. Robert E. Lerner, *The Feast of Saint Abraham: Medieval Millenarians and the Jews* (Philadelphia: University of Pennsylvania Press, 2000), 12.

10. Louisa Burnham, *So Great a Light, So Great a Smoke: The Beguin Heretics of Languedoc* (Ithaca, NY: Cornell University Press, 2008), 19.

11. The etymology of the name is unclear but probably derives from the Indo-European root *begg-* (meaning someone who mutters and mumbles, as in someone praying under his breath) and is related to the modern French *bégayer*, to stammer. Walter Simons, *Cities of Ladies: Beguine Communities in the Medieval Low Countries, 1200–1565* (Philadelphia: University of Pennsylvania Press, 2001), 122. The term and its relationship to other lay religious groups will be discussed further in chapter 5.

12. Barbara Newman, "The Heretic Saint: Guglielma of Bohemia, Milan, and Brunate," *Church History* 74 (March 2005): 1–30.

13. Bernard Gui, *The Inquisitor's Guide: A Medieval Manual on Heretics*, ed. Janet Shirley (Welwyn Garden City, UK: Ravenhall Books, 2006), 79.

14. Burr, *Spiritual Franciscans*, 163.

15. Burr, *Spiritual Franciscans*, 172.

16. Burr, *Spiritual Franciscans*, 195.

17. Burnham, *So Great a Light*, 112.

18. Burnham, *So Great a Light*, 35.

19. Gui, *The Inquisitor's Guide*, 96.

20. See Alison More, *Fictive Religious Orders and Feminine Religious Identities, 1200–1600* (Oxford: Oxford University Press, 2018).

21. Gui, *The Inquisitor's Guide*, 105

22. Gui, *The Inquisitor's Guide*, 109.
23. Gui, *The Inquisitor's Guide*, 118–27.
24. Courtney Kneupper, "Reconsidering a Fourteenth-Century Heresy Trial in Metz: Beguins and Others," *Franciscana* 8 (2006): 187–227.
25. Burnham, *So Great a Light*, 59.

Chapter Five

Mysticism, Lay Religious Women, and the Problem of Spiritual Authority

On June 1, 1310, a woman named Marguerite Porete, author of the mystical book *The Mirror of Simple Souls*, was burned at the stake in Paris as a relapsed heretic. Church authorities focused on what they feared was her claim that "a soul annihilated in the love of the creator could, and should, grant to nature all that it desires." In other words, they accused her of writing that a soul can become one with God and that in such a state it can ignore the moral law, bypassing not only the Church but its sacraments and code of virtues. Marguerite meant no such thing, for she clearly explained in the text that a soul in this state desires only good and would not wish to sin. However, in the face of repeated ecclesiastical attempts to suppress the book, Marguerite refused to stop disseminating the "errors and heresies" contained therein. Her silence in the face of inquisitorial pressure ultimately doomed her. The work not only circulated for centuries in multiple translations as a thoroughly orthodox mystical text but was attributed to famous male theologians and was published in English in the early twentieth century by the Benedictines. Only in the mid-twentieth century was Marguerite's authorship finally determined and the book enshrined as the brilliant work of a condemned heretic—and a woman. Questions about its meaning and nature have continued to interest modern historians as much as they did medieval theologians.

What is certain is that the determination of Marguerite's heresy had as much to do with her identity as a single, pious woman and her resistance to inquisitors as it did with the actual contents of the book. Equally certain is that Marguerite's book influenced another hereticized mystical writer of the early fourteenth century, the German Dominican Meister Eckhart. Although the male theologian occupied a vastly different world from Marguerite in terms of education and influence, they both moved within circles of pious laywomen, were deeply influenced by scriptural vocabulary and images, and shared a belief in a mystical process by which soul and God unite. And although some of Eckhart's ideas, and indeed Marguerite herself, were condemned in the early fourteenth century, inquisitorial hostility did little to quell the admiration and enthusiasm of like-minded souls during and after the Middle Ages.

In order to understand "the heretic who seemed orthodox and the great theologian who inspired heresy,"[1] let us examine more closely the historical context and spiritual currents that shaped both of their writings. The fierce criticism that so marked their later years erupted at a unique historical intersection shaped by four distinct developments: (1) a remarkable groundswell of active female spirituality from the early thirteenth through the fifteenth centuries; (2) the blossoming of a new and often vernacular Christian mysticism that, although deeply rooted in scriptural and patristic authorities, represented a perceived spiritual hazard to the souls of common folk; (3) mounting papal and ecclesiastical certainty that secret heretics, particularly women, were corrupting Christendom; and (4) the papacy's increasingly labored struggle to maintain the office's prestige and authority not only against secular leaders such as King Philip IV of France but also within its own ranks. The Great Schism (1378–1417), in which first two and then three rival popes battled one another for control of the see, was a crisis of disastrous proportion; so too were the cold rains that drowned western crops during the second decade of the century and the devastation of plague that wiped out huge swaths of the population and continued to return in wave after pestilential wave. These were hard times, and they prompted a stunning variety of responses and resolutions in Western Christendom.

One response, of course, was to crack down on belief and behavior. As we have seen, "heresy" exists only in the eye of the hostile beholder, and the late medieval Church's preoccupation with mysticism, "free spirits," and female religiosity is as much a story of clerical fears as of religious history. In order to trace the story of suspect mystics, annihilated souls, and the problem of authority in the early fourteenth century, we need to proceed thoughtfully to untangle the different strands. We should start with a few fundamental questions: What is mysticism? What place did it occupy in the orthodox Christian tradition? And on what authority did Christian mystics claim and communicate their ineffable experiences?

CHRISTIAN MYSTICAL TRADITIONS

The term *mysticism* is derived from the Greek word meaning "to conceal," which in ancient Christianity came to imply hidden truths and secret realities, such as allegorical scriptural meaning or Christ's presence in the Eucharist. Bernard McGinn offers the following definition: "that part, or element, of Christian belief and practice that concerns the preparation for, the consciousness of, and the effect of what the mystics themselves have described as a direct and transformative presence of God."[2] In the simplest possible terms, therefore, mysticism is the certainty in and search for ecstatic union between the human and divine.

Because of Jesus's unique relationship to God—"I and the Father are one" (John 10:30)—and the promise of God's transformative love for humanity, mystical thought and practice grew organically from Christianity's very origins. Scriptural passages inspired centuries of diverse Christian thinkers to ponder the nature of the spirit and to record the paths by which humans could follow Christ into the promised divine illumination: "Now we are children of God, and what we will be has not yet been made known. But we know that when he appears, we shall be like him, for we shall see him as he is" (1 John 3:2). What set mystical tendencies apart from mainstream doctrine once the latter was defined in the third and fourth centuries CE was the means or process of knowing God. All Christians were presumed able to reach God through belief in Jesus and, increasingly over time, through participation in the Church's sacraments and rituals. Mystical Christians, however, sought to gain spiritual truths by a more immediate and unmediated experience (although for many, sacraments such as the Eucharist played a key role in facilitating or initiating such experiences). Christian mysticism, like many other global traditions, was often expressed in terms of stages through which the human soul awakens to a greater reality, is stripped of material distractions, is illuminated through contemplation, and finally is merged blissfully and fully into divine union: "For now we see through a glass, darkly, but then face to face: now I know in part; but then shall I know even as also I am known" (1 Corinthians 13:12).

Although some early groups inspired by Jesus, such as the Gnostics, drew criticism for their belief in esoteric knowledge that would allow human beings to escape the confines of the material world, others laid the foundations of fully orthodox and deeply influential Christian thought. Church fathers such as Tertullian (155–222 CE), Origen (185–254 CE), and Gregory of Nyssa (335–398 CE) wove depictions of the relationship between God, humanity, and the universe threaded through with mystical concepts and images. St. Augustine (354–430 CE) told his local community of Hippo in North Africa how he interpreted a mystical passage in scripture based on his own experience:

> Seeking my God in visible and corporeal things, I did not find him. Seeking his substance in myself, as if he were something like me, I also did not find him.

> I am aware that my God is something above my soul, and therefore, so that I might touch him, "I thought on these things and poured out my soul above myself" (Psalm 41:5).[3]

Augustine drew on Greek Platonism to communicate his understanding of the soul's search for God, attaining to That Which Is "in the flash of a trembling glance."[4] Later medieval thinkers would incorporate both Augustinian and Neoplatonic concepts in their own struggles to express the inexpressible.

By the twelfth century, when Christian mysticism would enter a new phase of vitality and intensity, one of the most vivid and frequent metaphors for the joining of a yearning soul and a loving God was the dance of human courtship from desire to consummation. Again, the foundations were laid in scripture, such as in the following passage from the Hebrew Song of Songs 7:11–13:

> I belong to my lover and for me he yearns. Come, my lover, let us go forth to the fields and spend the night among the villages. Let us go early to the vineyards, and see if the vines are in bloom, If the buds have opened, if the pomegranates have blossomed; There will I give you my love.

That such richly erotic poetry resonated with medieval piety may surprise modern readers, given the Church's dour attitude toward sexuality, but sex was, after all, a familiar image and one that when elevated to the allegorical realm, had nothing to do with the carnal fact of coupling bodies.

The new and fully orthodox mysticism that blossomed in western Europe in the centuries that followed, as articulated and expanded by spiritual leaders such as Bernard of Clairvaux and Hildegard of Bingen, thus had deep historical and theological roots in scripture, theology, and Christian practice. The emerging problem with later medieval mysticism, however, was that the direct knowledge of and illumination by God did not depend upon Christian sacraments or clerical mediation. In theory, therefore, the essential point of contact between earth and heaven became potentially accessible to anyone at any time, removed from the exclusive confines of monastery, convent, and altar. As ecclesiastical authorities further calibrated their inquisitorial instruments in search of those claiming false or inappropriate spiritual powers, one implication of mysticism drew particular concern: the notion that the Church and its sacraments are unnecessary (antisacerdotalism) and that mystical union with God overrides the need to observe a virtuous, moral life on earth (antinomianism). Despite the fact that no Christian mystic ever embraced those ideas as such, theologians and inquisitors in the fourteenth century began to develop a new and largely fictional heresy based on anxiety about mysticism, female piety, and current crises in the Church. The history of the "Heresy of the Free Spirit," as this specter came to be known, provides a neat example of how inquisitors created not only heretics but entire heresies from their growing tool kit of texts and techniques.

In this chapter, I continue the argument begun earlier that the early fourteenth century represented a major turning point in the Church's attitude toward and response to heresy. Three particular events will occupy us here: first, the trial and execution of Marguerite Porete in 1310; second, the 1317 publication of the Council of Vienne's decrees against "Free Spirits" and certain lay religious women referred to as "beguines"; and third, the erudite mysticism of the German Dominican scholar Meister Eckhart and the posthumous papal condemnation of portions of his work in 1329. The common

Figure 5.1. The Mystic Embrace, Passionar of the Abbess Kunigunde, 14th c. ms. ***Source*****: University Library, Prague, Czech Republic. Erich Lessing/Art Resource, NY.**

thread binding these three moments is their relationship to post-Gregorian lay Christian movements, particularly among women, whose formation of religious sisterhoods provided a durable (if complicated) new strand to the pattern of late medieval religiosity. That unlettered women and simple men might claim inappropriate spiritual authority through mystical experience, whether or not they actually did, troubled many an early fourteenth-century inquisitor. We begin where they did, with lay religious women and their communities.

"BEGUINES," OR LAY RELIGIOUS WOMEN

Gregorian reform had unleashed broad waves of lay piety that rippled across twelfth- and thirteenth-century Europe, and many women sought to mimic the apostolic life or develop a spiritual practice that was not so traditionally bound by oaths and walls. We have already encountered the challenges faced by early female followers of Valdès and the Spiritual Franciscans. But what options awaited the many other women who desired to live a religious life outside of formally regulated convents and cloisters? As Herbert Grundmann wrote, a new women's religious movement was arising that would "form communities belonging to no order at all, following no specific rule, but binding themselves in all strictness to commandments of female piety in chastity and poverty, prayer and fasting."[5] As one might imagine, the openness and flexibility of this type of communal lifestyle allowed for nearly endless possibilities, and thus is it extremely difficult to generalize about "beguines," as they frequently (and problematically) came to be known.

We have already encountered the term *beguin* in the previous chapter, which in that context implied lay followers associated with Spiritual Franciscans. However, these names are not nearly as exclusive and precise as scholars have traditionally thought; simple distinctions between southern beguins and northern beguines simply do not hold, as etymology and medieval usage both reveal. The term *beguine* (in the north it refers to women and thus appears with an *e* at the end) first emerged in the context of the Low Countries during the thirteenth century to refer to single laywomen who pursued actively pious lives *within* the world rather than enclosed in a convent. The most plausible etymology is that it derives from the Old French *béguer* (to stammer), just as the Middle Dutch equivalent *popelen* (to mumble, as in quiet prayer) gave rise to another smear word for beguins, *papelard*. Another Middle Dutch word implying a mutterer, *lollaert*, yielded the epithet "Lollard" that would circulate on the continent as a term for the hypocritically pious and emerge in England as a label for a particular form of heresy in the fourteenth and fifteenth centuries. All of these names conjure images of a person who appears to be absorbed in her own world of private prayer, unreachable and incomprehensible: "The term also served to relegate the person to another, inferior realm with which 'reasoned' communication seemed impossible: the beguine would not or could not communicate clearly."[6]

Because the label "*beguine*" contained so many different meanings across time and place, burdened by centuries of historical baggage and complicated by varying interpretations, I prefer to use here the more general "*lay religious women*." The term refers to those who pursued the apostolic ideal in their own lives, not behind monastic walls or as members of an order, but as laypeople pursuing a specifically pious form of life in the world. This is a rather difficult concept because we are used to thinking in the black-and-white categories of clergy or laity, as were medieval clergy themselves. Yet there was a large, diverse, and colorful spectrum of piety between the poles of clerical and lay, none of which was necessarily heretical or even controversial.[7] Pope Innocent III's prohibition of new orders in 1215 did little to stop these new ways of life, particularly because most laid no claim to becoming a formal order shaped by an official rule, and thus the phenomenon of lay religious individuals and communities flourished.

Although the masculine category of "beghards" have often been characterized as the counterpart of "beguines," there were significant differences; for instance, men could pursue an itinerant, apostolically inspired life with relative ease compared with women, and although preaching continued to be the right of trained clergy, masculine voices had a better chance of being heard than those of women. Fourteenth-century Church officials periodically targeted such men as heretics, primarily because of their association with "scandalous" mystical ideas; as we will see, clerical authorities would link ideas of unregulated piety with fears of inappropriate sexual freedoms (even though such accusations were almost always spurious).

Women called beguines first appeared on the medieval religious scene in the late twelfth and early thirteenth centuries, emerging as a welcome new model of piety first in the Low Countries and parts of southern Germany. In the words of the noted cardinal, historian, and preacher Jacques de Vitry (writing c. 1230),

> We see many who, scorning the riches of their parents and rejecting the noble and wealthy husbands offered them, live in profound poverty, having naught else but what they can acquire by spinning and working with their hands, content with shabby clothes and modest food.[8]

The model should be familiar now: the apostolic inspiration of a simple life dedicated to chastity, obedience, and adherence to scripture. In contrast to nuns or other formally organized women in orders, groups of lay religious women were not considered "regular" or subject to a particular ecclesiastical rule or way of life. Like so many people inspired by the Gregorian reform, their rule was the Gospel, an apostolically inspired role that was at once both lay *and* religiously inflected; abandoning other means of sustenance, they adhered to communal life and wore special monastic-like garb, yet, like all other laypeople, they lived beyond any established order and were subject to the authority of their local parish priest and secular leaders.

The phenomenon of lay religious women's communities manifested across wide regions and yet was simultaneously highly localized, for different types of communities quickly cropped up across Europe as part of a vibrant new striving among Christian laywomen to live according to the apostolic model of chastity, poverty, and simplicity. They appeared most notably in the cities of the Low Countries, the Rhineland, northern France and Italy, and later, even Spain, but recent research has shown that they were taking root in rural areas as well. Often founded through bequests or charitable donations, the daily routine of beguine houses was generally shaped by house rules designating behavioral, financial, and spiritual expectations. Above all, the women were to live chaste, humble, obedient lives of prayer and service.

Once again, nomenclature or labels are tricky: such women appear in sources not only as "beguines," "*beatas*," "*bizzoche*," and "*pinzochere*," depending upon the region, but also simply as "sister," "poor sister," "poor woman," "holy woman," and sometimes only "virgin" and "widow." Although most of the northern women were single, either unmarried or widowed, many in the southern countries adopted this penitential way of life as married women. Some were old and some young, and some joined for part of their life and then left for marriage, or perhaps returned after a spouse had died. In the early years, many women lived alone or with their families, but more often (particularly by the late thirteenth and fourteenth centuries) they resided in communities that ranged in size regionally from one or two to hundreds.

In the Low Countries, beguines gathered in "courts," extended communities with residences extending, in some cases, to the hundreds. The pious French king Louis IX founded in 1264 a large royal *beguinage*, a communal house of lay religious women in Paris supported by his family and successors through the fourteenth century. In Germany, the model was frequently a household of residents numbering the apostolic twelve, though documents indicate a range from two up to about twenty. Sisters, mothers, and daughters sometimes joined together, whereas other communities were founded specifically for women with no other connections or family.

One of the most important aspects of local interactions was the relationship between lay religious women and the mendicant orders. As early as the

Figure 5.2. Statue of Two Beguines. *Source*: **Photo by Henri Haneveer.**

thirteenth century a large proportion of such women in France, Germany, and northern Italy sought spiritual direction from Franciscans or Dominicans and so were closely related with the penitential confraternities attached to both these orders. As a consequence of this spiritual focus to beguine life, prayer became an activity—a labor—of signal importance to the women and to their lay and clerical supporters: residents of lay religious communities were petitioned or even required in house rules and statutes to pray for their benefactors, and in some houses the daily prayer cycle was structured along lines similar to monastic schedules. Plainly garbed in clothing evocative of nuns' habits, they typically supported themselves and served the town or village through their labor—often weaving, spinning, performing domestic chores such as cleaning and laundry, tending the sick, or caring for the bodies of the deceased before burial.

Because of the women's combination of both active service and contemplative piety service, commentators frequently invoked the story of the sisters of Lazarus in Luke 10:38–42 when discussing lay religious women's piety:

As Jesus and his disciples were on their way, he came to a village where a woman named Martha opened her home to him. She had a sister called Mary, who sat at the Lord's feet listening to what he said. But Martha was distracted by all the preparations that had to be made. She came to him and asked, "Lord,

> don't you care that my sister has left me to do the work by myself? Tell her to help me!" "Martha, Martha," the Lord answered, "you are worried and upset about many things, but only one thing is needed. Mary has chosen what is better, and it will not be taken away from her."

In this passage, Jesus chastises Martha for her domestic busyness and tells her that Mary has the better part, yet among lay religious women, especially in the north, it was the active Martha who seemed most appealing and instructive. Lay religious women, it would seem, sympathized with the practical Martha, who opened her home and labored in service. The mistress of German beguine houses was frequently called a "Martha," for example, and such women were often associated with care for the sick and dying. Encounters with such women would even inspire the learned Dominican Meister Eckhart to develop a novel theological defense of Martha and her active service. Meanwhile, other women and their supporters would develop new understandings of a Christian life that blended the exemplars of both Mary and Martha.

At this point, we can venture a few generalizations: first, these lay religious women were single, either unmarried or widows, who took simple oaths (as opposed to "solemn," or canonically binding), vows to a life of poverty, chastity, humility, and obedience. Second, in the late twelfth and thirteenth centuries, the women tended to be more elite in origin; by the fourteenth and fifteenth centuries, we see a greater number of women who are lower on the social scale joining communities. Finally, there was extensive support and encouragement for this way of life, in some areas from elites and in others from local citizens and clergy. Like so many of the other movements we have studied, these women drew their inspiration from basic apostolic ideals and medieval Christian virtues; nothing in their various ways of life or spiritual claims were theologically unusual or canonically heretical.

Of the many women drawn to the lay religious life between the thirteenth and fifteenth centuries, few seem to have been mystically inclined. Fewer still could and did record their ideas and experiences in written form, but those who did left a stunning corpus of richly evocative vernacular texts. Famous "beguine mystics" such as Marie d'Oignies (1177–1213), Hadewijch of Brabant (mid-thirteenth century), Mechtild of Magdeburg (c. 1210–c. 1285), and Douceline de Digne (1215–1274) each communicated unique visionary experiences and spiritual revelations in her own language; working closely with secular clergy or mendicants, each also received crucial approval from Church authorities for her literary endeavors. None of the beguine mystics mentioned above were ever suspected of heresy, yet their lives and writings were subjected to careful scrutiny. The combination of an approving male mentor and the women's overt willingness to bow to clerical authority were vital elements in their "orthodoxy."

We may contrast their situation with the lay religious *pinzochera* Guglielma of Milan, whose simple yet charismatic spirituality attracted in the mid-thirteenth century a fiercely devoted group of lay followers and several nuns (including one spiritually ambitious Sister Maifreda). Despite her vigorous protests to the contrary, she was identified by her devotees as the incarnation of the Holy Spirit, come to save not only Christians, but pagans, Jews, and Muslims alike. After her death in 1281, a passionate cult grew up around Guglielma's memory, fed by contemporary strains of Joachite thought and apocalypticism. Believers insisted that after "Guglielma's resurrection and ascension, this utopian church would be led by her 'earthly vicar'—none other than Sister Maifreda, the *papessa* of the age to come."[9] Unsurprisingly, the circle of some dozens of male and female followers was eventually unraveled by Dominican inquisitors in 1300, and several, including Maifreda, eventually went to the stake. Based on confessions extracted under force, Guglielma was posthumously found guilty of heresy; inquisitors destroyed her tomb, burned her bones, and scattered her ashes along with those of her followers' writings. If locating the joining of heaven and earth in a single human man was heretical, how much more was the Guglielmites' loyal insistence that divinity, femaleness, and the lay religious life were not mutually exclusive.

Mounting concerns about lay piety and the growing establishment of inquisitorial procedures in the late thirteenth and early fourteenth centuries hardened concern about the distinction between "good" and "bad" beguines. Even the final arbiter of heresy, the papal office, could not conclusively decide where the division lay. The intersection of lay religious women's piety, questions of spiritual authority, and antiheretical legislation mark a rich site for exploring the ambiguities and possibilities of trying to live the Gospel in the world—particularly for women, who had no apostolic model of their own.

THE PROBLEM

If lay religious women's ideals of chastity, poverty, simplicity, and service were not in themselves controversial, and early beguine mystics such as Hadewijch and Mechtild were approved by the proper authorities, what was the problem? By the end of the thirteenth century, the crux of the matter lay once again in the questions of *who* possessed the right to enact apostolic and mystical ideals and what the proper method was of demonstrating authority to speak. Medieval clerical and lay leaders strove for centuries to maintain proper order, that fixed hierarchy of regulated estates and roles, in which women's place was scrupulously circumscribed. The seal of approval from an admiring male cleric and institutional authority such as Jacques de Vitry certainly bolstered one's claims. But as one mid-thirteenth century wit and critic of lay religious women put it,

This art arose only yesterday
Among the women of Brabant and Bavaria.
What kind of art can it be, Lord God,
If old women are more skilled in it than wise and learned men?[10]

As single women of any age, lay religious women in community were grudgingly granted only minimal social space and identity, and even that could be construed by clergy as sexually dangerous because of their proximity to male confessors or men in the secular sphere. Ecclesiastical authorities feared that lay sisterhoods would become a sexually charged presence in European cities, even though most remained entirely uncontroversial or even deeply supported by local communities. As specifically Christian women, moreover, whom the Church typically sought to channel into the irrevocable institutions of either marriage or monasticism, beguines represented to some an alarmingly unauthorized and disturbingly temporary way of life. In fact, due to the medieval concern for female sexual purity and its powerful cultural significance, such women were disparagingly associated with prostitutes, the only other publicly visible nonmonastic community of single women. Thus pious women were vulnerable to the damning cultural charge of hypocrisy, of being promiscuous "women on the loose."[11]

By the mid-thirteenth century, critics had begun to perceive beguines as the antithesis of the increasingly organized and administratively centralized monastic orders and were particularly upset by the women's apparent lack of regulated supervision. Ridiculing their false piety and pretense, their detractors turned their way of life into a joke and the name itself into a smear word. Jacques de Vitry explained it this way:

If a young maiden wishes to preserve her virginity and her parents offer her a wealthy suitor in marriage, she despises and rejects him . . . but secular prelates and other malicious men try to destroy her and convince her to give up her sacred purpose; they say: "Look, she wishes to be a *beguina*" (because that is what they call them in Flanders and Brabant), or *papelarda* (that is what they call them in France), or *Humiliate* (their name in Lombardy), or *bizoke* (their name in Italy), or *coquenunne* (as they are called in Germany). It is with such nicknames and insults that they intended to dissuade them from pursuing a life of purity.[12]

Clearly the rhetoric resonated across multiple regions and languages, and it grew more hostile as time passed. Clerical language equating lay religious women with "a pernicious sort of woman" had long been in play, as had a deep sense that the difference between their pious communities and whorehouses was more a matter of degree than of kind.[13] In other words, a community of women without husbands or a binding religious rule for protection were viewed as little better than a brothel.

From the secular side, a French poet and contemporary of the cardinal wrote a biting commentary that neatly encapsulates uncharitable stereotypes about such women:

> Whatever a beguine says, listen only to what is good. All that happens in her life is religious. Her speech is prophecy; if she laughs, it is good companionship; if she cries, it is out of devotion; . . . if she has a dream, it is a vision . . . if a beguine marries, that is her vocation, because her vows or profession are not for life. Last year she wept, now she prays, next year she'll take a husband. Now she is Martha, then she is Mary; now she is chaste, then she gets a husband.[14]

Referring to the thriving royal beguine house of Paris founded by Louis IX, he scathingly concludes, "But remember: say only good things of her because the King would not tolerate otherwise." On the other hand, Parisian churchmen and university scholars who preached to and interacted with the beguines drew on their example in their sermons and writings, employing them variously as models of humble piety and mystic spirituality or of hypocrisy and obstinance.[15]

Why were these lay religious women so troubling and such easy targets for mockery and abuse when their lives were rooted in a pious model? There are three factors. First, there was their unofficial status. As a Franciscan friar complained around 1274, "There are among us women whom we have no idea what to call, ordinary women or nuns, because they live neither in the world nor out of it."[16] Of particular concern was the women's legal status: having taken no permanent monastic vows, their life situation was theoretically open-ended and flexible: they could leave to marry if they chose and thus inhabited an ambiguous location between the secular and religious, between the contemplative and active. Second was the concern about hypocrisy, of "false seeming." Thinkers in the Middle Ages were deeply worried about the possibility that one was not what she seemed, and given medieval assumptions about the inherent depravity of females and the impossibility of retaining purity without direct supervision, beguines were mocked as two-faced liars and insufferable religious hypocrites. Third was the notion of female sexual aggression, which was certainly connected to the fear of such women as lying hypocrites. In the allegorical poem *The Romance of the Rose*, the characters of Constrained Abstinence and her companion False Seeming formulate a cunning plan to pass themselves off as pious pilgrims as a disguise for nefarious deeds: "At once Constrained Abstinence donned a robe of cameline and dressed as a beguine, covering her head with a large kerchief and a white cloth. She did not forget her psalter, and she had beads [paternosters] hanging on a white thread . . . a friar had given them to her." After suggesting that the friar was her father, her lover, or both, the author turns a venomous pen to the beguine:

> I would describe her as having a fine figure, but her face was a little pale. Wanton bitch, she was like the horse in the Apocalypse that signifies the wicked people, pale and stained with hypocrisy, for that horse has no colour but a deathly pallor, and Abstinence was coloured with that same sickly hue. Her face suggested that she repented of her state. Fraud had given her a pilgrim's staff of theft, darkened with somber smoke, and her scrip was full of cares.[17]

The vile pseudopilgrim and her vicious companion, False Seeming, proceed from this point on a murderous "pilgrimage." Of particular importance, however, is that the beguine's sin is not simply lustfulness but the even greater medieval crime of duplicity; associated with False Seeming, she claims to be that which she is not. Evidently the stereotype resonated sufficiently among popular imagination so as to be recognizable, even if it bore little resemblance to one's own personal knowledge of individual sisters. And thus cultural anxieties about unbridled female sexuality, hypocritical women, and inappropriate spiritual authority continued to brew, even as lay religious houses took welcome root in communities across Europe.

Readers might justifiably wonder what any of this has to do with heretical mysticism, so let me explain: Marguerite Porete, the woman executed in Paris in 1310, was by all accounts a beguine—whatever might have been meant by that term, she was probably not itinerant, and likely associated with the beguinage of St. Elizabeth's at Valenciennes. In fact, we might consider her the next generation of the literary-mystical virtuosae of the thirteenth century mentioned above, though much had changed by the time her book circulated. Her trial and execution thus represented a precise moment in the history of medieval heresy and inquisition, an opening salvo in the Church's burgeoning anxiety about the intersection of mysticism, female piety, and clerical control in the later Middle Ages. Marguerite's condemnation as a "false woman" and relapsed heretic must be understood within this context, as should the Church's ensuing attempt to regulate lay religious women.

MARGUERITE PORETE AND *THE MIRROR OF SIMPLE SOULS*

As is so often the case with medieval figures, there is much we do not know about Marguerite Porete's life. From clues in ecclesiastical records and her own writings, we know that she came from the county of Hainault, perhaps the vicinity of Valenciennes itself.[18] Although her date of birth is unknown, a reasonable guess would put it between 1250 and 1270, making her about fifty years old when her book first drew the critical eye of Guy II of Colmieu, the bishop of Cambrai. Analysis of her book reveals that she was remarkably well educated and was probably of either lower noble or wealthy urban origins; clearly enjoying access to expensive writing materials and books, she wrote with an aristocratic style and courtly vocabulary that would have resonated among educated circles of her day. Moreover, her vernacular literacy may also have been supplemented with knowledge of Latin as well: modern scholars have found in her work traces not only of scripture, but also of Augustine, Bernard of Clairvaux, Bonaventure, Richard of St. Victor, William of St. Thierry, and Pseudo-Dionysius. We cannot know where Marguerite obtained her unusual education, though scholars have recently begun to pay attention to the pedagogical role of lay religious women's communities, particularly teaching young girls. Given her likely contacts with the sisters of St. Elizabeth's, she probably also had acquaintances among wider circles of independent lay religious within and beyond the city. Opponents would repeatedly refer to her efforts to circulate the book among a broad swath of simple people; the aristocratic beguine was clearly no literary or spiritual snob.

Composed in Old French sometime between 1296 and 1306, *The Mirror of Simple Souls* was both a treatise and a handbook for guiding Christians on their spiritual journey. Following a popular medieval literary convention, she wrote it in the form of a courtly dialogue between many voices, including Love, Reason, and the Soul. In the 140 chapters of the book, she combines prose, poetry, and vivid metaphors to map her understanding of the soul's seven-stage journey to God. Although no excerpt can hope to do justice to the complexity of her ideas, the following is a sample of the flavor and shape of Marguerite's text:

> I have promised, says this Soul, to say something of the seven states which we call states of being, after Love has come and taken hold; and states of being they are. And they are the steps by which one climbs from the valley to the summit of the mountain, which is so isolated that one sees nothing there but God; and at each step is found the corresponding state of being.[19]

Of these seven stages, loving and blissful union with God is only the fourth; Marguerite extends the Soul's divine experience further than most other mystics, for whom ecstatic divine union consummates and thus concludes the human search for God. In the fifth stage, she continues,

> Now this Soul has fallen from love into nothingness . . . and this fall has been so low, if she falls as she should, that the Soul is not able to raise herself up again from such an abyss; nor must she do this, but rather remain where she is. And there the Soul loses her pride and her girlishness, for . . . her will has left her, which often, when she felt the stirrings of love, made her proud and overweening and fastidious, when she was exalted in contemplation in the fourth state. But the fifth state has subdued her in showing to the Soul her own self.[20]

In this painful and desolate stage, the Soul must die to herself, accepting the utter evacuation of self and human will.

Only through this annihilation of self in the fifth stage can a soul be perfected, emptied, and prepared to receive the divine: "The sixth state is when the Soul does not see herself at all . . . but God of his divine majesty sees himself in her, and by him this Soul is so illumined." Desolation, emptiness, and the abyss of annihilation are thus necessary preconditions of an inconceivably more rapturous joining with God than that of the human love of stage four: "And therefore this Soul knows nothing except him, and loves nothing except him, and praises nothing except him, for there is nothing but he. . . . And so there is no one except Him Who Is, and who sees himself . . . in such a creature."[21] Marguerite's summary of the seventh stage is both concise and oblique: "And the seventh state Love keeps within herself, to give to us in everlasting glory, of which we shall have no knowledge until our souls shall have left our bodies."[22]

If, as we saw earlier, medieval authorities had no problem with the wildly erotic love imagery of earlier mystics, why did they react so strongly to Marguerite's book? Put briefly, the answer lies in passages such as the following:

> This [annihilated] Soul no longer has any sentiment of grace, nor desire of spirit, *since she has taken leave of the Virtues* who offer the manner of living well to every good soul, and without these Virtues none can be saved nor come to perfection of life. . . . Is she not out of her mind, the Soul who speaks thus? [emphasis added][23]

Marguerite's suggestion that the annihilated soul would bid farewell to virtue was a red flag to inquisitors; it smacked of antinomianism, the terrifying prospect of unregulated sexual decadence in the name of spiritual freedom.

Marguerite, however, was no libertine and certainly did not advocate the abandonment of virtue. Her assertion that the liberated soul gave "to nature, without remorse, all that it asks" is qualified with the statement that nature "does not demand anything prohibited" of the liberated soul. Virtues, like sins, like will, like the self, are abandoned in the process, all remnants of the distracting and ultimately unreal material realm. According to Marguerite (and many other mystically inclined thinkers who had made similar claims), virtues are no longer necessary *because the liberated soul no longer needs such relatively artificial guides to reach God*; it is in the sixth stage, after all, fully illuminated by divine presence itself. Her opponents, however, were disinclined to grant the theological leeway demanded by the sophisticated text. Sometime in the first years of the fourteenth century, the bishop of Cambrai commanded her to stop circulating the book and had it publicly burned. In 1308, she was arrested again for spreading heresy and shipped to Paris. There she faced an inquisitorial board led by the formidable Dominican William of Paris, confessor to King Philip the Fair (the king simultaneously preoccupied with the Knights Templar). A panel of theologians analyzed the book and labeled thirteen extracts as heretical.

Lifting passages out of context to accuse her of wantonness, they claimed that she spread the wicked idea that a liberated soul was no longer subject to moral codes and could behave in any licentious way it desired. Accusations of antinomianism had also been hurled at the earliest Gnostics, but they were vastly more damaging when flung at an unmarried, independent, and evidently intelligent woman of the early fourteenth century. Central to her condemnation were two additional factors: her refusal to speak to inquisitors and her alleged distribution of the book among unlettered and vulnerable people. This book about simple souls was most emphatically not a book for simple minds. Marguerite herself acknowledged that it might be misunderstood, which makes it all the more surprising that she seems never to have uttered a word of explanation or defense to the inquisitorial forces soon arrayed against her.

Because of her earlier conviction in Cambrai, this second condemnation meant relapse and thus brought with it the sentence of death at the stake for heresy. Yet what might at first glance appear a straightforward case of heresy (an unlicensed female spreading antinomian error) was anything but. Marguerite's fate was surely shaped by the complex historical circumstances of her day, the various spiritual pressure points and authoritative fault lines that intersected at the Place de Grève in 1310.

ANTI-BEGUINE DECREES (1311–1312, 1317)

During the first decade of the fourteenth century, as you will recall from chapter 4, King Philip IV of France was busy intimidating Pope Boniface VIII, encouraging the papal shift from Rome to Avignon in 1305, and plotting the financially lucrative downfall of the Knights Templar. In fact, the primary act of the Council of Vienne (1311–1312) was Pope Clement V's royally induced withdrawal of support from the Templars. Nonetheless, a number of other issues were also debated at the council, including the place and orthodoxy of "beguines," a conversation evidently influenced by the Marguerite Porete trial. Two decrees seemingly directed against lay religious women, *Cum de quibusdam mulieribus* (*Since Certain Women*) and *Ad nostrum* (*We Have Heard*), were circulated in 1317 and opened a formal but confusing attack upon such sisterhoods. Why the confusion? Because no one could agree upon how to distinguish between a "good" beguine and a "bad" beguine. A "good" beguine was exactly the kind of chaste, obedient, humble Christian woman that the Church wanted to encourage, but because "bad" beguines looked very much like them, it became a tricky matter indeed to discern true goodness from the hypocritical semblance of goodness.

The decree *Cum de quibusdam* opened by referring to "certain women commonly known as beguines" who "neither promise obedience to anyone, nor renounce personal property, nor profess any approved rule, they are by no means considered religious, although they wear a so-called beguine habit and attach themselves to certain religious to whom they are drawn by special affection."[24] At the heart of the decree was the accusation that

> some of them, as if having been led into insanity, dispute and preach about the highest Trinity and the divine essence and introduce opinions contrary to the catholic faith . . . they lead many simple people who are deceived in such things into various errors, and they do and commit much else under the veil of sanctity.

Note that the heresy here is not the beguine way of life, but rather the women's alleged preaching and teaching of errors to simple people. Hypocrisy, that old charge against females who appear holy, is also stirred into the mix, a potent ingredient in the attack upon "beguines"—women who *look* like nuns but were not what they appeared.

The decree also assigned penalties for such suspect forms of life: "We expressly enjoin upon these and all other women under pain of excommunication . . . that they no longer follow this way of life in any way whatsoever." By "this way of life," one might presume that the entire beguine status is implied. Yet the document concludes in a surprising fashion:

> Of course by the preceding we in no way intend to forbid any faithful women, whether or not they promise chastity, from living honestly in their dwellings, doing penance, and serving the Lord in a spirit of humility, this being allowed to them as the Lord inspires them.[25]

The decree thus provides an escape clause for "good" beguines and a direct acknowledgment that female lay religious did not in themselves constitute a heresy. Pope John XXII, the pontiff responsible for the text, was evidently interested in safeguarding "orthodox" beguines. Both categories, of course, were artificially manufactured by Church officials, as no evidence of unusual ideas or practices among lay religious women exists.

Nonetheless, ambiguity and anxiety characterized early fourteenth-century attitudes toward lay religious communities, perhaps best illustrated by *Ad nostrum*, which circulated simultaneously with *Cum de quibusdam*. Targeting the "abominable sect of malignant men known as beghards and faithless women known as beguines in the Kingdom of Germany,"[26] *Ad nostrum* focused upon doctrinal rather than organizational issues and accused beguines of eight doctrinal errors. These included the beliefs that man becomes incapable of sin once attaining a certain degree of perfection; that prayer, fasts, and other forms of religious observance are superfluous to one in such a perfected state; and that such a person is so close to God that he need not subordinate himself to human or Church law because "where the spirit of the Lord is, there is Liberty" (2 Corinthians 3:17). If these tenets sound familiar, it is because they explicitly parrot the condemned extracts lifted from Marguerite's *Mirror*, combining them with spurious and decades-old reports from the German-speaking Rhineland region. And thus was the "heresy of the Free Spirit" brought into being, not by dissenting communities or charismatic preachers but rather by the very institution that sought to eradicate them. All evidence suggests that ecclesiastical fears rather than any real dissent or overreaching of spiritual bounds were responsible for the decrees and persecutions to come.

Ad nostrum became the touchstone for ensuing antiheretical pronouncements against what came to be seen as increasingly dangerous forms of mysticism. To use Lerner's phrase, it was the "birth certificate" of the heresy of the Free Spirit, though "it may have been an example of a birth certificate without a baby" because there is no evidence for an actual movement of libertine heretics.[27] By fall of 1317, lay religious women were beginning to be harassed in northern Europe. A synod of Mainz excommunicated in 1318 all women who could be considered beguines by status, habit, name, or any other means. A Franciscan chronicle in Strasbourg in 1318 recorded in horror that many German clerics (evidently not attentive to John's escape clause in *Cum de quibusdam*) were forcing pious women to give up their penitential clothes, revoke their vows of chastity, and return to the world; moreover, they were forcing members of the Franciscan Third Order to do the same. The Franciscans did not question the validity of suppressing laywomen's communities that followed no approved rule but, outraged at the treatment of their tertiaries, insisted that *Cum de quibusdam* exempted pious women who lived in houses and served the Lord in a spirit of humility.

John's response later that year (1318) was to issue another decretal, *Ratio recta* (*Right Judgment*). He was simultaneously preoccupied with the matter of Spiritual Franciscans and their followers, and no doubt the two issues appeared to him as part of a broader heretical attack upon Christendom and his pontificate in particular. In *Ratio recta*, he ordered the clergy to protect all beguines leading stable lives, women who did not dispute about the Trinity, divine essence, or sacraments of the Church. It was, in effect, an extension of the final section of *Cum de quibusdam*, but he was careful to add that these concessions did not mean that the beguines were an approved order (Innocent III had prohibited new orders in 1215, and the women took no oaths to follow a formal ecclesiastical rule). Moreover, John continued to support the search for heretics among them. So we are back where we started, with "good" and "bad" beguines and the apparent ambivalence of their vocation. Most were, of course, not mystics but rather the simple people whom Marguerite, and later Meister Eckhart, would be accused of misleading. In an era that powerfully defined feminine identity and status in black-and-white terms—married or single, religious or lay, regulated or unregulated—the ambiguous, flexible space inhabited by such women left them vulnerable to the old smears of promiscuity and heresy. Perhaps surprisingly, it was not that they were marginal but that they were in fact deeply connected that made them lightning rods for criticism, satisfying proxies through which male clergy could lash out against their enemies. It was this, more than any actual heresy, that provoked decrees and against beguines, tertiaries, and other female lay religious in the fourteenth century.

MEISTER ECKHART AND THE RHINELAND MYSTICS (1260–1328)

Before considering the inquisitorial response to lay religious women later in the century, however, let us first consider a vibrant strand of mysticism entwined with gender and heresy: the scholarly career and pastoral contributions of the Dominican theologian Meister Eckhart within the powerful ecclesiastical provinces of Strasbourg and Cologne. Although influenced by developments in and beyond Paris, it was in the German Rhineland that Eckhart preached to rapt audiences, mentored and interacted with lay religious women, and developed a mystical theology, key tenets of which would be condemned as heretical by Pope John XXII in 1329.

Born in Thuringia in 1260, the young Eckhart von Hochheim followed a well-trodden path for bright boys of his age and entered the Dominican Order, where he first learned Latin grammar and the liberal arts. Eckhart was clearly a capable student with a sharp mind and was sent for higher education to the Dominican school at Cologne, founded in 1248 by the great German theologian Albertus Magnus (Albert the Great). Albert had been a teacher of Thomas Aquinas himself at the University of Paris, and Eckhart would soon follow that path to Paris, the center of the Western intellectual world. It was a great honor to be selected to teach at Paris, and the young Eckhart was undoubtedly a rising star within the order. In 1286, Eckhart began his career involvement with the University of Paris—first as a student, then as master of theology and professor in 1302–1303. The academic title "Meister" was added to his name at this point. After a long stint as head of the new Dominican province of Saxony from 1303 to 1311, Eckhart returned to Paris to teach in 1311–1312.

These early years of the fourteenth century were tumultuous times, and Eckhart was certainly affected by the controversies in the air. Tension between pope and king had erupted with the assault upon and subsequent death of Boniface VIII, and contemporaries worried about the increasingly close relationship between the new Avignon papacy and the French monarchy. When Eckhart returned to Paris in 1311, King Philip IV was vigorously pursuing his case against the Knights Templar; Marguerite's trial and execution were still recent news; and the friary of St. Jacques, where Eckhart was staying, also housed one of the theologians who had sniffed out heresy in Marguerite's *Mirror*. It is very likely that Eckhart heard of her writings and ideas in Paris through his Dominican connections and that he had the opportunity to reflect on them at length before returning to the Rhineland. From 1314 to 1322, he preached to Dominican convents in Strasbourg; from 1323 on, he was preaching and teaching back in Cologne. During this vital juncture of vibrant lay piety, fierce antiheretical activity, percolating urban culture, and religiopolitical disarray, Eckhart's message of spiritual transformation through scriptural content and soulful detachment resonated powerfully with lay and monastic followers alike. Worlds apart in terms of the highly gendered and hierarchical social order, Eckhart and Marguerite nonetheless shared a distinct spiritual point of view—one not only focused upon the soul's journey to God but expressed in the native tongue and available to all souls.

An accomplished academic theologian, Eckhart was remarkable for his unusual use of the German vernacular in the bold and lively sermons he delivered to Rhineland communities. A prolific writer, he left a vast collection of treatises, books, and sermons in both Latin and German united by the common emphasis on scripture and the revelation of truth through the Word of God. Fundamental for Eckhart was the sense of alignment between scriptural revelation and the truths discoverable by reason. In his eyes, there was no conflict between intellect and revelation; instead, philosophy was his key to unlocking divine mysteries.

What qualifies him as one of the most influential Christian mystics, however, is his emphasis upon union with God within the soul. Key to his German sermons is the idea that God is present in the individual soul, and that one may come to recognize that presence through the practice of detachment. Uninterested in special or altered states of being, of rapture, Eckhart mocked those who "want to see God with the same eyes with which they behold a cow."[28] Rather, it is the birth of that word in the human soul that is union for Eckhart, the breaking through of the soul to God. He writes that

> when we turn away from ourselves and from all created things [detachment], to that extent we are united and sanctified in the soul's spark, which is untouched by either space or time. This spark is opposed to all creatures and desires nothing but God. . . . He who lives in the goodness of his nature lives in God's love; and love has no why. It is proper to God that He has no "why" outside or beyond Himself. Therefore, every work that has a "why" as such is not a divine work or done for God. There will be no divine work if a person does something that is not for God's sake, because it will have a "why"—something that is foreign to God and far from God. It is not God or godly.[29]

At the end of the mystical journey is a still heart and mind detached from the cares of "why," no longer seeking and wondering, but finally at infinite rest within the divine. All of this sounds very abstract and perhaps marginal to the question of how to live as a Christian in the world. Yet Eckhart also believed that the divine word and the soul's progress toward detachment were deeply integrated into the mundane details of human existence. It is a message that would certainly appeal to pious laywomen seeking spiritual satisfaction within their own local or domestic communities.

In his sermon 86, moreover, Eckhart expounds a novel understanding of the Martha and Mary story that inverts traditional approaches in an intriguing way. Instead of privileging Mary's contemplative role, Eckhart praises the spiritual maturity of Martha's labors *within* the mundane and the groundedness that her experience afforded her. Neither distracted nor hindered by the lived demands of her circumstance, Martha thus represents for Eckhart a noble detachment through which she could accomplish necessary activity *and* spiritual growth. In contrast, the rapt Mary at Christ's feet was, as Martha feared, at risk of losing herself to the unsustainable and passive bliss of spiritual satisfaction. Life in the world demands work, and for Eckhart, such efforts bore a significant meaning for individuals grappling with their place in God's universe.

Eckhart's emphasis on Martha should therefore not be read as a hierarchical preference for active over contemplative piety, but rather as an expression of his keen familiarity with the various pitfalls of spiritual life in the world. In the sermon's conclusion, Eckhart relates "that Mary eventually becomes a true servant, working and living 'without a why,' a joyful example of the 'living union' and harmonious continuity between the active and the contemplative life in Eckhart's mysticism."[30]

Like that of so many of his early fourteenth-century contemporaries, Eckhart's thought was intertwined with the spiritual concept of poverty, that fundamental theme in medieval piety that had proven such a fraught issue for the Franciscan Order. For Eckhart, however, true poverty means the utter abandonment of will—even, paradoxically, the will to follow God. Here he seems to evoke Marguerite's theory of the annihilated soul:

> If then, I were asked what is a poor person who wants nothing, I should reply as follows. As long as a person is so disposed that it is his will with which he would do the most beloved will of God, that person has not the poverty we are speaking about: for that person has a will to serve God's will—and that is not true poverty! . . . For I declare by the eternal truth, as long as you have the will to do the will of God, and longing for eternity and God, you are not poor: for a poor person is one who wills nothing and desires nothing.[31]

Acknowledging the difficulty of the concept, Eckhart reassures the reader, "But you do not need to understand this."

During this decade following the trial of Marguerite and the Council of Vienne, fear of Free Spirit heresy grew strong in the Rhineland cities of Mainz, Cologne, Strasbourg, and Basel. In 1317, for example, the bishop of Strasbourg investigated errors of "those whom the crowd calls beghards and 'bread-for-God' sisters . . . and who call themselves children, or brothers and sisters, of the Free Spirit and of voluntary poverty."[32] It was in this context that the first campaigns against Meister Eckhart began in Cologne, at the instigation of staunchly antiheretical Archbishop Henry II. One of the seven electors of the empire and a powerful territorial prince in his own right, the archbishop was a significant opponent of the theologian. In the summer of 1326, he gathered at least two lists of suspect beliefs extracted from Eckhart's writings and sermons and launched an inquisitorial proceeding against the theologian. In 1327, inquisitors pronounced his ideas heretical.

Eckhart vigorously denied the accusations and, with the support of the local Dominicans, appealed to the pope for support. In both public and trial forums, he asserted his innocence and willingness to recant any errors.

Unlike Marguerite, therefore, Eckhart deferred to ecclesiastical authority and signaled his intent to cooperate. Papal commissions were appointed to investigate the accusations filed against him, and Eckhart personally defended himself late in 1327 and may even have still been in Avignon when he died in January of 1328. He never accepted the Church's judgment that the ideas *themselves* were unorthodox. Pope John XXII, however, disagreed with the theologian. In March 1329, he issued the bull *In agro dominico* (*In the Field of the Lord*), condemning fifteen articles from Meister Eckhart's work as heretical; the additional eleven were characterized as "evil-sounding, rash, and suspect of heresy."[33]

For example, article 8 reads, "Those people honor God who do not look for possessions, nor honors, nor usefulness, *nor internal devotion, nor sanctity, nor reward, nor the kingdom of heaven*, but who renounce all these"; article 10 included the claim that "we are being totally transformed into God and converted into him. Just as in the sacrament the bread is converted into Christ's body, so in a similar way I am converted into him, because *he makes me his one being and not just similar to him. By the living God it is true that there is no distinction*"; article 14 posited that "a good person ought to so conform his will to God's will that he wills whatever God wills. *Because God wills me to have committed sin in some way, I should not will that I had not committed sin*. This is true penance" [emphases added].[34] Lifted out of their theologically sophisticated context, Eckhart's statements do sound antinomian, anticlerical, and generally alarming, as do those of Marguerite—particularly to the ears of one anxious about rumors of spiritually willful libertines on the loose.

However, the bull concluded with the acknowledgment that Eckhart was no conscious heretic, as he "professed the Catholic faith at the end of his life and revoked and also deplored the twenty-six articles which he admitted that he had preached . . . insofar as they could generate in the minds of the faithful a heretical opinion, or one erroneous and hostile to true faith."[35] As a trained Dominican preacher and renowned scholar, Meister Eckhart possessed all of the cultural privilege and voice denied to a laywoman such as Marguerite, yet his writings and interactions underscore the extent to which their worlds were not as clearly delineated in practice as in theory. Eckhart drew inspiration from the same spiritual well as beguine mystics, preached and tended to devout laymen and laywomen inspired by his words, and even wrote in the German vernacular for their benefit.

Had Eckhart only written in Latin, thus restricting the circulation of his works to highly educated circles, it is doubtful that they would have been so censured. Indeed, John was particularly infuriated by Eckhart's public preaching of these ideas to simple people or "the uneducated crowd" and held him accountable for "many dogmatic pronouncements that clouded the true faith in the hearts of many."[36] The pope thus circulated the news broadly within the Rhineland to ensure that any possible adherents of the theologian's more controversial ideas would be tarred with heresy. Two of Eckhart's young disciples, John Tauler and Heinrich Suso, carefully avoided any of the errors attributed to their master and thus avoided suspicion of heresy; by the mid-fourteenth century, each had added rich new material to the growing body of Rhineland mysticism begun centuries earlier by Hildegard of Bingen.

Several attempts have been made to clear Eckhart's name in recent decades, and he is generally now regarded as a great scholar of the Church. In 1985, Pope John Paul II queried, "Did not Eckhart teach his disciplines: 'All that God asks you most pressingly is to go out of yourself—and let God be God in you?'" In fact, in recent years, scholars have determined that both committees that found him guilty of heresy were not themselves aware that great Church fathers such as St. Augustine had already stated many of Eckhart's most objectionable ideas, or if they were aware, it was not enough to win their approval. For instance, one condemned statement read: "A good person ought to so conform his will to God's will that he wills whatever God wills. *Because God wills me to have committed sin in some way, I should not will that I had not committed sin*. This is true penance." Eckhart supported his claim by quoting St. Paul—"All things work together for good," to which St. Augustine had added, "Yes, even sins."[37] But in an age abounding with lay religious movements claiming apostolic purity and rejecting sacraments and the clergy, alarms sounded. In the eyes of the clergy, the claim that God somehow wills sin and that humans should not wish otherwise was a perversion that threatened to undermine the entire penitential structure of Christendom.

ANTI-BEGUINE PRESSURE IN THE FOURTEENTH CENTURY

With these papal decrees in place, episcopal and papal inquisitors initiated periodic waves of persecutions across the fourteenth century, although their frequency and significance (particularly in German-speaking lands) seem to be considerably less than once thought. In 1318, for example, the bishop of Strasbourg initiated a persecutory campaign in his diocese, a process that left behind a substantial number of records regarding perceptions of bad beguines and Free Spirits. As is generally the case with inquisitorial records, they offer a list of tenets culled from examinations, and they are "rich in scandalous propositions" far exceeding the details from the Vienne decrees. Were the people of this community really uttering such outrageous statements—for example, that they could have adulterous sex without consequence and that the sacraments were useless? It is very unlikely, not least because what made them stand out initially in their local community was their pious life. So where did the ideas come from?

One source was the texts themselves, which inquisitors used as tools and guides when interrogating the accused. Inquisitors could suggest tenets or gather ideas from the handbooks and cobble together a profile of a beguine "heretic" that bore little relationship to the actual point of view and ideas of the person being questioned. Only certain questions were asked, and the framework was imposed on them rather than built anew in each context. Students of heresy must always remember that the most consistent and frequent accusations are probably the most untrue: repetition does not constitute reliability.

In another example, lay religious women were examined for heresy in Magdeburg in 1334. According to a chronicle source, the women blasphemed against Christ and the saints in ways so horrific that the chronicler piously claimed that he could not bring himself to record them. Having gathered himself sufficiently to continue, however, he records that they repented and were immediately released without penalties. What was their heresy? The chronicler provides a clue when he says they described themselves as "of the high spirit," a phrase that suggests at worst spiritual arrogance and criticism of preachers for not being high or holy enough—uppity, in other words, though this is hardly the same as blaspheming against Christ. Bishops across the Low Countries and Germany conducted similar kinds of trials, drawing on local inquisitors and their own staff to weed out the "good" from the "bad" and to impose more stringent regulations upon the communities.

Inquisitions into beguine "depravity" were shaped far more by local personalities and pressures than by any coordinated effort among inquisitors. To the Bohemian southeast, between 1335 and 1355, the Dominican Gallus of Neuhaus interrogated thousands of people, consigning many hundreds to the stake for heresy—including beguines, although it is impossible to offer precise figures. Men called "beghards" and long presumed to be a kind of beguine equivalent often came under inquisitorial scrutiny as well during this period, though the masculine privilege of mobility certainly cast them in a familiar model of "wandering libertine preachers" akin to those encountered in the twelfth and thirteenth centuries. Executions did occur, though more groups were silenced or expelled from cities due to the conflation of their claimed piety with other "heretical" movements or unpopular groups.[38] In Basel at the beginning of the fourteenth century, for example, lay religious women (mostly Franciscan tertiaries) became caught in the rivalry between Dominican and Franciscan friars due to tangled interpretations of poverty and who bore the right to live poor in the world.[39] Papal interventions achieved only confusion until the women were finally expelled from the city some years later and their property confiscated.

Apparently, however, there were protests as well. In 1377, Pope Gregory XI stepped into the fray to support "good" beguines who were not the dreaded Free Spirits in yet another bull, *Ad audientam nostrum* (*It Has Come to Our Ears*). He carefully avoided the label "*beguine*," which had now become a smear word, and referred to them simply as "poor people" who had pure faith, and he ordered episcopal and papal inquisitors to leave them alone. As long as the women were orthodox, they should be protected; if they were not, the persecutions were appropriate. Back to square one: Gregory XI had just arrived at the same impasse that faced John XXII a half century earlier: What is a "good" beguine, and how is a pious Christian woman to live in the world? His solution was no more enduring than his predecessor's. In 1395, the next pope effected an about-face and issued a hostile bull against lay religious women, *Sedis apostolice* (*Of the Apostolic See*), which launched yet another wave of sporadic pressure through the early fifteenth century.

Thus, across the later Middle Ages, lay religious women and those accused of Free Spirit heresy were occasionally persecuted and sometimes burned, even as their sisters and brothers in other regions—or even neighboring communities—lived the same lives without controversy or criticism. In some areas, secular clergy led the criticism, usually where beguine connections with mendicants were strong. In others, feuding groups of regular clergy variously attacked each other and drew beguine communities into the fray, as in Basel, where the rivalry was between Dominican and Franciscan friars. Other related communities, such as the brothers and sisters of the Common Life in the Low Countries (or the Modern-Day Devout, as they were also known), also came under scrutiny, forced to articulate their orthodoxy and defend their way of life to increasingly suspicious authorities.[40] Responses to the Vienne decrees varied tremendously over time and place, but recent work indicates that there was more ink than blood spilled on the matter of beguines. The effects of this shifting legislation and occasional pressures on lay religious women were as wide-ranging as their chosen lifestyles, but nowhere did it actually involve the kind of intense persecution suffered (for example) by the accused Good Christians or "Cathars" of southern France in the twelfth century or by the communities of Waldensians executed in late fourteenth-century Germany.

In fact, beguine foundations seem to have actually increased in the fourteenth century, particularly those funded by widows and lay couples, a fact obscured by a shift away from the term "beguine." In late medieval Würzburg, for example, people from both the secular and religious spheres simply stopped calling their many lay religious women beguines after 1320, employing instead the more neutral language of "spiritual women," "holy women," "virgins," or "widows" as they continued to found communities. Although the language changed, the women's gatherings and way of life did not. It was an elegant, if largely unconscious, solution to the problem of broad ecclesiastical pronouncements against locally appreciated and supported women.

By the time of the Council of Constance in 1415, papal and episcopal attention had turned to other, more apparently pressing concerns such as ending the papal schism. It is worth noting, however, that lay religious women's communities played an important role in fourteenth- and fifteenth-century Bohemian reform, as they did in fifteenth-century religious reforms across Christendom. In some places by the sixteenth century, communities had transformed largely into poorhouses and civic associations; yet others maintained their status, melded with the mendicant orders, or developed other alternative forms of life. Despite ecclesiastical pressure, such sisterhoods continued through and beyond the fifteenth century, adapting and reconstituting themselves to meet changing local conditions.[41]

POLITICAL MYSTICISM AND HERESY IN THE FIFTEENTH CENTURY

By the early years of the fifteenth century, clerical rhetoric against beguines and libertine mysticism had quieted. Indeed, the spiritual claims of famous visionaries such as Bridgette of Sweden, Catherine of Siena, and Julian of Norwich had earned them significant moral and political authority within Christendom (though always with the prior approval of a clerical male mentor or spiritual companion). Yet leading theologians such as Jean Gerson and Pierre d'Ailly continued to write treatises distinguishing between true and false revelation and calling down scorn upon variously named but universally perverse heretics who performed the most debased carnal acts out of a "free spirit." No evidence suggests such theologians ever encountered a real libertine, and one may confidently place these repeated polemics in the same category as the other libelous smears against medieval heretics. As we will see in the following chapters, popes and inquisitors would soon shift their gaze to new foes on the horizon, including demonic magic, witchcraft, and anticlerical and nationalist reform movements in England and Bohemia.

Yet the vexed relationship between Christian revelation, Church authority, gender, and simple souls continued to shape the landscape of fifteenth-century Europe. Perhaps the best example with which to end is the case of a young peasant girl named Jeanne from the village of Domremy in France. Born in around 1412, Jeanne (or "Joan of Arc," as she would be known in the Anglophone world) came of age during a bitter phase of the Hundred Years' War (1337–1453), in which England and Burgundy battled the French for control of the throne. At the age of seventeen, Jeanne received mystical visitations from the archangel Michael and other saints, who directed her to lead an army in defense of the French heir, Charles VII. She began to speak of her visions and, surprisingly, to gather supporters around her—most significantly, the very soldiers whom local authorities expected to deride and dismiss her. By 1430, this most unlikely source of military and political authority had successfully inspired and personally led French soldiers in battle against the English.

God, she asserted, was using a simple peasant girl as a channel through which to restore order and to make the men of her land rise up and take charge once more. Jeanne's unique mystical voice allowed her to invert the normal gender roles of her day and to wield authority, paradoxically, *because* of her inferior status. That authority was not limited to the French throne and army, either, for she clearly held strong opinions about Christian piety more broadly. Intriguingly, in 1430 she directed her considerable literary force against Hussites in Bohemia, excoriating them for their heresy:

> What rage of madness consumes you? . . . As far as I am concerned, to tell you frankly, if I weren't occupied in the English wars, I would have come to see you a long time ago; but if I don't find out that you have reformed yourselves I might leave off [fighting] the English and go against you, so that by the sword, if I can't do it any other way, I will eliminate your mad and obscene superstition and remove your heresy or your life.[42]

But that miraculous moment in which all believed that God conveyed his will through a mere girl was fleeting. What was the king to do with such a troubling figure once she had served her purpose? What to do when her mystical conduit to God ran dry? No nun, she could not be kept behind convent walls, and her proclamations and directions could prove a greater threat than they were worth. More to the point, Charles was likely embarrassed that he had required the assistance of an uneducated and rustic female. Without a strong patron to protect her, Jeanne (like so many other "heretics" of the later Middle Ages) was vulnerable. Once on the throne, Charles famously decided that she had served her purpose and abandoned his former defender to the Burgundians, who in turn sold her to the English. Tried for heresy on trumped-up charges, Jeanne faced an ecclesiastical court that violated so many legal procedures as to make a mockery of the law. National politics were no prettier in the fifteenth century than they are today; Jeanne was inevitably found guilty of heresy, including the crime of cross-dressing—of wearing garb inappropriate for her station and for looking like something she was not. The English burned her at the stake on May 30, 1431. Although Jeanne was not a beguine, she shared two factors with them: first, her beliefs and behavior ran counter to traditional gender roles, which was on the one

Figure 5.3. Initial "D" shows Joan of Arc in Armor Holding a Flag Showing God the Father and Two Angels. *Source*: **Flemish. Archives Nationales, Paris, France. Erich Lessing/Art Resource, NY.**

hand her source of power and on the other a tremendous vulnerability; and second, her connection to a male authority meant his enemies were hers as well. Again, her bond with Charles was her strength until it became her liability; the English would never have troubled themselves with a peasant girl, no matter how she dressed, had she not brought power and esteem to the newly crowned French king. That he turned his back on her reminds us that the role of "court prophet" or visionary is a dangerous one.

If gender shaped antiheretical conversations and intensified ecclesiastical scrutiny over time, so too did the issue of status. In 1476, an uneducated peasant boy from Germany named Hans Böhm had a vision of the Virgin Mary, who directed him to preach moral virtue and, more controversially, social equality. The "Drummer of Niklashausen," as he came to be known, vigorously preached against clerical laxity and elite economic privilege and called for a radical leveling of the traditional social order in keeping with the Gospel.[43] First thousands and then tens of thousands flocked to hear his message, a phenomenon that deeply worried both secular and sacral leaders. Who was this boy, this upstart, and what kind of treasonous rabble was he stirring up? Authorities were right to be nervous, for a peasant revolt erupted almost immediately, precipitating Hans's trial and immediate execution at the stake for heresy. It is interesting that the very complaints of Hans and his followers would be echoed fifty years later during the better-known German peasant revolt of 1525, whose adherents were slaughtered by the princes and scorned as "robbing and murdering hordes" by the monk Martin Luther.

CONCLUSION

Between the twelfth and fifteenth centuries, therefore, the right to speak of religious matters or to challenge the traditional social order was a rare privilege. In the crisis-fueled late fourteenth century and schism, female mystics were sometimes granted access to voice criticism; however, the key point is that they all had male supervisors and advocates who effectively vouched for them and for their sanctity. They were the exceptions, for average lay Christians would increasingly be warned away from involving themselves in theological business. Church officials believed that this was for the protection of Christendom, whereas reforming or dissenting Christians believed that the clergy were simply protecting their own interests. Tension between the rule of the Gospel and that of the Church thus heightened by the decade, long before Luther voiced his own criticisms in the early sixteenth century.

Authority remained the problem at the center of medieval mysticism, lay female religiosity, and heresy. Both Marguerite and Meister Eckhart were accused of circulating their theological ideas among simple, unlettered people who (according to the Church) could not comprehend them and had no business discussing such matters, and both were convinced that all souls could embark upon the mystical itinerary to divine unity. Thus did inquisitors anxiously scan the horizon for phantom libertines of both sexes, their fears betraying just how subversive to clerical hierarchies and institutional authorities could be the simple soul's journey to God.

SUGGESTIONS FOR FURTHER READING

Böhringer, Letha, Jennifer Kolpacoff Deane, and Hildo van Engen, eds. *Labels and Libels: Naming Beguines in Northern Medieval Europe*. Turnhout, Belgium: Brepols, 2014.

Colledge, Edmund, and Bernard McGinn, ed. and trans. *Meister Eckhart: The Essential Sermons, Commentaries, Treatises, and Defense*. The Classics of Western Spirituality. New York: Paulist Press, 1981.

Elliott, Dyan. *Proving Woman: Female Spirituality and Inquisitional Culture in the Later Middle Ages*. Princeton, NJ: Princeton University Press, 2004.

Field, Sean L. *The Beguine, the Angel, and the Inquisitor: The Trials of Marguerite Porete and Guiard of Cressonessart.* Notre Dame, IN: University of Notre Dame Press, 2012.

Grundmann, Herbert. *Religious Movements in the Middle Ages: The Historical Links between Heresy, the Mendicant Orders, and the Women's Religious Movement in the Twelfth and Thirteenth Century, with the Historical Foundations of German Mysticism*. Notre Dame, IN: University of Notre Dame Press, 1995.

Hobbins, Daniel. *The Trial of Joan of Arc*. Cambridge, MA: Harvard University Press, 2005.

Hollywood, Amy M. *The Soul as Virgin Wife: Mechthild of Magdeburg, Marguerite Porete, and Meister Eckhart*. Studies in Spirituality and Theology 1. Notre Dame, IN: University of Notre Dame Press, 1995.

Lerner, Robert E. *The Heresy of the Free Spirit in the Later Middle Ages*. Berkeley: University of California Press, 1972.

Makowski, Elizabeth M. *A Pernicious Sort of Woman: Quasi-Religious Women and Canon Lawyers in the Later Middle Ages*. Washington, DC: Catholic University of America Press, 2005.

McDonnell, Ernest W. *The Beguines and Beghards in Medieval Culture: With Special Emphasis on the Belgian Scene*. New York: Octagon Books, 1969.

McGinn, Bernard. *The Essential Writings of Christian Mysticism*. Modern Library Classics. New York: Modern Library, 2006.

———. *Meister Eckhart and the Beguine Mystics: Hadewijch of Brabant, Mechthild of Magdeburg, and Marguerite Porete*. New York: Continuum, 1994.

Miller, Tanya Stabler. *The Beguines of Medieval Paris: Gender, Patronage, and Spiritual Authority.* Philadelphia: University of Pennsylvania Press, 2014.

More, Alison. *Fictive Orders and Feminine Religious Identities, 1200–1600.* Oxford: Oxford University Press, 2018.

Peterson, Janine Larmon. *Suspect Saints and Holy Heretics: Disputed Sanctity and Communal Identity in Late Medieval Italy.* Ithaca, NY: Cornell University Press, 2019.

Porete, Marguerite. *The Mirror of Simple Souls*. Edited by Ellen L. Babinsky. The Classics of Western Spirituality. New York: Paulist Press, 1993.

Ritchey, Sara. *Acts of Care: Recovering Women in Late Medieval Health.* Ithaca, NY: Cornell University Press, 2021.

Simons, Walter. *Cities of Ladies: Beguine Communities in the Medieval Low Countries, 1200–1565*. The Middle Ages Series. Philadelphia: University of Pennsylvania Press, 2001.

NOTES

1. Robert E. Lerner, *The Heresy of the Free Spirit in the Later Middle Ages* (Berkeley: University of California Press, 1972), 2.

2. Bernard McGinn, *The Foundations of Mysticism: Origins to the Fifth Century* (New York: Crossroad, 1991), xvii.

3. Bernard McGinn, *The Essential Writings of Christian Mysticism* (New York: Modern Library, 2006), 21–23.

4. Augustine, *Confessions (Book VII)*, ed. Henry Chadwick (Oxford: Oxford University Press, 2008), 127.

5. Herbert Grundmann, *Religious Movements in the Middle Ages: The Historical Links between Heresy, the Mendicant Orders, and the Women's Religious Movement in the Twelfth and Thirteenth Century, with the Historical Foundations of German Mysticism* (Notre Dame, IN: University of Notre Dame Press, 1995), 78.

6. Both the etymological discussion and quote are from Walter Simons, *Cities of Ladies: Beguine Communities in the Medieval Low Countries, 1200–1565* (Philadelphia: University of Pennsylvania Press, 2001), 122.

7. See, for example, the range of forms discussed in *Between Orders and Heresy: Rethinking Medieval Religious Movements,* ed. Jennifer Kolpacoff Deane and Anne E. Lester (Toronto: University of Toronto Press, 2022).

8. Penelope Galloway, "'Discreet and Devout Maidens': Women's Involvement in Beguine Communities in Northern France, 1200–1500," in *Medieval Women in Their Communities*, ed. Diane Watt (Cardiff: University of Wales Press, 1997), 92.

9. Barbara Newman, "The Heretic Saint: Guglielma of Bohemia, Milan, and Brunate," *Church History* 74 (March 2005): 4.

10. André Vauchez and Daniel Ethan Bornstein, *The Laity in the Middle Ages: Religious Beliefs and Devotional Practices* (Notre Dame, IN: University of Notre Dame Press, 1993), 226.

11. Anke Passenier, "Women on the Loose: Stereotypes of Women in the Stories of Medieval Beguines," in *Female Stereotypes in Religious Traditions*, ed. Ria Kloppenborg and Wouter Hanegraaff (Leiden: Brill, 1995).

12. Simons, *Cities of Ladies*, 121.

13. Elizabeth Makowski, *"A Pernicious Sort of Woman": Quasi-Religious Women and Canon Lawyers in the Later Middle Ages* (Washington, DC: Catholic University of America Press, 2005), 29.

14. Simons, *Cities of Ladies*, 119.

15. See Tanya Stabler Miller, *The Beguines of Medieval Paris: Gender, Patronage, and Spiritual Authority* (Philadelphia: University of Pennsylvania Press, 2014).

16. Gilbert de Tournai, *Collectio de Scandalis Ecclesiae*, ed. Autbertus Stroick, in *Archivum Franciscanum Historicum* 24 (1931): 58.

17. Guillaume de Lorris and Jean de Meun, *The Romance of the Rose*, ed. Frances Horgan, 3rd ed. (Oxford: Oxford University Press, 1995), 185.
18. Robert E. Lerner, "New Light on the Mirror of Simple Souls," *Speculum* 85, no. 1 (2010): 93.
19. McGinn, *Christian Mysticism*, 173.
20. McGinn, *Christian Mysticism*, 177–78.
21. McGinn, *Christian Mysticism*, 178.
22. McGinn, *Christian Mysticism*, 179.
23. Marguerite Porete, *The Mirror of Simple Souls*, ed. Ellen L. Babinsky (New York: Paulist Press, 1993), 85.
24. Norman Tanner, *Decrees of the Ecumenical Councils*, I (Washington, DC: Georgetown University Press, 1990), 374.
25. Tanner, *Decrees*, I, 374.
26. Tanner, *Decrees*, I, 383.
27. Lerner, *Free Spirit*, 48.
28. Edmund Colledge and Bernard McGinn, ed. and trans., *Meister Eckhart: The Essential Sermons, Commentaries, Treatises, and Defense* (New York: Paulist Press, 1981), 61.
29. Colledge and McGinn, *Meister Eckhart*, 59–60.
30. Charlotte Radler, "Living from the Divine Ground: Meister Eckhart's Praxis of Detachment," *Spiritus* 6 (2006): 36.
31. McGinn, *Christian Mysticism*, 439–40.
32. McGinn, *Christian Mysticism*, 295.
33. Colledge and McGinn, *Meister Eckhart*, 80.
34. McGinn, *Christian Mysticism*, 497.
35. Colledge and McGinn, *Meister Eckhart*, 81.
36. McGinn, *Christian Mysticism*, 496.
37. Augustine, "On Free Will," in *Earlier Writings*, ed. H. S. Burleigh (Philadelphia: Westminster Press, 1979), 186.
38. Richard Kieckhefer, *Repression of Heresy in Medieval Germany* (Philadelphia: University of Pennsylvania Press, 1979), especially 19–51.
39. On the ways in which beguine life could both resonate with and thwart mendicant ambitions (particularly observant reform), see Michael D. Bailey, "Religious Poverty, Mendicancy, and Reform in the Middle Ages," *Church History* 72, no. 3 (2003): 457–83.
40. John van Engen, *Brothers and Sisters of the Common Life: The Devotio Moderna and the World of the Later Middle Ages* (Philadelphia: University of Pennsylvania Press, 2008), especially 84–118.
41. My comparative study of lay religious women's communities in the German context is in progress, and there is much need for further analyses transcending regional, linguistic, and terminological boundaries.
42. Text translated at http://archive.joan-of-arc.org/joanofarc_letter_march_23_1430.html.
43. Richard M. Wunderli, *Peasant Fires: The Drummer of Niklashausen* (Bloomington: Indiana University Press, 1992).

Chapter Six

Medieval Magic, Demonology, and Witchcraft

In this chapter, we explore another channel of European religiosity that Christian thinkers of the high and late Middle Ages came to regard as explicitly heretical. In contrast to some of the previous topics, however, the fusion of magic and heresy did not emerge as a specific response to the Church, nor did it develop under the leadership of any charismatic individual. Rather, magic represented an enduring strand of European culture, transmitted from various ancient practices and continued in remarkably diverse forms across time and space. Ideas about magic—particularly regarding its specific relationship to heresy and the assumed danger it posed to Christendom—changed dramatically in the high and late medieval centuries, and these escalating concerns in turn laid an ecclesiastical, legal, and psychological foundation for the notorious witch trials of the sixteenth and seventeenth centuries. That said, just as notions of "The Inquisition" based on fifteenth- and sixteenth-century models should not be anachronistically applied back to medieval inquisitorial practice, one should avoid facile associations between medieval concerns about magic and early modern witch hunts. The Roman Inquisition and the early modern witch hunts (both small and large) came later and emerged out of specific historical contexts unique to the sixteenth century. Yet both were also outcroppings of earlier developments, of shifts in ideas and practices that influenced the centuries to come.

For a simple definition of magical practice, let's take the following: "the exercise of a preternatural control over nature by human beings, with the assistance of forces more powerful than they."[1] The two key elements here are *control over nature* and the manipulation or use of *forces more powerful* than humanity. One has only to reflect momentarily on the vulnerability of human life to understand the appeal of a system in which people can control the natural world. How much more keenly must this desire have been felt by those whose circumstances were unpredictable and unreliable—shaped by scarcity, famine, disease, violence, and warfare—and how irresistible would seem the power to compel the sun to shine, to summon rain upon the fields, or to bar pestilence from one's village. Beyond the most basic needs of food, water, and physical health, moreover, lie the demands of the heart and hearth, the desire to control *other people's* nature to attain love, passion, wealth, devotion, justice, vengeance, or any of the other aspects of human experience. Because a belief in powerful preternatural forces is one of the earliest features of human societies, it should come as no surprise that people have long sought to harness those forces to their own personal desires and drives.

But for the historian, magic is particularly tricky to study because (like heresy) it is more concept than reality, and because our sources (like those on heresy) are so often written by authors hostile to their topic. For our purposes, therefore, the term *magic* offers

> a way of categorizing a wide array of beliefs and practices, ranging from astrology and alchemy, charms and amulets, to sorcery and necromancy, trickery and entertainment, as practiced by both laity and clergy, by those of high and low social status, educated and uneducated, and found in diverse sources and contexts, including scientific and medical treatises, liturgical and other religious documents, and literary texts.[2]

Any subject that includes amulets, court tricks, and alchemy might sound obscure at best and thus not particularly relevant to the more traditional themes of European intellectual, political, and cultural histories. Surprisingly, the opposite is true: magic matters to history.

From the earliest to latest Middle Ages, the realm of magic represented a unique space in which otherwise segmented cultures and traditions mingled and influenced one another. So while peasant farmers muttered charms and priests blessed fields with holy water for a good harvest, young people flirted over love potions, healers cured infertility with animal testicles and incantations, learned university scholars pored over magical Arabic texts and ciphers, and court astrologers sought to divine the political future (and secure their own good fortune) in sign and sky. Indeed, this precise quality of magic—its powerful intersections and accessibility—increasingly worried theorists of the high and late Middle Ages, for whom proper social and moral order was of paramount importance. By the high Middle Ages, magic would be characterized and literally demonized in terms of those intersections, as inappropriate conjunctions of people, power, and purpose through which hell erupted on earth.

THE COMMON TRADITION OF MEDIEVAL MAGIC

Confidence in the effectiveness of magical practices was a hallmark of the premodern European world, sweeping not only across time and place but also extending broadly into all levels of society. However, certainty in a power is not the same as approval of that power; an astonishingly wide spectrum of people thus occupied themselves with pursuing *how* magic operated, *who* practiced it, and *what* they accomplished. In addition to the canon lawyers and theologians who pondered magic were other clergy such as popes, bishops, and inquisitors, and in the secular realm, royal, princely, and court authorities also frequently dedicated time and energy to studying the magical arts. Due to the essential Christian explanation of magic as operating by the power of demons and forces of evil, however, no one would have labeled himself a "*magician*" any more than medieval figures embraced the term *heretic* to describe themselves and their beliefs. Indeed, accusations of magic and witchcraft would increasingly come to echo the charge against other types of heretic in the later Middle Ages; in both cases, the presumption becomes that the problem is not so much what the person *does*, but what he or she *is*.

Before turning to the question of how magical practice became heresy in the later Middle Ages, it is worth reflecting on the depth and richness of the medieval magical tradition and the various strands of belief and practice that webbed through Western Christendom. One of the major complications in understanding medieval magic and its gradual reconceptualization into a category of heresy is that medieval people from all levels of society—from peasants to princes, laborers to lawyers, merchants to mendicants—often performed simple rituals or actions that seemed fully orthodox to them but that could appear "magical" to others. As with heresy, the meaning of "magic" lay very much in the eyes of the beholder, practitioner, theorist—or historian. For decades, scholars have attempted to isolate trends in "elite magic" as distinct from "popular magic," essentially categorizing them as two worlds that never met. But the model does not work, because the worlds were always in contact and influencing each other in a dialogue that profoundly influenced Western perceptions of evil up through the modern period. Thus, instead of an artificial distinction between "elite" and "popular" practices rooted in socio-economic distinctions, Richard Kieckhefer proposed instead that we consider a "common tradition" underpinning most magical practice across all social levels during the medieval centuries.

It is, of course, risky intellectual business to attempt a brief description of such a vast and varied set of human beliefs across a thousand-year period, for all of the rich local details and distinctions across time and place are obscured. Common magical practices were as fluid and flexible between the fifth and fifteenth centuries as the political, economic, social, and religious contours of Europe. With that caveat, however, a vivid and unbroken thread within common magic is its focus on outcomes: although intellectual and legal authorities tended to focus on *how* magic worked and the means or agency by which ritual activity achieved its ends, most of the people who performed common magical practice were interested in *what* it achieved. This consistent concern about the ends rather than the means of magical activity extended from the early to late Middle Ages and represents one unifying element in what we today call medieval "magic."

Healing, harming, and protecting were the basic purposes of such practice: rather than seeking extravagant wealth or powers, medieval people who engaged in common magic were typically responding to the threats and pressures of daily life. Village healers, such as barber-surgeons and midwives, often possessed extensive practical knowledge of the body and seamlessly employed herbs, unguents, and natural remedies with healing properties, and charms, on the one hand; amulets, rituals, blessings, and complex potions on the other. Although a modern reader is likely to discern two radically different approaches (the scientific and the religious), such a distinction was nonexistent in the medieval era. Healers not only employed these remedies as part of a single, unified understanding of the relationship between the material and the immaterial, but also combined and merged them in a kaleidoscopic array of forms.

Another outcome frequently sought in the common tradition of medieval magic was the prevention of disease and injury, not only among human beings, but also for animals and crops. Such magical practices reflect the keen sense of looming mortality that cut across medieval society and the desperate need to maintain vitality—not only in one's own body, but in those elements that provided crucial sustenance. Healthy domestic animals were often the lifeblood of medieval families, and magical rituals to cure or prevent harm to them were frequent. Not surprisingly in such a deeply agricultural society where the margin of existence was often appallingly thin, crops were also a regular object of protective spells and rituals. Because fertility of body, creature, and field often depended on weather conditions, other manifestations of common magical practice focused upon summoning rain, repelling insects, and generally protecting the often meager resources sustaining a family or village. Medieval fairy tales reflect this world, particularly stories in which a lucky individual is granted wishes; the wise choice in the story is rarely endless riches or power above one's station but instead the simple safety net of a never-ending soup pot or a domestic creature that lays coins or golden eggs.

Of course, sometimes those stories also tell of vengeance and the infliction of harm: the young man, for instance, who wishes for a pipe that when played forces his enemies to dance themselves to death, to run helplessly

Figure 6.1. Male Mandragora (Mandrake) Root, Said to Cure Sterility. ***Source*****: Page from the Hebarium of Trent, Italy, 14th c. Photo by Alfredo Dagli Orti. Biblioteca del Museo Provinciale d'Arte, Trent, Italy. Bildarchiv Preussischer Kulturbesitz/Art Resource, NY.**

and painfully through thicket and briar, or to fart upon command, shamefully and with devastating social consequences. Medieval Europe, particularly in the late tenth century, was a world of small communities and tight-knit relationships. Safety lay in community, but so did resentment, envy, and discontent—not only against the privileged members of this sharply divided socioeconomic structure but also against family members, friends, neighbors, rivals, and so on within one's own quotidian world. Harmful magic, or *maleficium*, could hurt and destroy. On some level, although people might utter beneficial spells or employ protective rituals without thinking twice, the performance of harmful magic was broadly understood as wrong, and those accused rarely admitted to doing it or even knowing how. As a consequence, it is impossible for us to know how widespread the actual practice of harmful magic was, much less to gain a sense of how often medieval people might have allowed themselves to reflect upon the possibility or daydream about taking vengeance on a perceived enemy through *maleficium.*

Love magic also claimed a central place within common magical practice, and a huge number of spells, charms, rituals, blessings, and potions were believed effective for inciting passion. What these diverse practices share is belief in a powerful agency that will help them dominate another's will; after all, no magical forces would be necessary if the desired figure were at all interested in relations. For the person casting the spell and seeking their beloved's embrace, the magic was of course beneficial and helpful. From the perspective of the enchanted one, however, such magic was no boon but rather an aggressive manipulation of her or his own will. Thus, although love charms and potions may seem innocuous in contrast to some of the more overtly malevolent practices, the intention of controlling the will of another human being would prove increasingly troubling to authorities.

A final major purpose of common magic was to determine the truth of a situation, to uncover a secret circumstance or condition, or to discern future events (termed "divining" in both ancient and medieval traditions, meaning that it worked through the involvement of supernatural powers). Like other common magical practices, divining was generally used to ensure a positive outcome or to avoid or deflect harm—in other words, to facilitate the safe continuation of the status quo—and was rarely wielded to secure enormous transformations in one's circumstances. For instance, people tried to establish auspicious days for major events such as marriages, harvests, or battles; family members sought to know whether their children would prosper and whom they would marry; and the victims of crimes or misfortune employed divination to locate lost or stolen items and to identify the guilty party. In the tight-knit medieval communities in which everyone lived in proximity and depended upon relationships for survival, such knowledge and skills were perhaps just as important as the physical protection of body, animals, and crops.

Throughout the Middle Ages, therefore, the purposes of medieval magic remained fairly constant as people continued to react to or attempt to control the immediate threats and challenges to their lives. But let us not take that to mean that medieval magic consisted of an unchanging set of practices: on the contrary, the different methods and systems employed in common magic varied tremendously, and only the barest hint of that diversity can be offered here. Among the most important and prevalent forms through which medieval magic was expressed were ritualized speech, including spells, incantations, blessings, curses, and other verbal formulas; material items from the natural world, or substances that could be fashioned and manipulated; and combinations of the verbal and physical, often involving ritualistic use of time and location. Very often such practices were organically infused into specifically Christian practices: a woman in labor might blend herbs, recite incantations, and pray to St. Margaret (the patron saint of childbirth), and a farmer might bury a consecrated wafer in his field to ensure a good crop. Educated churchmen would begin to scrutinize the array of practices in the eleventh and twelfth centuries, however, and their intellectual efforts would transform later medieval conceptions of magic from the complex realities of common practice into an increasingly uniform, monocausal (and largely fictitious) image of demonic magic.

But why did authorities begin to scrutinize magic so carefully in and after the eleventh century, and how did a preoccupation with demons come to dominate later medieval conceptions of magic? One of the reasons has to do with a new form of magical practice that grew out of and beyond the common tradition we have discussed so far. As early as the eleventh century, educated men—that is, clergy, because all university students were required to join orders—began to investigate and theorize magic, developing an exclusive, learned form that focused not on simple outcomes of healing, harm, or protection, but on deeper and potentially dangerous knowledge of powers both natural and supernatural. Although such men were trained in the most sophisticated theology of day, influenced by Aristotle, Plato, and other Greek thinkers, many of their esoteric practices were directly antagonistic to Church teachings. As we will see, ideas of medieval magic were profoundly shaped by members of the educated minority, who both participated in and railed against efforts to summon and control demonic forces. And it was with such concerns and considerations that the later (and historically lingering) category of medieval magic began to take form, as Church thinkers encompassed all the various forms of common magic we have discussed here under the umbrella of demonic magic.

LEARNED MAGIC IN THE MIDDLE AGES

The centuries between about 1000 and 1300 CE witnessed a vibrant resurgence of intellectual activity and the first major institutionalization of learning since the time of the Romans. Opportunities for advanced education remained sharply limited to men of a certain social, economic, or mental caliber, yet the percentage of literate men increased dramatically from earlier centuries. With the establishment first of schools and then universities in major European cities such as Bologna, Palermo, and Paris came increasingly sophisticated curricula and the organized exploration of topics ranging from law and medicine to theology, with texts including Aristotle, Galen, Augustine, and of course scripture. Magical practice also became a subject of serious study and analysis in this first blush of European intellectualism; although some highly educated figures put into practice what they learned while poring over new books and collections of magical knowledge, others simply studied the rites and rituals and the means by which they operated. The very involvement (pro or con) of learned men in magic lent a new weight to the subject, far beyond what the common practice had borne when earlier Christian thinkers deemed it the foolishness of rustics.

In addition to the classic texts mentioned above, students were deeply influenced by recently translated Arab and Hebrew works flooding in from the East. Many important Greek texts that had been lost to the West had survived in the Byzantine East and had become thoroughly incorporated into sophisticated Arab learning by the tenth century. Muslim and Christian scholars were not regularly interacting face to face, which is not surprising given the long-standing hostility inflamed by the late eleventh-century call to crusade and capture of Jerusalem. Yet there were isolated key points of interaction between intellectuals from Muslim, Jewish, and Christian traditions in locations such as Sicily, Spain, and Italy. Gerbert of Aurillac, for example, was a Christian cleric from southern France who studied Arab mathematics and astronomy before teaching at the northern cathedral school at Rheims. He rapidly ascended the clerical ranks and upon his election as Pope Sylvester II in 999, critics muttered that he had used his occult Arabic knowledge to secure the throne. In truth, both Muslim and Jewish scholars had absorbed much magical knowledge from the ancient Greeks, especially on the subjects of astrology and alchemy. Both topics became of great interest among certain circles of clerics, particularly those employed by secular authorities eager to discover (by whatever means necessary) what dangers and delights the future might hold.

In the growing body of texts that identified and criticized it, such magic was usually called *necromantia*, or necromancy, a term that originally meant the process of divining through the supplication of the dead. Not only pagan classical cultures but scripture itself lent weight to this tradition, as in the case of the Hebrew king Saul, who needed to know the outcome of a looming battle and thus consulted a diviner (the Witch of Endor) to summon the ghost of the dead prophet Samuel (1 Samuel 28). Christian authorities flatly rejected such divination, but more important, they dismissed the notion that ghosts could return from the dead: once in heaven or hell, there was to be no return. Isidore of Seville thus explained that necromancers only *appeared* to summon the spirits of the dead, and later writers asserted a crucial new interpretation: that the supposed spirits were in fact demons and that necromancy was thus a black art, an invocation of demons.

Necromantic magic usually consisted of many of the same basic forms and practices as the common tradition of medieval magic, but in more complex combinations. Simple verbal formulas were routinely used to command or control demons ("I conjure you," or "I adjure you") but were combined with elaborate and precise rituals. Magic circles inscribed on paper or earth might be filled with language and symbols to heighten the spell's power, and other objects such as plants, animals, food, wax, or any of a variety of natural materials might be cut, manipulated, burned, or otherwise offered up to entice the demons. Given their training and exposure to Greek, Arabic, and Hebrew texts, necromancers also frequently wove astrological and alchemical components into their magical practice. To make another person "abominable," for instance,

> so that he is held to be ugly and deformed and odious, set up a lead image and put the feet in place of the fingers and vice versa, and a twisted face, in the hour of Saturn and on its day [Saturday]. Then write the name for the one for whom it is made on the head and the name of the planet Saturn on the chest, and first suffumigate the image with a horrible and fetid odor, saying, "Oh spirit of most resplendent Saturn and those descending from higher places, hand over into strife and hatred this person named N, of whom this image is made, sad ones, and in torment, unquiet ones, the same person, choleric ones." Afterwards it ought to be buried in a deep, horrible and fetid place.[3]

In a sense, therefore, these clerical necromancers drew on the vocabulary of the existing common magical tradition but employed a new and uniquely demonic grammar so that the meaning of such magical practice, although an outgrowth of the common tradition, was nonetheless substantially different. By the high Middle Ages, the term *necromancy* had come to represent the learned and complex magical arts practiced by educated men whose illicit knowledge generally came from secret books and manuals. Purposes varied widely, from forecasting the future to generating powerful illusions that could affect the material world: for instance, creating an illusory horse that could actually transport a person or a satisfying banquet of delicious (but unreal) food. In any such necromantic magic, the assumption was that the agency was demonic and that appearances lied—the horse was actually a demon that only *seemed* an animal, and the delicious food only *appeared* wholesome. As a consequence, the twelfth and thirteenth centuries witnessed an outcropping of theories about the exact nature and extent of demonic power over the natural world and human beings: they could not, for example, control human will, although they could manipulate bodies and circumstances to *influence* a person to love, hate, or otherwise act according to another's wishes. Thus, no matter what the specific purpose of necromantic magic, its effectiveness and power came from demonic agency.

A wise reader might ask at this point whether such magic was ever actually practiced, or whether necromancy was largely a figment of inquisitors' imaginations (as was the case with so many of the "heresies" we have covered). Surprisingly, given the lurid nature of such magic and its underlying assumptions, the practice of necromancers was apparently real—limited, of course, to a small group of highly educated men, but real nonetheless, and documented by an array of guides to such magic. Many of these manuals still exist, and because the practitioners were usually clerics, there are striking parallels between the rituals of learned magic and the Church's own liturgical rites. Nor did they disappear out of circulation; in the thirteenth century, William of Auvergne (a University of Paris scholar and bishop of Paris from 1228 to 1249) recorded that he had seen several books of necromancy. A century later, the inquisitor Nicholas Eymeric recorded in his important inquisitorial manual *Directorium inquisitorum* (*Directory of Inquisitors*) that he had seized and destroyed many such magical Latin texts, the titles of which provide some insight into their condemned contents: *Clavis Salomonis* (*The Key of Solomon*) and *Liber iuratus Honorii* (*Sworn Book of Honorius the Magician*). Even as late as the fifteenth century, necromancers' manuals and other books of demonic magic were still being copied and transmitted; for example, the reforming Dominican Johannes Nider referred to a Viennese monk who had been a necromancer in his earlier life and possessed several such books.[4]

The tiny subset of clergy involved with necromantic magic was far outnumbered by their colleagues who either knew little about the practice or condemned it outright. Necromancers typically defended their practice with the claim that they were compelling rather than submitting to demons, that they possessed the knowledge and power to do so safely, and even that the Christian value of such practice was demonstrated by the fact that Christ's disciples themselves had the power to exorcise and thus control demons. Opponents such as Thomas Aquinas disagreed, echoing Augustine's vehement concern about evil associations between humans and demons and noting that even a magician's command over demons operates on the basis of a pact between the two. Whatever its purpose or form, Church authorities would tolerate no such practice.

As Latinate necromancy performed by a small clerical underground began to attract more and more attention among Christian authorities after the twelfth century, condemnations of demonic magic mounted. And because such magic also employed the various formulas and objects of the older common magical tradition, all forms of practice ultimately became tarred with the brush of demonic magic. In other words, mounting concern about demonic agency and necromancy provoked a major shift in the Church's stance on magic: by the later Middle Ages, simple healing charms, love potions, fertility rituals, and basic divination were now conceptualized as inherently diabolical, resting on demonic rather than divine agency. This reinterpretation of the common magical tradition in explicitly demonic terms is crucial for understanding how and why magic became linked to the legal category of heresy in the thirteenth century. At heart lay the issue of sovereignty and an emerging theological certainty that human beings faced a black-and-white choice between service to God or service to the devil.

THINKING ABOUT MAGIC AND HERESY (c. 1100–1300)

European thinkers had long criticized magic on two basic grounds: the moral, which viewed such practices as alien and antisocial, and the legal, which tended to focus on the malicious or criminal outcomes of those practices. In other words, one layer of condemnation was rooted in notions of the social fabric and the other in specific theories of crime and punishment. During the early centuries of Christian practice in the medieval West, ecclesiastical authorities had associated magic with pagan rites and specifically with evil powers; as a consequence, all magical activity was theoretically deemed illicit within early medieval Christianity. Yet because a wide variety of common practices (pagan or otherwise) were so thickly interwoven into the strategies early medieval people embraced for coping with their world, the same authorities actually responded mildly to actual cases of magical practice. Moral correction and penitential reconciliation, rather than outright punishment, were primary among the concerns of clergy. In cases in which royal or other secular leaders charged magicians, the trials tended to focus upon the legal (rather than moral) and criminal outcome of the act, whether theft, murder, or other *maleficium*. Such tendencies picked up momentum in the high and later Middle Ages: first was a further elaboration of evil in the world and the relationship between human beings and preternatural forces;

second was a shift from the "what" of magic to the "how" and "why" of the power *behind* the act.

As we have explored in other chapters, the economic and intellectual vitality of the high Middle Ages nurtured an explosion of legal innovations and institutions, including the shift from accusatorial to inquisitorial methods in court and the corollary establishment of new officials—the "inquisitors of heretical depravity." Scholars churned out legal texts and theories in ever-greater numbers, which served to buttress the growing sense that matters of faith were indeed matters of law as well. In other words, the category of magic (like that of heresy) was in many ways forged by the legal and intellectual preoccupation of high medieval thinkers; it was perhaps simply a matter of time before the two realms were linked in the minds of those authorities.

In 1140 in the city of Bologna, a monk named Gratian produced one of the most important legal texts in Western history, which also provides a useful litmus test for attitudes toward heresy of all types. In the *Concordia discordantium canonum* (*Concordance of Discordant Canons*, or the *Decretum*) Gratian collected and compared the previously diffuse array of earlier rulings on a wide variety of issues or "cases." The volume thus served as the first standard European legal text, became the foundation of canon law, and laid a profoundly important legal foundation for all aspects of Christian experience. Magic was no exception, although the space and thus significance allotted to it in the *Decretum* was relatively minor. In case 26, Gratian considered an array of important earlier rulings and largely echoed earlier medieval perspectives on magic and superstition. For Gratian, magical practices were generally understood to be the foolish error of simpletons, who (although deceived by the illusions and tricks of demons) posed no deep risk to Christendom. Persistent practice of sorcery and divination were to bear the penalty of excommunication—a consequence whose sting was of a moral or spiritual rather than specifically legal nature.

Within about a century of Gratian's publication, however, attitudes had begun to shift significantly as formative early ideas about the relationship between magic and demons were extended. Aquinas himself analyzed the relationship between magic, demonic agency, and heresy in a systematic way. In the *Summa Theologica,* for example, he considered the various assaults of demons in the following categories:

> Concerning this we have five points of inquiry: (1) Whether men are assailed by the demons? (2) Whether to tempt is proper to the devil? (3) Whether all the sins of men are to be set down to the assaults or temptations of the demons? (4) Whether they can work real miracles for the purpose of leading men astray? (5) Whether demons who are overcome by men, are hindered from making further assaults?[5]

He and other theologians demonstrated in practical terms, for example, how it was possible for offspring to result from sex between humans and demons (the demon obtains semen by seducing a man as a succubus, then taking the form of an incubus and impregnating a woman). Likewise, a pact with the devil came to be understood as an act akin to, but entirely subversive of, feudal homage.

As we have seen, the mid-thirteenth century witnessed the deputizing of papal inquisitors who began to bear down on newly categorized heretics, and ecclesiastical anxiety about organized, clandestine enemies of the Church mounted. The legal procedure of *inquisitio* allowed officials to investigate and charge potential suspects on the basis of their own authority rather than requiring an injured party to formally accuse a suspect. Interestingly, papal inquisitors were ordered in 1258 *not* to investigate cases of sorcery unless the practice specifically involved heretical practice, a decree that entered canon law forty years later in 1298 under Pope Boniface VIII (r. 1292–1303). But what was the distinction between sorcery and heresy in practice? Many inquisitors found the directive troubling. Escalating rumors of clerical necromancy and other forms of diabolical magic thus drew inquisitorial attention to magic by the mid-thirteenth century as well as to the belief that magical practices should fall within their purview as seekers of heretical depravity.

One intriguing early case linking heresy with magic was reported by a Cistercian monk named Ralph of Coggeshall. According to his account, authorities in the French city of Rheims discovered a group of heretics known as "Publicans" whom they thought related to Cathars. The archbishop and his clergy (responsible for pursuing heresy in this era prior to deputized papal inquisitors) summoned and interrogated one old woman, whose apparent obstinacy earned her a death sentence. As the execution fires were being prepared, however, she effected a dramatic escape: pulling a ball of yarn from her pocket, she tossed it out a window, shouted "Catch!" and was literally spirited away by demons. As historians we do not need to preoccupy ourselves with the literal truth of either event or account, of course, but the story does underscore that clerics were making those connections for themselves.

Likewise, one might recall the wild report filed by the early inquisitor Conrad of Marburg. As we discussed in chapter 3, Conrad's methods were neither official nor ultimately approved, and his excesses prompted a quick reevaluation of the inquisitorial role and scope of power by the papacy. However unorthodox his methods, the resulting description of heretics in the Rhineland appears to have had a tremendous impact on Pope Gregory IX. In 1233, the pope issued the decree *Vox in Rama*, which directly echoed Conrad's report, detailing the process by which heretics summoned and worshiped a demon. Capable of appearing in different forms (for example, a great toad, a pale man, a giant cat), the demon also inspired the heretics to acts of indiscriminate sexual depravity. These early reports by Ralph and Conrad influenced later ecclesiastical authorities in their clear association between heresy, demonic worship, and (particularly in the latter) the horror of untrammeled and criminal sexuality. As we saw in earlier chapters, thirteenth- and fourteenth-century authorities were convinced that people who claimed pious lives were actually behaving in the most demented and depraved of ways. The growing definition of magic as the intersection of the demonic and human worlds, the "intercourse" of Christian and demon, meant that accusations increasingly took on a sexualized element as well.

Ideas about Magic and Jews

Such perceptions of deviant behavior—wildly inaccurate imaginings rather than observations rooted in any kind of reality—would prove similarly crucial regarding Jews, as increasingly cruel and hostile stereotypes of their communities were folded into conceptions of diabolical magical practice by the late fourteenth century. As anxiety over nonexistent heretical conspiracies in the midst of Christendom escalated, so too did hysteria regarding the presence of Jewish communities, a visible group of religious outsiders and one whose long-standing presence in the Christian West was suddenly subjected to unprecedented violence and abuse in the high Middle Ages. Although the medieval Church tolerated Jews, claiming their presence was necessary for the eventual conversion of all Jews prophesied in scripture, ignorance of Judaism and suspicion of Jewish communities were endemic, as was the association of Jews, with heresy and dark magic. As people explicitly beyond the boundaries of Christendom, they could not, of course, be heretics in the technical sense of the term, but they had long been treated as enemies of the Church. The decrees of the Fourth Lateran Council in 1215, for example, included the demand that Jews wear distinctive garb to distinguish them from Christians and prohibited them from holding public office.

Like so many of their Christian contemporaries, Jews had of course engaged in various elements of the common magical tradition from the earliest medieval centuries. But as ecclesiastical condemnations of magic as essentially demonic and diabolical heightened, those old associations between Jews and magic became particularly dangerous. Already depicted by early Christian writers in the most negative terms due to their "rejection" of Christ, Jews were easily and frequently represented as particularly close to demons. For example, the legend of the sixth-century saint Theophilus, who was persuaded by a wicked Jewish sorcerer to sign a pact with the devil, became archetypal for later conceptions of magic as explicitly involving a demonic joining.

Such stories and theories quickly erupted into the material plane as accusations of ritual murder aimed at Jews began to escalate in the twelfth century. Perhaps the most famous example among many tragic cases was the accusation in 1144 that Jews murdered a little Christian boy named William near the English town of Norwich. Lurid fantasies of Jewish demonic conspiracy burst across Europe, frequently including accusations of (Christian) child murder and cannibalization. As devotion to the Eucharist and the sacred power of the host flourished in the thirteenth century, so too did the ugly parallel belief that Jews were intent upon destroying that power. Rumors of wafer stealing and desecration swirled across Europe in the thirteenth and fourteenth centuries, as did bloody attacks upon Jews and their communities. When plague erupted in the mid-fourteenth century, Jewish communities were scapegoated and slaughtered by the thousands, as new paranoia fanned the flames of twelfth- and thirteenth-century hatred.

Ideas about Magic and Satan

At the center of this rapidly developing story of battling demons was Satan himself, an entity shaped by ancient Near Eastern demons and spirits and whose powers and intentions were initially rather ambiguous in both the Hebrew and Greek scriptures. In the book of Luke, for example, Christ describes Satan as a rebellious angel cast down from heaven; the flash of lightning as he fell prompted Satan to be associated with Lucifer, the "light bearer," which was a name originally given to a fallen king of Babylon in the book of Isaiah. In the book of Revelation, which so fueled medieval apocalypticism, Satan appears as a dragon, "that old serpent, called the Devil, and Satan, which deceives the whole world" (Revelation 12:9). Early Church fathers such as St. Augustine further articulated the particular role of Satan in the fourth and fifth centuries, providing an essential bridge between the classical and medieval worlds. Yet in both popular and clerical worlds through the early Middle Ages, the devil served as a catch-all figure for temptation, deception, wickedness, or sometimes simple trickery: far from representing an indomitable evil, the early medieval devil was often represented as a character to be fooled or foiled by clever peasants whose skills of barter, persuasion, and trickery were celebrated in a variety of literary forms.

Not until the twelfth and thirteenth centuries did the terrifying notion of Satan as the single great, dragonlike adversary of God and lord of hell itself finally emerge, a product of the same intellectual world responsible for the new developments in law, theology, and inquisitorial procedure. And the "new Satan" fulfilled a crucial role in medieval authorities' understanding of magic after the twelfth century as well, as the single diabolical master of all demons whom magicians allegedly served and worshiped. In other words, the crime of magic became even more serious once authorities accepted the notion that all magicians invoking demons were actually venerating the ultimate lord of darkness. Once again, we are reminded that the condemnation of medieval magic had much less to do with the actual practices and outcomes than it did with theories of sovereignty and subservience.

MAGIC, HERESY, AND INQUISITION (c. 1300–1400)

Because ideas about magic and heresy were enormously diverse and transformed slowly over time, it is not possible to identify a single moment or place at which attitudes shifted. Nonetheless, one may reasonably argue that the first quarter of the fourteenth century ushered in a new era in the relationship between inquisitors, heresy, and magical practice. The unprecedented constellation of disasters that characterize the fourteenth century (ranging from natural catastrophes such as famine and plague to the man-made crises of papal schism and endemic warfare) doubtless heightened contemporary concerns about the source and causation of misfortune. In other words, the fourteenth century intensified and expanded existing concerns about who was wreaking disaster upon whom, and why, and how. As a consequence, violence against heretics and Jews mounted across the century, and both categories would become increasingly triangulated with that of the demonic magician or sorcerer. Common fears and hatreds would play out on the local level of village, town, and city, fed by the growing body of papal decrees, academic treatises, and inquisitorial procedures aimed at revealing (by force, if necessary) the demonic intersections of hell and earth within Christendom.

Already in the earliest years of the fourteenth century, royal and papal authorities were deeply preoccupied with demonic magic. Some cynically employed accusations as a means to an end; others appear to have fully believed in the diabolical wickedness of forces arrayed against them; all accepted that the strained political and religious circumstances of the day were rife with opportunities for demonic intervention. As we discussed in chapter 3, King Philip the Fair of France leveled charges of demonic involvement and magical practice at his opponent, Boniface, and also drew upon that same constellation of supposed magical practices to discredit and ultimately disband the wealthy military order of the Knights Templar. Historians agree that Philip deployed the power of such accusations for political and economic ends rather than out of any genuine belief that his declared enemies were invoking demons, but the fact remains that such charges were enormously damaging because so many contemporaries *did* fear the intrusion of

Figure 6.2. The Devil Riding Behemoth. From the illustrated manuscript *Liber floridus* by Lambert de Saint-Omer. Flemish, 15th c. Parchment, 50 cm × 35.8 cm. MS724 folio 42 verso. *Source*: Photo by René-Gabriel Ojéda. Musée Condé, Chantilly, France. Réunion des Musées Nationaux/Art Resource, NY.

diabolical forces. In fact, anxieties even at the same French court proved how real the intersection of political power and vulnerability to magical practice could seem: when Philip's queen died at the young age of thirty-two in 1305, rumors of murder by magic and poison flew through the court. Philip's own death in 1314 and those of his sons Louis X in 1316 and Philip V in 1322 were similarly scrutinized for evidence of diabolical causes.

Pure political motives mingled with overt fear of demonic magic in other courts as well, particularly that of the papacy, located since 1305 in the southern city of Avignon. During the reign of Pope John XXII (r. 1316–1334), the tangible effect of such concerns became particularly apparent. Accusations of magical practice became a staple of his political arsenal from the earliest days of his pontificate: in 1317, he accused Hugues Géraud, the bishop of Cahors, of attempting to murder him through sorcery; after confessing under torture, the bishop was convicted and burned alive. John's concerns about magic were also pulled into specific local and regional antiheretical currents; the Franciscan Bernard Délicieux, for example, was tried in Toulouse for possessing books of sorcery, and a range of accusations was launched against Spiritual Franciscan radicals in the March of Ancona. Nor were secular authorities safe from accusations of magical practice: in 1320, John accused Matteo Visconti, the ruler of Milan, and his son of plotting against him through magic and sorcery. To be fair to John, some of his opponents probably *were* contemplating various strategies for removing him from power—and whether or not any explicitly considered or performed demonic magic, few would have fundamentally doubted its efficacy.

John's accusations represent one source of evidence about the intersection of politics and demonic magic in the early fourteenth century, and his official letters and decrees provide another. In 1320, for example, he dramatically reversed the traditional papal stance regarding inquisitors and magic. Overturning Pope Alexander IV's 1258 injunction that inquisitors should not pursue magic and sorcery unless specifically heretical, John had a letter issued to inquisitors in Toulouse and Carcassonne (the heart of the earliest inquisitorial tribunals) ordering them to proceed against *all* sorcerers who infected Christendom by summoning, sacrificing to, worshiping, and joining with demons. A few years later, John himself issued the crucial decree *Super illius specula* (*Upon His Watchtower*), which automatically excommunicated anyone who invoked demons:

> Grievingly we observe . . . that many who are Christians in name only . . . sacrifice to demons, adore them, make or have made images, rings, mirrors, phials, or other things for magic purposes, and bind themselves to demons. They ask and receive responses from them and to fulfill their most depraved lusts ask them for aid. Binding themselves to the most shameful slavery for the most

> shameful of things, they ally themselves with death and make a pact with hell. . . . We hereby promulgate the sentence of excommunication upon all and singular who against our most charitable warnings and orders presume to engage in these things, and we desire that they incur this sentence *ipso facto*.[6]

Of particular interest here is that his language evokes the elaborate necromantic practice of a clerical underworld rather than the broad, common tradition of medieval magical practice. By now, the specifically demonic element of necromancy had been thoroughly—if mistakenly—applied to the entire spectrum of medieval magic.

MAGIC IN INQUISITORS' TEXTS

The widening scope of inquisitors' authority over magicians and sorcerers in the early fourteenth century is reflected in their handbooks and manuals. In 1326, Pope John XXII published a list of forbidden magical acts that inquisitors could investigate, including invoking or sacrificing to demons or their images, making a pact with the devil, or abusing the sacraments of baptism or Eucharist. One of the local papal inquisitors responding to John's directives in these years was Bernard Gui in Toulouse, who finished compiling his comprehensive manual *Practica inquisitionis heretice pravitatis* (*The Practice of Inquisition into Heretical Depravity*). Although Gui seems never to have sentenced anyone for sorcery during his years as an inquisitor, his handbook clearly indicates that magic fell under the umbrella of his authority. Such manuals were intended for practical use, and although later compilations were often simple copies or repetitions of old material, Gui wrote his based upon personal experience. In his eyes, and thus in his manual, sorcery and divination are categorized as one of six standard varieties of heresy that an inquisitor would likely encounter. To effectively respond to and persuade practitioners of magic away from their heresy, Gui proposes that an inquisitor pay careful attention to the status and nature of the person being interrogated, since various methods could be used effectively on different sorts of people. Individual interrogations, he continues, can be developed from questions regarding

> children or infants put under a spell or released from one; lost or damned souls; thieves who should be imprisoned; quarrels or reconciliation between spouses; making barren women fertile; things given to eat, hairs, nails and so on; the condition of the souls of the dead; foretelling future events; female spirits whom they call Good People who go about, they say, by night; enchantments and conjurations using songs, fruit, plants, straps and other things.[7]

In contrast to John, whose ideas about magic were drawn from the elite clerical practice of necromancy, Gui seems familiar with both the common *and* learned magical traditions. In his manual, he directs inquisitors not only to interrogate suspects about common magical practices such as healing and love charms but also to pursue demonic rituals and the superstitious misuse or abuse of sacraments. Gui's quite practical manual circulated widely across Europe in the fourteenth and fifteenth centuries, and his assumptions (including his certainty in the demonic essence of most magic) powerfully influenced subsequent inquisitorial theory and practice.

Over the course of the fourteenth century, inquisitors increasingly fixated upon defining and dismantling systems of demonic magic. At the end of the fourteenth century, an important stepping-stone in the linking of magic, demonology, and heresy emerged under the pen (once again) of the Catalan inquisitor Nicolas Eymeric. In his *Directorium inquisitorum*, Eymeric adopts a more theoretically inflected approach to the work of inquisition and the categories of heresy, considering

> whether magicians and diviners are to be considered heretics or as those suspected of heresy and whether they are to be subjected to the judgment of the inquisitor of heretics . . . [and] whether those who invoke demons, either magicians or heretics or those suspected of heresy, are subject to the judgment of the inquisitor of heretics.[8]

In the manual, he draws on authorities ranging from Augustine, Peter Lombard, Thomas Aquinas, and even Pope John XXII. In response to necromancers who claimed that they were in full control of the demons they invoked (and thus not guilty of serving or venerating evil), Eymeric insisted that the mere invocation of demonic power, regardless of intention, was prohibited for Christians.

As a growing body of antiheretical and antimagical expertise circulated through the texts and tribunals of the fourteenth century, concerns about malevolent magic rippled through court and college, particularly in France. Two related developments from the end of the century illustrate how magic had become perceived as (1) a very real and effective (if illegal) tool, (2) a potent political weapon, and (3) an increasingly dangerous legal category. In 1398, rumors and accusations flew once again at the French court when two Augustinian monks were put to death in Paris after accusing the king's brother of employing sorcery to harm him; suspicions of magic at court returned in the early fifteenth century. In direct response, the theologians at the University of Paris (who served as the medieval equivalent of a modern-day think tank) issued that same year a list of twenty-eight articles condemning sorcery, divination, and superstition. The eighteenth article, for example, proclaimed it an error to believe that "by such arts and impious rites, by sortilege, by incantations, by invocation of demons, by certain glances and other sorcery, no effect ever follows by aid of demons."[9] Likewise condemned were the notions

> that the blood of a hoopoe or kid or other animal, or virgin parchment or lion skin and the like have efficacy to compel and repel demons by the aid of arts of this sort, [that] our intellectual cogitations and inner volitions are caused immediately by the sky, [and] that by certain magic arts we can reach the vision of the divine essence or of the holy spirits.[10]

By categorizing so many different types of activities as magical and idolatrous, the theology faculty continued to mistakenly link common and learned practice in terms of the demonic underpinnings of both. Prosecutions for magic (now explicitly understood as heresy) had already begun to escalate by the late fourteenth century, particularly in the regions of modern-day Switzerland and Italy. Moreover, such developments laid the foundation for a major shift in the fifteenth century: a steep escalation of concern about magic and superstition, perceived association of women with magic, and a consequent explosion of trials for diabolical witchcraft.

FIFTEENTH-CENTURY THINKERS AND THEORISTS

Just as the historical contexts and conditions of the fourteenth century shaped contemporary dialogues about magic and heresy, so too did the changing set of issues and pressures of the fifteenth century. First, a series of late fourteenth-century university foundations within imperial lands (including Heidelberg in 1386, Cologne in 1388, and Erfurt in 1392) contributed a crop of impassioned new scholars to join the ranks of Europe's professional thinkers, dedicated to reforming Christendom, ending magical corruption, and exposing the precise nature of demonic agency and human interaction. Leading figures such as Jean Gerson, the chancellor of the University of Paris, were joined by a talented cohort of scholars who focused their considerable intellectual sights on magic, superstition, and heresy in the early decades of the fifteenth century. Gerson denounced common and elite forms of magic alike in his many treatises, as did Nicholas Magni of Jauer at Heidelberg. In 1412, another theologian at Heidelberg, Johannes of Frankfurt, concluded in his analysis of demonic coercion that any invocation of diabolical powers *did* presume some form of worship or subservience. Many other such works followed throughout the 1420s, produced by some of the finest and best-trained minds of the day. Indeed, the potential eruption of demonic power into the material world was one of the most pressing issues of the day, and university scholars were deeply involved in the effort to discern and defuse the threat.

Second, just as earlier heretical categories and inquisitorial decrees emerged out of twelfth- and thirteenth-century councils and reform movements, major fifteenth-century shifts in perspective also reflected new initiatives in ecclesiastical administration. Church officials and scholars were jointly engaged in reforming Christian governance and institutions in the early fifteenth century, efforts that culminated in key conciliar gatherings focused in no small part on issues of heresy, piety, and the proper relationship between the divine and mundane. At the Council of Constance (1414–1418), for example, clerical officials and authorities met to end the papal schism and deliberate on a variety of strategies for reviving Christian devotion. A few decades later, participants at the massive Council of Basel (1431–1439) sought, among other ambitious agendas, to replace the individual authority of the pope with the broader authority of a conciliar administrative system. Given the highly politicized context and concern for spiritual safeguards, it is not surprising that many attendees wanted to talk about the growing satanic threat to Christendom. Christian regeneration and rejuvenation was the issue of the day, and fifteenth-century reformers were quick to perceive magical practices as the devil's work.

Among the most important of these reforming authorities in terms of witchcraft was the Dominican Johannes Nider, whose moral treatise *Formicarius* (*The Anthill;* 1437–1438) laid out a model for orderly, pious Christian society. In the fifth book of the treatise, he turns to the subject of "Witches and Their Deceptions," claiming that his information came directly from the mouth of a secular judge who led trials between 1397 and 1406 in one of those western Alpine regions. According to the judge, the supposed community of demonic baby eaters was tortured until confessing *maleficia* of murder, infertility, and divination; in this case, the primary witch was a man named Stedelen, who provided a step-by-step overview of the group's diabolical practices. Yet as a male witch, Stedelen was unusual. Already by the later fourteenth century, women were a clear majority of those accused of witchcraft; by the first half of the fifteenth century, women would represent nearly 70 percent of the accused. And contemporaries began to wonder why.

Nider was one of the first theorists to address gender as a fundamental element of profiling witches and to set forth an argument about the relationship between women and *maleficium*. The evidence he gathered was typical for a medieval cleric and drew on deeply established Greco-Roman and early Christian sources: for as "proved" by Aristotle and scripture, women were inferior to men in all matters, ranging from the physical and mental to the emotional and religious. Given the innate incapacity of females, then, why did men like Nider consider them capable of powerful and deeply destructive magic? As Nider had a bewildered student express it in the *Formicarius*, "I cannot wonder enough that the fragile sex should dare to rush into such presumptions," to which the sage master responded, "Among simple ones like yourself, these things are wonders, but in the eyes of prudent men they are not rare."[11] But why was the association of women and magic "not rare"? Why did the deep misogyny of clerics not prompt them simply to dismiss women's magic as merely foolish, the harmless babblings of fundamentally lesser beings? Necromancy, after all, had been a decidedly masculine act requiring skill, intelligence, and extensive education, qualities or resources denied most women.

Nider provided a crucial explanation of how witches' magic differed from that of necromancers: once again, it focused more upon the source of power rather than the act itself. For example, he described how a witch might *appear* to cause rain by dipping a broom in water, whereas the true agent in fact lay elsewhere: "The broom that the witch immerses in the water, so that it should rain, does not cause the rain, but a demon who sees [her do it] . . . the witch gives a sign with the broom, but the demon acts, so that it rains through the action of the demon."[12] Thus the easy power that female witches seemed to wield was actually not their own; their actions (spells, incantations, charms) were merely passive signs enacted upon by diabolical forces. Within Nider's framework, the apparent contradiction between female incapacity and witches' power was collapsed. Because of their weakness, carnality, deviousness, and self-seeking, women were deemed particularly prone to demonic temptations, inclined to respond to diabolical seductions, and likely to grasp at any form of available power—even the satanic. In short, women's weakness was perceived by the fifteenth century as an exceedingly dangerous soft spot in the spiritual barrier between humanity and the devil.

Nider was not alone in his interests and passions, for many other mid-fifteenth-century theorists dedicated themselves in these decades to questions of witchcraft, heresy, and women's particular proclivity to the crime. French inquisitors such as Jean Veneti in the south and Nicolas Jacquier in the north each argued in scholarly treatises that the witches of their day were a new heretical sect, one unknown in the earlier centuries of Christendom, and thus a particularly dire threat. Approaching the subject from a different milieu and set of assumptions was the brilliant poet Martin Le Franc, another figure who spent significant time among reformist circles in Basel and whose long poem *Le champion des dames* (*The Defender of Ladies*) contains an extended section on the linkage of women and witchcraft. In contrast to Nider and others who reinforced those connections, however, Le Franc challenged them, defending women from the charges and particularly rejecting the supposed "night flight" of witches to their diabolical orgies.

By the mid-fifteenth century, contemporaries were not only thinking about witchcraft and heresy but intent upon exposing its darkness and secrecy—including the clear depiction of what one *looked* like. Marginalia from Le Franc's text offer the first known depiction of witches riding broomsticks, whereas an illuminated manuscript of Johannes Tinctoris's treatise from 1460 garishly rendered witches' scandalous worship of the devil (here in the form of a goat). In the later fifteenth century, the development of printing allowed for the much wider dispersion of written materials and also of visual images in the form of woodcuts. Many early printed treatises on witchcraft contained illustrations, and other works dealing with moral virtues and vices often included images of witches. Woodcuts also appeared in widely distributed pamphlets and on their own. By the end of the century, visual images of witchcraft in various forms circulated throughout European society.

A NEW CONSPIRACY THEORY

The intersection of new reformist concerns and a new generation of university men to implement them gave rise to the fusion of magic and heresy in the early fifteenth century, when authorities began to regard magical practice as a deeply threatening and specifically *conspiratorial* act. As noted above, in previous centuries, a man or woman's dabbling in healing or love charms or divination might have been dismissed as an act of pagan nonsense to be lightly punished, whereas by the fifteenth century such acts came to be evaluated less in terms of the act itself and more in terms of its symbolic meaning—that the magical action (assumed to be demonic) meant that the individual her- or himself belonged to a diabolical cult of witches, a debased and demonic community of humans in league with Satan, intent upon overthrowing Christian sovereignty and unleashing hell on earth. Evidently, the more time these scholars dedicated to the task of thinking about demons, the more elaborate and terrifying their theories became. By the early fifteenth century, therefore, "magic" had taken on a much darker and more dangerous meaning that sent ripples of fear through even the highest ranks of the Church.

In 1409, the newly installed Pope Alexander V warned of new sects appearing in Europe and of novel dangers posed by sorcerers, diviners, and other practitioners of magic and superstition. In 1437, Pope Eugenius IV likewise affirmed the threat of such demonic sorcerers and proclaimed not only that Christian magicians were apostates for abandoning religion in the service of demons, but that they were members of conspiratorial, diabolical cults. By the early fifteenth century, therefore, the traditional vocabulary of *maleficius* (male) or *maleficia* (female) was still employed by clerical opponents, but the words' meaning had shifted with profound consequences: the terms no longer simply referred to the practice of harmful magic of various sorts, but bore the specific and sinister implication of conspiratorial crime. This stereotype of magical practitioners as members of wicked communities bent on serving demons and loosing evil into the world would prove an exceptionally enduring image in the minds of European authorities up through the early modern period. Such broad new fantasies also tended to blend with local traditions and tensions, which helps to account for the diversity of accusations, inquisitorial procedures, penalties, and consequences across different regions and time periods. Thus the contribution of thinkers such as Johannes Nider and others was that witchcraft came to be perceived as a doubly heinous evil, consisting not only of the mundane crimes of *maleficium* but in the fundamentally heretical act of apostasy and idolatrous worship of the devil—an act increasingly depicted as a feminine crime.

FIFTEENTH-CENTURY WITCHCRAFT TRIALS

One documented consequence of the new theories was a dramatic increase in the number of trials for magic and witchcraft in the mid-fifteenth century. Fewer than a hundred references to sorcery trials exist prior to 1420, whereas the subsequent decades witnessed an explosion in both the number (roughly between three hundred and four hundred trials) and the intensity of prosecutions. These trials were centered in the Alpine regions of Italy, French-speaking Switzerland, and France, where the language employed betrays the growing link between heresy, magic, and witchcraft. In a particularly vivid example of how porous were categories of magic, heresy, and pejorative terminology, Alpine communities grafted the local term for Waldensian (*Vaudois*) onto witches.

In 1426, the popular sermons of Italian reformer Bernardino of Siena stirred up a frenzy of fear among Roman citizens that local healers were guilty of sorcery and that to protect such people was in itself a despicable crime. It is interesting that the people he and the Romans targeted were local practitioners of healing magic, folks who provided a useful service to those who turned against them. The accused tended to be women, although men were also charged, and were often accused of slaughtering children by sneaking into their rooms at night and sucking their blood—a charge rooted in ancient folk beliefs in a vampiric creature known as the *strix*.[13] Even more significant was the nearly contemporary incident in 1428 in the Italian town of Todi, which clearly reveals the new pattern of accusation and condemnation that would become typical of fifteenth-century trials. A woman named Matteuccia Francisci was charged at first with performing basic spells and love magic in the common tradition; by the end of the trial, however, she had been accused of being a *strix* who murdered children and who magically traveled to a distant town to worship demons at a diabolical gathering of witches.

The last element represents a dramatically new element in the relationship of magic and heresy, for although *maleficium* had always been considered

Figure 6.3. Witches Leaving for the Sabbath. Marginalia of Le Champion des Dames by Martin Le Franc, 1440. ***Source*****: Snark/Art Resource, NY.**

criminal in the eyes of medieval authorities, it had been an individual act (and thus an individual threat). Satan's newly expanded role in the late medieval period heightened the stakes of such activity, of course, but even the devil himself was apparently less terrifying to authorities than the notion of collective, conspiratorial behavior in his service. As would so many other women and men in the decades and centuries to come, Matteuccia died at the stake. Laity and clergy had different worries about *maleficium*: the former feared the particular outcome or end of harmful magic, whereas ecclesiastics were concerned instead with its means. The numbers and penalties involved ranged widely, although some trials sent up to a hundred victims to the stake. Such trials inspired still more, as the events traveled by word of mouth and ignited fears elsewhere. Near Savoy, an anonymous mid-fifteenth-century inquisitor penned a widely circulated treatise called *The Errors of the Gazarii* (a local term for witches) that provided a vivid silhouette of contemporary fears: not only were the accused seduced by the devil into using *maleficium* to kill and destroy, but they met regularly in secret nighttime gatherings to desecrate the holy, worship demons, eat babies, and defile themselves with illicit sex. If that accusation rings a bell, it is because we have encountered it repeatedly as a stereotype with which different communities were bludgeoned between the ancient and late medieval worlds. By the mid-fifteenth century, the centuries-old set of smears first applied to early Christian movements and then medieval heretics was now harnessed to fifteenth-century notions of diabolical conspirators meeting in "sabbaths" that specifically inverted and denigrated sacramental grace.

Clerical authorities echoed the claim, as in the graphic description penned by an inquisitor in Savoy in the mid-1430s who described cultic gatherings of witches who worshiped demons at their "synagogues" (a term certainly reflecting festering late medieval anti-Semitism), renounced Christianity, and forged pacts in their own blood. In the northern French city of Arras, thirty-four men and women were accused of witchcraft between 1459 and 1462; twelve were burned at the stake for devil worship and "attendance at the synagogue of the Vaudois." Thus the elements of the late medieval witches' cult represented reformers' concerns cast upside down: instead of reverently taking the Eucharist, witches gorge themselves on disgusting matter; instead of pious devotion within the domestic realm, they are women on the loose, riding broomsticks in prurient night flights to Sabbath gatherings; they subvert rites of traditional homage by kissing the devil's backside and granting him sovereignty; they dissolve boundaries of sexual propriety by fornicating with demons and one another; and they desecrate the bonds of motherhood and kinship by slaughtering and eating babies. In the minds of fifteenth-century reformers and theorists, therefore, witches' sabbaths were literally hell on earth.

MALLEUS MALEFICARUM (THE HAMMER OF WITCHES; 1486)

In 1486, the Dominican inquisitor Heinrich Krämer (also known by the Latin surname Institoris) drew on both previous literary tradition and his own trial experiences to publish the famous witch-hunting handbook *Malleus Maleficarum* (*The Hammer of Witches*). As papal inquisitor, Krämer had conducted inquisitions in southern German lands since 1474, where he worked in tandem with another Dominican inquisitor, the theologian Jakob Sprenger of the University of Cologne. Apparently the inquisitors' concerns about the spread of witchcraft in Germany were not shared by local authorities, as leading officials and citizens in the cities he visited frequently resisted his findings and methods. In one town, he was contemptuously dismissed as a senile old man; evidently the comment rankled, for Krämer petitioned the papacy in 1484 for support of his efforts. Shortly thereafter, a sympathetic Pope Innocent VIII issued the bull *Summis desiderantes affectibus* (*Desiring with Supreme Ardor*), which decried the extent of witchcraft in Germany, supported Krämer's and Sprenger's efforts, and insisted that local authorities cooperate with the papal inquisitors. The bull does not seem to have eased the inquisitors' path, however, for leaders in Innsbruck still resisted their procedures in 1485. It is within this context of frustrated ambition, therefore, that Krämer began the task of bolstering his own authority by writing a handbook that detailed the supposed actions of witches, proper procedures for identifying and prosecuting them, and thorough explanations as to how these diabolical communities aligned themselves with the devil. The *Malleus* included a copy of the papal bull when it first circulated, and it received approval in 1487 from the theological faculty of the University of Cologne.

Organized in scholastic question-and-answer form, the handbook consisted of three separate parts addressing the essential components of witchcraft, the means by which dark deeds were accomplished and methods for counteracting witches, and judicial procedures for handling such cases. A sense of Krämer's concerns and priorities may be gleaned from some of the key questions addressed in part 1, which included:

- Whether the belief in witches is so essential a part of the Catholic faith that to maintain the opposite opinion is heresy
- Whether children can be generated by *incubi* and *xuccubi* [types of demons]
- By which devils the activities of *incubus* and *xuccubus* are made possible
- Why the practice of witchcraft has increased so notably in recent years
- Concerning witches who copulate with devils, why it is that women are chiefly addicted to evil superstitions

Figure 6.4. Three Sorceresses. *Source*: Drawing by Hans Baldung Grien. Bibliothèque Nationale, Paris, France. Scala/White Images/Art Resource, NY.

- Whether witches can sway the minds of men to love or hatred
- Whether witches can make men impotent
- Whether witches can make a penis appear to be entirely removed and separate from the body
- Whether witches can by some glamour change men into beasts
- That witches who are midwives in various ways kill or abort children or offer infants to devils
- Whether the permission of Almighty God is an accompaniment of witchcraft[14]

At the heart of the lengthy manuscript were three key assumptions: first, that witchcraft was a real and diabolical heresy; second, that anyone who claimed otherwise or challenged the notion of witchcraft at all was also a heretic; and, third, that women, being lustful and weak, were particularly susceptible to the devil's seduction and thus more likely to become witches. The circular logic of the first two ideas served simultaneously to bolster Krämer's authority and to render resistance to witchcraft prosecutions even more dangerous, whereas the third claim eventually became a major underpinning of sixteenth- and seventeenth-century witchcraft theory. Although Krämer was not the first to link women and witchcraft explicitly (Nider had already made such a connection in the *Formicarius*, from which Krämer drew some of his theories), he was the first to dwell at such length and in such depth upon the topic.

Krämer has been represented for decades as a fierce misogynist, an example of a medieval friar and inquisitor innately—and perhaps pathologically—hostile to women. Yet recent scholarship into the final years of Krämer's life has revealed that the Dominican's attitude toward women was actually much more complex. Between 1487 and his death in 1505, for example, Krämer was actively involved in promoting the cults of four Italian holy women, *living saints* rather than spiritual exemplars safely in the tomb, and female humans still tempted by the world and potentially corruptible.[15] In other words, the inquisitor did not reject *all* females as inherently wicked and worthless but rather perceived the feminine as a particularly susceptible vessel for spiritual communion. Although lustful and depraved women became a channel for the devil, modest and virtuous women could become vibrant conduits for Christian grace. Rooted in a misogynist Greco-Roman tradition to which complex Christian theories had accrued over time, this split perspective of women (Madonna/Mary Magdalene, or virgin/whore) was a fundamental element of late medieval culture. By reinforcing both the potential horror and holiness of women, Krämer turned out to be, like Nider, very much in stride with the cultural and religious trends of his day.

Whatever Krämer's own motivations, however, there is no disputing that the contents of the *Malleus* took on a literary and legal life of their own, reprinted in fourteen separate editions between 1486 and 1520, and again

Figure 6.5. Crucifix, Roughly Carved from a Mandrake Root, Popular Object of Magic and Superstition in the Fifteenth and Sixteenth Centuries. *Source*: Schloss Ambras, Innsbruck, Austria. Erich Lessing/Art Resource, NY.

in sixteen editions between 1576 and 1669 (the peak of the great European witch trials). Although Krämer, Sprenger, and their late medieval associates did not initiate or participate in trials of the scale witnessed in the sixteenth and seventeenth centuries, their theories and the ensuing theological and legal frameworks ultimately accrued an authority far beyond that of their individual roles and responsibilities. Their ideas and procedural apparatus, in other words, became a weapon that later theorists and hunters would wield—hammerlike—against witches.

CONCLUSION

By the end of the fifteenth century, ideas about magic had changed dramatically from the early medieval period. Linked specifically with heresy by the time of the high Middle Ages and associated further with diabolical, conspiratorial witchcraft in later centuries, magic serves as an intriguing litmus test for charting medieval shifts in anxiety, authority, and antiheretical activity. By 1500 no definitive, overarching concept of "magic" or "witchcraft" would prevail any more than there would be a stable or immutable category of "heresy." For all their crudity, stereotypes are subtle, malleable instruments easily tuned to the peculiar pitch of local communities' own circumstances, conditions, and complaints. Perhaps the only common thread binding medieval attitudes toward magic was the certainty in the existence of evil powers and the capacity of certain people to forge hellish channels to depravity on earth. Although trial procedures varied tremendously across European regions, and men and women would continue to die at the stake, the stereotype of lustful women in voluntary bondage to Satan would become a particularly potent and bitter legacy to the early modern world.

SUGGESTIONS FOR FURTHER READING

Bailey, Michael. *Battling Demons: Witchcraft, Heresy, and Reform in the Late Middle Ages*. University Park: Pennsylvania State University Press, 2003.

———. *Fearful Spirits, Reasoned Follies: The Boundaries of Superstition in Late Medieval Europe*. Ithaca, NY: Cornell University Press, 2017.

———. "From Sorcery to Witchcraft: Clerical Conceptions of Magic in the Later Middle Ages." *Speculum* 76, no. 4 (2001): 960–90.

———. *Magic and Superstition in Europe: A Concise History from Antiquity to the Present*. Lanham, MD: Rowman & Littlefield, 2007.

Blumenfeld-Kosinski, Renate. *The Strange Case of Ermine de Reims: A Medieval Woman between Demons and Saints.* Philadelphia: University of Pennsylvania Press, 2015.

Boureau, Alain. *Satan the Heretic: The Birth of Demonology in the Medieval West.* Chicago: University of Chicago Press, 2006.

Cohn, Norman. *Europe's Inner Demons: The Demonization of Christians in Medieval Christendom*. Chicago: University of Chicago Press, 2000.

Elliott, Dyan. *Fallen Bodies: Pollution, Sexuality, and Demonology in the Middle Ages.* Philadelphia: University of Pennsylvania Press, 1999.

Fanger, Claire. *Conjuring Spirits: Texts and Traditions of Medieval Ritual Magic.* University Park: Pennsylvania State University Press, 1998.

Jolly, Karen Louise, Edward Peters, and Catharina Raudvere. *Witchcraft and Magic in Europe.* Vol. 3, *The Middle Ages*. London: Athlone, 2002.

Kieckhefer, Richard. *Forbidden Rites: A Necromancer's Manual of the Fifteenth Century.* Philadelphia: University of Pennsylvania Press, 1998.

———. *Magic in the Middle Ages*. Cambridge: Cambridge University Press, 1989.

Kors, Alan, and Edward Peters, eds. *Witchcraft in Europe 400–1700: A Documentary History*, Second edition. Philadelphia: University of Pennsylvania Press, 2001.

Page, Sophie. *Magic in Medieval Manuscripts*. Toronto: University of Toronto Press, 2004.

Peters, Edward. *The Magician, the Witch, and the Law*. Philadelphia: University of Pennsylvania Press, 1978.

Rampton, Martha, ed. *European Magic and Witchcraft: A Reader.* Toronto: University of Toronto Press, 2018.

NOTES

1. Valerie Flint, *The Rise of Magic in Early Medieval Europe* (Princeton, NJ: Princeton University Press, 1990), 3.

2. Karen Louise Jolly, Catharina Raudvere, and Edward Peters, *Witchcraft and Magic in Europe*, vol. 3, *The Middle Ages* (London: Athlone, 2001), 3.

3. Claire Fanger, *Conjuring Spirits: Texts and Traditions of Medieval Ritual Magic* (University Park: Pennsylvania State University Press, 1998), 57.

4. Alan Kors and Edward Peters, eds., *Witchcraft in Europe 400–1700: A Documentary History*, 2nd ed. (Philadelphia: University of Pennsylvania Press, 2001), 155.

5. Kors and Peters, *Witchcraft*, 97.

6. Kors and Peters, *Witchcraft*, 119–20.

7. Bernard Gui, *The Inquisitor's Guide: A Medieval Manual on Heretics*, ed. Janet Shirley (Welwyn Garden City, UK: Ravenhall Books, 2006), 150.

8. Kors and Peters, *Witchcraft*, 122–23.

9. Kors and Peters, *Witchcraft*, 132.

10. Kors and Peters, *Witchcraft*, 132.

11. Quoted by Michael Bailey, *Battling Demons: Witchcraft, Heresy, and Reform in the Later Middle Ages* (University Park: Pennsylvania State University, 2003), 151.

12. Michael Bailey, “The Feminization of Magic and the Emerging Idea of the Female Witch in the Late Middle Ages,” *Essays in Medieval Studies* 19 (2002): 127.

13. Michael Bailey, *Magic and Superstition in Europe: A Concise History from Antiquity to the Present* (Lanham, MD: Rowman & Littlefield, 2007).

14. See part 1 in Christopher MacKay, *The Hammer of Witches: A Complete Translation of the Malleus Maleficarum* (Cambridge: Cambridge University Press, 2009), 91–258.

15. Tamar Herzig, “Witches, Saints, and Heretics: Heinrich Kraemer’s Ties with Italian Women Mystics,” *Magic, Ritual, and Witchcraft* 1 (2006): 24–55.

Chapter Seven

Wyclif, the Word of God, and Inquisition in England

By the late fourteenth century, the contours of piety and religion on the Continent had already been shaped by centuries of apostolic preachers, acerbic reformers, and ascetic laypeople. In England, however, separated geographically by a major waterway and politically through the Anglo-Norman legacy of powerfully centralized kingship, a somewhat different pattern emerged. Although many of the same arguments about the proper joinings of heaven and earth rippled across England, and did periodically crest into accusations of heresy, such concerns were relatively mild compared with contemporary events farther south. Why, then, did English authorities issue and implement new, Continental-inspired inquisitorial legislation at the turn of the fifteenth century? Of what crimes were suspects accused? And how did those who came under inquisitorial scrutiny understand and practice their own faith? In this and the next chapter, we visit medieval universities such as Oxford, Cambridge, Paris, and Bologna to consider how blurred the line was between teaching and preaching (particularly since all medieval faculty were clergy), and how faculty engagement with theological matters could both inspire a movement and enrage opponents. We begin with the Oxford theologian John Wyclif, around whom a small group of followers began to gather in the 1380s. Within a few decades, that first intimate circle would widen dramatically as its ideas found purchase in communities across England, forging networks and relationships that would endure through the sixteenth century.

Although the context in which Wycliffite complaints emerged was specific to England, the struggles focused, as they did elsewhere, on the fundamental issue of spiritual authority and, in particular, the relationship between scripture and ecclesiastical hierarchy. Englishmen and women inspired by Wycliffite ideas also found rich and relevant meaning in the apocalyptic book of Revelation and other scriptural passages anticipating the advent of the Antichrist; yet in England those ideas were able to take took root without the associations southern beguins had formed with Francis, Peter Olivi, or Spiritual Franciscans. Indeed, Wyclif was a far cry from the charismatic Continental preachers described in earlier chapters and appears at first glance an unlikely hero for a popular reformist movement. However, his increasingly strident embrace of scripture and rejection of certain core tenets and practices of the institutional Church became the heartbeat of a new phenomenon. Representing different geographic, socioeconomic, and intellectual backgrounds, its adherents found that their interests aligned upon a common agreement: that the top-heavy institutional Church interfered with the individual Christian's unmediated contact with scripture and the Word of God. Once harnessed to specifically English debates over the proper exercise of power, the drive for direct access to vernacular scripture took on potent (and potentially inflammatory) new dimensions that would influence English piety and the relationship between politics, religion, and literacy on the island.

Historians have long debated the question of why England had so little heresy compared with its Continental neighbors, where the matrix of religious reform, dissent, and repression emerged by the twelfth century. Part of the answer undoubtedly lies within the complex constellation of legal, political, and religious factors unique to the island, including the strong centralized kingship and relatively stringent ecclesiastical oversight that prevented the sort of abuses that enraged reformers on the Continent. There were, however, at least a dozen heresy proceedings in England prior to the Wycliffite controversy, two of which involved Oxford academics whose propositions never made it past the university community. It is telling that the so-called geographical isolation that scholars have argued shielded England from Continental heresy did little to hinder the transport of ideas to Bohemia, where, as we will see in chapter 8, their fusion with powerful regional currents of Czech religious reform and political resentment would bear lingering consequences through and beyond the Reformation.

LIFE AND WRITINGS OF WYCLIF

As is typical for those historical figures not of royal background or otherwise unusually well documented, we know few details about John Wyclif's origins. Historians have made a plausible case for his birth around 1328 to parents of the lesser nobility in the Yorkshire town of Wycliff-on-Tees. That the family's lands lay under the lordship of John of Gaunt, the Duke of Lancaster, also sheds some light on the duke's later influence on Wyclif's career. Evidently a talented boy, John was taught locally by the rector of the church on the family manor before departing Yorkshire for Oxford. Ordained in 1351, he earned his bachelor of arts degree from Merton College by 1356.

An increasingly renowned teacher of philosophy through the 1360s, he then turned to theology, earning his doctorate by 1372.[1] As his reputation spread, he accrued parish responsibilities and a growing reputation within ecclesiastical and scholarly circles.

In 1365, Wyclif was involved in the first of many controversies during his career when he was chosen to be warden of the new Canterbury College

Figure 7.1. Portrait of Theologian John Wyclif. *Source*: **Getty Images.**

at Oxford: the college hosted an unusual mixture of "regular" and "secular" clergy among its students: the former were monks who followed a particular rule (hence "regulated") and were not involved in secular pastoral care, while the latter belonged to no monastic order. As a secular priest, Wyclif was unpopular among the monastic contingent and tensions periodically flared; after the new archbishop of Canterbury tried to remove him from office, Wyclif appealed to Pope Urban V for support. The appeal was unsuccessful, and he was removed from office in 1370, an event that likely cemented his hostility toward the institution of monasticism and its place within Christendom.

Other ideas were similarly taking shape for him during these formative years as a student, teacher, and administrator at Oxford. For example, Wyclif grew up intellectually steeped in one of the major philosophical debates of the day, an argument begun among the ancient Greeks over the nature of "universals." Consider an animal: What is the relationship between the essence of "animal" (the object or known thing within the idea of "animal") and a material animal in the real world? Is there an essence that exists universally in every individual cat, dog, monkey, and so on? Or does the fact that each of these creatures is labeled "animal" simply reflect the workings of mind, rather than a real, universal essence in itself?

The subject is an enormously complex and vital strand in medieval thought. For our purposes, however, it is reasonable to simplify matters and focus on two distinct medieval positions: realism and nominalism. Put simply, the question had to do with whether entities existed independently of one's mind (having real existence, the position of "realists") or only existed within one's mind (existing just as a name, the solution of "nominalists"). Drawing on Platonic belief in the realm of abstract forms (or universals) independent of the material world, realists tended to identify physical objects as dim reflections of an ideal universal. In other words, material animals represent only a pale copy of the ideal Platonic form of "animal," which exists in itself. Nominalists, on the other hand, rejected the notion that these universals existed in any real sense, claiming instead that "animal" is merely a label for imposing similarities where there were perhaps none. The word *nominalism* comes from the Latin for "name," and for nominalist thinkers, such descriptors were indeed merely names. Any perceived similarity between objects that allowed one to categorize them (for example, as "table," "light," or "cloud") was therefore just a name. Though such disagreements might not immediately strike modern students as compelling, at heart was a series of fundamental questions about the universe: What can be known by human beings? How? What separates the material from the immaterial? And, by extension, what is the relationship between the mundane and divine?

As a young man, Wyclif had been drawn to the nominalism of the English Franciscan and theologian William of Ockham, but he was troubled by Ockham's denial of the reality of universals. Over time, he developed a carefully articulated position predicated on the authority and indestructibility of universals. Following a line of thought proposed by early medieval theologians such as St. Augustine and St. Anselm, Wyclif conceived of universals as prototypes emerging first and foremost from the divine. In other words, for Wyclif a divine idea gives birth to universal archetypes, which only then, derivatively, manifest in material creation. Although traditional scholarship has oversimplified Wyclif's perspective as "ultrarealist," recent work has illuminated the great sophistication and complexity of the doctor's theology.[2] Emerging out of a deep conviction in the universal reality of the eternal church and in scripture as the timeless and perfect Word of God, Wyclif's stance became the foundation for his philosophical and theological writings. Those in turn became the wellspring of novel conclusions about ecclesiastical authority and the sacraments, controversies that soon landed him in hot water with the Church. In contrast with the eternal, "invisible" church, for example, the visible Church of the fourteenth century increasingly appeared to him as not only lesser but corrupted and debased—the seat of the Antichrist himself.

Modern professors are sometimes pulled into the orbit of political circles, particularly in certain fields (such as political science or economics), when their expert opinion is deemed significant for matters beyond the university; in a similar vein, late medieval professors (particularly theologians and canon lawyers) could also be called on for their specialized doctrinal and legal knowledge by Church leaders and secular rulers alike. Wyclif notably found a powerful patron and protector in John of Gaunt, Duke of Lancaster, uncle to the young king Richard II, and thus in practice the ruler of England. John of Gaunt was an imposing figure determined to check the power of the Church; recognizing the political potential of Wycliffite thought as a weapon against ecclesiastical authority, he took the scholar under his wing.

In 1371, Wyclif appears to have entered the political arena for the first time, jumping headlong into a parliamentary debate over one of the major controversies of the fourteenth century: secular taxation of the clergy. Defending the position of two Austin friars who claimed that secular authorities were justified in seizing Church property in times of emergency, he rejected the claims to dominion of the established Church and its head, the pope. It was not a new claim, for tensions between secular and sacral authority had represented a major axis of European history since the eleventh century, but the emergence of increasingly powerful secular authorities in the later Middle Ages had sharpened its edge. In 1302, for example, Pope Boniface VIII had responded to the French king's attempt to tax the clergy by thundering forth in the bull *Unam Sanctam* (*One Holy Church*) that "we declare, we proclaim, we define that it is absolutely necessary for salvation that every human creature be subject to the Roman Pontiff."[3] During the subsequent decades, theorists such as Marsilius of Padua and John of Jandun, who explicitly critiqued papal claims to supremacy, were hailed by emperors and kings on the Continent eager to employ scholars to bolster their political agendas.

In his defense of the friars, therefore, Wyclif was walking a similar path to those earlier critics, in this case encouraged by John of Gaunt and the English king. The theological outgrowths of these early ideas about proper authority and dominion would first bring Wyclif under suspicion of heresy. Yet Wyclif's political star rose for several more years, and he took on increasingly visible political appointments through the decade, protected by his relationship with John of Gaunt: in 1374 he served as a diplomatic representative of the English king to papal envoys in Bruges, and in 1376 he helped his patron fight an opposing faction in Parliament. An academic to the end, he also continued to write during these years, refining and sharpening his stance on certain theological issues that, when extended to their logical outcome, challenged the very basis of the Roman Church.

Wyclif's theological writings flooded from his pen almost immediately upon completion of his doctoral degree. In the early 1370s, he developed the *Postilla super totam bibliam* (*Commentary on the Entire Bible*), probably presented first as a series of lectures, and continued to produce works on issues of law and dominion and the relationship between secular and sacral authority through the rest of the decade. Influenced by other late medieval political theorists, Wyclif argued in works such as *De mandatis divinis* (*On Divine Commandments*) and *De civili dominio* (*On Civil Dominion*) that only a man currently in a state of righteousness could properly wield power. In other words, authority came not from the office but rather from the moral and spiritual wellness of its occupant. Such a bold claim rang particularly true in the final decades of the fourteenth century, when the papal see was riven by competing and mutually excommunicated contenders, and when accusations of clerical corruption and laxity were gaining momentum. In his *De ecclesia* (*On the Church*), around 1379, Wyclif even more clearly articulated his perspective on the nature and composition of the Church and its relationship to the divine: the membership of pope and clergy among those of grace was not a foregone conclusion. Once again, the logical implications of the idea proved radical, for if Church officials could not be known as members of the true Church, not men of righteousness, then adherence to their edicts could not be required. For Wyclif, *dominium*, or proper power, whether civil or ecclesiastical, resided only within those in a state of grace. Because God alone could discern those in grace from those who are damned, the institutional Church's sacraments of absolution, excommunication, and so on could not logically serve in themselves as a vehicle for grace.

Scripture, rather, was for Wyclif the only and ultimate source of Christian knowledge and doctrine. In his *De veritate sacrae Scriptura* (*On the Truth of Sacred Scripture*) of 1378, he explored the Christian foundation set forth in scripture and called for the stripping away of all growths and practices not rooted specifically in the Word of God. One of the most venerable of the offices and institutions condemned by Wyclif was the monastic tradition, which he excoriated as a biblically unwarranted separation of some individuals from the rest of the Church. Unsurprisingly, English monks and friars vehemently defended their ancient communal way of life against what the professor called "private religion." Thus, because Wyclif's years of secular political service were intertwined with doctrinal criticism of ecclesiastical authority, members of the monastic orders were among the most vocal of his growing numbers of enemies.

The increasingly radical stance of the Oxford professor did not escape the notice of Rome; encouraged by the scholar's Benedictine foes, Pope Gregory XI issued in 1377 a list of eighteen "erroneous conclusions" gleaned from the writings of the "professor of holy writ—would that he were not also a master of error!" The pope accused him of having

> burst forth in such execrable and abominable folly, that he does not fear to maintain dogmatically in said kingdom and publicly to preach, or rather to vomit forth from the poisonous confines of his own breast, some propositions and conclusions . . . which threaten to subvert and weaken the condition of the entire church.[4]

Such criticisms, however, did little to dampen Wyclif's theological commitment or scholarly productivity. At other times and places, papal and archiepiscopal wrath had proved a formidable obstacle to those who would preach or teach prohibited ideas. By 1378, however, this was no longer the case; the conflict between rival popes would not only distract clerical authorities from the matters at hand and temporarily overshadow the Wycliffite controversy, but over time lent even greater force to growing English anticlericalism and vernacular scripturalism. Wyclif was popular at Oxford, having drawn to him a large group of like-minded colleagues and students; in addition, he had protection from powerful secular patrons. Repeated attempts to secure a formal condemnation of the professor in England failed, due in large part to the intervention of the Black Prince's widow, Joan. Thus even in these tumultuous times, Wyclif continued for several years to teach, write, and participate in political spheres—until, that is, the context shifted in the early 1380s.

ECCLESIASTICAL RESPONSE

What finally tipped the scales against Wyclif were the implications of his theology for the Eucharist, that ultimate joining of heaven and earth. The ideas that he began to teach in 1379 and that prompted an Oxford commission in 1381 are summed up in a papal condemnation the following year: "that the substance of material bread and wine remains after the consecration in the sacrament of the altar," "that accidents do not remain without a subject after the consecration in the same sacrament," and that "Christ is not in the sacrament of the altar identically, truly, and really in his bodily person."[5] Simply put, Wyclif was denying the doctrine of transubstantiation, refuting the Church's explanation that although the appearance of bread and wine remain, the reality is Christ's body and blood, and rejecting orthodox doctrine that Christ's presence in the consecrated wafer and wine is the same bodily Christ born to Mary. These long-standing certainties within the Church could not be subjected to dismissal by an upstart theologian, and thus Wyclif's Eucharistic theories provoked Rome (even in the midst of the papal schism) to respond.

Despite support from his Oxford colleagues, the now-famous—or infamous, depending on one's point of view—scholar was forcibly retired from the university, and he withdrew to a quiet domicile in Leicestershire, where he continued to write and preach. Church authorities, however, were not finished. In May of 1382, Archbishop William Courtenay summoned a council in London to investigate Wyclif's propositions. The gathering, which came to be known as the Earthquake Council due to the coincidental geological event, decided that twenty-four of Wyclif's conclusions were errors or outright heresies. Followers and opponents alike deemed the earthquake an ominous sign of divine displeasure, though they naturally disagreed as to the cause of that displeasure. The tide was also beginning to turn at the university as increasing pressure was brought to bear on the faculty by the Church. Chancellor Robert Rygge withdrew his former support.

Some of Wyclif's followers were compelled to recant, such as his close disciple Philip Repingdon, but the professor himself was surprisingly unscathed. Allowed to return to his country rectory in Lutterworth, he not only curtly refused Pope Urban VI's summons to Rome in 1384 (perhaps as a consequence of pressure from the duke), but even underscored in his letter the possibility that the pope was the Antichrist. Wyclif appears to have been unperturbed by the possibility of papal wrath, though whether because of principled commitment, an idiosyncratic personality, or confidence in protection by secular allies, we will never know.

Personally unscathed by the controversies his ideas provoked, the scholar continued writing in relative peace until his death from stroke on December

31, 1384. Although he was posthumously condemned for heresy at the Council of Constance in 1415, Wyclif suffered little clerical pressure during his lifetime, and although his corpse would be exhumed in 1428, burned, and the ashes tossed into a river to ensure his utter destruction, he was never confronted with the stake. The same would not be true for many of those who followed, particularly once the relationship between Wyclif's ideas and the early fifteenth-century Hussite revolution in Bohemia became clear. In the centuries that followed, English authorities paid ever closer attention, acknowledging that geographical insularity and royal strength were no longer a bulwark against the forces of change.

WYCLIF, WYCLIFFISM, AND "LOLLARDY"

Even in the face of the condemnation of 1382 and the subsequent edicts outlawing Wycliffite thought, the Oxford professor's ideas continued to attract support. Part of the appeal no doubt had to do with their resonance with contemporary attitudes and the eagerness with which discontented populations reached for the intellectual tools he first provided. Yet the relationship between Wyclif and those criticized for adopting, adapting, or extending his ideas (particularly those who came under fire in the late fifteenth and sixteenth centuries) is no easier to determine than it was for the generations who followed Valdès centuries earlier on the Continent.

Once again, we are faced with difficulties of terminology. Those hostile to the followers of Wyclif generally called them either "Wycliffites" or "Lollards," that latter being an epithet rooted in the Middle Dutch verb *lollen* (to mumble) that skewered the perceived hypocrisy of those who mumble and mutter prayers under their breath. On the Continent, it served as a general designator for wandering men of suspicious piety, as they were described in the antiheretical tract *Against the Beghard, Lollard, and [Beguine Sister] Heretics*, written by the Rhineland inquisitor John Wasmod in 1398. In England, the term *Lollard* was already being specifically applied to Wycliffites in episcopal registers and other ecclesiastical documents. Within the growing circles of like-minded adherents, however, simpler names akin to those we have already encountered in these pages emerged, such as "True Men," "Known Men," and "Sons of Grace." The masculine quality of these names reflects a particularly gendered element within these late medieval English communities that will be discussed below. Since much scholarly confusion has derived from imposed (and often pejorative) terms such as *Lollard* and *Wycliffite*, we will instead use the designation *True Men and Women* when referring to the perspective of members and believers: while not a universally employed term, it at least conveys an element of self-conception and community identity and avoids unduly privileging inquisitorial categories.

Such multiplicity of terms and names reinforces the fact that the overlapping circles of self-conscious believers never constituted a formal or organized institution but instead represented a shared worldview shaped by distinct attitudes toward the contemporary Church, key texts, and local rural or urban circumstances. Like the Poor, beguins, Apostolic Brethren, and others, the True Men and Women in England perceived themselves as embodying the true original Church set in signal opposition to the corrupted institutional authority of pope and clergy. I follow here J. Patrick Hornbeck's recent proposal that we consider such communities across time and space in terms of a "family resemblance" model that allows for gradations and variations rather than reducing them to a falsely uniform and static set of theological principles.[6] As we have now observed in many contexts, pious notions were hardly fixed or homogenous: the beliefs of members of the same community (or family) sometimes overlapped and were at other times distinct; major theological variations appear across time and space much as family characteristics across generations may recur or disappear; and many believers blended localized or eccentric ideas with standard tenets, contributing to an ultimately kaleidoscopic array of ideas and practices.

What, then, can we learn about these clusters of people who picked up on the ideas rippling through early fifteenth-century England and aimed them at the hallowed rituals of the institutional Church? How did ecclesiastical authorities respond, and with what consequences? Let us turn to the history of those communities and the mounting inquisitorial response through a chain of circumstances that can be divided roughly into three stages: the first begins in Wyclif's lifetime and traces his early followers' experience through the controversies surrounding his work and writings; the second considers early inquisitorial response to "Lollards" and the explosion of seething political and economic resentments into outright revolt; and the last addresses the growth and prosecution of English communities of True Men and Women through the first quarter of the sixteenth century and the ways in which communities' spiritual convictions developed, transformed, and spread until the arrival of Protestantism in the 1520s and 1530s.

EARLY CIRCLES OF INFLUENCE

The process by which Wyclif's arguments first circulated within and then extended beyond the walls of Oxford can be at least partially reconstructed using various Church documents that reflected the growing anxiety in the final decades of the fourteenth century.[7] In 1382, four of Wyclif's most ardent supporters (Nicholas Hereford, John Aston, and two unnamed men) were chastised by Bishop Wykeham of Winchester for teaching Wycliffite errors in north Hampshire. By the year of his death, 1384, the trickle of injunctions against Wyclif and his followers had broadened into a steady stream and would continue to swell through the early fifteenth century, particularly under the stern direction of William Courtenay, Archbishop of Canterbury (r. 1381–1385), a forceful opponent of the university master and his followers. Yet support for Wyclif continued within Oxford circles long after the theologian's death: Nicholas Hereford, for example, stood firm in his commitment to Wycliffite principles through the 1380s, while figures such as William James, Robert Lechlade, Thomas Turk, William Taylor, and Peter Payne held fast even longer.

Members of the lower clergy such as chaplains and unemployed priests also made up a significant proportion of early preachers within the movement. Although technically members of the ecclesiastical hierarchy, these men often found themselves economically disadvantaged; moreover, pastoral responsibilities brought them into regular contact with people either familiar with or receptive to the new teachings. Men such as William Swinderby of Leicester thus played an important role in the early spread of Wycliffism beyond Oxford's forbidding walls. A dynamic and experienced preacher accustomed to the hardships of the road, Swinderby harnessed his evident rhetorical skill to the cause, stirring up local populations, challenging authorities, and enticing new recruits into the swelling ranks. Although he disappears from the historical record in 1392, his influence extended far beyond through the message he spread and the members he converted.

Wyclif's supporters did not limit themselves to academic arguments and charismatic preaching, however, but quickly extended their reach directly into the public eye of English politics. In 1395, a group of his most influential followers penned a declaration known as the Twelve Conclusions, which was not only publicized by being nailed to the doors of Westminster Abbey and St. Paul's Cathedral (cathedral doors being the late medieval version of a bulletin board), but even presented to Parliament. Among the issues tackled in the document were the sorry state of the Church and the flight of faith, hope, and charity; the failure of the priesthood to achieve the apostolic model; clerical abuse of confession; the false doctrine of transubstantiation that "induces all men but a few to idolatry, for they ween that Christ's body . . . by virtue of the priest's word should be essentially enclosed in a little bread"; rejection of exorcisms, ritualistic blessings, prayers for the dead, and pilgrimage; condemnation of Christian warfare as contrary to the New Testament; the immoral consequences of imposed celibacy, including sodomy, contraception, and abortion; and the wastefulness of frivolous craft. Reserving special ire for clergy in secular offices, the authors of the Twelve Conclusions insisted that the spiritual and secular were to be kept apart, scornfully observing that "hermaphrodite or ambidexter were a good name to such men of double estate."[8] Although Parliament did not respond, the text circulated widely thereafter and was soon part of the growing Wycliffite canon.

The Twelve Conclusions cannot be taken to represent the beliefs of all those in Wyclif's circles, but they do point to the visibility and vehemence of his early adherents. More than twenty years after Wyclif's death, moreover, his influence was evidently still so strong at Oxford that William Courtenay's successor, Thomas Arundel, insisted in 1407 that its undergraduates be interrogated monthly by hall wardens about their theological opinions. Such an infringement upon the traditional liberties of the university underscores fifteenth-century authorities' perception of Wycliffism as an alarmingly vital, even viral force whose suppression would require increasingly bold action.

Wycliffite ideas evidently not only appealed early on to the colleges of Oxford but also resonated with secular nobility and elites. Contemporary chroniclers report the affiliation of a group of knights with the movement, men who wielded significant power at the court of King Richard II. In an entry for 1382, for example, an Augustinian canon named Henry Knighton from Leicester records that among the followers of Wyclif were some knights, including "Sir Thomas Latimer, Sir John Trussel, Sir Lewis Clifford, Sir John Peachey, Sir Richard Storey, Sir Reginald Hilton, and some dukes and earls." They were, he continued, "the strongest promoters and most powerful protectors of the sect, and its most effective defenders, and invincible champions."[9] Several years later, the St. Albans chronicler Thomas Walsingham likewise reported that "there were knights who were enthusiastic followers of this sect and who gave it their support."[10] Part of the appeal of Wycliffite thought to this cluster of elites was its usefulness in combating Church authority and reinforcing secular claims to power. In this respect, the ideas proposed by Wyclif and circulated by his followers provided ammunition to the side of secularism in the centuries-old struggle between pope and king. Influential knights contributed in turn to the movement, providing not only protection from Church authorities but also the financial backing necessary for the writing and distribution of Wycliffite texts.

Most important among these writings was the first full vernacular translation of the Bible, which was completed by 1397 through contributions by Wyclif himself and through the work of his associates. The completed version was an initially rough text that later circulated in more polished form to feed English scriptural yearnings. On the basis of translated biblical passages, adherents from all levels of society could mark for themselves the yawning gap between apostolic ideals and the institutional Church; inquisitorial bonfires did little to suppress the text, and more than 250 copies of the Bible survive. Perceptions of ecclesiastical failure also fanned the flames of incipient apocalypticism, as in a Wycliffite Latin commentary on the Apocalypse known as the *Opus arduum* (*Hard Work*). *Its anonymous but apparently scholarly author claimed to write from prison in early 1390, but little else is known about its origins; the text survived and circulated for decades, however, finally drawing the approving gaze of a reforming monk named Martin Luther in the early sixteenth century. Other early texts included the vast Floretum*, an anthology (or "garden") of quoted materials compiled by 1396 that drew extensively from Wyclif's own writings; an abridged version circulated as the *Rosarium*. As with the *Opus arduum* and the extensive Wycliffite *Glossed Gospels* or commentaries, the driving force here clearly consisted of trained scholars with access to superior libraries.

The scholarly quality of these works may help explain why Wyclif's ideas did not ripple out into the broader population until talented preachers and teachers set themselves to the task of explaining them to local communities. Once that process began, however, a large body of sermons, teaching tracts, and other forms of Wycliffite texts were shared and copied within sympathetic circles. The movement's early written productivity peaked by 1415, and scholars suggest that few, if any, new texts were written after about 1430; yet the core of extant materials took on a powerful new life, serving as the

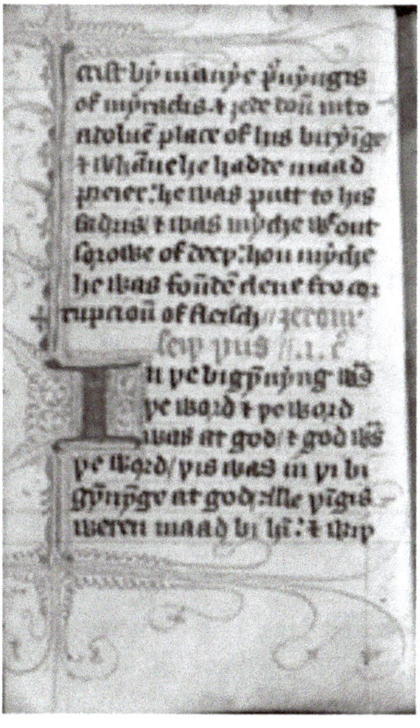

Figure 7.2. Pocket Wycliffite Bible, Introduction to Gospel of John. Folio 2v of MS Hunter 191 (T.8.21). *Source*: **University of Glasgow Library, Department of Special Collections.**

medium through which communities solidified their own doctrinal identities and secured contacts with other like-minded groups. Thus, texts and literacy were fundamental to what would soon become a diffused but nevertheless widespread phenomenon.

ANTIHERETICAL LEGISLATION (1401–1409)

Unlike their counterparts farther south, the English clergy possessed few administrative tools or procedures to arrest, prosecute, or condemn heretics. In 1397, therefore, prelates successfully urged Parliament to implement the centuries-old Continental procedures and penalties for heresy, whereby diocesan authority could imprison and interrogate suspects; those found recalcitrant were to be handed over to secular authorities for execution. The deposition of Richard II in 1399 and crowning of the Lancastrian Henry IV opened the door to fiercer prosecutions than had previously been the case, and the new archbishop of Canterbury, Thomas Arundel, seized the opportunity. Key among prohibited practices were unapproved preaching and vernacular translations of scripture, but further legislation was required to give teeth to the new antiheretical mission.

Two documents issued in the first decade of the fifteenth century provided such traction. First was the decree *De heretico comburendo* (*On the Burning of Heretics*), issued by Henry IV in 1401; second was the *Constitutions* of Arundel, which are discussed later. Targeting "diverse false and perverse people of a certain new sect," *De heretico comburendo* charged Lollards with meeting in unlawful conventicles, holding schools, making and writing books, "wickedly" instructing others in error, and making "great strife and division among the people" as they "commit subversion of the said Catholic faith and doctrine of the Holy Church, in diminution of divine Worship, and also in destruction of the estate, rights, and liberties of the said Church of England." Any who refused to abjure or who relapsed into heresy after abjuring were to be handed over to secular authorities for burning, "that such punishment may strike fear into the minds of others, whereby no such wicked doctrine and heretical and erroneous opinions, nor their authors and fautors . . . be sustained or in any way suffered." Specifically tasked with aiding inquisitorial efforts were the "sheriffs, mayors and bailiffs of the said counties, cities, bouroughs and towns."[11] Thus was execution by fire first mandated and implemented against English heresy.

If the Council of Verona's decrees of 1184 were the foundation of Continental inquisition (see chapter 3), one might argue that *De heretico comburendo* served the same purpose in England 217 years later. Although the decree reflected the escalation of royal anger and ecclesiastical anxiety, it did not elicit the intended surrender of souls; rather, it seems to have provoked a stiffening of resistance among many Wycliffites. Akin to the experience of the Poor on the European mainland, the once-public True Men went underground and sought to evade diocesan inquisitors wherever possible. A number of trials took place after 1401, particularly under the leadership of the archbishop of Canterbury, but also with participation by bishops, university masters, and panels of various ecclesiastical authorities.

One of the first to be executed was the parish priest William Sawtrey, the curate of Lynn. During an early round of questioning in 1399, he had apparently proclaimed that instead of adoring *the cross on which Christ suffered*, he adored *Christ who suffered on it*. After recanting and returning to the faith shortly thereafter, Sawtrey was interrogated again in the presence of Arundel himself in 1401. In a list of charges clearly echoing his earlier claims, the inquisitors focused particularly upon the priest's Lollard rejection of three monumental Christian issues: holy relics, sacramental authority, and transubstantiation. Because Sawtrey had sworn never again to preach Lollardy when he was charged with heresy the first time, the congregation found him guilty of relapse into heresy, thus earning the death penalty. Before his execution, the priest was first formally deposed from clerical status and stripped of the symbols of his office; to underscore his degraded status, a layman's cap was placed on his head to hide the tonsure (the ring of hair marking a member of the clergy). The decree of condemnation came from the pen of Henry IV, directing the mayor and sheriff of London to arrest and burn the relapsed Lollard. Many others convicted of "the new heresy" would soon follow Sawtrey to the flames.

Adding to the antiheretical momentum of combined inquiry and targeted legislation, in 1409 Archbishop Arundel issued the draconian *Constitutions*. The second major legal contribution to English inquisition, the document regulated licenses to teach and preach, specified punishments for disobedient preachers, mandated monthly theological interrogations of Oxford students, prohibited the ownership or reading of unapproved Wycliffite material, and forbade the unauthorized possession or translation of scripture into English. Because the last prohibition applied not only to full biblical texts but to any works even citing scripture, it was a significant blow. The *Constitutions* concluded with the specific penalties and procedures that would be suffered by those who refused to follow its rules. Although ostensibly casting a net of orthodoxy wider than the Wycliffite community, the *Constitutions* achieved its aim of hereticizing the preaching and teaching of True Men leadership.

Bonfires of Wyclif's books blazed on Arundel's watch. Intriguingly, they simultaneously also burned in Prague, far to the east, where students and other couriers between England and Bohemia had transmitted many of his major works in the years following 1407. Perhaps first introduced through the marriage of Anne of Bohemia to Richard II in 1382 and the opening of formal political and economic relationships between the two realms, people inspired by Wycliffite ideas sustained a mutually beneficial dialogue between England and Bohemia up until about 1415. Letters, books, and documents traveled to and fro among self-identified, sympathetic networks. Before his burning at the Council of Constance in 1415 for heresy (as we will see in chapter 8), the Czech reformer Jan Hus would close his response to an Englishman's letter as follows: "The church of Christ from Bohemia salutes the church of Christ in England, desiring to be a sharer of the profession of the holy faith in the grace of the Lord Jesus Christ."[12]

In 1414, the volatile mixture of anticlericalism, extant political resentment, and gospel ideals exploded into rebellion. The Lancastrians, who had been laboring to demonstrate links between religious and political dissent, could not have asked for a better opportunity to make their case. At the heart of these events was Sir John Oldcastle, a politically elite leader of the movement, whose background included the rare combination of wealth, literate education, military experience, and connections to the future king, Henry V. First accused of heresy in 1410, Oldcastle was later interrogated due to the incriminating contents of his library and brought to trial in 1413; faced with the choice of recanting or being executed, Oldcastle held firm to his beliefs. In a dramatic turn of events, however, he managed to escape imprisonment in the Tower of London, where he had been awaiting execution, and went into hiding.

Inspired by the sudden reversal of fortune, Oldcastle's allies hastily summoned supporters from London and surrounding areas to mount a bold uprising scheduled for January 9, 1414. Unfortunately for them, success depended upon the elements of secrecy and surprise. When the authorities caught wind of the plan through leaked information, they easily captured and defeated the rebels as they arrived in London. Over the course of the ensuing massive inquisitorial action, many of Oldcastle's followers were fined, forced to recant their heresy, or executed. Oldcastle himself managed to avoid arrest for years until he was finally captured and burned at the end of 1417.

The failure of Oldcastle's rebellion temporarily cooled political aggression infused with evangelical and apocalyptic sentiment, and suspected Wycliffites drew ire from their neighbors. (Margery Kempe, an eccentric but orthodox pilgrim, visionary, and the first English autobiographer, was taunted as a Lollard at this time, much to her dismay.) Executions and public scorn did not, however, permanently quell brewing resentment, and small uprisings continued to erupt periodically in subsequent decades. In 1431, for example, a group of artisans and a few nobility were apparently at the center of an uprising in Berkshire and Wiltshire, a campaign focused upon stripping the wealth from monastic and mendicant houses (those bastions of "private religion")

Figure 7.3. Martyrdom of Sir John Oldcastle, Lord Cobham, 1583. *Source*: **British Library. HIP/Art Resource, NY.**

as well as from some leading secular lords. Although inquisitorial scrutiny of Lollards remained fierce in the decades following Oldcastle's rebellion, the appeal of Wycliffite ideas was apparently stronger than any ecclesiastical warning. Those who followed his teaching in the fifteenth and sixteenth centuries extended Wyclif's critique to mine the rich vein of anticlerical hostility, particularly toward monastic privileges and ancient papal claims to material wealth and sovereign power.

CONTACTS AND CONTINUITIES IN THE FIFTEENTH CENTURY

Between the early fourteenth and mid-sixteenth centuries, textually driven ideas about spiritual authority, the role of the Church, and the Gospel model took root in English lay communities of both city and countryside. Informed by scripture, shaped by family structures, and linked by contact between traveling leaders, such small groups of True Men and True Women flourished within local (usually orthodox) populations. Who were they, to what extent were they influenced by John Wyclif, and what did they believe? Inquisitors, usually local bishops, were increasingly eager after 1415 to know the answers to those questions. Yet, as with any decentralized and diverse historical movement rooted in a cluster of shared but not identical ideas, it is impossible to determine precisely the beliefs or tenets held at any one time by any one of its self-identified members.

It is equally difficult to ascertain any direct link between the late fourteenth-century professor and the much later lay communities—this is in marked contrast, for example, to the southern French beguins' explicit veneration of the scholar Peter Olivi. Although many of the ideas embraced by those accused of Lollardy have a genealogical relationship with Wyclif's work, there were other significant issues, conclusions, and contexts that accrued to the movement over time. Many True Men and Women pushed beyond the scholar's original ideas in various directions: some insisted upon the priesthood of all believers, others called for the radical disendowment of the Church and the establishment of communal property, and still others embraced an explicitly pacifist agenda that was nonetheless derived from the same theological claims that fueled the arguments of their nonpacifist brethren. It is therefore no easier to answer the question, "Who was a Lollard?" than it was to ascertain the inner beliefs of people labeled Cathars or Waldensians.

Historians of the mid-twentieth century tended to be skeptical about linkage between Wyclif and the subsequent movement bearing his name, arguing that the largely lay and rural Lollards represented a separate historical movement fueled by economic and social forces distinct from elite intellectual programs. Yet recent research suggests that those later groups previously characterized as economically resentful illiterates were apparently stimulated as much or more by texts and ideas—even among those who could not read themselves—than by dismay over social injustice. Thus it is perhaps more useful first to consider Wyclif's texts as a significant, but hardly the sole, influence on the subsequent century and a half of dissenting lay piety in England and, second, to look more closely at the diverse circumstances in which self-conscious pious communities developed and defended themselves. As we will see, the communities targeted for persecution in the late fifteenth and early sixteenth centuries were thriving, usually in the same locations at which much earlier groups had emerged, and they maintained regular contact with other long-standing regional groups.

During the early years of activity, up to about 1430, a major role was played by individual itinerant preachers who (akin to the traveling masters of the Poor) linked communities through their visits and teaching. Of clerical status and academically trained, these men were responsible for first establishing and then maintaining belief in regional pockets: the central to eastern region of the Midlands, Kent, and East Anglia held some of the most deep-rooted communities, particularly those of Coventry, Salisbury, Norwich, and London.

By the late fifteenth century, however, when sympathetic communities had been well established and ecclesiastical pressure heightened, it seems that the significance of peripatetic clerical teachers declined. Literate leaders continued to journey between households of True Men and Women, but sources suggest that they were more commonly laymen instead of clergy. Moreover, laypeople in their local communities, women and men "who in the course of their everyday activities proselytized, encouraged and upbraided the wavering, and fostered the faithful,"[13] were increasingly taking on the task of teaching and converting. This new emphasis on domestic space as a channel for the Word was, of course, paralleled among other hereticized communities, for whom "house" and "church" were not mutually exclusive. East Anglian groups, for example, met not in a chapel or traditionally sacral space, but in the humble "chesehous chambr" of a Friend's home. One major consequence of this fusion of sacred and secular space was that it enabled each group to conduct its own affairs with minimal interference or risk of discovery; a second was that a community's deep local roots allowed it to survive even if individual members were accused of or condemned for heresy.

In response to the growing threat of detection, True Men and Women (who sometimes referred to themselves and their communities as the Known) seem to have increasingly conformed to the expected rituals and behavior of Catholicism across the middle decades of the fifteenth century. For the

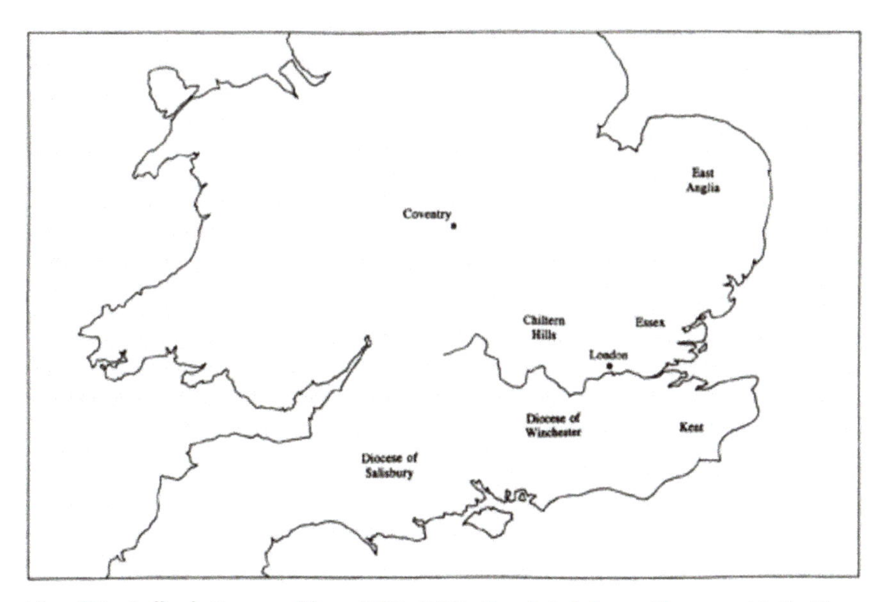

Map 7.1. Lollard Communities, 1420–1530. Reprinted from Shannon McSheffrey, *Gender and Heresy: Women and Men in Lollard Communities, 1420–1530. Source*: **Copyright © 1995 by the University of Pennsylvania Press. Reprinted with permission of the University of Pennsylvania Press.**

appearance of orthodoxy, they attended Mass, received the Eucharist, confessed orally, and generally blended into parish life in order to evade detection. Scholars have suggested that the relative scarcity of information about such communities in the middle decades of the century is a consequence of their strategy's success; apparent conformity may have prompted ecclesiastical officials to conclude that the danger had passed. Meanwhile, however, believers continued to read books among their groups and share them with one another, memorizing scripture, studying Wycliffite texts, and listening to sermons infused with their own truths.

INQUIRY INTO "LOLLARDY" (c. 1415–1525)

Inquisitorial tribunals had not been established in England during the early thirteenth century but emerged nearly two hundred years later under pressure from Wycliffism. Reports of suspected heresy were routinely gathered by episcopal visitations, during which the bishop gathered information about the spiritual and behavioral state of his diocese.[14] Once concerns were raised about their heterodoxy, individual suspects were procedurally separated from other types of criminals in order to facilitate a more effective ecclesiastical response. During the early years of the fifteenth century, commissions were quickly established under the authority of bishops such as William Alnwick of Norwich or designated episcopal representatives.

The general protocol set forth for inquiry was similar to that on the Continent. Suspects were brought forth to face a panel of experts and presented with charges, which usually included having uttered heretical statements, possessing forbidden books, or coming into contact with known Lollards. Inquisitors deposed witnesses, interrogated suspects, and then presented the accused with a dossier of the evidence against them. Those who chose to recant their heresy for the first time at that point were provided with a formal abjuration text and assigned penance.

Penances frequently made use of social pressure and public shame. Suspects who recanted their beliefs were assigned humiliating penance that served to reinforce through public performance the exact division between orthodoxy and heresy and the precise consequences of challenging ecclesiastical authority. Some were commanded to walk humbly and barefoot in a procession or minipilgrimage carrying a burning torch as a reminder of the stake that awaited anyone who relapsed. Others had symbolic badges or crosses imposed on their clothing or brands seared into their skin, marks that underscored their simultaneous exclusion from and reconciliation with the orthodox fold. Of course, anyone who returned to heresy after previously abjuring was deemed relapsed (and thus incorrigible) and transferred to secular authorities for burning.

As in the papally established tribunals across the channel, careful records were maintained as an aid to inquisitors who would need to cross-reference testimony compiled over years of interrogations. Thus the antiheretical techniques and methods that had developed over decades in France, Italy, and Germany were implemented quickly and under specifically episcopal authority in England. Yet we cannot assume standardization or uniformity across the English diocese in which Lollardy was reported any more than we could for earlier Continental contexts. First, bishops had many other obligations and no doubt approached the pursuit of heresy with varying levels of urgency and skill. Second, there was little coordination among dioceses or even within individual prosecutions; for example, only by 1430 did episcopal authorities begin to develop a standard set of questions, and sources do not indicate whether all those accused were subjected to the same questions. Finally, methods of record keeping varied because some processes allowed wider-ranging queries and responses than others. Moreover, those interrogated employed strategies of evasion or resistance similar to those used earlier on the Continent, which certainly shaped or distorted the inquisitorial record. These efforts were informed both by internal texts such as *Sixteen Points on which the Bishops Accuse the Lollards* and personal strategy.[15]

According to surviving sources, sustained persecution of heretical communities took place in England for over a century under the supervision of bishops John Chedworth of Lincoln (1476), John Hales of Coventry and Lichfield (1486), Thomas Langton and John Blyth of Salisbury (1491–1499), Geoffrey Blyth of Coventry and Lichfield (1511–1512), Richard Fox of Winchester (1512), Edmund Audley of Salisbury (1514–1518), and Archbishop William Warham of Canterbury (1511–1512). Episcopal and specifically inquisitorial texts from the trials that took place between Oldcastle's rebellion and the early years of the Protestant Reformation offer intriguing insight into diverse Lollard communities. In the English context, two major sources of evidence are bishops' registers and court books. Registers are best described as "collections of incoming and outgoing letters, mandates, statutes, and commissions, put together in the episcopal chancery by a member of the bishop's household staff . . . in one sense then they were not original documents but copies of original instructions and communities."[16] Decisions about what to record in the registers could be quite personal or eccentric, and because they varied tremendously from one diocese to another, one cannot draw many conclusions across regions based on these sources. A second type of source, court books, recorded the proceedings and rulings of the episcopal court and might contain information not necessarily included in the registers; many fewer of these sources survive, however, since they were apparently not intended for long-term usage. When surviving court books contain reference to heresy, however, the material is richly informative.

Bishop Alnwick's court book, for example, offers a detailed picture of the origins, beliefs, structure, communication, and contacts of communities embedded in several Norfolk and Suffolk villages, as do the records of Bishop Blyth and Archbishop Warham. Of course, sources must be read with the usual caution: as compilations of testimony and formulas profiling a certain kind of criminal and reducing diffused sets of ideas into a single category, they lump together complex ideas and variants and record only that which clerical authorities deemed relevant. The texts are frequently copies of original texts, abbreviated or adapted at the whim of the copyist. Moreover, trial records note only what doctrines and practices heresy defendants *rejected* (always from a preset list framed by inquisitors) rather than indicating what they positively believed or advocated. Nonetheless, scholars have gleaned crucial details from their pages about the beliefs and behaviors of the accused.

For example, all communities appear to have emphasized textual study—particularly of scripture. Inquisitors thus shone a searchlight on questions of literacy and book ownership in their attempts to unravel heretical networks. After the release of Arundel's *Constitutions*, ownership of, familiarity with, or interest in vernacular scriptures became red flags in ecclesiastical eyes, as did a preoccupation with apocalyptic concerns—even though many traditional Christians were equally enthusiastic about both. A book preserved by a believer named Morden in the early sixteenth century, for example, contained English versions of the epistle of James, the letters of Paul to the Romans, Titus, and Timothy, and the epistle to the Hebrews, including annotations to guide a reader; and a family from the Berkshire village of Ginge had copies of all the epistles, the Gospels of Luke and John, *Wycklyffes Wicket*, a gloss of the Apocalypse, "a book of our Lady's Matins in English, a book of Solomon in English, and a book called 'the Prick of Conscience.'" The mother, Alice, was famous for her ability to recite whole the epistles of Peter and James.[17]

In general, the key elements of Lollardy, as depicted within inquisitorial documents, are (1) a scorching critique of priestly authority; (2) denial of the doctrine of transubstantiation; (3) explicit rejection of the spiritual value of images, pilgrimage, and saints' feasts; and (4) a deep familiarity with scriptural, Wycliffite, and other vernacular texts. Over the intervening generations between about 1420 and 1530, one finds a gradual de-emphasis of the earlier theological concerns that emerged out of the university setting and a mounting concern for the daily issues of scripture, lived Christianity, and ecclesiastical critique. With this in mind, let us look more closely at how these ideas shaped the lives of people who read and talked (and listened) about God in linked pockets of faith.

Communities and Conventicles

Whether they were known as True Men and Women, the Known, or sometimes simply as Friends, the defining characteristic of a group, no matter its size, was the internal, ongoing conversation about scripture, revelation, and Christian authority. Among the various gatherings, the most central were gatherings or congregations at which adherents came together for sermons and instruction by their teachers. Such communities formed the movement's spine, the channel through which ideas were transmitted across generations and family lines and maintained through repetition and personal solidarity. Never self-identified as an organized movement, communities of True were nonetheless bound by the travels of such leading figures as William White of Norwich or Robert Silkby of Coventry, whose visits and outreach to other groups created networks of affiliation and affection. Such contacts among spiritual neighbors kept their shared worldview refreshed and revitalized, even under inquisitorial pressure.

The texts read and heard within True communities were not limited to hereticized writings such as vernacular translations of scripture or Lollard tracts but also included a range of popular orthodox works that adherents might nonetheless interpret differently from the institutional Church. Because a person's act of reading is complex, idiosyncratic, and impossible to reconstruct precisely, we cannot know in exactly what manner True adherents used books or what meanings they drew from them. Again, inquisitorial sources obscure as much as they illuminate: aimed at securing confessions to a predetermined list of heretical errors, interrogation protocols were not designed to elicit a holistic understanding of any single individual's worldview. Limited questions yield limited responses.

Although these gatherings were private, even secret events closed to outsiders, they were public insofar as the community was concerned; as such, they seem to have echoed traditional gender hierarchies even as they criticized traditional institutions. Public leadership and teaching were primarily male roles, for example, a circumstance likely rooted in several factors. Literacy rates were certainly lower among women than men, particularly within the booming ranks of artisans and laborers whose work increasingly required at least some level of familiarity with letters. Moreover, women's contributions were limited by contemporary taboos on female mobility, which curbed the travel necessary to attend gatherings or for maintaining personal connections between relatively distant rural communities. Although Lollardy was a phenomenon of both city and countryside, rural areas were particularly associated with the heresy, and entire villages periodically turned toward the new ideas.

In urban centers, by contrast, large populations could support localized gatherings with minimal travel, where women were thus more likely to appear and participate. In Coventry, an entirely female congregation met with the approval of leaders, providing a setting where single women could discuss matters of the faith free of the taint associated with singledom, mobility, and contact with men. It was an apparently unique solution, however, as no other solely female gatherings are mentioned in the record. Only a tiny number of influential female leaders appear in the sources, such as the intriguing Alice Rowley of Coventry; inquisitors seem to have decided to lean rather more heavily on masculine rather than feminine targets, though women (perceived as more fragile and likely to break down under interrogation) were often brought in first for initial questioning to elicit information about their brethren.

Public leadership was not the only way of participating in or contributing to the community, however, and many hundreds of women would find themselves before inquisitors because of their active involvement in private settings. As we have observed in many other medieval contexts, teaching and talking about God often took place at home, over the dinner table and hearths tended by women. Mothers instructed children, husbands and wives murmured in bed, and friends listened to one another over bread and beer. Women could and did seize these informal opportunities to share oral knowledge of scripture, to instruct other women in the faith, and to exhort coreligionists to piety. Akin to the household settings of the Good Christians and Poor on the Continent, the piety and principles of True Men were passed on within family structures. A great majority of the women interrogated were related to someone else in the community, and marriage was often the door through which females came to Lollardy. Yet unlike circumstances farther south (such as in Languedoc and Provence), women do not seem to have been a driving force behind the teachings and networks of religious dissent in England.

Texts and the Word

Fundamentally, the group's appeal lay in the promise of a direct connection among soul, Word of God, and Holy Spirit, and its coherent answer to brewing late medieval anticlericalism and spiritual dissatisfaction. Members not only engaged individually with the meaning of scripture and its implications for their salvation but were also aided by the community as they linked arms (metaphorically speaking) with similarly inclined Christians. Preaching represented a primary instrument of conversion, as passionate defenders of True precepts rendered the Word into vernacular speech, their perspectives reinforced by written texts on which believers could meditate long after a teacher's departure. Thus were converts made beyond family circles, particularly through male contact in the working world. Occupational links among members of different crafts (for example, carpenters, wrights, parchment makers, shoemakers, tailors) provided vital channels through which ideas flowed, transmitted from True members to receptive potential converts. The concentration of heresy in some economic centers with developed industry is a familiar pattern, since the ideas of the Poor had resonated along similar frequencies in the thirteenth and fourteenth centuries. However, older representations of Lollardy as a lower-class phenomenon have had to be revised in recent years, given evidence of significant participation by educated men and women of higher socioeconomic status.

Whether from urban craft centers, rural villages, artisanal circles, or higher up on the social scale, members' earthy skepticism about the Church and its theology surface occasionally even through English inquisitors' filters: in 1428, for example, a True Man from Norwich asserted that he would rather touch a woman's privates than the sacrament of the altar; similarly, a woman named Margery Baxter from the same community independently arrived at a criticism that had reverberated on the Continent for centuries when she claimed that "if that sacrament were God, the true body of Christ, there would be infinite gods, because a thousand priests and more every day make a thousand gods, and afterwards eat those gods, and once they are eaten discharge them through their hinder parts into the stinking latrine, where you can find plenty of such gods, if you care to sift through it."[18] In other words, despite significant differences in doctrinal content and historical context, the appeal of such ideas directly paralleled those of self-proclaimed Good Christians and Poor across Europe—not because of any links among the groups themselves, but because they all focused to some degree on the increasingly apparent gap between Gospel and ecclesiastical authority. Each person had his or her own thoughts and each community its own structures and traditions, therefore, even as they shared a questioning spirit and textual dedication.

Among the few clergy who clearly discerned the font of Lollard beliefs and attempted to persuade them on the basis of those points was Reginald Pecock. Appointed bishop of Chichester in 1450, Pecock acknowledged the effectiveness of Lollard teaching and scriptural memorization, even as he scorned their attempts to comprehend scripture without trained clerical guidance. Fundamentally, Pecock took seriously the pressing late medieval concern over access and interpretation of scripture and dedicated himself to writing persuasive texts aimed at what he clearly perceived as a rational and eager, if misguided, community. Attempting to counter the True Men and Women's insistence on the Word of God as the single source of authority, he argued in his extensive vernacular writings that scripture alone was "inadequate as an embodiment of the plenitude of God's law" and defended reason and humanity's rational capacity as "the real 'text' on which God has written."[19] Ironically, however, Pecock soon found himself under suspicion for these claims by the archbishop of Canterbury and was accused of heresy. After publicly recanting in 1457, he was stripped of his episcopal position and sent to a small abbey for the remaining few years of his life. Ecclesiastical authorities were not amenable to reasoning with heretics: coercion trumped persuasion in England.

PERSECUTION

As discussed above, inquisitorial procedures unfolded differently in England than they did farther south, although episcopal authorities employed a similar set of tools and texts to uproot heresy.[20] To develop a clearer picture of late medieval encounters between adherents and inquisitors in England, let us consider a specific set of trials and their outcomes: specifically, Archbishop Warham's proceedings against heretics in Kent from 1511 to 1512. Norman Tanner and Shannon McSheffrey's study of the inquisitorial records provides us with the following information: fifty-three suspects were closely linked, even though they originated from more than a dozen separate towns or villages, consisting of seventeen women and thirty-six men of ages ranging from twenty to seventy-four. All were laypeople, evidently from moderately prosperous artisan circles, including cutlers, weavers, tailors, fletchers, and glovers.

Between April 1511 and June 1512, interrogations were held at different locations within the diocese, including parish churches, archiepiscopal residences, and Canterbury Cathedral. Of the fifty-three interrogated, one was released, another abjured without a record of penance, and the fate of a third is unknown. Five defendants found guilty of relapsed or recalcitrant heresy were sent to the stake. The charges on which Robert Harryson of Canterbury, William Carder and Agnes Grebill of Tenterden, John Browne of Ashford, and Edward Walker of Maidstone were condemned focused primarily upon their attitudes toward sacraments, religious rituals, or holy objects. Despite initial protests, "the depositions against them, however, made clear that all of them had been leading Lollards in the region over a long period of time."[21] Illustrating the extent to which English heresy trials required cooperation between Church and Crown, the archbishop here followed the bureaucratic formality of addressing the document of condemnation to Henry VIII himself:

> We signify to your royal highness . . . that certain sons and daughters of iniquity . . . have been legitimately and canonically convicted and judged to be heretics by us . . . [and since] holy mother church may not do what ought to

> be done further in this matter, we relinquish the said heretics . . . to your royal highness and your secular arm.[22]

Of those remaining, all of the other fifty were found guilty of some level of heresy and thus received varying types of penitential sentences. The penances handed out to the Kentish True provide a snapshot of the different carrots and sticks employed to win heretical souls back for salvation. In order of frequency indicated in parentheses, they included: carrying a bundle of wood on a public occasion (thirty-three); confinement to the parish (thirty-one); informing on other suspects (twenty-five); wearing a badge (seventeen); surrendering heretical books (thirteen); attending services on Sundays and feast days (twelve); recitation of the Lord's Prayer, Hail Mary, and creed (ten); fasting or abstinence (nine); imprisonment (seven); confession (seven); reception of the Eucharist (seven); restrictions in dress, particularly for women (six); offering a candle (three); and the unique injunction to treat one's wife well (one). Forced witnessing of executions also appeared in the documents; for example, seven people were required to watch William Carder's burning as part of their own penitential duty. Whether this served to discourage the accused from heresy or to steel their commitment (as it did among many southern beguins), we cannot know.

Processes similar, if not identical, to these had unfolded periodically across the English landscape, escalating steeply in the final decades of the fifteenth century and early years of the sixteenth. Rough estimates suggest that more than five hundred trials took place between 1423 and 1522, out of which approximately thirty people were burned. In contrast to the tenacious pursuit of Good Christians and beguins in France, however, episcopal authorities never succeeded in fully uprooting the Lollard foe. Dozens of men and women went to the stake, their ordeals both devastating and inspiring to the friends who looked on. English authorities, however, never invested the time or resources to ensure the full annihilation of the movement; as some branches were destroyed, new seeds fell and roots flourished. As a consequence, those whose quiet underground existence was either tacitly or overtly tolerated by neighbors survived the periodic waves of persecution unleashed by motivated inquisitors. Early academic Wycliffism echoed only faintly in the daily devotions of later English adherents, whose call to apostolic and Gospel authority rang out in the schools and house-churches of multiple generations. Wyclif's legacy is thus perhaps best understood as genealogical, a "family" relationship that weakened over the generations as other influences came into play but whose trace might still be detected in certain beliefs, practices, and community stories. One might say that the English communities who survived to encounter Protestant reformers in and after the 1520s shared some of the same theological DNA but had, over the intervening decades, responded to and transformed within such different contexts that no direct connection to Wyclif may be ascertained.

Many contemporaries nonetheless retained a strong sense of continuity between Wyclif and the later Lollards. Just as Martin Luther was affixing his theses to the door of Wittenberg Cathedral and launching his critique of papal authority, recruitment among the True was apparently surging, the original strands of anticlericalism and Gospel authority once again vibrating along with growing lay disaffection. Indeed, once the German monk's ideas made their way to the island, leading clerics understood it as an extension of Lollardy. As Bishop Tunstall put it in a letter to the humanist scholar Erasmus, "It is no question of pernicious novelty . . . it is only that new arms are being added to the great crowd of Wycliffite heresies."[23] Luther himself, moreover, recommended that his brethren read an apocalyptic treatise with the statement that "we are not the first to interpret the papacy as the rule of Antichrist . . . [for this author is] a witness preordained by God for the confirmation of our doctrine so many years before us."[24] The text was a German translation of the Wycliffite *Opus arduum.*

CONCLUSION

Across the generations following Wyclif's death, groups linked by overlapping ideas and influences not only survived but flourished underground until they resurfaced to blend with Protestant reformers in the 1520s and 1530s. Indeed, some antiheretical investigations in the mid-sixteenth century did not distinguish between Lutherans and Lollards but were intent upon containing and eradicating "heresy" no matter what its label or point of origin. Certainly the attitudes of True Men and Protestants resonated, committed as they were to the principles of anticlericalism, vernacular scriptural access, and the individual's relationship with God. Within the turbulent context of King Henry VIII's reign (1509–1547) and the peculiar challenges of Church and Crown facing the kingdom in these years, such issues of scriptural and ecclesiastical authority were more fraught than ever in European history. Thus the brilliant scholar William Tyndale met death at the stake in 1536 due to his erudite but illegal printed translations of scripture after being summarily dismissed by Lord Chancellor Thomas More as a wicked Wycliffite. By the 1530s, concerns for Church reform and vernacular Gospel access had become so widespread that the otherwise distinct perspectives of True men and Renaissance humanists became (at least on these issues) virtually indistinguishable.

Ascertaining the impact of Wyclif's legacy is therefore no small challenge, particularly because it requires consideration of how these complex ideas were transformed across time and space into only tenuously linked families of resemblance. But we have already strayed beyond the chronological boundary of this volume, so let us return to the fifteenth century and shift our attention to Prague, where Wycliffite ideas would meet a volatile brew of seething political, religious, and cultural tensions, igniting a full-scale Bohemian revolution whose "heresy" would ultimately win unprecedented concessions from Rome.

SUGGESTIONS FOR FURTHER READING

Aston, Margaret. *Lollards and Reformers: Images and Literacy in Late Medieval England.* London: Hambledon Press, 1984.

Barr, Helen, and Ann M. Hutchison, eds. *Text and Controversy from Wyclif to Bale: Essays in Honor of Anne Hudson.* Turnhout, Belgium: Brepols, 2005.

Biller, Peter, and Anne Hudson, eds. *Heresy and Literacy, 1000–1530.* Cambridge: Cambridge University Press, 1994.

Bostick, Curtis V. *The Antichrist and the Lollards: Apocalypticism in Late Medieval and Reformation England.* Leiden: Brill, 1998.

Cole, Andrew. *Literature and Heresy in the Age of Chaucer.* Cambridge: Cambridge University Press, 2008.

Duffy, Eamon. *The Stripping of the Altars: Traditional Religion in England,* c. 1400–1580. New Haven, CT: Yale University Press, 1992.

Forrest, Ian. *The Detection of Heresy in Late Medieval England.* Oxford: Oxford University Press, 2005.

Ghosh, Kantik. *The Wycliffite Heresy: Authority and the Interpretation of Texts.* Cambridge: Cambridge University Press, 2001.

Hornbeck, J. Patrick, II. *What Is a Lollard? Dissent and Belief in Late Medieval England.* Oxford: Oxford University Press, 2010.

Hudson, Anne. *Lollards and Their Books.* London: Hambledon Press, 1985.

Janin, Hunt. *The University in Medieval Life, 1179–1499.* Jefferson, NC: McFarland, 2008.

Lahey, Stephen E. *John Wyclif.* Oxford: Oxford University Press, 2009.

———. *Philosophy and Politics in the Thought of John Wyclif.* Cambridge: Cambridge University Press, 2003.

McSheffrey, Shannon, and Norman Tanner. *Gender and Heresy: Women and Men in Lollard Communities, 1420–1530.* Philadelphia: University of Pennsylvania Press, 1995.

———. *Lollards of Coventry 1486–1522.* Cambridge: Cambridge University Press, 2003.

Russell, Alexander. *Conciliarism and Heresy in Fifteenth-Century England: Collective Authority in the Age of the General Councils.* Cambridge: Cambridge University Press, 2017.

Somerset, Fiona, and J. Patrick Hornbeck, trans. *Clerical Discourse and Lay Audience in Late Medieval England.* Cambridge: Cambridge University Press, 2005.

———. *Feeling Like Saints: Lollard Writings after Wyclif.* Ithaca, NY: Cornell University Press, 2014.
———. *Wycliffite Spirituality*. Mahwah, NJ: Paulist Press, 2014.

NOTES

1. For a thoughtful and up-to-date treatment of Wyclif's life, see Stephen E. Lahey, *John Wyclif* (Oxford: Oxford University Press, 2009).

2. Paul V. Spade, "The Problem of Universals and Wyclif's Alleged 'Ultrarealism,'" *Vivarium* 43, no.1 (2004): 111–23.

3. New Advent, https://www.newadvent.org/library/docs_bo08us.htm (accessed May 9, 2022).

4. Joseph Dahmus, *The Prosecution of John Wyclyf* (New Haven, CT: Yale University Press, 1952), 39.

5. Dahmus, *The Prosecution of John Wyclyf*, 93–94.

6. This argument is a fundamental claim in J. Patrick Hornbeck II, *What Is a Lollard?* (Oxford: Oxford University Press, 2010).

7. See Anne Hudson, *The Premature Reformation* (Oxford: Oxford University Press, 1986).

8. Edward Peters, *Heresy and Authority in Medieval Europe: Documents in Translation* (Philadelphia: University of Pennsylvania Press, 1980), 279.

9. Henry Knighton and G. H. Martin, *Knighton's Chronicle 1337–1396* (Oxford: Clarendon Press, 1995), 295.

10. John Taylor, Wendy R. Childs, and Leslie Watkiss, eds., *The St. Albans Chronicle: The Chronica Maiora of Thomas Walsingham* (Oxford: Clarendon Press, 2003), 821.

11. Peters, *Heresy and Authority in Medieval Europe*, 212–15.

12. Michael van Dussen, "Conveying Heresy: 'A Certayne Student' and the Lollard-Hussite Fellowship," *Viator* 38, no. 2 (2007): 224.

13. Hudson, *Premature Reformation*, 449.

14. Ian Forrest, *The Detection of Heresy in Late Medieval England* (Oxford: Oxford University Press, 2005). See in particular "The Social Contours of Heresy Detection," 207–41.

15. Anne Hudson, *Selections from English Wycliffite Writings* (Cambridge: Cambridge University Press, 1978), 19–24.

16. Forrest, *Detection of Heresy*, 4.

17. Hudson, *Premature Reformation*, 461–64.

18. Steven Justice, "Inquisition, Speech, and Writing: A Case from Norwich," in *Criticism and Dissent in the Middle Ages*, ed. Rita Copeland (Cambridge: Cambridge University Press, 2006), 315.

19. Kantik Gosh, "Bishop Reginald Pecock and the Idea of 'Lollardy,'" 251–65, in *Text and Controversy from Wyclif to Bale: Essays in Honor of Anne Hudson*, ed. H. Barr and A. M. Hutchison (Turnhout, Belgium: Brepols, 2005), 260.

20. Forrest, *Detection of Heresy*, offers a thorough examination of the process by which antiheretical techniques and procedures developed in England.

21. Shannon McSheffrey and Norman Tanner, *Lollards of Coventry 1486–1522* (Cambridge: Cambridge University Press, 2003), 233.

22. McSheffrey and Tanner, *Lollards of Coventry*, 246.

23. Malcolm Lambert, *Medieval Heresy: Popular Movements from the Gregorian Reform to the Reformation, 3rd ed.* (Oxford: Blackwell, 2001), 372.

24. Curtis V. Bostick, *The Antichrist and the Lollards: Apocalypticism in Late Medieval and Reformation England* (Leiden: Brill, 1998), 54–55.

Chapter Eight

Reform, Revolution, and the Lay Chalice in Bohemia

On July 6, 1415, a popular Bohemian university professor, priest, and preacher named Jan Hus (the anglicized pronunciation is "Yawn Huss"; it is pronounced "Hoos" in the original Czech) was condemned for heresy and handed over to secular authorities by Church officials at the Council of Constance. Stripped of his ecclesiastical vestments, the Czech-speaking reformer was forced to don a tall paper hat with the label "heresiarch" (a leader of a group of heretics) before being burned alive along with his books. According to observers, Hus maintained his innocence and faith in Christ to the last, demonstrating a steadfastness of spirit that would inspire followers after his death as much as it had during his life. The execution, or martyrdom as it seemed to some, ignited tensions that had been smoldering in the Bohemian kingdom of the Holy Roman Empire for decades—matters not only of religion and reform, but of national identities, imperial politics, and socioeconomic rifts as well.

Hus's name thus became a rallying point around which various forms of protest cohered: the general principles for which he stood, including scriptural primacy, Church financial reform, vernacular preaching, and lay access to the communion chalice, soon became the channels through which the first officially sanctioned and independent national church emerged. As Howard Kaminsky put it, "The Hussite movement was both a reformation and a revolution, in fact *the* revolution of the late Middle Ages, the history of which period cannot be properly understood if the Hussites are left out."[1]

In the preceding chapters we explored a variety of contexts in which crucial elements of medieval Christianity were adopted, challenged, questioned, reconceived, repressed, or reformed. We traced the debates over issues such as the authority of scripture, the appeal and enactment of apostolic life; concern about correct order, hierarchy, and the observance of Christian rules; the desire to access, control, and protect the various sacred intersections of heaven and earth; the symbolic influence of bread and wine, as well as its material importance; the nature of the "true" Church; and the proper relationship between Christendom, Christ, and Christians. In this chapter, we remain in the fifteenth century but move from English Wycliffism to the related tangled strands of reform and revolution in the Bohemian kingdom, a turning point that marks, chronologically and thematically, the end of medieval heretical movements as well as of the unified Roman Church.

Before we examine Jan Hus and his beliefs, therefore, let's start with a few questions: Why did the issues above play out so dramatically in this particular region? Why did the definition and repression of heresy become fused with political and linguistic controversies? And why were university professors and students at the heart of the controversy? Although inquisition plays less of a role in these events than crusade (a weapon the Church continued to wield against its enemies through the early modern period), the late fifteenth century arguably marks a watershed in the history of institutionalized *inquisitio* in Europe. We will return to the matter in the epilogue.

THE BOHEMIAN CONTEXT

The movement for reform and revolution in Bohemia did not begin with the execution of Jan Hus in 1415: instead, its roots lie deep in the matrix of local politics and a native reform movement that was already under way in Prague by the mid-fourteenth century. Unlike the outskirts of the urbanized and sophisticated regions we focused on in previous chapters, the kingdom of Bohemia was essentially a frontier province on the margins of the Holy Roman Empire in the tenth and eleventh centuries. A "latecomer to the circle of advanced nations,"[2] its population grew in the thirteenth and fourteenth centuries due to an influx of German colonists, and its political influence grew as well. Its capital city of Prague was well positioned at the intersection of trade routes between Germany and Italy, a lucrative spot for merchants. The late medieval city's fairs and markets enticed thousands of visitors, and its increasingly powerful and influential court drew artists and intellectuals from many lands.

Under King Charles IV (1346–1378), later crowned emperor of the Holy Roman Empire, Prague became a thriving cultural and economic center. Although Charles had been raised in France and did not even speak Czech when he was first enthroned, his lively intellect prompted him to master not only Czech but also German, Italian, and, of course, Latin. A man of many talents who personally designed and planned the city's New Town quarter, Charles embarked on a number of ambitious projects to raise the profile of both the city and the country. Yet Charles's interests and ambitions were not limited to the secular, and he also fostered a flowering of religious life in the city. A conventionally pious man, he enthusiastically collected relics and made Prague a center for saints' cults and wealthy churches.

Three decisive steps early in his reign would prove particularly formative for what became known as the Hussite movement fifty years later. First, in 1348, he established Charles University in Prague, a vital intellectual and cultural institution and the first university in the Holy Roman Empire and central Europe; although Charles would not live to see it, the school would in the future become a hotbed of theological and political dissent. Second, he fostered a close relationship with the pope in France and opened the Bohemian Church to broader papal influence than desired by many local citizens. And third, he invited a famous Austrian cleric, Conrad Waldhauser, to preach reform in his lands. Under the weak reign of Charles's son, Wenceslaus IV, the combination of royal ties to the papacy, a vital new intellectual institution with a concentrated population of scholars, and the reforming momentum of persuasive preachers would explode into an indigenous Czech movement—first of reform, but eventually of full-scale revolution.

Figure 8.1. Hradcany Castle, Seen from the Charles Bridge. Prague, Czech Republic. *Source* **: Vanni/Art Resource, NY.**

THREE PREACHERS IN PRAGUE

At first, there was not much to distinguish the fourteenth-century reform movement in Bohemia from similar ideas that had been rippling across Europe since the Gregorian reform. Waldhauser, a lively German-speaking preacher who also served as Charles's personal confessor, launched scathing attacks on the usual suspects of clerical sexual misbehavior, including simony and mendicant hypocrisy. In consequence, he was unpopular among the clergy and died in Avignon in 1369 while defending himself to the pope, but his words had formed a community of listeners among the citizens and students of Prague, sowing the seeds of radical reform. Women as well as men responded to the exhortation to apostolic purity: at least eighteen communities of pious lay religious women existed in late medieval Prague, supported by private donors and supervised by parish authorities.[3] And men, both within and beyond clerical circles, increasingly trained their attention on the Gospel and its meaning for individuals in a rapidly changing world. As elsewhere in Europe, the spiritual climate was ripe for a new message.

One of Waldhauser's disciples, Jan Milič of Kroměříž (pronounced "MIL-ich"—Hus himself profoundly influenced the Czech language by introducing diacritical marks that regularized spelling and pronunciation) carried on where his master left off and developed a particular interest in female roles and religiosity. Milič was a former imperial notary and cathedral canon who converted to the life of an itinerant and impoverished preacher of repentance in 1364, a midlife conversion akin to that of the orthodox wandering preachers of the twelfth century: "the same fiery asceticism, the refusal of meat and wine, sleeping on the hard ground, long prayers and lack of rest, combined with a certain vein of eccentricity, demonstrated in his obsessive interest in the coming of the Antichrist."[4] Speaking in Czech, Milič continued preaching reform of Church and laity, and (again, like those twelfth-century preachers) was particularly keen on rehabilitating prostitutes into good Christian women. The reform effort should be read as a desire not only to transform "fallen" women but to liberate them from the otherwise inescapable conditions of economic bondage that undermined Christian ideals of both sexual purity and charity.

To that end, he took over a number of houses in the prostitutes' quarter of town (a designation that suggests that nightlife in Prague was as lively as its flourishing intellectual scene) and transformed them into a kind of apostolic community for reformed women that flourished parallel to the existing lay religious women's houses. While Milič himself avoided contact with the women, he occasionally paid off their debts to madams and enlisted feminine help in getting former prostitutes established in a new way of life. Charles

IV himself had granted him possession of one of the city's leading brothels, known as "Venice." Indeed, the houses shared much in common with Western lay religious women's communities: women were bound by simple rather than formal oaths, lived a routinized life of piety and prayer, and developed strong bonds with their male brethren, who also resided in the community and continued to preach.[5]

Milič chose to name the new community "Jerusalem," after that supreme umbilicus between heaven and earth. He could not have chosen more potent language with which to baptize the new community of reformed sinners nor a more resonant symbol of his own apocalypticism. Although apocalypticism held a central place within Christian theology and medieval people had regularly and repeatedly anticipated the End of Days since the early Middle Ages, the fourteenth century presented many reasons to suspect that the end really was near. Thus, Milič was far from alone in his millenarian convictions, and his preaching evidently struck a particularly resonant chord in the hearts of many listeners.

Not everyone was impressed, however, and the clergy were nettled by his criticisms and their exclusion from the community's organization. You may recall from chapter 5 the ease with which medieval people associated uncloistered pious women (or single women generally) with prostitutes, and the Jerusalem community proved no exception—except in Prague the scenario was reversed, for here the former prostitutes were being denigrated as beguines! Milič himself was smeared as a beghard (although he explicitly rejected the model as heretical), and in 1373 a group of clergy mounted a coordinated attack and prepared a list of accusations. As a result, Milič was summoned to the papal court to defend himself. When the friars of Prague learned that the reformer had been thrown into prison in Rome, they cheered, "Ah, now Milič will be burned!" No doubt many were disappointed when he died of natural causes the next year. Jerusalem was dismantled, the buildings were granted to the Cistercians as a college for their members at the university (certainly with many a lewd joke for years to come), and the "pernicious" women presumably either struggled to maintain a reformed lifestyle under new patronage or returned to their former trade.

The third reformer shaping late fourteenth-century Bohemia was, in turn, a disciple of Milič—a rising intellectual and cathedral canon named Matthew of Janov. Trained at the University of Paris, Matthew shared the longing of so many others across European lands for a return to the primitive Church, one unencumbered by false relics, superstition, corrupt indulgences, formulaic prayers, expanding hierarchies, and the theological hairsplitting of canon lawyers. And it was Matthew who contributed the major written work of early Bohemian reform, *The Rules of the Old and New Testament*. This text presented a series of twelve rules of behavior drawn from scripture (four from the Old Testament and eight from the New Testament) designed to shield the faithful from the Antichrist.

Insisting on his respect and reverence for holy mother Church, Matthew's basic intent in the *Rules* was nonetheless to criticize changes that had occurred within its structure since about 1200, when "the church of Christ abounded . . . in riches and in glory."[6] He chastised popes and other ecclesiastical leaders for attempting to fuse the holy and the mundane and for polluting the Church with material values; for Matthew, secularized Christianity was the apocalyptic whore described in Revelation, seated upon her hellish scarlet beast. Thus the mingling of sacral and secular realms had destroyed the Church's early purity, creating a corruption through which the Antichrist himself would erupt.

Matthew's Eucharistic focus was both a consequence of and a remedy for the crisis of his day. Since the Fourth Lateran Council of 1215, Christians had been required to take Communion at least once a year, but more frequent reception of the Host had by the fourteenth century become a popular devotional practice among many Christians. Matthew was not alone in his conviction that Christendom was in a time of utter emergency and that only a return to the evangelical law of scripture and the practice of frequent Communion would defend the faithful from the hypocrisy and formalism of the Church. Indeed, only greater piety and sacrality among the laity could counter the horror he perceived in a monstrously swollen, corrupt, and greedy Church.

It was a message that gained greater urgency in Prague as the fourteenth century (scarred by plague, warfare, and papal schism) came to a close. Unlike his reforming predecessors, Matthew was never summoned to defend himself before the pope, but authorities were certainly paying close attention. In 1388 and 1389, the authorities attempted to counter his increasingly popular message: university lawyers and theologians criticized the practice of frequent Communion, and clerics at a Prague synod forbade taking Communion more than once a month. Although his position was not heretical in any doctrinal sense, Matthew was an annoyance and irritation to clerical authority, and he was harassed by local Church officials until his death in 1394. Attempts to curtail his influence failed, for Matthew's writings left an important textual legacy for his Bohemian successors—men who would be increasingly convinced not only that abuse within the Church had reached intolerable levels, but that the only means for permanent reform might be force.

In 1391, two years before Matthew's death, others in his circle built a new church in the center of Prague that would become the heart of Czech reformist impulses in the decades that followed. Its name, Bethlehem Chapel, underscores once again the yearning of fourteenth-century Bohemians for a tangible connection to the primitive Church and to Christ himself. A plain but enormous structure that could (and frequently did) seat thousands, it was intended as a place for vernacular preaching, where ordinary Czechs could come and hear the Word of God in their own language. Like Waldhauser's "Jerusalem" before it, Bethlehem Chapel represented a man-made pious site, a "linking of heaven and earth" conceived by Christians inspired by scripture and increasingly dissatisfied with the spiritual program offered by the institutional Church.

LATE-FOURTEENTH-CENTURY CRISES, SCHISMS, AND SCANDALS

One of the reasons Prague became the epicenter of reform and revolution was that it lay at the intersection of three major fault lines: one ecclesiastical, one ethnic/linguistic, and one of royal authority. Crises in the late fourteenth century triggered upheavals along all three fault lines, driving a movement that in turn energized the nascent reformist tendencies in the city and the surrounding Bohemian kingdom. Thus, the story of the Hussite movement cannot be understood purely in terms of religious issues, for these were inextricably knotted with local, regional, ecclesiastical, and even imperial circumstances.

First was the problem of papal authority, an issue exacerbated by the unprecedented 1378 election of rival popes—Urban VI in Rome and Clement VII in Avignon. Attempts to resolve the schism failed, and secular leaders lined up behind one pope or the other, motivated variously by carefully considered equations of piety and politics. Nor did the death of either man resolve the crisis, because Roman and French successors continued to be named in their stead. Thus the schism continued unabated, year after year. In fact, it would be the central agenda item at the Council of Constance in 1415; Hus's execution occupied only a fraction of the attendees' time and attention. And because each pope excommunicated the Christians in lands supporting the other, the final decades of the fourteenth century cast a dark shadow of intense spiritual anxiety across Christendom. If the pope is the heir to St. Peter, the rock on which the Church was founded, what was one to make of this terrible rift? Who belongs to the rightful Church? How could one know? Understanding the continuing schism is vital to comprehending the context of Bohemian reform because it forced both laity and clergy to consider the nature of the Church and its leadership. Moreover, it of course distracted ecclesiastical officials and dramatically undermined the moral authority of the papacy at the very moment when Bohemian reform was entering territory soon to be labeled "heretical."

The second fault line whose weakening in the late fourteenth century fueled the Hussite movement was the fierce ethnic and linguistic rivalry between Germans and native Czechs in Bohemia. German colonists had arrived early in the kingdom, invited and encouraged by kings willing to parcel out choice lands and positions to these desirable immigrants. By the time of Wenceslaus's reign, they dominated elite positions of government, trade, and the Church—and the Czechs hated them, seething in their resentment such that one abbot compared the hostility between Germans and Czechs to that of Jews and Samaritans. Universities, with their concentrated populations of well-educated men influenced by cutting-edge theories and methods, were often at the forefront of political or social agitation in the Middle Ages, and this was nowhere more true than at Charles University.

Although university governance might not seem a particularly exciting topic, what might at first appear a dull administrative detail turned out to be a flash point of revolution. As at the University of Paris, faculty and students at Charles University were divided into four "nations," or units, based on language and origin (Saxon, Bavarian, Polish, and Bohemian), with Germans outnumbering Czechs by a ratio of three to one. Anger over that disproportion festered among the native Bohemians. Ugly disputes among professors and with their administrators are nothing new, and the battles were particularly fierce in medieval Europe, where the institutions claimed enormous spiritual, legal, and political influence. University faculty soon found themselves at the center of a cultural maelstrom fed by the raw antagonism between Czechs and Germans, royal maneuvering in response to the Great Schism, and reforming zeal.

Each of these crises was in turn exacerbated by problems in the royal family. Charles IV died in 1378 and was succeeded as king of Bohemia by his far less capable son, Wenceslaus IV (r. 1378–1419), the year the schism erupted. The list of problems was daunting. First, because the Luxembourg family's inheritance had been divided among six relatives, Wenceslaus was forced to expend a great deal of energy in attempting to pacify or suppress family disputes and keep his powerful brother Sigismund (then king of Hungary) at bay. Second, he faced unrelenting hostility from the nobility within the Bohemian kingdom and was even imprisoned for a period of time by his own subjects. Third, he suffered the profound humiliations of never being crowned emperor and of actually being deposed as king of the Romans and replaced instead by his bitter dynastic rival, Count Rupert of the Palatinate. In contrast to Wenceslaus, Rupert understood the political value of prosecuting heresy during the papal schism and thus aligning himself with Rome; a decade earlier, he had joined forces with clergy in Mainz and theologians from the University of Heidelberg (which had been founded by his family in 1385) to eradicate heresy in the region. The Roman pope was evidently impressed, and it is no coincidence that he was instrumental in arranging Rupert's coronation in 1400.

These circumstances, combined with Wenceslaus's own apparently volatile and vacillating personality, ensured that he would not develop a firm stance either for or against the Hussite movement or on the issue of heresy in Bohemia. Lacking a keen strategic sense, Wenceslaus juggled political factors as they arose, reacting to shifting circumstances rather than shaping a strong royal policy. As a result, both the Western Church and Bohemia entered a difficult period in the final two decades of the fourteenth century.

But what does any of this have to do with religious reform? Although the intersecting crises of schism, ethnic hostility, and royal weakness could in themselves certainly have undermined stability in Bohemia, it was to be the drive for Church reform that triggered the massive historical quake in fifteenth-century Bohemia. By the end of the fourteenth century, reformist momentum would spread far beyond Bethlehem Chapel and the enthusiastic congregations of the popular preachers, aggravated in large part by undeniable abuses within local Church administration. Wealth was a problem. In contrast to the ideal of a pure and unadulterated Church (based on the apostolic model), the Bohemian ecclesiastical hierarchy faced problems of excess.

First, there were probably too many clergy: of the approximately thirty-five to forty thousand residents of late fourteenth-century Prague, approximately twelve hundred were clergy; two hundred of these worked at the cathedral itself. A superabundance of clergy was not unique to Prague, as many late medieval cities found themselves in a similar predicament, but that fact did not ease local anxieties—without either sufficient work or financial support, clergy might become spiritually lazy or professionally unscrupulous. On the other hand, it seems that too much wealth had been funneled by means of endowments for particular Church offices and positions; critics charged not only that fighting over such prizes was unseemly for clergy, but that offices were being filled with unworthy candidates. As discussed previously, the influence of lay aristocracy over Church positions was a long-standing practice in the German-speaking lands—and one of the specific targets of the eleventh-century reform movement. Charles IV was sufficiently pious to support reform in terms of general principles but would not take the fatal step of alienating his nobility.

The late fourteenth century was an even more difficult time to be an archbishop of Prague because any hope for royal support for reform evaporated under Wenceslaus. A particularly compelling example is the case of Archbishop Jan of Jenštejn, whose spiritual convictions and commitment to reform brought him into a series of confrontations with the king over schism politics. Not only did Jan hold firmly to the Roman side, whereas Wenceslaus shifted to Avignon to further his political agenda, but he had to fend off what he saw as royal intrusions into Church administration. In 1393, however, his key official, Jan of Pomuk, was murdered; the reformer archbishop's resignation shortly thereafter symbolized the now-unbridgeable gap between royal power and religious reform in Bohemia.

After Jan of Jenštejn's archiepiscopate, abuses within the Church not only continued but were made worse by the king himself. In 1393, for example, Wenceslaus—now engaged with Rome instead of Avignon—worked out a deal with the pope whereby pilgrims to churches in Prague received the same indulgence (or spiritual benefit) as pilgrims to the great ancient destination of Rome. What accounted for Wenceslaus's sudden interest in pious pilgrims? Half of the pilgrims' offerings at one of the major churches would end up in the king's coffers. It was a neat arrangement for all involved, but it would prove to be a dangerous precedent.

WYCLIFFITE INFLUENCE

By the early 1390s, therefore, an increasingly vocal population of thinkers, students, and idealists in Prague had reform on their minds and Czech on their lips. Within a few years, they would also have the books of John Wyclif in their hands, and his ideas served as a vehicle for a new and specifically Czech religiopolitical agenda. Initially it was Wyclif's philosophical writings that first attracted the attention of Bohemian thinkers, but attention quickly shifted to his more controversial theological works. But how did the works of an English theologian make their way to Bohemia in the first place? One key avenue was pure politics at the level of royal marriage. In 1382, Charles IV's daughter and Wenceslaus's sister Anne was married to the English king Richard II. The union not only fostered political and economic contacts between the two realms but also served as an early conduit for spiritual exchanges and reformist impulses. After Anne's death in 1394, Bohemian courtiers returned to Prague with further Wycliffite ideas and texts, which they introduced into the already active currents of local controversy. Channels of communication between the English and Bohemian networks continued through the early fifteenth century through letters, couriers, writings, and more: two Czech students from Charles University visited England and brought back with them not only books, for example, but a fragment of Wyclif's tomb as well.

Just as Oxford had been the center of original Wycliffite thought in England, Charles University was to be the incubator of Wycliffism in Bohemia. Once Wyclif's arguments were introduced in Prague, masters and students approached his realist ideas with the same combination of fascination and fear earlier felt by the professor's English colleagues. One major reason for the mounting popularity of Wyclif's ideas in Prague had to do with the conflict between Germans and Czechs at the university and the passion with which the latter wanted to remove the former from their positions of influence and authority. Indeed, the Bohemian theologians at Charles University had not established a particularly strong reputation in the field; typically embracing a fairly conservative realism rooted in Augustinian theology, they were eager to establish a counterpoint to the nominalist Germans but did not have the tools with which to construct a strong platform. Wyclif gave them those tools.

Particularly appealing to Czech scholars was Wyclif's rooting of universal prototypes in the original divine idea, a theory that contrasted directly with William of Ockham's insistence that the divine idea was unnecessary. In Prague, ontology (the study of being) became enmeshed with local rivalries. To put a complicated subject simply, Ockham's nominalism was not only the dominant philosophy in European universities of the late fourteenth century but particularly popular among the German masters in Prague. Wyclif offered the Czechs a new philosophical point of view with which to challenge the nominalists; the search for an intellectual weapon that could be used against the Germans may well have led the Czech masters to Wyclif in the first place. One Wycliffite manuscript bears a jubilant marginal note written by a Czech speaker at the university: "Haha, Germans, ha ha, out, out!"

Thus translated copies from the period abounded, though many readers found cause for concern: the boldness of Wyclif's stance, for example, provoked one reader to note in the margins, "O Wycleff, Wycleff, more than one head you have turned," a comment tinged with as much alarm as admiration. One of the central elements of Wycliffite thought (as discussed in chapter 7) was that every Christian was to have equal access to salvation—and to help ensure accessibility, he himself translated portions of the Bible into English so that it could be read by, or to, everyone. Of particular interest to his followers, first in England and later in Bohemia, was his doctrine of the true church. To Wyclif, of course, Christian society was not the true body of Christ, nor was the hierarchical institution that administered to this motley assortment of human souls. In response to the vexed question, "How do we know who is saved?" Wyclif offered no easy answer: moral living might reflect one's salvation, but there could be no proof. Because Wyclif also claimed that effective authority in both secular and sacral government depended upon the spiritual status of the officeholder (again, impossible to determine with certainty), the tainted Church—with its sinful priests, corrupt officials, and self-serving bureaucracies unrooted in scripture—could claim no sacred power. In Bohemia, such criticism of Church abuses—and the challenge to its institutional authority—harmonized sweetly with the rising currents of anticlericalism and apocalypticism.

Nobles also recognized the utility of Wyclif's position. Although his message that clergy were to serve as exemplars to the Christian laity of apostolic poverty, humility, and simplicity spoke to local disgust at clerical pomp and laxity, wealthy aristocrats and lords appreciated his argument for creating territorial churches under the authority of secular leaders. Eager to co-opt his claim that the papacy and cardinals merited respect only insofar as they demonstrated evangelical purity (and of course few did in this period of papal schism), the nobility seized the opportunity to defend its territorial interests. And where there are territorial interests, economic concerns cannot be far behind; in his rejection of papal and clerical authority, Wyclif also called for the secularization of Church property, a bold proposition whose enactment would necessarily upend the entire foundation of the Western Church.

Wyclif's ideas thus became simultaneously a reformist tool for critiquing the wealthy and formalist Church, an intellectual weapon to combat the influence of Germans at the university, and a political club with which to drive home the message of Czech identity. The mid-century preachers' emphasis upon personal piety and individual moral regeneration had been transformed into a strident insistence upon the need to rectify Church failings with major institutional reform—a reform that might even require the use of force. These are, of course, potent and potentially dangerous ideas whose implications had not been lost on English contemporaries, either lay or secular.

The impact and legacy of Wycliffism was as complex in Bohemia as it was in England: it lent intellectual tools and theological structure to the reformist movement, as well as a new energy and edge to its advocates; it fused the interests of otherwise disparate Bohemian populations, such as popular reformers, university masters, and nobility; and it alarmed and alienated some who simply could not accept its radicalism (even if they were initially sympathetic to reform). One particularly significant consequence of the fusion of reform and Wycliffism is that critics of the reformers would increasingly be able to wield charges of "Wycliffite heresy" against their opponents. As we will see, the very concept of heresy in the fifteenth-century Bohemian kingdom would ultimately prove impossible to extricate from an increasingly tangled knot of political, economic, social, and religious issues. Such was the historical stage onto which Jan Hus stepped upon arriving in Prague as a young university student in 1390.

JAN HUS (1372–1415)

The son of peasants from the village of Husinec in southern Bohemia, Hus is a remarkable exception to the rule that the Middle Ages offered little in the way of social mobility. Like most mothers, his thought her child was brilliant. Unlike most mothers, however, she was right, and his local schoolteacher sent him directly to Charles University. Life in cosmopolitan Prague was a change from his sleepy rural village, both shocking and exhilarating. Hus quickly made a name for himself in the university; working odd jobs to scrape together a living and studying late into the evening, he quickly finished his bachelor of arts. In 1396, already known as a brilliant lecturer and scholar, he became a master of arts and began to teach in the same institution. Evidently a charismatic and devoted teacher, Hus drew flocks of students and earned the admiration of his former teachers as well.

The first few years of the fifteenth century would be the turning point for Hus, both professionally and personally. In 1400, Hus decided to enter the priesthood, more as a means of furthering his career than as an expression of deep piety. Later, however, after his profound conversion to the religious life, he recalled,

> Before I became a priest I often, and gladly, played chess. I wasted my time. I bought fashionable gowns and robes with wings, and hoods trimmed with white fur. I thought that I would become a priest quickly in order to secure a good livelihood and dress well, and be held in great esteem. Alas! The goose was plucked of its virtue by the devil.[7]

(In Czech, *hus* means "goose," a pun enjoyed by his critics and supporters alike.)

Yet something powerfully changed for Hus after he decided to enter the priesthood at the age of thirty-one. What seems to have driven that transformation was not the ordination itself but a step in the process along the way: the requirement that he carefully and closely read the Bible. Although he retained his academic appointment at the university (even serving as dean of the arts faculty in 1401–1402), this internal conversion prompted the young Hus to focus his talents on preaching, studying scripture, and taking ideas out of the classroom and introducing them to Bohemian society. By 1402, he had become not only the personal confessor of Sophie, the queen of Bohemia, an increasingly active supporter of his program, but also the primary voice heard at Bethlehem Chapel.

For the next ten years, Hus combined teaching and service, both to the university and to the wider public who attended his regular sermons at Bethlehem Chapel and received spiritual direction from the scholar. Hus's appeal went deep into Prague society: elite citizens, nobility, gentry, and even members of the royal court sought his guidance, evidently impressed as much by his character and personality as by his principles. Queen Sophie (r. 1389–1413), the wife of Wenceslaus, made Hus her personal confessor and was one of the many women from different socioeconomic backgrounds who became actively involved in the new reformist circle.[8] The archbishop of Prague even invited Hus periodically to preach to gatherings of clergy, approving his tendency to point out clerical lapses in morality. Such support from Church and castle would not, however, be permanent.

At Bethlehem and in every other pulpit from which he spoke, Hus's central message had to do with the primacy of scripture and the importance of individual Christian access to those sacred texts. For Hus, as for Wyclif, the individual's encounter with the sacred word was crucial and yet depended upon rendering God's Word into the vernacular. Thus Wyclif's commitment to translating scripture into English was matched by Hus's interest in preaching in Czech. As a student, Hus had copied some of Wyclif's writings, and the Englishman's thought had a profound impact upon the Czech master, one that became stronger as he grew older. Although he would prove generally more cautious than some of his associates (rejecting, for example, Wyclif's attack on transubstantiation), he did agree with the Englishman's critique of the Roman Church.

ANTI-WYCLIFFISM IN PRAGUE (1403–1408)

As one might expect, it was the Germans who tended to lead the attacks against Wyclif and those who defended him, and among the latter was Jan Hus. The Germans were quick to point out that many of Wyclif's claims had been condemned as heretical by Pope Gregory XI, and they were no less quick to wield the label of "heresy" as a weapon against the entire Czech intelligentsia. In 1403, a German master fired the first shot in the battle by presenting to the cathedral chapter at Prague a list of forty-five articles compiled from Wyclif's books; the clerics, in turn, sought an informed opinion from the university. As expected, the German nations voted to reject the articles, including Wyclif's Eucharistic ideas, political ecclesiology, and philosophical position. The disputes continued, and in 1408 the stakes were raised: some members of the Czech faculty were accused of having taught Wyclif's disputed theory of the Eucharist to students, and two fled to Italy even as charges were filed against them in the court of Pope Gregory XII. Archiepiscopal pressure on the sixty Czech masters at the university to condemn the forty-five articles yielded only a conditional response, for the Bohemians were not about to submit to what they regarded as a power play by the Germans.

Hus, who was involved in all of these events, although not yet in a leadership position, did not agree with the condemnation of the forty-five articles and also had to defend his position against opponents. As noted previously, he embraced only some of the principles ascribed to Wyclif, but he was certain that the Englishman was right to insist that all doctrine be rooted in scripture. Under Wycliffite influence, therefore, Hus became increasingly convinced of certain truths: that the Word of God must be accessible to all believers, that the Bible *and* services ought to be in Czech, that the distinction between priest and congregation in the mass should be eliminated, and that the chalice of wine should be offered to the laity as well. The issue of the lay cup might not appear particularly important, but it would prove to be one of the most explosive and enduring issues of the entire Bohemian reform.

Traditionally, laity were given only the wafer, and the cup was reserved for the clergy. In contrast, some reformers in Prague maintained that Christ had shared both bread and wine with his disciples at the Last Supper, as noted in the Gospel of John (6:53): "Except ye eat the flesh of the Son of Man and drink his blood, ye have no life in you." Both camps (pro- and antichalice) agreed that the body and blood of Christ were fully contained in the bread, as they were in the wine; the problem was the decision of the hierarchical Church to change the custom in violation of Christ's words at the Last Supper. The issue of the chalice, therefore, provoked consideration of a particularly challenging question: What authority did the Church bear over scripture? For the increasingly vocal reformers who believed that the institutional Church was a corrupted body, the answer could only be "none." Although Hus himself did not actually offer the cup in practice, he refused to denounce his more radical followers who did administer the chalice to the laity and raised more than a few ecclesiastical eyebrows in the process.

THE TURNING POINT (1409–1412)

For decades, the Czech intelligentsia had remained focused on transforming the balance of power between themselves and the German majority; even Hus was to insist that "The Czechs in the realm of Bohemia, according to human law, divine law, and natural instinct, should be first in the realm's offices, just like the French in France and the Germans in their lands."[9] If conditions and procedures at the university had remained in their traditional form, such an outcome would have been most unlikely. But historical circumstances favored the Czechs, specifically King Wenceslaus's political needs and his relationship to the Great Schism. In an attempt to resolve the thirty-year-old crisis, cardinals summoned a great council to meet in the city of Pisa in the spring of 1409. Secular leaders were asked to withdraw obedience from their respective popes and to back the election of a single new candidate. Wenceslaus, still smarting from the humiliation of being deposed in 1400, was willing to play political hardball in a last-ditch effort to secure an imperial coronation. Standing in his way, however, were two forces: first, Archbishop Zbyněk, who refused to relinquish support for Rome (it was evidently no easier to be archbishop of Prague under Wenceslaus during the fifteenth century than it had been decades earlier); and second, the German nations at the university, who knew that to turn on the pontiff would mean professional suicide, since German lands and their universities remained staunch supporters of Rome.

Seizing the moment, Hus and some key colleagues, Jan of Jesenic and Jerome of Prague, developed an alliance with the Czech burghers of the city and some members of the royal court, and together they managed to persuade King Wenceslaus to adopt a dramatic new course. In 1409, the king intervened in both city politics and the university's disputes in order to further his own (not particularly religious or intellectual) agenda. The consequence was a dramatic reversal of power at the university and a new platform of support for the reformers. First, to pacify embittered burghers, he replaced the majority of German officials in the city government with Czechs. More important, however, was the tactic to sidestep the obstacle of the three German nations and their refusal to back his plan to withdraw obedience from Rome: in 1409, he issued the Decree of Kutná Hora that simply reversed the voting power of the university nations. The Bohemian nation (which had no stake in papal politics) was granted three votes, the combined German nations were reduced to one, and Wenceslaus gained the support he needed for his royal politicking. As a consequence, the faculty quickly voted to support Wenceslaus's planned action at the Council of Pisa—a council that met as planned but proceeded merely to add a third pope (Alexander V) to the schism.

When the Germans realized they were not going to be able to duck or repeal the Decree of Kutná Hora, they voted with their feet. Almost a thousand masters and students furiously abandoned Prague, most ending up at one of the several new universities recently founded in German lands (Heidelberg, established in 1386; Cologne, in 1388; Erfurt, in 1392; and, in particular, Leipzig, founded in 1409). Their vacated positions were immediately filled upon royal authority by Czechs, an action that was so welcome that even the Czech masters who did not support Wycliffite ideas were on board. For a short period, ethnic/linguistic rivalry had trumped theology. It would not do so forever, however, because Hus and the rest of the new leadership specifically underscored via sermons and writings that they fully intended this as part of a Wycliffite program, shaped by his doctrine of secular authority over territorial churches. Hus's rising visibility and centrality were amplified when he was named rector of the university in the same year (1409–1410), and although he was not the most radical of reformers in Prague, he became the symbolic head and voice of the movement.

Much as the departure of the Germans delighted most Czech masters, it did not settle the controversy over Wyclif because the ethnic rivalry had been only part of the problem. Opposition to Wycliffism and to Bohemian reformist impulses lingered, even among some Czechs, who worried about the radicalism of Wyclif's ideas. Archbishop Zbyněk, an old supporter and friend of Hus, began to regard the professor's movement with a new wariness. Seeking support from Alexander V, Zbyněk warned the pope of the dangerous new association formed in Prague between Wycliffite doctrines and royal power. Alexander, eager for supporters and allies, issued a bull later in 1409 condemning the forty-five articles, outlawing preaching in chapels such as Bethlehem, and supporting archiepiscopal attempts to suppress Wycliffism. Now armed with papal approval (that is, approval from *one* of the popes), Zbyněk launched a massive confiscation of Wyclif's works in Prague and publicly burned two hundred volumes as heretical works in July 1410. Hus scorned the action, claiming that

> such bonfires never yet removed a single sin from the hearts of men. Fire does not consume truth. It is always the mark of a little mind that it vents anger on inanimate objects. The books which have been burned are a loss to the whole people.[10]

Many students and residents agreed, and they took to the streets to protest and jeer, harassing priests, disrupting services, and denouncing Zbyněk and his prelates as the servants of the Antichrist—apocalyptic rhetoric that would soon rise to an unprecedented pitch.

Flouting the archbishop's command, Hus continued preaching. And although there was nothing necessarily doctrinally suspect about his words, one must recall that medieval heresy lay first and foremost in disobedience—Hus's decision to defy the archbishop's command thus signaled a rejection of Church authority. Herein lay the first steps toward the hereticization of Hus and the movement he came to both symbolize and inspire. Archbishop Zbyněk excommunicated Hus in 1410, and by the end of the summer, like so many other reformers we have discussed, Hus was "invited" to speak with the pope in Rome about his position. Hus refused. The refusal prompted the papacy to excommunicate him in February 1411, an event that sparked more street demonstrations and protests in Prague; the archbishop ended up fleeing the city and dying soon after, having been unable to check the peculiar tide of Bohemian reform and rebellion.

By 1412, the driving force within the movement was no longer the university faculty (most of whom were completely satisfied by the elimination of German dominance at the school), but a new and more radical generation of reform-minded leaders such as Jerome of Prague and Jakoubek of Stříbro, fierce critics of the Church whose anticlerical and apocalyptic strains fueled, and were in turn energized by, the growing momentum of street protests by citizens and students. Although Hus was never as radical as his colleagues, a striking (ultimately fatal) element of his character was refusal to dissociate himself from them or even from those Wycliffite articles that he himself did not embrace. As a consequence, Hus became the figurehead of—and thus target for—a movement known for ideas that he did not necessarily personally embrace. Before long, his foes were organized in a formidable array against him, including lingering German enemies, local clergy, Czech anti-Wycliffites, and various papal authorities. And in a neat example of the looming complexity of Hussite politics and reform, the radical Jakoubek would end up leading the relatively conservative Prague wing by 1419. Agendas and alliances shifted quickly during the decades to come, and close attention to chronology is vital as we explore the relationship between reform and revolution in Bohemia.

PROTEST FROM PULPIT AND STREET (1412–1414)

Royal support had granted Hus the power to defy papal summons and prohibitions in 1410, but such protection would not last; controversy with the king over the issue of indulgences soon proved to be Hus's undoing (as well as one of the major sparks of Luther's reform movement a century later). First used when the pope needed to raise money for crusades against the infidels, indulgences had developed over the intervening centuries into an exchange of spiritual merit (i.e., release from years in purgatory) in exchange for military service or, with increasing frequency, money. The theology is complicated, but indulgences had essentially become a fundraising mechanism for the papacy—heaven for sale on earth, said critics. And in 1411, a lucrative opportunity was presented to King Wenceslaus by Pope John XXIII. The pope needed to raise money for a crusade against the king of Naples and saw a rich market for indulgences in Bohemia; upon securing a promise that the indulgence revenues would be split between pope and king, Wenceslaus enthusiastically supported their sale in the kingdom. Hus was appalled by this practice, as were others.

By early 1412, the reformist community in Prague was flourishing in both size and enthusiasm, in part due to the arrival of a reformist group of Germans from Dresden (a further indication that the period of Czech versus German had passed). Adhering to a set of tenets redolent of the Poor (or Waldensians), the radical newcomers apparently supported free preaching, the stripping of Church wealth, and the supremacy of scripture. In addition, they rejected a wide spectrum of traditional practices, from the swearing of oaths to obedience to papal authority. Led by Nicholas of Dresden, the radical German contingent was no doubt highly involved in the street uprisings. By autumn of 1412, Nicholas had written *The Tables of Old and New Colors*, a collection of images and texts sharply contrasting the original and pure Church with the corrupted contemporary Church.

Further radicalized by Nicholas, the weight of the Hussite movement was already shifting from an emphasis upon reform to rejection—not only the rejection of certain practices but the explicit condemnation of an irredeemably corrupt Church. Rather than providing examples of apostolic morality, churchmen under papal leadership (according to the growing number of radicals in and beyond Bohemia) had turned the Church into a whore. Rather than guiding Christians via scripture and example, they had become degraded minions of the Antichrist and his hellish reign on earth. And if the lay chalice were a symbol of the former, indulgences were about to become a symbol of the latter.

In June 1412, Hus publicly condemned the sale of indulgences and their cynical marketing in Bohemia, and in a move demonstrating that the major rift was no longer ethnic/linguistic, he and his followers were opposed by the Czech anti-Wycliffite theologians at the university. The new precariousness of Hus's position was ominously signaled in the king's response to his preaching: "Hus, you are always making trouble for me . . . if those whose concern it is will not take care of it, I myself will burn you."[11] Prague residents and students once again poured into the streets, shouting, destroying property, and waving placards on which the pope was represented as the Antichrist. Violence erupted on July 10 when three young students opposed to the indulgences were seized and executed by Prague city officials. The movement that was consolidating around Hus had its first martyrs, whose bodies were brought to Bethlehem Chapel and mourned. By September, not only was Hus excommunicated by the pope, but the entire city of Prague was placed under interdict because of his presence. In other words, Prague and all of its residents were excised from the body of Christendom, from the sacraments, and thus from God's grace. To prevent Prague from suffering unduly, Hus left and lived for two years in the castles of his elite rural supporters in southern and western Bohemia.

During these years of exile, he traveled widely around the countryside, preaching, mulling over his ideas, and writing a treatise, *De ecclesia* (1413), which was later read out loud at Bethlehem Chapel. In this text, he drew deeply on Wycliffite radicalism to reject the papacy's claim to divine origins, which made the papacy dispensable. Although the rest of his interpretations of Wyclif tended to be fairly moderate, with his claims about the papacy he was finally treading on doctrinally heretical ground. He also wrote *On Simony*, also inspired by Wyclif, which was a direct response to the sale of indulgences in Bohemia. He criticized all sales and purchases of offices, sacraments, property, and grace, rebuking clergy who wasted revenues that might be better managed by secular leadership. The years of exile afforded Hus the opportunity to develop a coherent articulation of his position on the all-important issue of the nature of the Church. From this point on, the momentum of Bohemian reform carried it to an increasingly unresolvable impasse amid mutually hostile Bohemian conservatives and radicals, Church officials worried about heresy in Bohemia, and a king whose attempts to mend the rift proved consistently fruitless.

Even during the years of Hus's exile, Prague continued to earn its own reputation for heresy, and King Wenceslaus's anxiety mounted. The issue of the lay chalice (or Utraquism, as it came to be known) was central to agitation in Prague prior to 1415. Jakoubek had begun to introduce the chalice at mass in Prague, with support from men such as the German radical Nicholas of Dresden and the scholar Jan Příbram (another figure who would take an increasingly conservative position as time passed). Access to the cup appealed enormously to both laity and clergy in the city, and the services at which it was offered drew throngs of impassioned supporters. Many others, however, were repelled by what they regarded as an innovation specifically condemned by the Church. Thus the city was quickly divided over the issue of the lay chalice, split into congregations offering the cup to laity and congregations that did not. Rhetoric and resentment escalated, as each side accused the other of heresy, and each Christian had to consider his or her own position before deciding where to attend mass. The controversy quickly reached an intolerable pitch, and in April 1415 the city council intervened to insist that both sides stop the name-calling. Although Hus was not present in Prague, the Utraquists continued to unite under the Hussite banner—the university master and preacher wielded enormous influence even in absentia.

Attempts to persuade the university to come to a compromise between the papacy and the ideas of Wyclif and Hus failed, and the latter remained obstinate:

> Even if I should stand before the fire prepared for me, I hope that death will sooner remove me, either to heaven or to hell, than that I agree. . . . [I]t is better to die well than to live wickedly . . . truth conquers all.[12]

At this point, the king washed his hands of him and handed over the case to his brother Sigismund, who had been crowned the Holy Roman emperor in 1411.

HUS AT THE COUNCIL OF CONSTANCE (1414–1415)

In the spring of 1414, Emperor Sigismund summoned Hus to the Council of Constance to plead his case but made clear that it was a minor issue compared to the council's principal purposes of reforming the Church and the empire. Sigismund offered a safe conduct to Hus, namely in the form of a group of Czech nobility who supported the master. Many supporters became increasingly uncomfortable under pressure at this time: in 1414, for example, the Oxford scholar Peter Payne fled England for Bohemia, where he would spend the remainder of his life working for the Hussite cause. Hus did not wait for the safeguard of an escort, confident in the virtue of his position and the value of the letters he had gathered attesting to his orthodoxy and morality.

Constance, however, afforded him none of the opportunities he had anticipated. The council's focus was not heresy but rather the very nature of authority within Christendom: for more than thirty years, the papal see had been split between two (and for a period, even three) rivals, an event with catastrophic spiritual implications for Christians and equally damaging consequences for ecclesiastical structures. Bishops in attendance at the Council of Constance sought to diminish papal influence and channel the Church's power instead through episcopal channels, whereas papalists insisted that a single head was necessary to prevent the Church from suffering further factionalism. In other words, the traditional supporters of the pope as the head of Christendom doubted that a decentralized system would be sufficiently strong to defend the Church against its enemies—including secular powers, infidels (Muslims), and, of course, heretics.[13] As a result, the upper clergy who sought to diminish papal influence at the Council of Constance needed to demonstrate that they could and would act decisively to protect Christendom. These underlying circumstances meant that Hus was walking into a particularly dangerous situation, one he could not easily have anticipated; no fool, however, he made out his will before he left.

After only a few weeks at Constance, he was soon outflanked by enemies, their representatives, and hostile leading scholars such as the Parisians Jean Gerson and Pierre d'Ailly, who succeeded in having him imprisoned in November as a dangerous Wycliffite. Hus's attempts to explain himself to the assembled prelates changed no minds; indeed, he would certainly have been safer with papal inquisitors, who at least tended to conduct interrogations thoroughly, patiently, and with an eye toward rehabilitation of Christian souls. Instead, he was faced with a list of Wycliffite articles culled from his own works and asked whether he held those ideas—yes or no, with no opportunity to explain further. This was not the open debate that Hus had (perhaps naively) expected, a forum in which he could articulate and defend the broad reformist position that he could prove was rooted in the traditional authorities of scripture and the Church fathers.

Meanwhile, once his noble followers back in Bohemia got wind of what was happening, their vociferous intervention resulted only in a single public hearing after seven months of interrogation and imprisonment. The Bohemians were aghast and furious at the manner in which their leader was being treated. In prison, Hus too was dejected, though he wrote in thanks to supporters such as Lady Petra of Říčany, founder of one of the leading lay religious women's communities.[14] Evidently disappointed in the emperor, from whom he had (again, perhaps too optimistically) expected more, he wrote to a Czech supporter that "I am surprised that Sigismund has forgotten me, and never sends a word."[15] It might have been better for Hus if Sigismund *had* forgotten him, for the emperor's final directive to the assembled prelates at Constance was, "If he will not recant his errors and abjure . . . let him be burned."[16]

And so they did, after weeks of unsuccessfully pressuring him to recant. When asked whether he abjured the heretical articles, he once again refused on principle, insisting that he could not actually withdraw ideas that he had never embraced—or at least, not in the form set forth by the Council of Constance. On July 6, 1415, Hus was formally condemned as a heretic guilty of having propagated the doctrines of John Wyclif, stripped of his ecclesiastical vestments, and burned at the stake in a field outside the city before an assembled group of officials and onlookers. Witnesses reported that he died with serene confidence in his innocence, and perhaps also in the strength his martyrdom would provide to the Bohemian reform.

Back in Prague, Hus's supporters had to decide upon a course of action, a significant challenge considering the variety of agendas and ambitions among its heterogenous members. For instance, the university masters who had been Hus's first defenders were primarily motivated by the hope that both Hus and Wyclif would prove useful in consolidating their power within and beyond the university. It is doubtful that any would have independently chosen to continue pursuing Bohemian reform, but their hand was forced by Church pressure (including the looming threat of an actual papal crusade to crush the Hussites). Help was vital, but where to seek it? Given the king's history of unreliability, the professors joined forces with the hundreds of Bohemian nobility who had already agitated on Hus's behalf while he was in prison. It was a wise decision, for the nobles quickly organized a formal protest to the Council of Constance, signed by 452 nobles who emphatically declared Hus's innocence and insisted there was no heresy in Bohemia. Letter writing in itself was not sufficient, however, for it was clear that reform preachers and other adherents of the movement were about to be harassed and repressed by Church authorities. Thus within a few days, leaders among the nobility created a Hussite League to physically protect Hus's followers; the masters of Charles University were appointed their verbal and legal defenders, charged with the arbitration of all theological questions.

Proclaiming the right of Hussites to preach freely on the basis of holy scripture, the league's new alliance between noble and scholar effectively barricaded the kingdom of Bohemia from royal, conciliar, and Church authorities: "The doctrinal authority of the international Church was replaced by that of the university, and the jurisdiction of bishops made subject, in a way

Figure 8.2. Burning at the Stake of Reformer Jan Hus in 1415.c. *Source*: **From the Chronicle of the Council of Constance by Ulrich von Richenthal, 15th c. Bildarchiv Preussischer Kulturbesitz/Art Resource, NY.**

now characteristic of Hussite proceedings, to the private conscience of members of the league."[17] Ecclesiastical summonses and proceedings initiated against the nobles who protested Hus's execution were ignored in Bohemia because the league was so much more powerful than Church forces within the kingdom. Although pro-Hussite lords represented only a fraction of the Bohemian nobility, they were nonetheless sufficiently powerful to protect the burgeoning Hussite reform platform. Thus, they contributed to the crucial early victories of both moderate and radical wings.

UTRAQUISM AND GROWING RESISTANCE IN BOHEMIA (1415–1419)

Hus's martyrdom gave the movement one powerful symbol; the lay chalice would become another, particularly for the radical wing. In particular, the league served during these crucial years of 1415–1416 to shield the rapidly growing community of Hus supporters and their practice of the lay chalice from the furious decrees of the Council of Constance. The main leader of the emerging radical wing was Hus's old associate Jakoubek of Stříbro, a strident figure inspired both by Wyclif's ecclesiopolitical framework and Matthew of Janov's notion of the true church as an evangelical community of pious men and women. From both models, Jakoubek drew an image of the Roman Church and its officials as sinful, defiled, and the very body of the Antichrist himself—that final joining of hell and earth prophesied in the book of Revelation. The clerical hijacking of Christ's blood in the now traditional practice of denying the cup to laity thus became a potent symbol to Jakoubek of the Church's swollen institutional power, wealth, and authority. Thus, he and his followers adopted Wyclif's concept of a simple church comprising pious Christians and governed by secular rather than papal power. Although the specific agitation for access to the chalice was a regional issue, Jakoubek and his followers were very much of their day with their emphasis upon the centrality of the Eucharist to Christian piety; earlier Bohemian reformers such as Jan Milič and Matthew of Janov had promoted frequent Communion, and the entire issue must be viewed in the framework of a broad European preoccupation in the fourteenth and fifteenth centuries with the body and blood of Christ.

Thus, the sharing of the common cup in the Eucharist quickly became one of the primary weapons Hussite reformers wielded against the son of perdition and his tool, the pope. Once again, the central issue was the nature of the Church itself and the power of its representatives to interpret scripture. On the one hand, conservatives maintained that the pope and other officials could justly decide against Communion "in both kinds," even given its precedent in the Bible; the Hussites vehemently disagreed. How could officials whose authority derived from a stained and corrupted institution rightfully instruct Christians to deviate from the holy Word? Why should pious Christians accept the decision of wicked clergy to withhold Christ's blood for themselves? And how much longer would God tolerate the cynical sale of heaven through papal indulgences? The end must have seemed very near in 1415.

A few short weeks before Hus's death, the Council of Constance responded to Jakoubek's revolt by prohibiting offering the cup to the laity; on June 15, 1415, the shared cup was officially condemned by the authorities. Hus, who had always tried to avoid open revolt, did not favor the introduction of Utraquist Communion at the time, nor did he agree with Jakoubek that it was necessary for salvation—he apparently cautioned his colleague, "Go slow, Kubo." However, he refused again to criticize the beliefs or actions of his fellows, and thus the association between Hussites and the lay chalice was cemented. Ironically, the conciliar decree against the common cup served more to provoke than limit its spread: the council's almost simultaneous decisions to outlaw the cup and burn Hus ensured that the furious Bohemians would forever link both symbols into a single representation of their oppression by the Church (which to some meant by the Antichrist himself).

In the wake of Hus's execution, a new wave of protest swirled with the preexisting currents of Hussite anticlericalism and apocalypticism. Utraquism became a rallying point among a number of otherwise distinct populations in Prague, ranging from pious laity to radical university students. The latter proved to be an especially vital force as they flooded into the Bohemian countryside preaching about the evils of the Roman Church and the need for a revitalized Christianity rooted in scripture. Preachers encountered many pockets of latent reform in the Bohemian countryside, particularly of a long-standing Waldensian-type disenchantment with ecclesiastical traditions and trappings. Such communities were particularly common among German speakers who, in some cases, had been reading and hearing the vernacular Word of God for generations. Thus radical Czech Hussites found themselves energized by new recruits from older and often German "heretical" communities. Within a few months, the radicals were gaining momentum in Prague as well.

As the months and years passed, the gap between the moderate Hussite Utraquists and the radical reformers became wider and increasingly evident. What did this mean in practice? Put baldly, the new radicals in both town and countryside sought a new form of church service and Christian leadership so reformed as to be almost unrecognizable. Services were conducted in the vernacular (Czech or German rather than Latin), with an emphasis upon simple hymns and prayers and lay Communion in both kinds. Priests shed their vestments in favor of simple or ordinary garments, and they replaced their vessels of precious metals with those of homely materials instead. Saints' images and relics, that mainstay of late medieval piety, were taken away or destroyed so as to focus Christian attention upon Christ. The radical Hussites, again sympathetic to the apostolic model upheld by "Waldensian" friends, simplified several of the sacraments (including baptism and penance) while eliminating others (confirmation and extreme unction).

Thus the dual symbols of the martyred Hus and the lay chalice ignited a bold radical movement in and beyond Prague that lasted two years. On one level, it was fought by the nobility of the Hussite League, who rejected the council's execution of Hus and the Church's verdict of Bohemian heresy; on

Map 8.1. Poor in Bohemia. Reprinted from Euan Cameron, *Waldenses: Rejections of Holy Church in Medieval Europe*. *Source*: **Copyright © 2000 by Euan Cameron. Reprinted with permission of the publisher, Blackwell Publishing.**

another level, the opposition came from the increasingly radical reformers and their flocks who benefited from the league's protection as they established explicitly anti-Roman congregations and communities throughout Bohemia. Yet not all those who were sympathetic to the cause of Hussite reform were radicals. Many Utraquists continued to adhere to the traditional Roman model, such as Hus's friend Christian of Prachatice, who continued to chant the full Latin Mass in elegant vestments even as he passionately defended the Hussite reform. By the end of 1416, a gap had also emerged between the radicals and the nobility. Both the relatively conservative nobles and university masters had managed to secure their goals by this point: the nobles had drastically pruned clerical power in Bohemia and enhanced their own political and religious influence in the kingdom, and the masters had successfully secured Czech control of Charles University. All accepted Utraquism because the university had officially rejected Roman practice and declared that Communion of both kinds was to be available for all laity. Despite the hostility between radicals and moderates, a shared commitment to the lay chalice would provide sufficient unity to the movement to ensure its survival through the tumultuous years ahead.

If Hus's heresy and the question of the common cup had been the only issues, an agreement might have been reached among the Church, the king, and the reformers in 1417. But these were symbols of the struggle, not the central problem itself. At the heart of the matter lay the still-unresolved question of the nature of the true Church—an issue exacerbated by the radical new communities sprouting up throughout the Bohemian kingdom founded in explicit opposition to what they perceived as the corrupted body of the Roman Church. The composition and ambition of the Hussites were about to change again under the influence of the radical wing. Before long, many of its former supporters (nobles and masters) would peel away from Hussitism and return to Catholic obedience.

Meanwhile, the Great Schism had ended with the election in 1417 of Pope Martin V, who immediately turned his attention to Bohemia. Early in 1418, he tasked King Wenceslaus with a long list of steps necessary for restoring the Bohemian Church to its former condition—including the demand that Hus's followers formally and publicly approve his execution for heresy, an utterly implausible scenario given the current mood in Bohemia. Two potent weapons were employed against the "heretics": law, especially proceedings against Hussites for infringing upon the Church's rights and possessions; and physical force, the grant of full powers to Emperor Sigismund to intervene militarily against the Hussites.

FROM REFORM TO REVOLUTION (1419)

Early in 1419, the forces of religious reform, political rebellion, and royal anxiety reached the boiling point. Intimidated by the prospect of a crusade against the Hussites in his kingdom, King Wenceslaus finally moved to pacify Catholics by ejecting Utraquists and restoring many of the churches that had been seized by the "heretics." By late February, Catholic services had resumed alongside Hussite services in Prague. Attempting to forge a temporary peace, Wenceslaus did not entirely ban Hussites from Prague or persecute them directly, but they were forbidden to agitate against or decry Catholic practice. The awkward compromise was largely accepted by moderates but rejected by radicals, who refused to be silenced on the issue of Catholic perfidy.

Among the most dynamic of these new Hussite leaders were Jan Želivský (pronounced "zhe-liv-ski"), a popular urban priest, and Jan Žižka (pronounced "zhee-shka"), a battle-experienced veteran and rural landowner. Each in turn played a powerful role in channeling brewing Bohemian discontent into revolution—not only in Prague, but most dramatically in new communities gathering in the rural south. A contemporary chronicler succinctly described the events as follows:

> In the year 1419 evangelical priests, who were followers of Master John Hus and who propagated communion in both kinds for the laity, and who at that time were called Wyclifites or Hussites, began to frequent a certain mountain near Bechyně castle, with the sacrament of the Eucharist and along with men and women from various regions, cities, and towns of the kingdom of Bohemia. They called this mountain Tabor, and there, particularly on feast-days, they gave communion with the holy Eucharist to the laity, with great reverence, for the enemies of that sort of communion [Utraquism] would not permit the laity to take communion in that way in the neighboring churches.[18]

Tabor, the mountain designated here after the biblical Mt. Tabor, became the most important of the new apostolic hilltop communities to which faithful Hussites of all social orders were being called across Bohemia; those who participated in such communities came to be known as Taborites. Gentry provided the leadership, Hussite priests the spiritual care, and both retained ties of one sort or another to Želivský's urban Hussite core in Prague. John Klassen suggests that these radicals also offered a specific message to women, a "hope of release from domestic drudgery . . . and end to the old order and the beginning of a new utopia in which there would be no hunger or thirst and no pain even in childbirth."[19] Soon the radicals who had once agitated in the city of Prague would be put to flight by the city's growing conservatism, and Tabor would become the rallying point for a new radicalism so distinct from urban Utraquism that the two functioned as distinct movements at certain points throughout the following decades.

In July 1419, clear evidence of those ties surfaced to redirect the course of Bohemian Hussite history. At one of the huge open-air congregations that had become a hallmark of the Taborite movement, thousands of men and women committed to the Hussite cause gathered from across Bohemia. The agenda included a plan of action against their perceived oppressors—the Church and royal authority. Within a week, the Taborites had struck, launching a massive demonstration in the heart of Prague fueled by reformist rage, anticlerical and antiroyal sentiment, and the seething despair of peasants and other impoverished men and women so long denied a political voice. "Power to the people" is flammable rhetoric, especially in times of socioeconomic stress, and Hussite street demonstrations had already demonstrated their inherent potential for violence. On July 30, as Želivský led his supporters through the streets to demand the release of Hussite prisoners, someone hurled a stone at them from a window of the town hall. Incensed, the Hussite demonstrators stormed the hall and, under the leadership of the rural Hussite squire Jan Žižka, threw the judge, mayor, and several other officials out the window to their deaths in the street below. This particular form of political dissent apparently held enduring appeal in Prague, for the event would later come to be known as the *First* Defenestration of Prague (*defenestration* comes from the Latin: "de" = out of, and "fenestra" = window). Faced with such aggression and the very real threat of a full-scale political revolution, King Wenceslaus was forced to accept Hussite demands to install new, sympathetic city councillors. The shock probably contributed to the heart attack that killed him within a matter of weeks.

Although Wenceslaus had long been hated by both moderate and radical wings of the movement, he had been a relatively manageable force compared with the new Bohemian king. Thus, his death was a blow to the recently jubilant Hussites. Sigismund, king of Hungary, Holy Roman emperor, and the secular ruler who abandoned Jan Hus to his enemies at the Council of Constance, would prove to be a much tougher opponent. Sigismund summarily rejected Hussite attempts to propose a compromise, and moderates and radicals disagreed sharply on the right course of action. The impasse quickly turned into a schism. Prague elites and Bohemian nobility (both Hussite and Catholic) joined ranks to accept Sigismund's condition of full submission in exchange for the right to the lay chalice and some other concessions. Radical Hussites in both city and country condemned the move, rioting in the streets, tearing down images, and destroying monasteries. A new era of Bohemian history was begun. What followed were decades of argument about the Eucharist and lay chalice and infighting between moderate Utraquists and radical Taborites inspired by apocalyptic and apostolic themes. Thus the reformist movement originally sparked by linguistic divisions and ethnic privileges had been transformed into a political revolution fueled by anticlericalism and socioeconomic complaints. By 1419, the primary division in Bohemia was no longer between Czechs and Germans, but between elite conservatives and impoverished radicals.

The split would never be healed because both Catholic and Hussite elites turned their formidable arsenal against the Taborites. As radicals were hunted down and assassinated by their former allies as well as by royalists, the movement became more extremist, and members sought refuge in rural communities led by increasingly radical figures preaching a potent apocalyptic message of the impending End of Days. It is not hard to understand how Prague might have seemed a new Babylon to them (full of wickedness, treachery, wealth, and sin) and why the persecuted radicals believed that they were the only true adherents of a righteous reform. Thus the new radical communities that formed around Bohemia were specifically conceptualized in terms of the communal primitive church (Acts 4:32ff). Members shared

IOANNES ZISSKA.A.TROCZNOW SVPERBIÆ SIMVLET
AVARICIÆ CLERICORVM SEVERVS VLTOR.

Figure 8.3. Jan Žižka [Johann Ziska von Trocnov] (1370–1424), Leader of the Bohemian Hussites and Taborites Who Won Two Battles against Imperial Armies in 1420 and 1422, 15th c. Inv. 2743. ***Source*****: Portraitgalerie, Schloss Ambras, Innsbruck, Austria. Erich Lessing/Art Resource, NY.**

goods equally in piety and service. Doctrines were also transformed in this radical environment, as people such as Nicholas of Hus denied transubstantiation and claimed instead that the Eucharist was a commemoration. These were no pacifist communities—their members also made up armies under the capable leadership of people such as Jan Žižka, whose career reveals much about the ensuing era of violence known as the Hussite Wars.

JAN ŽIŽKA AND THE COMMUNITY AT TABOR (1420)

In contrast to the urban Hussites of Prague, Jan Žižka represented a different population within the movement. A minor landowner from Budweis (Ceske Budejovice) in southern Bohemia, he had not only served as a captain in King Wenceslaus's palace guard but also as a mercenary—possibly even at the famous Battle of Tannenberg against the Teutonic knights in 1410.[20] Battle scarred and strategically minded, the one-eyed Žižka was a formidable commander whose leadership fueled the radical Hussites' military strength against the increasingly daunting crusading forces arrayed against them. Infuriated by the Prague Hussites' capitulation to Sigismund in 1419 and by the royalists' subsequent brutal persecution of rural Hussite communities, Žižka had withdrawn from the city to Pilsen in the south; however, he would not remain there for long.

Two crucial developments emerged in March of 1420: the establishment of a new radical Hussite center in the south and the calling of an anti-Hussite crusade. Under attack by royalist forces, early in the year the beleaguered southern radicals were pressured to yield their positions and seek new ground, which they did at an abandoned fortress. Establishing a new Hussite settlement there, the fleeing men, women, children (clergy, soldiers, preachers, and peasants among them) christened it Tabor. When Pilsen came under attack, Žižka too shifted his location to the revitalized town, which would become the base of Hussite military operations for years to come. Royalist soldiers who tried to prevent Žižka's men from reaching Tabor were defeated along the way on March 25, a minor battle but a major psychological victory in terms of enhancing Hussite confidence and solidifying Žižka's reputation as a formidable leader.

New recruits flooded to this second Tabor, now fortified by Žižka's men and the newly constructed fortress walls he supervised. The settlement became the heart of a vibrant complex of radical congregational communities where religious reform and apostolic piety were channeled through basic systems, ensuring social order. Overseen by joint civil and religious authorities, the communities centered on a single church, simple services, and strict adherence to a code of apostolic morality. Tabor and the other radical Bohemian communities were thus analogous to later but similarly self-conscious Christian locales such as Calvin's Geneva or the Massachusetts Bay Colony.

A strong military edge underlay these towns as well, one sharpened not only by their self-perception as an embattled and righteous minority but also by Žižka's martial innovations. Working with the resources on hand (peasants and agricultural equipment), he organized bands of men to modify farm wagons with reinforced sides and portholes for visibility. Once transformed, the wagons were placed into large circles called *wagenburgs* that essentially served as mobile fortresses. Their purpose was not merely defensive, however: within the wagons, Žižka stationed soldiers, armed with crossbows and little handguns (*pistola*), who could kill at a distance, as well as others with pole arms to pull down knights from their equestrian mounts. Once knights in their heavy armor had been yanked off their horses, a third group of soldiers hiding underneath the wagons could dart out and quickly dispatch them. Finally, Žižka developed a brilliant use of heavy artillery (*houfnitze* in Czech; later the modern military term *howitzer*), mobile offensive weaponry that would not be similarly employed for another five hundred years.[21]

EARLY WAR AND RESPONSE (FROM 1420)

In March 1420, Pope Martin V picked up the blunt weapon of crusade with which to fight the "Wycliffites, Hussites, and other heretics." It was an odd decision given the likelihood that such an action would provoke a reunified Czech resistance. Once the crusade bull was read aloud in the city and formally proclaimed, masses of crusaders drawn from across Europe (but particularly from German-speaking lands) quickly gathered outside of Prague,

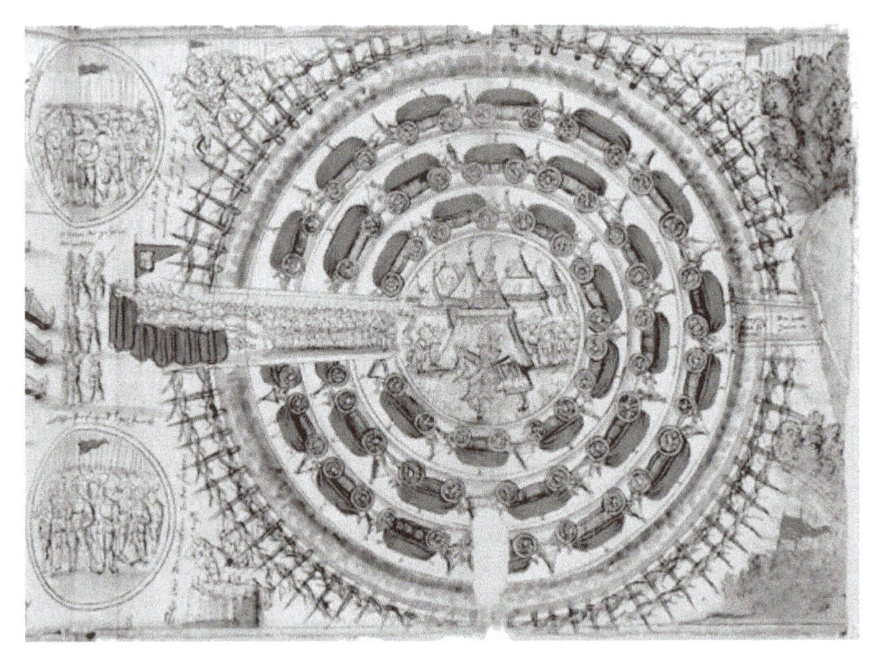

Figure 8.4. Barricade of Wagons of the Hussites during the Hussite War, 1419–1434. Illustration from a codex around 1450. *Source*: **Bibliothèque Municipale, Amiens, France. Erich Lessing/Art Resource, NY.**

probably motivated as much by the prospect of pillage as by the promised benefit to their souls. Hussites in Prague tried to take Hradčany Castle before the intimidating mass of crusaders arrived, but they failed and could only wait for reinforcements to arrive. Žižka and his army of about nine thousand marched north and, quickly surveying the scene, decided to cut off the crusaders by seizing a strategic position on an eastern rise (Vitkov Hill) and cutting through enemy flanks to the south. It was a stunning defeat for the crusading army; indeed, Vitkov Hill is still known as Zitkov Hill in Žižka's honor, topped with an imperious statue of the general.

Sigismund's fortunes continued to decline through 1420, as the unlikelihood of securing either the city of Prague or his own authority through military means began to become clear. On July 28, he enacted a symbolic victory by crowning himself king of Bohemia in the city cathedral, but his army was already dissolving as a consequence of illness and poor morale. In the wake of many German soldiers' departure home, Sigismund too withdrew from Prague (whose citizens were increasingly enraged by the army's brutality) to the safety of Kutná Hora. By early 1421, the southern Hussite armies' minor but regular territorial victories had persuaded him to leave Bohemia entirely.

The Four Articles of Prague (1421)

The weakening of royalist and crusader antagonists in 1421 provided a window of opportunity in which the Hussites managed to secure holdings even in Prague, including Hradčany Castle itself. In response to the successes, Želivský and others in Prague managed to bring together all wings of the movement to form a militarized Hussite Union in defense of the chalice. Decrying the crusade and its armies composed of "our natural-born enemies, the Germans," the unified Hussites were determined to resist both pope and emperor, and together with many rural brethren who arrived in the city as representatives, negotiated an agreement that would become known as the Four Articles of Prague:

1. We stand for the ministering of the body and blood of the Lord to the laity in both kinds, for . . . this was Christ's institution and . . . that of the first apostles and of the holy Primitive Church . . . , as the Council of Constance admitted to us.
2. We stand for the proper and free preaching of the word of God and of his every truth.
3. All priests, from the pope on down, should give up their pomp, avarice, and improper lordship in superfluity over temporal goods, and they should live as models for us.
4. We stand for the purgation of and cessation from all public mortal sins, by each in his own person; and for the cleansing of the Bohemian realm

> and nation from false and evil slander; and in this connection, for the common good of our land.[22]

These core demands far exceeded, of course, what Emperor Sigismund or the Roman Church were willing to accept. Even more galling to royalists, moreover, was that the Hussites so publicly denounced Sigismund and sought to replace him on the Bohemian throne with Grand Duke Alexander Vytautas (Witold) of Lithuania. No mending of the religiopolitical breach was possible from this point on: hostilities continued unabated and battles flared across Bohemia between Hussite recruits and Sigismund's troops. Žižka continued to serve as a key military commander, despite the fact that he was hit by an arrow in June of 1421 in his remaining good eye. Now completely blind, he nonetheless managed to lead armies successfully for another four years.

DISSENT AMONG THE TABORITES

Although Žižka provided the military backbone and strategic leadership vital for sustaining the Taborite cause against its foes, other threats loomed against which the *wagenburg* would offer little defense. Radical movements fracture easily, and there were many distinct groups under the general Taborite umbrella whose differing visions of proper behavior, Eucharistic interpretation, or the imminence of the Apocalypse proved a barrier to settled communal life. As the message of Tabor spread across the land, for example, sympathetic men and women from related circles of reform or dissent answered the call: lay religious women, members of Poor communities, charismatic preachers, and others for whom the apostolic model of simplicity, spiritual equality, and Christian renewal resonated. The mixture of differing interpretations of scripture and its implications for behavior on earth with increasingly bloody persecution fueled fierce disagreement from within their own ranks.

Perhaps most notable in this enormously complex array of perspectives was a chiliastic mood, manifested in some cases by groups pooling their goods into a communal chest in expectation of the imminent apocalypse (expected by many in 1420): some believed that, in keeping with Revelation 20:4, the subsequent new age would last a millennium, while others predicted that the harmonious age of renovation would last for eternity. In its most radical expression, the chiliasts believed that they were the only true Christians and that the lives of their opponents (of any theological stripe) were thus forfeit, a tenet that exonerated the escalating bloodshed of the day. Represented by leaders such as Martin Húska, chiliasts followed a particularly apocalyptically inflected line of historical reasoning quite similar to that articulated centuries earlier by Joachim of Fiore and raised sensitive issues such as the nature of the sacraments and pious rituals; historians have recently emphasized the extent to which various flavors of beguin, Free Spirit, and other hereticized pieties cropped up at Tabor. Húska, for example, led a group rejecting the real presence of Christ in the Eucharist, replacing the sacrament with informal and commemorative "love-feasts" of bread and wine.[23] Eucharistic piety was, however, only one issue on which groups disagreed, as controversies raged over everything from the proper interpretation of scripture to the legal regulation of Taborite society. One faction among Húska's followers (called Adamites) was said to have claimed that they were living in a state of innocence akin to that before the Fall and that nakedness and even intercourse were no sins. The claim smacks of the prurient charges made against all kinds of hereticized movements, but the fevered climate of Tabor no doubt gave rise to startling expressions of human yearning. Believing the Adamites to be sodomites, murderers, and heretics of the worst possible kind, Žižka himself annihilated them both in battle and at the stake after reporting their errors to Prague.

Húska had distanced himself from Adamite claims but remained a figure of enormous controversy. Taborite leaders were soon communicating regularly with conservative Hussites in Prague over the matter of the "free" interpretation of scripture and presumed licentiousness it provoked. In another example of how complex the issue of names and labels can be, the Prague contingent referred to this type of heresy as "Pikartism," derived from "Pikart," which was a regionalized corruption of "beghard." In other words, even the radical Hussites (heretics in the eyes of both Church and state) were employing the categories and assumptions of traditional authorities as they attempted to establish their own heaven on earth. Almost immediately, the fragile unity of the radicals' hoped-for Eden was shattered as leaders turned on the "heretics" within their community. After being captured and imprisoned, Húska was (with the agreement of both Taborite majority and Prague Hussites) burned at the stake in the summer of 1421. In the long run, such internal feuds proved even more damaging to the Taborite cause than the furious combined enmity of conservative Hussites and royal forces.

Not all Hussites were turning upon their enemies with violence, however. A Taborite farmer by the name of Peter Chelčický turned away from the rampant bloodshed and directly questioned how one might square murderous warfare with God's commandment not to kill. Denouncing even Hussite victories as a spiritual breach, Peter removed himself to the countryside, where he lived quietly and pacifically, writing treatises exhorting Christians to abandon the struggle for political authority. Akin to the Poor, he refused to swear oaths, believed the Donation of Constantine to have corrupted the church, and sought a restoration of the original, primitive, apostolic church.

Throughout the course of the wars ahead, he would maintain contact with Hussite leaders, many of whom admired his position; simultaneously, however, Peter gathered like-minded brothers and sisters into a morally rigorous community dedicated to making scripture accessible to the illiterate. Other such groups emerged elsewhere to become the basis of the later pacifist Unity of Brethren, or *Unitas Fratrum*.

THE HUSSITE WARS (1419–1434)

During the first decades of the fifteenth century, antagonism was the dominant theme of Bohemian history. The fifteen years of warfare between is best understood not as sustained combat but rather a slow (yet violent) series of crusading waves met, sometimes defensively and sometimes offensively, by Hussite armies. Already in midsummer of 1421, Sigismund was coordinating an assault on Bohemia with German support, hoping to cut the Hussites' ground out from beneath them. Crusaders' early success in sieging the town of Zatec northwest of Prague soon failed, however, when news of the rehabilitated Žižka's imminent arrival prompted many of their number to flee. Undaunted, Sigismund augmented his army with expensive mercenaries (many experienced from fighting Turks) and turned his attention east. Pointing the army (now conceived as crusaders) toward his old base of Kutná Hora, Sigismund hoped to seize the largely German Catholic town whose minority Czech population had recently joined the Hussites. The armies met in late December 1421, clashing at strategic external positions, while royal supporters within Kutná Hora secretly opened a gate to the crusaders. Soldiers massacred the Hussites within the city.

After desperately fighting their way through the opponents' ranks, Žižka and his forces made their way to safety north of the city. Regrouping within only a matter of weeks, they charged back south in early January of 1422 with renewed force that so overwhelmed a crusading army that Sigismund decided to evacuate Kutná Hora. Royalist attempts to face off against the Hussites were repulsed along the way, and morale was finally shattered when fleeing troops jammed a bridge at the town of Nemecky Brod. Žižka's army devastated both town and army, forcing the defeated Sigismund to flee east to Moravia for safety.

To rub salt in the wound, the grand duke of Lithuania (whom the Hussites had "elected" king in Sigismund's place) chose this moment to make his move. Writing to the pope in early March, the duke offered to protect the Czechs and heal the religiopolitical rift, bringing them back safely to Roman Catholicism. And to make his presence directly felt in Bohemia, he sent his own nephew, Prince Charles Korybut of Lithuania, to act on his behalf.

Sigismund, safe but isolated in Moravia, doubtless felt the ground shifting uncomfortably beneath him. In the autumn, a new wave of crusaders (this time invading Bohemia from the north and west) encountered Prince Korybut at the castle of Karlstein, where the outcome was an armistice signed on November 8, 1422.

Interestingly, the settlement and ensuing lull turned out to be more damaging to the Hussite cause than the furious warfare had been. External foes had always served to temporarily unite the riven Hussite ranks—in the absence of such pressure, however, religious disputes once again splintered the Czech cause, as did the social and economic divisions of urban and rural culture. By the summer of 1423, rival groups of Hussites were fighting one another, a breach in which Žižka himself played a role. Abandoning the extreme radical community at Tabor in August 1423, the commander relocated to eastern Bohemia as leader of a more moderate group known as the Orebites. In June 1424, Žižka's army defeated Hussite rivals from Prague, and the rural Orebites and Taborites reconciled. On October 11, the old soldier died of disease while besieging an enemy position; distraught at his loss, his followers among the Orebites now called themselves "the Orphans."

Among the most influential leaders after Žižka's death was the surprising figure of Prokop Velicky, a married priest and Utraquist from Prague who headed up Taborite armies in their many battles against royalist crusaders in the following years. Prokop the Great, as he became known, shifted Hussite warfare to a more deliberately offensive strategy of raiding into territories that had previously yielded crusading forces. After another failed crusader attack in 1427, no further Catholic armies tried to invade Bohemia for four years. Far from dampening the Czech martial spirit, however, the crusading lull merely provided the Hussites an opportunity to raid expansively and destructively on what they called "beautiful rides" through Germany, Austria, Hungary, and even Poland. Sigismund's repeated efforts to intercept and rout the Hussite armies failed, despite his increasing familiarity with their methods and technologies, and a final devastating defeat of the crusaders in 1431 paved the way for a final settlement. Yet divisions among Hussites had been deepening across the years, and the process by which peace finally emerged had as much (or more) to do with internal conflicts as with pressure from royalist Catholics.

THE COMPACTS OF BASEL (1434)

In 1434, the newly formed Council of Basel approached the radical Hussites with a settlement offer based on the Four Articles of Prague drafted fourteen years earlier, an agreement intended to ensure their return to the Roman

Church. When negotiations failed due to schisms among the Hussites (discussions in which the Englishman Peter Payne took part), key figures among their conservative members decided that a final burst of force was required: joining with Catholic forces after taking Prague, their gathered army confronted the combined Taborites and Orebites at the town of Lipany on May 30, 1434. It was a rout. Thousands of radicals, including Prokop, were slaughtered in this decisive demonstration of baronial Hussite power, a force that would thereafter continue to define Bohemian politics for centuries to come.

After crushing the radical movement, the barons resumed negotiations with the Council of Basel and imperial authorities. In 1436, Emperor Sigismund was finally accepted as king of Bohemia: on August 16, he proclaimed peace between the Bohemian "heretics" and his Christian kingdom, sagely tabling plans to eliminate Utraquism until his position was secure. In 1437, a final settlement was reached on the Compacts of Basel, which set forth a significantly weaker version of the Four Articles of Prague from 1420: Bohemian and Moravian Christians were to be offered the wine as well as the host at Communion; sins were to be punished by those officially authorized to do so; the preaching of God's word fell to priests and worthy deacons; and priests should claim no ownership of worldly possessions. The compacts thus confirmed the legitimacy of core moderate Hussite tenets, verifying that although Bohemia was full of Hussites, there was no heresy in Bohemia. Hus's followers had succeeded not only in resisting a papal crusade but in institutionalizing key elements of a locally grown reformist movement into the Reformed Church of Bohemia. Perhaps its most visible success was in the elevation to the throne of Bohemia's first and only Hussite king, George of Poděbrady (r. 1458–1471), who had himself fought at the Battle of Lipany.

Formal religiopolitical agreements did not satisfy everyone who had been a part of the Hussite movement, however, and some among the surviving Taborites and moderates still yearned for a community based upon religious principles. Emphasizing brotherly love, devotion to Jesus, and disengagement from the mundane world of politics and power, the Unity of the Brethren (rooted in Peter of Chelćický's pacifist stance, as mentioned above) emerged in the 1450s. Later known as the Moravian Brethren, the pietistic movement became an influential spiritual model in northern Europe; stripped of Taborite apocalypticism and Hussite political quarrels, it survives today in what might well be described as a direct legacy of Hus and the original Bohemian reform.

CONCLUSION

In 1512, the Roman Church confirmed the equal rights of Catholics and Utraquists, effectively sanctioning a new and independent Bohemian Church.

Thus the forces of pluralism were well under way within official European Christianity years before a German monk posted his theses on the door of Wittenberg Cathedral criticizing papal indulgences. Martin Luther's criticism of the institutional Church and the attendant movements he sparked in the sixteenth century were shaped by the momentum of medieval reform and debates over the meaning of orthodoxy. Although the historical landscape had shifted in the century after Hus's burning, Luther would also be smeared by opponents with the label of "heretic"; in a neat about-face, however, he embraced the mocking title given him by his enemies of "the Saxon Hus." (What Hus himself would have thought of such links to later German reform is another matter entirely.)

The Bohemian reform had, through its long journey through revolution, succeeded in establishing the first formally distinct regional church within the Roman structure. On the one hand, it was a unique circumstance shaped by the singular Bohemian context. On the other hand, the moderate and radical wings of the Hussite movement drew initially from concern about Christian scripture and the meaning of bread and wine, which fed reform, criticism, and thus "heresy" across medieval Europe. Utraquism continued to be the definitive Bohemian creed until Catholic forces of reaction set in during the Thirty Years' War of the seventeenth century. And although the revolution was over by 1436, its effects have lasted into the twenty-first century and are likely to continue into the future. The Hussite motto "Truth Prevails" was publicly invoked by Czechoslovakia's first president, Thomas Masaryk, in 1918 and by its last president, Vaclav Havel, in 1992. It remains the motto of the Czech Republic today.

SUGGESTIONS FOR FURTHER READING

Bartos, F. M. *The Hussite Revolution 1424–1437*. New York: Columbia University Press, 1986.

Berend, Nora, Przemyslaw Wiszewski, and Przemysław Urbańczyk. *Central Europe in the High Middle Ages: Bohemia, Hungary and Poland, c.900–c.1300*. Cambridge: Cambridge University Press, 2014.

Fudge, Thomas A. *Origins of the Hussite Uprising: The Chronicle of Laurence of Březová, 1414–1421*. New York: Routledge Press, 2020.

———. *The Crusade against Heretics in Bohemia, 1418–1437: Sources and Documents for the Hussite Crusades*. Burlington, VT: Ashgate, 2002.

———. *The Magnificent Ride: The First Reformation in Hussite Bohemia*. Aldershot, UK: Ashgate, 1998.

Grollová, Jana. "The 'Clever Girls' of Prague: Beguines, Preachers, and Late Medieval Bohemian Religion." In *Between Orders and Heresy: Rethinking*

Medieval Religious Movements, edited by Jennifer Kolpacoff Deane and Anne E. Lester (Toronto: University of Toronto Press, 2022).

Heymann, Frederick G. *John Zizka and the Hussite Revolution*. Princeton, NJ: Princeton University Press, 1955.

Housely, Norman. *Religious Warfare in Europe, 1400–1536*. Oxford: Oxford University Press, 2002.

Kaminsky, Howard. *A History of the Hussite Revolution*. Berkeley: University of California Press, 1967.

Klassen, John M. *The Nobility and the Making of the Hussite Revolution*. Boulder, CO: East European Monographs 47, 1978.

———. *Warring Maidens, Captive Wives, and Hussite Queens: Women and Men at War and at Peace in Fifteenth Century Bohemia*. Boulder, CO: East European Monographs 527, 1999.

Lambert, Malcolm. *Medieval Heresy: Popular Movements from the Gregorian Reform to the Reformation*. Third edition. Oxford: Blackwell, 2002.

McGinn, Bernard. *Visions of the End: Apocalyptic Traditions in the Middle Ages*. New York: Columbia University Press, 1979.

Soukup, Pavel. *Jan Hus: The Life and Death of a Preacher.* West Lafayette, IN: Purdue University Press, 2019.

Spinka, Matthew. *The Letters of John Hus*. Manchester, UK: Rowman & Littlefield, 1972.

Turnbull, Stephen R., and Angus McBride. *The Hussite Wars, 1419–1436*. Oxford: Osprey, 2004.

Wolverton, Lisa. *Hastening toward Prague: Power and Society in the Medieval Czech Lands*. Philadelphia: University of Pennsylvania Press, 2001.

NOTES

1. Howard Kaminsky, *A History of the Hussite Revolution* (Berkeley: University of California Press, 1967), 1.

2. Malcolm Lambert, *Medieval Heresy: Popular Movements from the Gregorian Reform to the Reformation*, 3rd ed. (Oxford: Blackwell, 2001), 285.

3. Jana Grollová, "The 'Clever Girls' of Prague: Beguines, Preachers, and Late Medieval Bohemian Religion," in *Between Orders and Heresy: Rethinking Medieval Religious Movements*, ed. Jennifer Kolpacoff Deane and Anne E. Lester (Toronto: University of Toronto Press, 2022).

4. Lambert, *Medieval Heresy*, 290.

5. Klassen, "Women and Religious Reform," 6.

6. Kaminsky, *Hussite Revolution*, 19.

7. Theodore K. Rabb, "Jan Hus," in *Renaissance Lives: Portrait of an Age* (New York: Pantheon Books, 1993), 28.

8. On Sophie, see John M. Klassen, *Warring Maidens, Captive Wives, and Hussite Queens: Women and Men at War and at Peace in Fifteenth Century Bohemia* (Boulder, CO: East European Monographs 527, 1999).

9. Matthew Spinka, *John Hus: A Biography* (New York: Columbia University Press, 1968), 76.

10. Cited in Rabb, *Renaissance Lives*, 25.

11. Matthew Spinka, ed. and trans., *John Hus at the Council of Constance* (New York: Columbia University Press, 1965), 177.

12. Rabb, *Renaissance Lives*, 28.

13. On the Council of Constance and the issue of conciliar and papalist approaches to authority, see Francis Oakley, *The Conciliarist Tradition* (Oxford: Oxford University Press, 2003) and Brian Tierney, *Foundations of the Conciliar Theory* (Cambridge: Cambridge University Press, 1955).

14. Klassen, "Women and Religious Reform," 205.

15. H. B. Workman, "The Last Letters of John Hus," *London Quarterly Review* (1902): 25–43, at 36.

16. Thomas Fudge, *The Magnificent Ride: The First Reformation in Hussite Bohemia* (Abingdon, UK: Routledge, 1998), 86.

17. Lambert, *Medieval Heresy*, 319.

18. Kaminsky, *Hussite Revolution*, 279.

19. Klassen, "Women and Religious Reform," 207.

20. Frederick G. Heymann, *John Zizka and the Hussite Revolution* (Princeton, NJ: Princeton University Press, 1955).

21. On his military strategy, see Heymann, *John Zizka*; see also Stephen R. Turnbull and Angus McBride, *The Hussite Wars, 1419–1436* (Oxford: Osprey, 2004), especially 8–41.

22. Kaminsky, *Hussite Revolution*, 369.

23. Lambert, *Medieval Heresy*, 359.

Epilogue

By the time young Hans of Niklashausen was piping followers to the tune of his lay visionary authority, the contours of Christendom were much changed from the era of Adémar of Chabannes, Hildegard of Bingen, and James Capelli. In contrast to the vital ecclesiastical authority of the twelfth and thirteenth centuries, critics of the fourteenth and fifteenth had fiercely challenged the papal role, kings and councils alike asserted themselves against the power of St. Peter's see, and the bold new challenges of movements inspired by localized and vernacular renderings of gospel messages would bear lingering consequences for the traditional hierarchies of the Roman Church. So too would that medieval emergence of an educated, administratively talented, and specifically masculine workforce (including mendicants, university masters, and bureaucratic clerics) continue to play a central role in early modern conceptions of power, authority, and orthodoxy.

Two key developments of the sixteenth century bring our survey of medieval heresy and inquisition to a close. First is the shattering of formal confessional and institutional unity of the Protestant Reformation and the consequent explosion of meanings and uses for the construct of "heresy." The Church's flip sides of orthodoxy and heresy had always been illusory, a necessary fiction for its defense of traditional doctrine and hierarchies, but the sudden explosion of new Christian positions in the sixteenth century exposed the label's inherent fluidity: "Heresy increasingly acquired an unfocused quality as an all-purpose term of religious derision. Christians of differing affiliations employed the language of heresy to fling accusations at each other—Catholics against Protestants as well as Protestants against one another and against Catholics—so that eventually the epithet 'heretical' came to denote nearly any form of apostasy or infidelity."[1]

The second development is a marked transformation in the organization of formal inquisitions. In contrast to the independently operated tribunals staffed by mendicant friars, itinerant inquisitors, or episcopal authorities tasked with uprooting local heresy, the late fifteenth and sixteenth centuries witnessed the establishment of new, organized, and highly centralized institutions for persecuting dissent. In the final quarter of the fifteenth century, for example, the increasingly powerful monarchs of the Iberian Peninsula built upon medieval inquisitorial experience to launch, with papal blessing, the highly organized Spanish Inquisition. Spanish clergy particularly targeted *conversos*, or Jews suspected of false conversion to Christianity, as well as the few Protestants who made their way to southwestern lands; in 1492, shortly after conquering Muslim Granada in the south, Ferdinand and Isabella expelled all Jews from their lands. A decade later, the monarchs insisted that any Muslim who wished to remain in Spain must convert to Christianity; however, those converted Muslims, or *moriscos*, fared little better than the *conversos*, as they were themselves expelled in 1609. Spain's rapid ascent to political dominance in the sixteenth century cannot be understood without recognizing the fusion of powers both secular and ecclesiastical and the influence of inquisitorial techniques of classification, record keeping, and persecution on the shaping of a national state.

Rome also continued to fight for religious dominance, not against "false" converts but against the Protestant threat. In 1542, Pope Paul III revived papal campaigns against heresy via the new and highly organized Roman Inquisition staffed largely by Jesuits answerable directly to him. Smaller and local inquiries continued to take place, of course, but the legal authority for the persecution of heresy came to be increasingly associated with centralized bureaucracies. The powerful administrations of the Spanish and Roman (or papal) inquisitions are structurally distinct from their medieval predecessors, although the former certainly laid the theoretical and procedural groundwork.

Yet the world did not suddenly and entirely change in 1500, and many powerful continuities shaped European history across the subsequent centuries. Martin Luther and his contemporaries, for example, were indebted to the medieval religious critiques and conversations inherited by their age. Concerns about the individual's relationship to scripture, sacraments, and the other joinings of heaven and earth also continued to be a vital thread of European thought, as did interest in the authoritative role of texts and teachers in shaping Christian life. Traditional gender models and limitations on women held sway unabated through the early modern centuries, even as female religious expression thrived in both convent and lay communities. Belief in the threat of dissent survived, as did the conviction that institutionalized mechanisms of power could annihilate the "other"—demonized humans refused their place within the social body of Christendom. Finally, family networks (those bonds of blood and belovedness) would continue to shape faith profoundly across subsequent centuries; that inquisitors' techniques and technologies were primarily aimed at uprooting and destroying those relationships points to the inherently social aspect of what the Church identified as "heresy." One could continue in this vein *ad infinitum*, marshaling evidence of either disjuncture or continuity between the medieval and early modern: the point is that neither the judicial categories of heresy and inquisition nor the individual, local, and regional beliefs across which they painfully intersected so much end as they do transform, much as they had across time and space for the preceding centuries.

Interpretations of heresy, whether by medieval contemporaries or modern historians, also change over time. As much as one may strive for objectivity, struggling to avoid imposing ourselves upon the past, it is impossible to escape entirely the burden of the present; such histories are perhaps among the most difficult to approach because ideals of justice, tolerance, and religious identity resonate so powerfully and controversially in today's world. One way in which this volume represents current strands of thought, for example, is in its emphasis on the multiplicity of past perspectives and the constructedness of heretical categories. Scholars of the late twentieth and early twenty-first centuries have been particularly interested in the agency of individuals in history and have drawn on diverse methodologies and interdisciplinary influences (anthropology, gender studies, literary theory, sociology, etc.) to develop more fully dimensional understandings of past worldviews.

As a consequence, this volume has tried to balance the history of ecclesiastical institutions with attention to the various ways in which individuals experienced and engaged with the world about them—and although some distillation of belief was necessary for a short survey, the greater goal was to sketch the many patterns of life with which those beliefs were variously shaped. Emphasis on the mounting conviction with which people on all points of the institutional and theological spectrum struggled to define righteousness reveals a rich cross-section of medieval culture, only one of the infinite ways in which the past may be explored. Perhaps as important, however, is that today's interpretations will also communicate to the future, presenting an image of our own concerns about authority, belief, institutions, and power, as well as our own ideas about what it means to live well in the world.

NOTE

1. John Christian Laursen, Cary J. Nederman, and Ian Hunter, *Heresy in Transition: Transforming Ideas of Heresy in Medieval and Early Modern Europe* (Aldershot, UK: Ashgate, 2005), 4.

Index

Ad Abolendam (Lucius III), 45
absolution, 56
accusatorial procedure, 77–78
Acre, 97
Adamites, 269
Ad audientam nostrum (Gregory IX), 161
Adémar of Chabannes, ix
Ad nostrum, 152–53
agriculture, xx–xxi, xxi*f,* 172
Aimersent, 16–17
Albertus Magnus, 155
Albi, 24
Albigensian crusade, 29–31, 57, 73–74
Albigensians:
term, 30.
See also Good Christians
alchemy, 176
Alexander III, pope, 19, 21, 42–43, 45
Alexander IV, pope, 186
Alexander V, pope, 192, 250–51
Alexius, saint, 36
Alnwick, William, 222
Amegiardis, 129
Angermeier, Henry, 96
Anne of Bohemia, 218, 244
Anselm, saint, 207
Anselm of Alessandria, 20
Antichrist:
beguins and, 126;
Joachim of Fiore on, 116, 118;
Wyclif on, 210
antinomianism, 138, 150–51
antisacerdotalism, 138
anti-Semitism, xxvii, xxviii, 182, 195
apocalypticism, xxvii;
Hussites and, 239, 251, 263, 268–69;
Joachim of Fiore on, 115–19, 118*f*;
Olivi on, 119–20;
Spiritual Franciscans and, 115–21;
True Men and, 224
Apostolic Brethren, 121
apostolic model, xxvi;
beguines and, 141–42;
Good Christians and, 1;
Innocent III and, 28;
mendicant orders and, 70–71;
Poor Men and, 35–63;
versus social order, 36–37;
Spiritual Franciscans and, 103–4
apparallamentum, 11
Ariald (deacon), 20
Aristotle, 112
Armanno Punzilupo, 23–24
Arnaude de Lamothe, 16
Arnaud Picoc, 88

Arnold, John, x
Arnold of Brescia, 20
Arnold of Villanova, 120
Arundel, Thomas, 214, 216–17
Aston, John, 213
Astorgue, 16
astrology, 176
Audisio, Gabriel, 52–54
Audley, Edmund, 223
Augustine, saint, 4, 29, 117, 136–37, 159, 207
authority, ix–xxxii;
 beguines and, 145;
 Council of Constance on, 255;
 Franciscans and, 106, 111;
 and heresy, x;
 Hussites and, 249;
 Joan of Arc and, 162;
 in Languedoc, 13–15;
 Poor Men and, 36, 45, 47, 51, 58–59;
 True Men and, 217;
 women and, xxvii, 145–48;
 Wyclif on, 208
Avignon, 121, 122*f*, 186, 241

baptism:
 Good Christians and, 1, 10–11;
 Poor Men and, 51
Barcelona, 14, 129
Basel: Compacts of, 271–72; Council of, 190
Baxter, Margery, 227
beghards, 141, 153, 160, 269
beguines, 140–45, 143*f*;
 Church response to, 152–54, 159–62;
 persecution of, 159–62;
 resources on, 166–67;
 term, 126, 140–42, 161
beguins, 132n11;
 inquisitors and, 126–30;
 Olivi and, 120;
 Spirituals and, 126;
 term, 126
Benedictines, xviii
Benedict XI, pope, 96–97
Benedict XII, pope, 82–83, 94
Benedict XVI, pope, 119
Bergamo, Council of, 50–52
Bernarda of Pomas, 62
Bernard dels Plas, 89
Bernard of Clairvaux, xxvi, 1, 3–4, 24–26, 65, 138
Bernard of Fontcaude, 46
Bernarta Verziana, 88
Bernart Bofilh, 17
Bernart de Caux, 87, 93
Bernart Mir Arezat, 16
Bethlehem Chapel, 240–41, 247
Béziers, 103, 112, 123–24, 126;
 Council of, 120
Bible. *See* Scripture
Blanche of Laurac, 17
Blyth, Geoffrey, 223
Blyth, John, 223
Bogomils, 9
Bohemia:
 context in, 236–37;
 England and, 204;
 Hussites in, 235–74;
 Poor Men in, 53, 56;
 resources on, 273–74;
 True Men and, 218, 244–46;
 war in, 264–71
Böhm, Hans, 165
Bologna, xxi, 94, 106;
 university of, xxii, xxiv*f*
Bonaventure, saint, 112–13, 118–19, 126
Boniface, saint, xviii
Boniface VIII, pope, 96, 152, 155, 181, 184, 207–8
boundaries of beliefs, as unfixed, 2;
 Good Christians and, 23–24;
 Poor Men and, 56–57
Bridgette of Sweden, 162
Brown, Peter, xx
Browne, John, 228
Bulgaria, 9

Burgundy, 24, 52, 162–63
Burnham, Louisa, 129
burnings, xxvi, 76, 92–94, 103;
of Apostolic Brethren, 121;
of beguines, 160;
of beguins, 120, 129;
of books, 151, 218, 235, 251;
emperor on, 71;
Étienne de Bourbon and, 80;
forced witnessing of, 229;
of Good Christians and, 2;
of Hans Böhm, 165;
Henry IV on, 216;
of Jan Hus, 235, 256, 257*f*;
of Joan of Arc, 163;
of Marguerite Porete, 135;
of Martin Húska, 269;
of Sir John Oldcastle, 218, 219*f*;
of Spiritual Franciscans, 125;
of witches, 195
Burr, David, 103

Caldwell Ames, Christine, 66
Cambrai, 76
Canterbury College, Oxford, 205–6
Capelli, James, ix
Carcassonne, 9, 28, 31*f*, 78, 112, 123
Carder, William, 228–29
categories, contested, x, xiii, 2, 65;
and beguines, 147;
and Cathars, 6;
Gui and, 82;
Lateran IV and, 69;
and magic, 171–72, 178
Cathars:
term, xiv, 5–6.
See also Albigensians; Good Christians
cathedrals, xxi–xxii
Catherine of Siena, 162
Catholic Church:
administrative developments in, 190;
and beguines, 152–54, 159–62;
development of responses to heresy, 65–102;
and Good Christians, 24–29;
Hussites and, 235, 252–54, 259, 261, 266–69;
Jakoubek on, 258;
and magic, 186–87;
and Poor Men, 41–50;
Wyclif and, 207–8, 210–11, 245.
See also papacy
Celestine III, pope, 26
Celestine IV, pope, 161
Le champion des dames (Le Franc), 191–92
Charlemagne, xvii
Charles IV, king of Bohemia, 236, 238–39, 242
Charles University, 237, 242, 245–46, 250, 256–57
Charles VII, king of France, 163
Chedworth, John, 223
Chelčický, Peter, 269–70
Chiara Offreduccio, saint, 107–8
chiliastic:
term, 268.
See also apocalypticism
choice, and heresy, xii, 71–73
Christian life, xxv–xxviii;
Good Christians and, 12, 18;
Valdès and, 36;
women and, 161
Christian of Prachatice, 260
Cistercians, 28, 37, 82–83, 181
Clare of Assisi, saint, 107–8
class. *See* social status
Clavis Salomonis, 178
Clement V, pope, 97, 120–24
Clement VII, pope, 241
clergy:
Audisio on, 52;
behavior of, xxiv–xxv, 14, 243;
and Franciscans, 109–10;
Hildegard of Bingen on, 4–5;
Hus on, 247;
manuals for, xix–xx;

as new class, xxix;
and Poor Men, 41;
taxation of, 207–8
Clifford, Lewis, 214
clothing:
beguins and, 126;
Franciscans and, 122–25;
Hus and, 247;
Jews and, 182;
Joan of Arc and, 163
Clovis, xvii
Cologne, 155, 157;
Jews in, xxviii*f*;
university of, xxii, 189, 250
Commentary on the Apocalypse (Olivi), 119
Common Life, communities of, 161
Communion. *See* Eucharist
communities:
of beguines, 140, 142, 161;
of beguins, 127, 129;
of Good Christians, 14, 17–18;
of Hussites, 259, 262–66;
magic and, 174;
in medieval Europe, xix–xx;
of Poor Catholics, 48;
of Poor Men, 54, 56, 61;
in Prague, 238–39;
of Reconciled Poor, 49–50;
and resistance, 91;
of True Men, 219–22, 221*f*, 225–26
Concordia discordantium canonum, 180
Confession (sacrament), 56, 69
confinement, as penance, 92
Conrad of Marburg, 75–76, 181–82
consolamentum, 10–11
conspiracy theories:
on Jews, xxvii–xxviii, 182–83;
on magic, 192–93
Constance, Council of, 131, 162, 190, 211, 218, 241, 254–58
Constantine, emperor, 58
Constantinople, xviii
Constitutions (Arundel), 216–17
Conventual Franciscans, 119, 123, 126
converts, and inquisitorial procedures, 89
court books, 223–24
Courtenay, William, 210, 213
courtship metaphor, 138, 139*f*, 149
Coventry, 226
Crescentius of Iesi, 112
Crestina, 62
crusades:
Albigensian, 6, 29–31, 57, 73–74;
Fourth, 68;
against Hussites, 265–69;
Innocent III and, 26;
term, xxv
Cum de quibusdam mulieribus, 152, 154
Cum dormirent homines (Zwicker), 84
Cum ex officii nostri (Innocent III), 67–68
Czech Republic, 273.
See also Bohemia

d'Ailly, Pierre, 162, 255
Dante Alighieri, xxiii
d'Antuson, Raimon and Bernarda, 129
debates:
with Good Christians, 25, 28;
with Poor Men, 46–47
De civili dominio (Wyclif), 208
Decree of Kutná Hora, 250
De ecclesia (Hus), 253
De ecclesia (Wyclif), 208
Defenestration of Prague, 263
De heretico comburendo (Henry IV), 216–17
Délicieux, Bernard, 186
De mandatis divinis (Wyclif), 208
demonic concerns, xxvii, 169–202;
Gregory IX on, 75–76;
Gui on, 82;
and magic, 183–84;
resources on, 200–201;
and Templars, 97;
women and, 191–92
detachment, Eckhart on, 156

De veritate sacrae Scriptura (Wyclif), 209
Diego of Osma, 28, 47
Directorium inquisitorum (Eymeric), 178, 188
divining, 176–78; term, 174–75
Dominicans, 12, 73*f*;
and beguines, 143;
Eckhart, 135–36, 144, 154–59;
and inquisition, 78–82
Dominic de Guzmán, saint, 28, 67, 70–71
Donation of Constantine, 58
Donatism, 21, 47–49, 51–52, 58
Douai, 76
Douceline de Digne, 144
Dresden, 252
Drugunthia, 9
Drummer of Niklashausen, 165
dualism, 7–9, 23;
Good Christians and, 9–12;
and women, 60
Dulcie Faure, 17
dunkings, 77
Durand of Huesca, 40–41, 47–48

Earthquake Council, 210
Eberwin, prior, 1–3
Eckbert, abbot, 4, 6
Eckhart, Meister, 135–36, 144, 154–59
education:
women and, 62, 149.
See also universities
Elect, 11, 17
England, xviii;
and Bohemia, 204, 244–46;
Good Christians and, 24;
and Joan of Arc, 163;
legislation in, 216–19;
persecution in, 228–30;
True Men and Women in, 203–32
Erfurt, university of, 189, 250
Ermengaud of Beziers, 47
The Errors of the Gazarii, 195
Esclarmonda Durban, 129
Esquiva, 16
Étienne de Bourbon, 80–81
Eucharist, xxvi, xxix;
Good Christians on, 10;
Hussites on, 264, 269;
Jakoubek on, 258;
and Jews, 183;
Lateran IV on, 69;
Matthew of Janov on, 240;
and mysticism, 137;
Poor Men and, 51–52;
True Men and, 213, 217, 227;
Wyclif on, 210.
See also lay chalice
Eugenius III, pope, 25
Eugenius IV, pope, 192
Europe, medieval:
cultural flowering in, xvi, xxi–xxv;
culture of, and magic, 169, 171–75;
intensifications in, xx–xxv;
landscape of, xvii–xix, xvii*f*
excommunication:
of beguines, 153;
of Hus, 251, 253;
magic and, 186–87;
papal schism and, 241;
of Poor Men, 45;
of Spirituals, 123
execution. *See* burnings
Exiit qui seminat (Nicholas IV), 119
Exivi de paradisi (Clement V), 123
Eymeric, Nicholas, 90, 178, 188

family networks:
and Good Christians, 16–17, 23;
inquisitors and, 87–88;
magic and, 174;
and Poor Men, 54, 61;
and True Men, 226
fear:
Étienne de Bourbon on, 80–81;
and record keeping, 86
Ferdinand II, king of Aragon, 278

fifteenth century, personalities in, 189–92
flight, as resistance, 90, 129
Florence, 22
Floretum, 215
Formicarius (Nider), 190
Fournier, Jacques, 82–83, 94
fourteenth century, disasters in, 136, 184
Fox, Richard, 223
France:
 Albigensian crusade and, 30;
 Franciscans in, 103, 114;
 magic in, 188–89;
 Poor Men in, 35–63.
 See also Languedoc
Franciscans, 12;
 and beguines, 143, 147;
 challenges for, 106–9;
 and Clementine settlement, 121–24;
 and inquisition, 78–79;
 institutional stage of, 104–6;
 leadership of, 104–6, 112–13;
 and papacy, 109, 112;
 Rule of, 104, 105*f,* 107, 109, 119, 131–32;
 Spiritual, 103–33;
 Third Order, 108–9, 154
Francisci, Matteuccia, 193–95
Francis of Assisi, saint, 67, 70, 72*f,* 104–6, 105*f*;
 Testament of, 109–12
Frederick Barbarossa, emperor, 19, 21
Frederick II, emperor, 28, 71
Free Spirits, 138–39, 153, 157;
 persecution of, 159–62;
 term, xiv
Friars Minor. *See* Franciscans
Friends of God. *See* Poor Men

Galdinus, archbishop, 21
Gallus of Neuhaus, 95, 160
gender, xxvi–xxvii;
 Joan of Arc and, 162–64;
 Poor and, 60–62;
 roles, narrowing of, 22, 39;
 True Men and, 211, 225–26.
 See also women
George of Poděbrady, king of Bohemia, 272
Géraud, Hugues, 186
Gérauda of Cabuet, 16
Gerbert of Aurillac, 176
Germany, Germans:
 beguines and, 142, 153–54;
 in Bohemia, 241–42, 248–50, 252;
 Hussites and, 259, 266;
 images of heresy in, 75–76;
 and inquistion, 83, 89;
 missionaries to, xviii;
 Poor Men and, 53, 57.
 See also Rhineland
Gerson, Jean, 162, 189, 255
gnosis, xxv, 7
Gnostics, 137
Good Christians (Men, Women), 1–34, 31*f*;
 beliefs of, 9–12;
 Church response to, 24–26, 94;
 and dualism, 9–12;
 in Languedoc, 15–18;
 in northern Italy, 18–24, 19*f*;
 origins of, 8;
 Poor Men and, 40, 44;
 resources on, 32, 33n8;
 term, xv
Gotzlin of Jareschau, 95
Gratian, 180
Grebill, Agnes, 228
Gregory VII, pope, xxiv–xxv, 20
Gregory IX, pope, 52, 71, 73, 75–78;
 and beguines, 161;
 and demons, 181;
 and Franciscans, 106, 110–12
Gregory of Nyssa, 137
Gregory XI, pope, 57, 209
Grosseteste, Robert, xii, 71, 101n8
Grundmann, Herbert, 140
Guglielma of Milan, 121, 145

Gui, Bernard, 57, 81–82, 98, 121;
on beguins, 127–29;
on evasion, 90;
and magic, 187–88;
and Poor Men, 61;
and punishments, 93–94;
on questions, 88
Guichard de Pontigny, archbishop, 37–38, 42, 44
Guilhabert de Castres, 17
Guilhelma Michela, 62
Guy II of Colmieu, 149

Hadewijch of Brabant, xxiii, 144
Hales, John, 223
The Hammer of Witches (Krämer), 196–200
harm, magic and, 172–74, 190–91
Harryson, Robert, 228
Havel, Vaclav, 273
healing, magic and, 172, 193
health metaphor, 69–70
Heidelberg, university of, 189, 242, 250
Heinrich of Jareschau, 95
Henricus de Allemania, xxiv*f*
Henry II, archbishop, 157
Henry II, king of England, 24
Henry IV, king of England, 216–17
Henry of Le Mans, 36
Henry of Marcy, abbot, 26
Henry the Monk, xxvi
Henry V, king of England, 218
Henry VIII, king of Endland, 228, 230
Hereford, Nicholas, 213
heresiarch, term, 235
heresy, ix–xxxii, 277–79;
as category, x, 6–7, 45;
Church responses to, 26–29;
definitional issues with, x–xiii, xiv–xv, 71–73;
development of responses to, 65–102;
Eckhart and, 157–58;
Franciscan Rule on, 109;
Good Christians and, 1–34;
Hussites and, 235–74;
Lateran IV on, 68–69;
locales prone to, characteristics of, 9, 53, 142;
magic and, 179–84;
nature of, 31;
Poor Men and, 35–63;
scholarship on, xv–xvi;
True Men and, 203–32
Hildegard of Bingen, ix, 4–5, 138
Hilton, Reginald, 214
history, Joachim of Fiore on, 115–19, 118*f*
Holy Roman Empire, 18–21, 97, 155
Honorius III, pope, 71, 107
Hornbeck, J. Patrick, 212
Hugolino, 106. *See also* Gregory IX
humanism, 230
Humbert of Romans, 81
Humiliati, 27, 43–44
Hundred Years War, 162
Hus, Jan, 218, 238, 246–50, 253;
execution of, 235, 254–58, 257*f*;
True Men and, 248–49
Húska, Martin, 268–69
Hussite League, 256–57, 259
Hussites, 235–74, 260*f*;
Joan of Arc and, 163;
resources on, 273–74;
wars of, 270–71
Hussite Union, 267
hypocrisy:
and beguines, 147, 152;
Hildegard of Bingen on, 5

In agro dominico (John XXII), 158
indexes, 85
indulgences, 59–60;
in Bohemia, 244, 252;
Hus on, 253
inheritance, in Languedoc, 14
Innocent III, pope, xiv, xxv, 29–30, 56, 141;
background of, 26;

and clergy, 14;
and Fourth Lateran Council, 68–69;
and Francis, 70, 72*f*, 104, 105*f*;
and Good Christians, 26–29;
and heresy, 67–68;
and inquisition, 78;
and Jews, xxviii;
and papal authority, 70–71;
and Poor Men, 48–51
Innocent IV, pope, 89, 111
Innocent VIII, pope, 196
inquisition, ix–xxxii, 277–79;
and beguines, 159–62;
consequences of, 94–96, 98–99;
definitional issues with, xiv–xv, 66;
early tribunals of, 78–79;
in England, 203–32;
goal of, Gui on, 98;
Good Christians and, 30;
and magic, 181, 187–89;
mendicant orders and, 78–79;
personnel of, 75–76, 80–84;
and Poor Men, 57;
scholarship on, xv–xvi;
texts on magic, 187–89;
and True Men, 222–28
inquisitorial procedures, 86–90;
development of, 65–102;
problems with, 79;
resources on, 99–100;
shift to, 77–78
interrogation, 87–88
Ireland, xviii
Isabella, queen of Castile, 278
Isarn de Castres, 17
Isidore of Seville, 177
Italy, xviii;
Franciscans in, 114;
Good Christians in, 18–24, 19*f*

Jacques de Molay, 97
Jacques de Vitry, 141, 146
Jacquier, Nicolas, 191
Jakoubek of Stříbo, 251–52, 254, 258/259
James, William, 213
Jan of Jenštejn, 243–44
Jan of Jesenic, 250
Jan of Pomuk, 243
Jean de Bellesmains, archbishop, 44–45
Jean de Saint-Pierre, 87, 93
Jerome of Prague, 250–52
Jerusalem, xxv, 239
Jesuits, 278
Jews, xxvii–xxviii, xxviii*f*, 101n8;
Gui on, 82;
in Languedoc, 14;
and magic, 182–83, 195
Joachim of Fiore, 115–19
Joan, countess of Kent, 209
Joan of Arc, 162–64, 164*f*
Johannes of Frankfurt, 189
John of Gaunt, duke of Lancaster, 204, 207–8
John of Jandun, 208
John of Parma, 111–12
John Paul II, pope, 159
John XXII, pope, 82, 103;
and beguines, 152–53;
and beguins, 129;
and Eckhart, 158;
and Franciscans, 124–26;
and indulgences, 252;
and magic, 186–87
joinings, xx, xxxi;
beguins and, 130;
cathedrals as, xxi–xxii;
Jerusalem as, xxv, 239;
magic and, 170;
mysticism and, 138;
women and, xxvi
Julian of Norwich, 162
just war theory, 29–30

Kaminsky, Howard, 235
Kempe, Margery, 217–18
Kieckhefer, Richard, 171
Klassen, John, 262

Knighton, Henry, 214
Knights Templar, 97, 184
Known. *See* Poor Men
Korybut, Charles, 270–71
Krämer, Heinrich, 196–200
Kutná Hora, 250, 270

labels:
  Albigensians, 30;
  beguines, 126, 140–42, 161;
  beguins, 126, 132n11;
  Cathars, xiv, 5–6;
  heresy, x–xiii, xiv–xv, 71–73;
  inquisition, xiv–xv, 66;
  issues with, x–xiii, xiv–xv, 5–7, 46, 211–12;
  Lollards, 140, 211–12;
  magic, 169–70;
  Waldensians, xiv, 39, 46;
  Wycliffites, 211–12
labor:
  beguines and, 143;
  Poor Men and, 40, 51
Lambert, Malcolm, 21, 25
Langton, Thomas, 223
language. *See* labels; vernacular
Languedoc, 15*f*, 94;
  Albigensian crusade and, 29–31;
  Council of Toulouse and, 74;
  Good Christians in, 15–18;
  Innocent III and, 28;
  society and rulership in, 13–15;
  term, 12
Lateran Councils:
  Fourth, xxviii, 50, 68–70, 182;
  Third, 26, 42–44
Latimer, Thomas, 214
lay chalice, 249, 254, 258–61, 272;
  Articles of Prague on, 267;
  prohibition of, 258
lay piety:
  development of, xii, xxiii–xxvi;
  Franciscans and, 108–9;
  Good Christians and, 19–20;
  Poor Men and, 35;
  women and, 135–68
Lea, Henry Charles, 102n34
leadership:
  of Franciscans, 104–6, 112–13;
  of Poor Men, 51;
  of True Men, 226
learning, institutionalization of, xxi–xxiii, 176
Lechlade, Robert, 213
Le Franc, Martin, 191–92
legal system:
  and beguines, 147;
  development of, 65–102;
  and Franciscan poverty, 106–7;
  and Joan of Arc, 163;
  and magic, 179–80;
  Poor Men and, 59;
  shift in, 77–78
Leipzig, 250
Lerner, Robert E., xv, 116
Le Roy Ladurie, Emmanuel, 83
lex talionis, 77
Liber Antiheresis (Durand of Huesca), 40–41
Liber iuratus Honorii, 178
Lollards, term, 140, 211–12
Lombarde, 16
Lombardy, 20–21, 81, 94;
  Poor Men in, 39–40;
  Reconciled Poor in, 49–50
Lombers, 25
Louis IX, king of france, 142, 147
Louis of Bavaria, emperor, 126
Louis X, king of France, 186
love magic, 174
Lucius III, pope, 26, 45, 116
Luther, Martin, 131, 163, 215, 230, 273
Lyon, Poor of, 35–63;
  expulsion of, 44–45

magic, 169–202;
  common tradition of, 171–75;
  definitional issues with, 169–71;
  existence of, 178;
  and heresy, 179–84;

importance of, 170;
learned, 176–79;
resources on, 200–201
Magni, Nicholas, 189
Maifreda, 145
Mainz, 4, 53, 56, 84, 90, 96, 153
Maistre, Raimon, 130
maleficium, 172–74, 190–91
Malleus Maleficarum (Krämer), 196–200
mandrake, 173*f,* 199*f*
Manichaeism, ix, 7–8
manuals:
for clergy, xix–xx;
for debates, 25;
for inquisitors, 82, 85, 187–88;
on magic, 178, 196–200
Map, Walter, 43
March of Ancona, 81, 112
Marie d'Olgnies, 144
Marseilles, xxi
Marsilius of Padua, 208
Martha and Mary image, 143–44, 156–57
Martin V, pope, 261, 266
martyrs:
Hus as, 235;
victims as, 94, 129–30, 253
Masaryk, Thomas, 273
material world, Good Christians on, 9–12
Matthew, saint, xi*f*
Matthew of Janov, 239–40, 258
Maury, Bernard, 129
McGinn, Bernard, 137
Mechtild of Magdeburg, 144
medieval Europe:
cultural flowering in, xvi, xxi–xxv;
culture of, and magic, 169, 171–75;
intensifications in, xx–xxv;
landscape of, xvii–xix, xvii*f*
melioramentum, 12
mendicant orders, 12, 22, 70–71;
and beguines, 143, 161;
and inquisition, 78–79;
Wyclif and, 218
merchants, xxi, xxii*f*
Messalians, 8
methodology, ix–x, xiii–xiv;
on Good Christians, 2–5;
on inquisitorial records, 84–86;
on Poor Men, 37–38;
on True Men and Women, 212
Metz, 53, 129
Michael of Cesena, 124–26, 128
Milan, 186;
Good Christians in, 20–21;
Poor Men in, 40
Milič, Jan, 238
The Mirror of Simple Souls (Porete), 135, 149–51
misogyny. *See* women
Modern-Day Devout, 161
monastic orders, Wyclif and, 209, 218
Montaillou, 83, 94
Mont Aimé, 76
Montségur, 94
Moore, R. I., xxviii
Moravian Brethren, 272
More, Thomas, 230
Muir, Edward, xiii
Muslims, 101n8, 176
mysticism, 135–68;
beguines and, 144;
Christian traditions of, 136–40;
Joachim of Fiore and, 116;
Marguerite Porete and, 148–51;
resources on, 166–67;
term, 136–37

Narbonne, 48, 85, 103, 112–13, 120, 123–24
necromancy, 176–79;
term, 166–77
Nemecky Brod, 270
Neoplatonism, 138
Nicaea, Council of, x
Nicetas, papa, 8, 21

Nicholas IV, pope, 109, 119–20
Nicholas of Dresden, 252, 254
Nicholas of Hus, 264
Nider, Johannes, 178, 190–91
nobility:
and Good Christians, 15–16;
and Hussites, 256–57, 259;
and True Men, 214, 245–46
nominalism, 206, 245

oaths, Poor Men and, 47, 59
Observants, 131
occupations, of True Men, 225, 227
Oldcastle, John, 218–19, 219*f*
Olivi, Peter, 115, 119–21, 126–27
On Simony (Hus), 253
On the Manichaeans (Augustine), 4
ontology, 245
Opus arduum, 215, 230
ordeals, judicial, 77
Order of Friars Minor. *See* Franciscans
Order of Preachers. *See* Dominicans
Orebites, 271–72
Origen, 137
Orléans, xxv
Orvieto, 22, 23*f,* 94
Oxford, xxi, 204–6, 209, 213

papacy: 253, 254;
Charles IV and, 237;
and Franciscans, 109, 111, 124–26;
and Good Christians, 22;
and magic, 186;
schism in, 121, 136, 241, 249–50, 255, 261;
status of, xvii, xxiii, 18–21, 71, 96–97, 136, 155;
Wyclif on, 210.
See also Catholic Church; *specific pope*
papelards, term, 140
Paris:
Treaty of, 30, 74;
university of, xxii, 155, 188–89
Patarene movement, 19–20, 26
Patchovsky, Alexander, 96
Paul, saint, x
Paulicians, 7
Paul III, pope, 278
Payne, Peter, 213, 255, 272
Peachey, John, 214
Pecock, Reginald, 227–28
Peirone, 16
penance, 91–94;
True Men and, 222, 229
Penitential of Theodore, xx
Pepin, xvii
perfecti, 11
persecution:
of beguines, 159–62;
society of, formation of, xxviii–xxxi;
of True Men, 228–30, 248–49
persuasion, 25, 28, 65
Peter of Bruys, 36
Peter of John Olivi, 115, 119–21, 126–27
Peter of Verona, 81
Petra of Ricany, 255–56
Philip IV (the Fair), king of France, 96–97, 136, 151–52, 184, 186
Philip V, king of France, 186
Pierre Bofilh, 17
Pierre de Castelnau, 29
Pikartism, term, 269
Piphles, term, 6
Pisa, Council of, 250
plague, xxvii–xxviii, 136, 183
Plato, 7
Platonism, 138, 206
politics, xxiii, xxvii;
Albigensian crusade and, 30;
in Bohemia, 242, 246, 249–50, 263, 270–72;
imperial-papal struggle, 18–21, 96–97, 155;
and inquisition, 96–97;
in Languedoc, 13–15;
and magic, 184–86;

and mysticism, 162–65;
taxation issues, 207–8;
Wyclif and, 207–9
Poor Catholics, 48–49
Poor Men, 35–63;
beliefs of, 51, 57–60;
Church response to, 41–50;
dissent among, 50–52;
Étienne de Bourbon and, 80;
inquisition and, 94–95;
reconciliation with Church, 48–50;
resources on, 62–63;
social structures of, 54–57;
spread of, 52–54, 55*f*;
term, xv
Porete, Marguerite, 135, 148–51
Postilla super totam bibliam (Wyclif), 208
poverty:
beguines and, 141–42;
challenge of, 106–9;
Eckhart on, 157;
Good Christians and, 1;
Olivi on, 119;
Poor Men and, 35–63;
Spirituals and, 103–33;
Ubertino on, 122
Practica officii Inquisitionis heretice pravitatis (Bernard Gui), 82
Prague, 236–37, 237*f*;
anti-Wycliffism in, 248–49;
demonstrations in, 262–63;
Four Articles of, 267–68;
Hus in, 246–47;
True Men and, 244–45
preaching, xxiii;
beguins and, 127;
Dominicans and, 28–29, 71;
Eckhart and, 158;
Hussites and, 251;
in inquisitorial procedure, 87;
Lateran IV on, 69;
Poor Men and, 41–44;
in Prague, 238–41;
Third Lateran Council on, 45;
True Men and, 220, 226;
women and, 152
Príbram, Jan, 254
prostitutes, 146–47, 238–39
protection, magic and, 172
Protestant Reformation, 277
Prous Boneta, 120
Provence, 15*f*, 52, 78, 123
Publicans, 181
purgatory, Poor Men and, 58–59
Pythagoras, 7

Quéribus, 94
questions:
for beguins, 128;
inquisitorial, 88–90;
on magic, 187–88, 196–98;
for True Men, 224
Quo elongati (Gregory IX), 110–12
Quorundam exigit (John XXII), 125

Ralph of Coggeshall, 181
Ratio recta (John XXII), 154
Ratzinger, Joseph, 119
Raymond IV, count of Toulouse, 13–14
Raymond V, count of Toulouse, 25
Raymond VI, count of Toulouse, 28–30
realism, 206
Reconciled Poor, 49–50
record keeping:
development of, xxix, 84–86;
and True Men, 222–24
Regensburg, 78
registers, 223
relics:
Hussites and, 259;
True Men and, 217
Repingdon, Philip, 210
resistance:
beguins and, 129–30;
in Bohemia, 258–61;
forms of, 90–94;
Franciscans and, 112;
True Men and, 217

retaliation, law of, 77
Revelation, book of:
Joachim of Fiore on, 116–17;
on Satan, 183;
True Men on, 215
revolution, Hussite movement as, 235, 261–64
Rheims, 181
Rhineland, xviii, 1, 3–4;
mysticism in, 154–59;
Poor Men in, 53.
See also Germany
Richard II, king of England, 207–8, 216, 218, 244
Rixen of Limoux, 62
Robert le Bougre, 75–76
The Romance of the Rose, xxiii, 147–48
Roman Inquisition, 98, 278
Roman law, 66, 89
Rosarium, 215
Rowley, Alice, 226
Ruggiero, Guido, xiii
The Rules of the Old and New Testament (Matthew of Janov), 239–40
Rupert, count of Palatinate, 242
rural environments:
beguines in, 142;
Poor Men in, 53, 56;
True Men in, 225
Rygge, Robert, 210

Sacconi, Rainier, 8, 11, 81
saints:
Hus and, 259;
Poor Men and, 59
Sancta Romana (John XXII), 128
Satan, 184*f*;
Good Christians on, 9–10;
magic and, 183–84
Sawtrey, William, 217
Scandinavia, xviii
Scripture, 39*f,* 41;
Council of Toulouse on, 74;
Hus on, 247–48;
Joachim of Fiore on, 116;
Matthew of Janov on, 239–40;
and mysticism, 137–38;
on necromancy, 177;
Poor Men and, 45;
on Satan, 183;
True Men and, 203–32;
in vernacular, xxiii, xxv, 38, 59, 214–15, 215*f,* 217, 224
Sedis apostolice (Celestine IV), 161
Segerelli, Gerard, 121
Sermons against the Cathars (Eckbert), 4
sexuality:
beguins and, 127;
fear of, 146–48, 150;
Good Christians and, 11;
Hussites and, 269;
magic and, 182;
and mysticism, 138, 139*f*;
stereotypes of, 75–76
Sicard le Cellerier, bishop, 25
Sigismund, emperor, 242, 254, 256, 263, 265, 267–68, 270–72
Silkby, Robert, 225
social order, xxix;
versus apostolic model, 36–37;
Good Christians and, 22;
inquisition and, 94–96;
magic and, 195;
Nider on, 190;
penance and, 91
social status (class):
and beguines, 144;
and Good Christians, 15–16, 22;
and Hussites, 247, 263;
and mysticism, 164–65;
and Poor Men, 53–54;
and True Men, 214, 220, 227
Song of Songs, 3
Sophie, queen of Bohemia, 247
sorcery. *See* magic
Spanish Inquisition, 98, 278
spectacle, penance and, 91–94
Spiritual Franciscans, 103–33;
condemnation of, 124–26;

resources on, 129–32
spiritual realm, Good Christians on, 9–12
Sprenger, Jakob, 196
stake. *See* burnings
stereotypes:
of heretics, xi, 75–76;
scholarship on, xv;
of witches, 193, 194*f*, 195
Storey, Richard, 214
Stradigotto, 22–23
strix, 193
Summus desiderantes affectibus (Innocent VIII), 196
Super illius specula (John XX), 186–87
Supra montem (Nicholas IV), 109, 119
Suso, Heinrich, 159
Swinderby, William, 213
Sylvester, pope, 58
Sylvester II, pope, 176

The Tables of Old and New Colors (Nicholas of Dresden), 252
Taborites, 262–63, 265–66, 268–72
Tanchelm (preacher), 36
Tannenberg, battle of, 265
Tanner, Norman, 228
Tarragon, Council of, 87
Tauler, John, 159
taxation, of clergy, 207–8
Taylor, William, 213
terminology. *See* labels
Tertullian, 137
Testament of Francis of Assisi, 109–12
Teutonic knights, 264
Texerant, term, 6
texts:
Audisio on, 52;
Benedictines and, xviii;
burnings of, 151, 218, 235, 251;
and community, xxv;
Franciscans and, 115;
Good Christians and, 2–5, 10;
inquisition and, 84–86;
on magic, 187–89;
methodology and, xiii–xiv;
True Men and, 224–28.
See also Scripture
Theodore, archbishop, xx
Theophilus, saint, 182
thirteenth century, personalities in, 67
Thomas Aquinas, 155, 178–80
time, Joachim of Fiore on, 117–18
Tinctoris, Johannes, 192
tonsure, 217
torture, 89
Toulouse, 13–14, 87, 89, 128;
Council of, 74
Tours, Council of, 25
trade networks, xxi
translation. *See* vernacular
transubstantiation:
Hussites on, 264;
True Men on, 213, 217;
Wyclif on, 210
treason, heresy as, 27–28, 67
Trencavel, Raymond, 25
Treviso, 27
Tripoli, 13–14
True Men and Women, 203–32;
beliefs of, 219–22, 224;
and Bohemia, 218, 244–46;
communities of, 219–22, 221*f*, 225–26;
early circles of influence, 212–16;
inquisition and, 222–28;
legislation on, 216–19;
persecution of, 228–30, 248–49;
resources on, 231–32
Trussel, John, 214
Tunstall, Cuthbert, 230
Turk, Thomas, 213
Twelve Conclusions, 213–14
Tyndale, William, 230

Ubertino of Casale, 120, 122
ultramontanes, term, 51
Unam Sanctum (Boniface VIII), 207–8
uniformity of beliefs, lack of, 6;
beguines and, 160;

beguins and, 127;
Free Spirits and, 138–39, 153;
Good Christians and, 18;
inquisition and, 66;
and interrogation, 86;
magic and, 175;
Poor Men and, 57;
scholarship on, xiv;
Wycliffites and, 212
Unity of Brethren, 270, 272
universals:
Bohemians on, 245;
Wyclif on, 206
universities, xxi–xxiii, xxiv*f,* 176, 189, 237, 250
University of Bologna, xxii, xxiv*f*
University of Cologne, xxii, 189, 250
University of Erfurt, 189, 250
University of Heidelberg, 189, 242, 250
University of Leipzig, 250
University of Paris, xxii, 155, 188–89
urban centers, xxi, xxvi;
Franciscans in, 111;
Good Christians and, 22–23;
In northern italy, 18;
papacy and, 28;
True Men in, 226
Urban II, pope, xxv
Urban V, pope, 206
Urban VI, pope, 210, 242
usus pauper principle, 106–7, 110, 113–15, 119, 123, 125, 131
Utraquism. *See* lay chalice

Valdès of Lyon, 35–40, 42–45, 51, 58, 60
Valla, Lorenzo, 58
van Eyck, Jan, xxx*f*
Vaudois, term, 193
Velicky, Prokop, 271–72
Veneti, Jean, 191–92
Vergentis in senium (Innocent III), 27–28, 67
vernacular:
Eckhart and, 155;
Hus and, 249, 259;
literary forms, xxiii;
Marguerite Porete and, 135, 149;
Scripture in, xxiii, xxv, 38, 59, 214–15, 215*f,* 217, 224
Verona, Council of, 44–45, 93
Vienne, Council of, 152
vineyard motif, 3, 28, 65, 124
Visconti, Matteo, 186
vita apostolica. See apostolic model
Viterbo, 22, 27
Vitkov Hill, 267
Vivetus, 51
Vox in Rama (Gregory IX), 75–76, 181
Vytautas, Alexander, 268, 270–71

wagenburgs, 266, 266*f*
Waldensians:
term, xiv, 39, 46.
See also Poor Men
Waldhauser, Conrad, 237–38
Walker, Edward, 228
Walsingham, Thomas, 214
Warham, William, 223, 228
Wasmod, John, 211
Wenceslaus IV, king of Bohemia, 237, 242–44, 249–50, 252–54, 261, 263
wheat and tares motif, 27
White, William, 225
William of Auvergne, 178
William of Newburgh, 24
William of Ockham, 207, 245
William of Paris, 151
witchcraft, 169–202;
resources on, 200–201;
trials, 193–95
witches, appearance of, 192, 194*f,* 195, 197*f*
Witold, Alexander, 268, 270–71
women, 135–68;
and authority, xxvii, 145–48;
and Franciscans, 107–8;
and Good Christians, 16–17;
and Hussites, 238–39, 247–48, 262;

Joan of Arc, 162–64;
Krämer and, 198;
and magic, 190–91, 198;
and mobility, taboos on, 38, 90;
and Poor, 38–39, 60–62;
resources on, 166–67;
and True Men, 225–26
Wyclif, John, 203–32, 205*f*;
Church response to, 210–11;
life and writings of, 204–9, 230
Wycliffites:
term, 211–12.
See also True Men and Women
Wykeham, bishop, 213

Zbyněk, archbishop, 249–51
Želivský, Jan, 261–63
Zitkov Hill, 267
Žižka, Jan, 261–66, 264*f,* 267–69, 271
Zoroaster, 7
Zwicker, Peter, 57, 83–84, 96

About the Author

Jennifer Kolpacoff Deane is professor of history at the University of Minnesota, Morris. She earned her PhD at Northwestern University, studied at the Johann Wolfgang Goethe-Universität in Frankfurt am Main, Germany, and teaches courses on medieval, Renaissance, and Reformation history. A specialist in late medieval German religiosity, she has published on a variety of topics, including heresy, inquisition, piety, prophecy, and women's religious communities.

CRITICAL ISSUES IN WORLD AND INTERNATIONAL HISTORY

Series Editor: Morris Rossabi

The Vikings: Wolves of War
by Martin Arnold

Magic and Superstition in Europe: A Concise History from Antiquity to the Present
by Michael D. Bailey

War and Genocide: A Concise History of the Holocaust, Third Edition
by Doris L. Bergen

Peter the Great, Second Edition
by Paul Bushkovitch

A Concise History of Hong Kong
by John M. Carroll

Ming China, 1368–1644: A Concise History of a Resilient Empire
by John W. Dardess

A History of Medieval Heresy and Inquisition, Second Edition
by Jennifer Kolpacoff Deane

Remaking Italy in the Twentieth Century
by Roy Palmer Domenico

A Concise History of Euthanasia: Life, Death, God, and Medicine
by Ian Dowbiggin

The Work of France: Labor and Culture in Early Modern Times, 1350–1800
by James R. Farr

The Idea of Capitalism before the Industrial Revolution
by Richard Grassby

Women and China's Revolutions
by Gail Hershatter

Public Zen, Personal Zen: A Buddhist Introduction
by Peter D. Hershock

Chinese Migrations: The Movement of People, Goods, and Ideas over Four Millennia
by Diana Lary

The Concise History of the Crusades, Third Edition
by Thomas F. Madden

The Catholic Invasion of China: Remaking Chinese Christianity
by D. E. Mungello

The Great Encounter of China and the West, 1500–1800, Fourth Edition
by D. E. Mungello

A Concise History of the French Revolution
by Sylvia Neely

The British Imperial Century, 1815–1914: A World History Perspective
by Timothy H. Parsons

The Second British Empire: In the Crucible of the Twentieth Century
by Timothy H. Parsons

The Norman Conquest: England after William the Conqueror
by Hugh M. Thomas

Europe's Reformations, 1450–1650: Doctrine, Politics, and Community, Second Edition
by James D. Tracy

Lightning Source UK Ltd.
Milton Keynes UK
UKHW021314221222
414328UK00016B/71

9 781538 152942